Greek and Latin Love

Greek and Latin Love

The Poetic Connection

Edited by
Thea S. Thorsen, Iris Brecke, and Stephen Harrison

DE GRUYTER

ISBN 978-3-11-125579-8
e-ISBN (PDF) 978-3-11-063303-0
e-ISBN (EPUB) 978-3-11-063061-9

Library of Congress Control Number: 2021939452

Bibliographic information published by the Deutsche Nationalbibliothek
The Deutsche Nationalbibliothek lists this publication in the Deutsche Nationalbibliografie;
detailed bibliographic data are available on the Internet at http://dnb.dnb.de.

© 2023 Walter de Gruyter GmbH, Berlin/Boston
This volume is text- and page-identical with the hardback published in 2021.
Cover Image: Cupids playing with a lyre. Roman fresco from Herculaneum (detail) © The
Picture Art Collection / Alamy Stock Foto
Printing and binding: CPI books GmbH, Leck

www.degruyter.com

Preface

The volume arises from a conference entitled *Greek and Roman Literature: The Erotic Connection* which was held at Corpus Christi College, Oxford, on 11th June 2016, and which was organized under the auspices of the Corpus Christi College Centre for the Study of Greek and Roman Antiquity, the Norwegian University of Science and Technology, Trondheim (NTNU), and the Research Council of Norway. It includes most of the papers from that event plus a number which were subsequently commissioned. The conference was organised as part of NTNU's research project *The Heterosexual Tradition of Homoerotic Poetics* (2015–2020), headed by Thea S. Thorsen and funded by the Research Council of Norway. The editors wish to express their gratitude to all the above-mentioned bodies for their support.

Abbreviations follow those of the *Oxford Classical Dictionary*, 4th edition, or alternatively, those of *L'année philologique*.

Thea S. Thorsen/Iris Brecke/Stephen Harrison
Trondheim/Oxford
October 2020

Contents

Preface —— V

Thea S. Thorsen, Iris Brecke and Stephen Harrison
Introducing Greek and Latin Love: The Poetic Connection —— 1

Thea S. Thorsen
Love: Ancient and Later Representations —— 7

Benjamin Acosta-Hughes
There Falls a Lone Tear: Longing for a Vanished Love – Tracing an Erotic Motif from Homer to Horace —— 29

Peter Astrup Sundt
Orpheus and Sappho as Model Poets: Blurring Greek and Latin Love in *Lament for Bion*, Catullus 51, and Horace *Odes* 1.24 —— 39

Alison Sharrock
***Amans et Egens* and *Exclusus Amator*: The Connection (or not) between Comedy and Elegy —— 59**

Iris Brecke
Rape and Violence in Terence's *Eunuchus* and Ovid's Love Elegies —— 83

Boris Kayachev
Love and Poetry in Virgil's Sixth Eclogue: A Platonic Perspective —— 105

Paola D'Andrea
***Longum Bibebat Amorem*: Virgilian Adaptation of Sympotic Poetry —— 125**

Alison Keith
Philodemus and the Augustan Poets —— 145

Aaron Palmore
Love and Politics in Horace's *Odes* 4.10 —— 167

Jennifer Ingleheart
***Amores* Plural: Ovidian Homoerotics in the Elegies —— 185**

Thea S. Thorsen
The Beloved: Figures and Words —— 213

List of Contributors —— 231
Bibliography —— 233
Index Locorum —— 255
Index Rerum —— 261

Thea S. Thorsen, Iris Brecke and Stephen Harrison
Introducing Greek and Latin Love: The Poetic Connection

Without trying to reduce the scope and diversity of the various contributions to this book, it is reasonably fair to say that – as a whole – this volume substantiates three interrelated observations: 1) that there is a connection between the conceptions of love in Greek and Latin literature, 2) that this love is related to sexual desire (fulfilled and otherwise) without distinction between other- and same-sex configurations, and 3) that this love is found in the mainstream of poetry throughout the ancient world, from Homer to Ovid.

Covering this timeline, the contributions of this volume are organized according to an approximate chronology. The adaptation of an exact chronology of the authors and texts treated in each chapter is not possible given that most contributions range widely within ancient literary history. Hence, the order of the contributions reflects the point in antiquity at which the most important material which is discussed in each chapter can be dated.

In this way, the present volume not only covers an important landscape in ancient literature, but also unites a number of research areas that are frequently studied separately, simultaneously turning some central priorities in classical scholarship on their head. For while the kind of love that engenders care as well as sexual desire for the beloved is a massive topic in ancient literature, and even if poetry, which is closely connected to song and music, is a main vehicle of this topic in antiquity as in our day and age, classical scholarship on erotic topics tends to focus on sexuality rather than love,[1] and also on prose rather than poetry.[2]

Indeed, sexuality is a vast issue in antiquity that does not necessarily have anything to do with love, if love is understood as encompassing an interest in the beloved's wishes, wellbeing and happiness. Rather, ancient conceptions of sex-

---

1 See e.g. Dover 1973, 1978, Lilja 1983, Carson 1986, Cantarella 1992 (on bisexuality), Licht 1994, Foxhall 1998, McGinn 1998, Calame 1999, Davidson 2001, 2007 = 2008, Detel 2005, Skinner 2005, Younger 2005, Veyne 2005, Faraone/MacClure 2006, Boeringher 2007, Ormand 2008, Golden/Toohey 2011, Hubbard 2014. For a more extensive bibliografy, the *Oxford Bibliographies* entry 'sexuality' provides a useful overview. See also the literature of the respective chapters in this volume.
2 See below.

uality tend to pivot on domination and submission in asymmetrical relationships.[3] However, in cases where love is in play, sexuality follows as only one, subordinate aspect of the lover's interest in the beloved. For love, even when it is realized in sexual congress, tends to strive towards that which is the opposite of hierarchical power-relations, namely equality and reciprocity. Even in so-called pederastic poetry, where the asymmetrical relationship is an undeniable reality, the older, male lover's aim, however unattainable, is to be loved (and exclusively so) in return by the beloved boy.[4] By also encompassing issues related to sex, while mainly focusing on love, this volume contributes to tipping the balance in existing scholarship, where studies on the theme of love are currently outweighed by explorations of sexuality.

Similarly, the current dominance of studies in ancient sexuality compared to the scarcity of explorations of conceptions of love *per se*, is arguably mirrored in a focus on prose over poetry. Pre-eminent in this regard are the second and third volumes of Michel Foucault's *History of Sexuality*, on ancient Greece (*The Usage of Pleasure*, 1985a) and imperial Rome (*The Care of the Self*, 1985b), respectively. Here, the focus on sexuality is accompanied by a concentration on prose authors, while only glimpses are offered of great love poets such as Propertius or Ovid (1985b, 138–9). This approach, however justified concerning Foucault's line of enquiry, offers a distorted and marginalized view of such poets and the profound complexity of the love and corollary sexuality they portray. It is the hope that the focus on poetry in this volume, whose chapters also naturally make detours into prose and drama, can contribute to a recalibration of this imbalance, which is arguably still influential in classical scholarship.

Outline of the volume

In the first chapter, Thea S. Thorsen investigates what seems to be a mismatch between sources and scholarship regarding Greek and Latin love. Thorsen first posits the existence of conceptions of true love in ancient literature, then proceeds to probe the divides that hamper our understanding of this phenomenon,

---

[3] Important works are e.g. Dover 1978, Patzer 1982, Halperin 1990, Williams 1999, Cantarella/Lear 2008.
[4] An example of such longing for reciprocity (and exclusivity) can be found in Theognis' pederastic poems concerning the beloved boy Cyrnus (Thgn. 1231–1389), whom he repeatedly accuses of being faithless.

both outside and inside classical philology, and finally she launches the 'homo-poetic model of love' in an attempt to better adapt the scholarly map to the actual landscape of the ancient sources. Along the way, Thorsen discusses the story of Phrygius and Pieria, Alciphron's letter from Glaucippe to her mother, poems about Plato and Agathon, Ovid's Pyramus and Thisbe and his Leander and Hero, as well as Sappho's Frr. 1, 16, 31, 130 and 188, Anacreon's Fr. 402c and the matching couples of the Greek novel.

Beginning with Homer, Benjamin Acosta-Hughes argues in the second chapter that the poetic image of one single tear, almost photographically captured, falling from the eye of Achilles as he mourns the loss of Patroclus in the *Iliad*, sets in motion a complex of longing, memory and love that may be traced throughout classical literature up until Horace, and beyond. The 'single tear' thus becomes emblematic of a special kind of love, not necessarily sexual, but certainly passionate, that occurs predominantly, but not exclusively, in homoerotic contexts in both Greek and Latin poetry. The argument emerges from the close readings of patterns of allusions between passages from Homer (from book 19 and 24 of the *Iliad* and book 18 of the *Odyssey* in particular), Callimachus' epigrams 2 Pf. (34 GP) and 31 Pf. (1 GP), Catullus' poem 50, and Horace's *Odes* 4.1. The focus on loss and grief that necessarily blend with love and longing thus reveals a strikingly sustained trajectory across classical literature.

In the next chapter, Peter Astrup Sundt detects – between loss of and love for preceding poet-models – an erotic pattern of rivalry. Orpheus and Sappho emerge as particularly important poet-models in this dynamic that focuses on suffering, longing, death and metapoetics. The conspicuous blend of hetero- and homoeroticism evoked by these two figures, Sappho in her love poetry to other girls alongside her heterosexual *epithalamia*, and Orpheus as husband of the woman Eurydice and lover of the boy Calaïs, function as a particularly fruitful point of reference for the fashioning of poetic identities, also relating to other poets, in the Greek hexameter poem known as the *Lament for Bion*, Catullus 50 and Horace's *Odes* 1.24, simultaneously evoking the figure of Virgil.

Shifting the focus from longing and death as expressions of love, in a metapoetic sense too, which are at the heart of the preceding chapters, the next contributions critically revisit the established connections between comedy and elegy. Alison Sharrock demonstrates in her chapter that the two genres of Attic New/ Roman Comedy and Latin love elegy, and particularly the two types of lovers (the comic *adulescens* and the elegiac *amans*), are more different than is often thought – especially where money is a key issue. The chapter shows how connections between the two figures and genres are better understood in terms of intertextuality than as organically connected. Mainly focusing on descriptions of comic and elegiac young lovers, this chapter compares passages from Menander (*Dyskolos*), Plautus (*Persa, Curculio* and *Bacchides*) and Terence (*Eunuchus*) with several passages from the love elegies of Tibullus (1.1, 1.2) Propertius (1.6, 1.8a, 1.8b, 2.8, 3.25) and Ovid (e.g. *Amores* 1.6, 1.10 and passages from the second book of the *Ars amatoria*). Thus, the chapter celebrates the uniqueness of each genre, in particular as regards the nature of the love it espouses.

While Sharrock explores in depth one of the differences between comedy and elegy, in the incompatibility between money and 'true love', Iris Brecke tackles the irreconcilability between such love and violence head on in her chapter. Here, Brecke critically revisits the occurrence and use of violence, especially rape, in both comedy and elegy. Departing from the famous rape in Terence's *Eunuchus*, which is portrayed as particularly upsetting, Brecke proceeds to examine Ovidian instances of violence and rape in his love elegies. These instances include the rape of the Sabine women (*Ars am.* 1.89–134), the regret of Ovid's poet-lover at having assaulted his beloved physically (*Am.* 1.7, in a poem where he simultaneously asks why he can legally give his girl a beating, but cannot even touch another male citizen without violating the law), the rape of Rhea Silvia by the river Anio (*Am.* 3.6) and the unique female first-person account by Oenone of her own rape by Apollo (*Her.* 5.139–44). Brecke shows how violence and rape in Ovid's amatory poetry are linked to Augustan law, ideals and legends in a highly disquieting manner, amounting to a subtle critique of the institution of marriage and Augustus' moralizing programme.

The next two chapters represent another pair in the volume, focussing on Virgil. First Boris Kayachev discusses in depth the significance of love in the song of Silenus in Virgil's sixth *Eclogue*, which famously sports a wide array of loves: that of Hylas, the object of the homoerotic interest of Heracles and the heterosexual desire of the nymphs who abducted him; Pasiphae's mad desire for and mating with a bull; Scylla's betrayal of her father as an act of love for Minos; and Tereus' lecherous rape of Philomela. Tracing evocations of Epicurean and Platonic philosophy against the background of Lucretius' *De rerum natura*, Plato's *Symposium* and fragments of Parmenides, Kayachev reveals an underlying programme of an erotic poetics, where the poet's love of art *qua* ontological reality is centre stage.

In the course of his argument, Kayachev shows how the depiction of Silenus is reminiscent of the setting of the Greek symposium. This very same setting – with its predominantly homoerotic configurations according to convention – constitutes an important background for the chapter of Paola D'Andrea. She seeks to recontextualize one of the erotic *chef d'oeuvres* of ancient literature, namely Book 4 of the *Aeneid*. Building on recent scholarship that detects evocations of Greek lyric poetry not only in Book 4, but in all the books that lead up to it, D'Andrea presents Dido in the guise of the lyric poet Sappho and Aeneas in the role of the elegist Solon. Through the sounding-board of Greek lyric and sympotic poetry, D'Andrea brings out aspects of love in *Aeneid* 1–4 that illuminate Virgilian poetry, metapoetics, and the figure of Dido as both a loving self and beloved other.

Picking up on the Epicureanism discussed in Kayachev's chapter, that of Alison Keith offers unique glimpses into Augustan poetry in the making through the lens of Philodemus. For while there is a conspicuous Horatian and even Propertian reception (in elegy 3.5) of Philodemus' erotic epigrams (not forgetting Ovid *Amores* 1.5), Tibullus shows little concern with the Epicurean framework in which Philodemus' erotic epigrams were set. In fact, in spite of Horace's repeated invitations (*Carm.* 1.33, *Epist.* 1.4) to Tibullus to reject the theme of amatory obsession conventional for elegy and embrace the more instrumental sexuality of Epicurean erotics on display in Philodemus' poems, Tibullus eschews extended treatment of Philodemean epigram. Tibullus' indifference to Philodemus' erotic epigrams cannot, however, be explained as indifference to the genre in general, since his elegies' extensive debt to epigrammatic models is well documented. The chapter consequently discusses this conundrum's possible explanations, which include the role of Maecenas and Messalla and the increased literary prestige of Latin love elegy, which may have prompted its practitioners to exhibit a newly confident literary authority independent of contemporary Greek epigrammatic models.

Picking up on the Horatian traces of Philodemus, Palmore's chapter argues that Horace's *Odes* 4.10 has a political angle that ties in with its erotic qualities through a reading that is informed by psychoanalysis. *Odes* 4.10, one of Horace's shortest compositions, is a homoerotic poem that appears in a collection that seems to focus largely on the achievements of Augustus and his regime. Building upon the work of the psychoanalyst Jacques Lacan, the chapter constructs a theoretical basis for understanding the unity of *Odes* 4 through the rubric of desire, which can manifest itself not only in love but also in politics and poetry. *Odes* 4.10 is a valuable case study in this regard, as Horace associates Ligurinus (an erotic interest) with Augustus (a political interest) around key words like *incolumis* ('unharmed', 'safe and sound'). In addition to exploring Horace's *Odes* 4.10, this chapter also includes a discussion of Hellenistic epigram, represented by Asclepiades 46 (=*Anth. Pal.* 12.36) and Diocles 4 (=*Anth. Pal.* 12.35). In implicating politics in homoerotic love poetry, Horace suggests an ideological connection between the language of *Odes* 4.10 and the portrayal of Augustus as having been a *puer*, with all the connotations that follow. Using this perspective, Palmore suggests, we can further understand the coherence of *Odes* 4, and especially the place of *Odes* 4.10 as a link within the trajectory of desire in the collection.

The next chapter, by Jennifer Ingleheart, takes as its point of departure the fact that Ovid is often seen as the most heterosexual representative of the genre of Latin love elegy. Yet, as Ingleheart points out in her chapter, Ovid's *Amores* open with a poem in which Ovid contemplates having either a *puer* or a *puella* as his elegiac beloved (*Amores* 1.1.19–20). Ingleheart's chapter takes Ovid's homoeroticism seriously, interrogating the stereotype of Ovid as overwhelmingly focused on heteroerotic love and thus uncovering how homoeroticism plays an important role in his earlier amatory poetry. By exploring passages from Ovid's *Amores* (1.1, 1.2, 1.3 and 3.9 in particular) and several passages from the *Ars amatoria* and *Remedia amoris*, as well as reading them in light of passages from Catullus (50), Tibullus (1.4, 1.8) and Propertius (1.1) in particular, and via this poem, also Meleager, *Anth. Pal.* 12.101 (= 103 GP), this chapter argues that Ovid engages in detail with homoerotic passion and with homosociality in poems that are not limited to interest in *puellae*, but that truly treat *amores* ('loves') in the plural and across the genders.

Finally, picking up on the new perspectives on Ovid opened up by the preceding chapter, as well as on the closure of Chapter 1, the final chapter by Thorsen pursues the figures and words used of the beloved in Greek and Latin. In this context the *puella* ('girl') stands out. As an alternative to the established comparison between the *puella* and the figure of the comic *meretrix* ('prostitute'), this chapter traces the etymology of the word *puella* to that of the *puer* ('boy'), which in antiquity was furthermore linked to the grammatically gender-inclusive Greek word παῖς ('child'). Thorsen then pursues the many links between these three designations of the beloved in Greek and Latin. At the same time, she outlines a trajectory from a state of gender-fluidity to a state of stricter distinction between male and female, favouring heterosexual configurations, in line with Antony Corbeill's findings in his *Sexing the World: Grammatical Gender and Biological Sex in Ancient Rome* (2015). The argument emerges from discussions of Ovid's *Amores* 1.4 and 1.10, [Tib.] 3.16, Varro's *De lingua Latina*, Anacreon's Fr. 360, Catullus 99, Tibullus 1.4 and the Callimachean and Ovidian versions of the story of Acontius and Cydippe, the latter of which is most likely the last *puella* of Ovid.

Thea S. Thorsen
Love: Ancient and Later Representations

This chapter argues that although concepts more or less overlapping with the idea of true love may be found in ancient literature, the academic appreciation of such concepts is today complicated by certain divides in scholarship. The chapter identifies the theory that true love was invented in mediaeval France, here dubbed 'the mediaeval model of love', as particularly challenging, and suggests that this scheme should be recalibrated to include classical antiquity. It therefore launches an alternative model and outlines how it might help to bridge several divides in the research so that a scholarly map might be drawn that fits the landscape of ancient love literature more accurately.

Introduction

Today it seems that everyone across the globe knows what 'true love' is. This is a kind of love that may go under different labels in scholarship,[1] but whose common denominator is a combination of affection for the beloved's person and sexual desire, the fulfilment of which through actual sex with the beloved is of secondary importance compared to the state of being in love itself. Moreover, it is not true love if the lover acts against the will of the beloved, for example by means of obsessive stalking, offering money to achieve intimacy or, worse, using violence to that end. Acts of harassment, payment and violation are incompatible with true love. Indeed, even if the aim of true love should be to live 'happily ever after', it can never serve as a mere stepping stone on the way to acquiring marital or formal partnership status, if the purpose of such a status is to uphold a successful social façade and propagate one's own genes through offspring. True love is, in other words, unconditional. It has no extraneous cause and no extraneous purpose. It is love for love's sake. Its beginning and end cannot be anything other than the very person of the beloved (which may, of course, be idealized by the lover); and this person's will and well-being is the lover's care, to the extent that he or she is willing to sacrifice everything, even life, for the beloved's sake.

---

1 Lyne's concept of 'whole love', which includes both passionate desire and affectionate care, is perhaps the most accurate designation that has been launched in classical scholarship of the phenomenon in question; see Lyne 1980, *passim*. For the terms 'courtly' and 'romantic', see below.

https://doi.org/10.1515/9783110633030-002

Love in ancient literature

This chapter argues that – broadly speaking – such a concept of true love, which is marked by a willingness to fulfil the beloved's wishes, male *and* female longing, an urge to merge into one, and a death-defying fearlessness, was known in ancient Greek and Latin texts.

One example of such 'making of classical love'[2] is that of the Milesian king Phrygius, whose wish to fulfil the will of his beloved Pieria was so great that it became proverbial. The tale, which is found in Callimachus (fr. 80–1 Pf.), Plutarch (*De mul. vir.* 16) and Aristaenetus (1.15 Drago), is like a topsy-turvy reflection of the story of Judith and Holofernes, which is found in the book of Judith in the *Septuagint*, the *koine* translation of the *Old Testament*. Pieria's city Myus is at war with that of Phrygius, Miletus. During an armistice, Pieria, in order to attend a festival in honour of Artemis, visits Miletus, where Phrygius sees her and immediately falls in love. Straight away the two of them go to bed together. But instead of having his head cut off, which is what Judith did to Holofernes, the enemy leader, Phrygius, 'makes loving love' (ἐρασμίως ἐναφροδισιάσας, Aristaenetus 1.15.33) to Pieria. Nonetheless, Pieria, like Judith, does still save her people. For, eager to please his beloved in every way, Phrygius asks Pieria what he can possibly give her as a token of his love. And so, modestly blushing, Pieria asks not for jewels or precious clothes – 'all those things that the female sex is utterly crazy about' (Aristaenetus 1.15.41–2, οἷς ἅπασιν ἀτεχνῶς ἀγάλλεσθαι τὸ θῆλυ πέφυκε γένος; cf. Callim. fr. 80.8) – but for peace between the two cities. Phrygius happily fulfils her wishes and stops the war. According to Plutarch, '[t]here was, consequently, in both cities repute and honour for Pieria so that the women of Miletus pray even to this day that their husbands may love them as Phrygius loved Pieria' (Plut. *De mul. vir.* 16, ἦν οὖν ἐν ἀμφοτέραις ταῖς πόλεσι δόξα καὶ τιμὴ τῆς Πιερίας, ὥστε καὶ τὰς Μιλησίων εὔχεσθαι γυναῖκας ἄχρι νῦν οὕτως τοὺς ἄνδρας ἐρᾶν αὐτῶν, ὡς Φρύγιος ἠράσθη Πιερίας; cf. also Aristaenetus 1.15.67–9). So remarkable an act of love was Phrygius' eagerness to fulfil his beloved's wishes.

While the love of Phrygius is recognized in the proverb that was later cherished by other women, we learn little about the feelings of Pieria in the extant versions of the story. However, ancient literature also accommodates female desire, as seen in Alciphron's fictitious letter from Glaucippe to her mother Charope, in which the daughter also pays tribute to the poet of female desire par excellence, Sappho, to whom I shall return below:

---

[2] If I may be allowed a twist on the title of Reddy 2012; see also below.

Οὐκέτ' εἰμὶ ἐν ἐμαυτῇ, ὦ μῆτερ, οὐδὲ ἀνέχομαι γήμασθαι ᾧ με κατεγγυήσειν ἐπηγγείλατο ἔναγχος ὁ πατήρ, τῷ Μηθυμναίῳ μειρακίῳ τῷ παιδὶ τοῦ κυβερνήτου, ἐξ ὅτου τὸν ἀστικὸν ἔφηβον ἐθεασάμην τὸν ὠσχοφόρον, ὅτε με ἄστυδε προὔτρεψας ἀφικέσθαι Ὠσχοφορίων ὄντων. καλὸς γάρ ἐστι, καλός, ὦ μῆτερ, καὶ ἥδιστος, καὶ βοστρύχους ἔχει βρύων οὐλοτέρους, καὶ μειδιᾷ τῆς θαλάττης γαληνιώσης χαριέστερον, καὶ τὰς βολὰς τῶν ὀφθαλμῶν ἐστι κυαναυγής, οἷος τὸ πρῶτον ὑπὸ τῶν ἀκτίνων τῶν ἡλιακῶν ὁ πόντος καταλαμπόμενος φαίνεται. τὸ δὲ ὅλον πρόσωπον – αὐτὰς ἐνορχεῖσθαι ταῖς παρειαῖς εἴποις ἂν τὰς Χάριτας τὸν Ὀρχομενὸν ἀπολιπούσας καὶ τῆς Ἀργαφίας κρήνης ἀπονιψαμένας· τὼ χείλη δὲ τὰ ῥόδα τῆς Ἀφροδίτης ἀποσυλήσας τῶν κόλπων διήνθισται ἐπὶ τῶν ἄκρων ἐπιθέμενος. ἢ τούτῳ μιγήσομαι ἢ τὴν Λεσβίαν μιμησαμένη Σαπφὼ οὐκ ἀπὸ τῆς Λευκάδος πέτρας, ἀλλ' ἀπὸ τῶν Πειραϊκῶν προβόλων ἐμαυτὴν εἰς τὸ κλυδώνιον ὤσω.

(*Letters of Fishermen* (11 = iii.1 Benner and Fobes))

I am no longer myself, mother; I cannot endure the thought of being married to the boy from Methymna, the sea-captain's son to whom father recently promised to betroth me; I have felt this way ever since I saw the young guardsman from the city, the one who carried the vine-branch when, at your bidding, I went there on the occasion of the Oschophoria. He is beautiful, mother, beautiful, the sweetest thing, and his locks are curlier than sea-moss, and his smile is more charming than the sea in a calm, and the radiance of his eyes is like the dark blue of the sea, as it appears in the first moment of illumination by the sun's rays. And his whole face – you might say that the Graces themselves have left Orchomenus and, after bathing in the Argaphian spring, are dancing in his cheeks; and his lips – he has filched the roses from the bosom of Aphrodite and tipped his lips with their bloom. I intend to have this man, or, if I can't, I shall follow the example of Lesbian Sappho: not indeed from the Leucadian cliff[3] but from the jutting rocks of the Peiraeus I shall hurl myself into the surf.

(Transl. Benner and Fobes)

Glaucippe is suffering due to the distance between her and her beloved, which is increased by the prospect of marriage to someone she does not love.

A striking – and humorous – example of how not even the physical intimacy of a kiss is sufficient to satisfy the lover's sustained urge to merge with the beloved, soul to soul, is found in a set of poems that evoke the figures of Plato and Agathon, recorded by Aulus Gellius (and later by Macrobius). The first of the two poems is an epigram attributed to Plato:

Τὴν ψυχὴν Ἀγάθωνα φιλῶν ἐπὶ χείλεσιν ἔσχον·
 Ἦλθε γὰρ ἡ τλήμων ὡς διαβησομένη.[4]

---

[3] The legend that Sappho threw herself from the Leucadian cliffs out of lovesickness for her beloved Phaon is not attested in Sappho's own poetry, but in the later tradition; see Thorsen 2014 and Thorsen/Berge 2019, 309, 329 and 350.
[4] The epigram is also recorded under Plato's name in the *Anth. Pal.* 5.78 = FGE, 162.

My soul, when I kissed Agathon, did pass my lips; as though, poor soul, it would leap across.

(Transl. Rolfe)

Gellius claims that a friend of his, when young,[5] translated this couplet *licentius liberiusque* – 'with license and freely' – into Latin iambic dimeters, thus:

dum semihiulco sauio
meum puellum sauior
dulcemque florem spiritus
duco ex aperto tramite,
†animat aegra et saucia
cucurrit ad labeas mihi,
rictumque in oris peruium
et labra pueri mollia
rimata itineri transitus,
ut transiliret nititur.
tum si morae quid plusculae
fuisset in coetu osculi,
Amoris igni percita
transisset et me linqueret,
et mira prorsum res foret,
ut fierem ad me mortuus,
ad puerum intus uiuerem.

(Gell. NA 19.11.4; Macrob. Sat. 2.2.16 = Apuleius 6 Courtney)

While kissing my boy with half-parted lips, drawing his breath's sweet bloom from its open course, my poor wounded soul raced up to my lips and strained to leap across to the passage of the boy's parted mouth and soft lips. If we had lingered a moment more in the union of our kiss, then – roused by love's fire – it would have passed over and left me: a strange thing that would be, leaving me dead to myself but alive to the boy, within him.

(Transl. Kaster, from Macrobius)

Even Gellius casts doubt on the Platonic authorship[6] of the original epigram, and introduces the Greek couplet and Latin iambic dimeters in a playful context, which suggests that the epigram is a witty dramatization of the bewildered presence of 'Platonic love', in the shape of the soul's sustained longing (perhaps a hint at penetration), in the non-Platonic act of kissing. Be that as it may, the two poems are also an elaboration on a deeply romantic notion, namely that love is an urge to connect with one's soulmate.

---

5 Since Dahlmann 1979, the poem has commonly been assumed to be by Apuleius; see Harrison 1992 and Courtney 1993.
6 See also Ludwig 1963, 71.

However amusingly, the two poems, and the Latin more than the Greek, evoke the shadow of death, which is commonly envisaged as the departure of the soul from the dying person's body in ancient literature. In this literature, we also find examples (that are markedly less humorous than that of Gellius) of a willingness to risk one's life or even choose death for the beloved's sake. This willingness to die for the beloved readily emerges as an ultimate proof of 'true love'. One story of such a choice is that of Ovid's Pyramus and Thisbe (*Met.* 4.55–166), two young lovers from mutually hostile families who live next door to one another and who manage to communicate through a crack in the wall. One day they agree to stealthily leave their houses during the night so that they may finally meet. But, having successfully left her house and found the spot where she and Pyramus have agreed to come together, Thisbe discovers a lioness, whose mouth is bloody from a recent kill. Terrified, she flees from the site, but drops her cloak, which the lioness soon finds and starts to chew on; when Pyramus subsequently arrives at the spot, he finds not Thisbe, but a bloody piece of her garment, and believes that she has been killed by the beast. Desperate with grief, he stabs himself with his own sword. When Thisbe soon returns, she finds her love already dying, and so she too throws herself on his sword and dies.

Shakespeare knew the story, and integrated a famous version into his *Midsummer Night's Dream* (c. 1596). Moreover, several aspects of Ovid's basic plot are repeated in Shakespeare's *Romeo and Juliet* (c. 1595), possibly *the* love story that is most famous in our day and age. However, Ovid himself also recasts the same plot in his story of Leander and Hero in the double *Heroides* 18–19.[7] Ovid's Leander and Hero arguably knew love at least as profoundly as Romeo and Juliet did (cf. Act III, scene v), because they certainly enjoyed the physical pleasures of erotic embraces. Indeed, Leander and Hero's corporeal encounters allow them to remember past joys and fantasize about future bliss when they are separated against their will, thus, according to Leander:

> excipis amplexu feliciaque oscula iungis,
>   oscula, di magni, trans mare digna peti,
> eque tuis demptos umeris mihi tradis amictus
>   et madidam siccas aequoris imbre comam.
> cetera nox et nos et turris conscia nouit,
>   quodque mihi lumen per uada monstrat iter.
> non magis illius numerari gaudia noctis

---

[7] For the story of Leander and Hero from antiquity up until the Renaissance, see Montiglio 2017. For the likelihood that Ovid's double *Heroides* belong to the end of his poetic career, see Thorsen 2013c n. 10.

> Hellespontiaci quam maris alga potest.
> quo breuius spatium nobis ad furta dabatur,
>   hoc magis est cautum, ne foret illud iners.
> iamque fugatura Tithoni coniuge noctem
>   praeuius Aurorae Lucifer ortus erat.
> oscula congerimus properata sine ordine raptim
>   et querimur paruas noctibus esse moras,
> atque ita cunctatus monitu nutricis amaro
>   frigida deserta litora turre peto.
> digredimur flentes, repetoque ego uirginis aequor
>   respiciens dominam dum licet usque meam.
>
> (Ov. *Her.* 18.101–18, Kenney)

You welcome me with your embrace, share happy kisses with me – kisses, O you great gods, worth seeking across the deep! – and from your own shoulders you strip the robes to give them over to me, and dry my hair all dripping with the rain of the sea. For the rest – night knows of that, and ourselves, and the tower that shares our secret, and the light that guides me on my passage through the floods. The joys of that dear night may no more be numbered than the weeds of the Hellespontic sea; the briefer the space that was ours for the theft of love, the more we made sure it should not idly pass. And now Aurora, the bride of Tithonus, was making ready to chase the night away, and Lucifer had risen, forerunner of the dawn; in haste we ply our kisses, all disorderly, complaining that the night allows brief lingering. So, tarrying till the nurse's bitter warnings bid me go, I leave the tower and make for the chilly shore. We part in tears, and I return to the Maiden's [Helle's] sea, looking ever back to my lady while I can.

(Transl. Showerman, rev. by Goold)

Similarly, Hero fantasizes about Leander's arrival and is tormented by his delay:

> nam modo te uideor prope iam spectare natantem,
>   bracchia nunc umeris umida ferre meis,
> nunc dare, quae soleo, madidis uelamina membris,
>   pectora nunc nostro iuncta fouere sinu
> multaque praeterea linguae reticenda modestae,
>   quae fecisse iuuat, facta referre pudet.
> me miseram, breuis est haec et non uera uoluptas ;
>   nam tu cum somno semper abire soles.
> firmius o cupidi tandem coeamus amantes,
>   nec careant uera gaudia nostra fide!
> cur ego tot uiduas exegi frigida noctes ?
>   cur totiens a me, lente morator, abes?
>
> (Ov. *Her.* 19.59–70, Kenney)

For now I seem to see you already swimming near, and now to feel your wet arms about my neck, and now to throw about your dripping limbs the accustomed coverings, and now to warm your bosom clasped to mine – and many things else a modest tongue should say nothing of, whose memory delights, but whose telling brings a blush. Ah me! brief pleasures these, and not the truth; for you are ever wont to go when slumber goes. O more firmly let our eager loves be knit, and our joys be faithful and true! Why have I passed so many cold and lonely nights? Why, o tardy loiterer, are you so often away from me?

(Transl. Showerman, rev. by Goold)

Leander and Hero are not only separated by the Hellespont; his parents also condemn their love. That is why Leander steals out at night as often as he can and swims over to Hero's side of the strait, guided only by the moon and the stars, and the light in Hero's tower. On the night when their Heroidean letters are written, a terrible storm has been obstructing Leander for days from entering the waves; only a sailor dares to defy the wild waters in his boat, and Leander sends his letter with him to Hero. She receives it, reads and sits down immediately to write back. At the same time, Leander has thrown himself into the waves at last, willing as he is to sacrifice everything, even life, for his beloved. And, as Virgil (*G.* 3.258–63) and Musaeus record in their versions of the couple's story, the light in Hero's tower goes out, most likely due to the storm, Leander gets lost, drowns and is washed ashore on Hero's side the next day, whereupon she throws herself from her tower to her death. Notably, although this sad outcome infuses Ovid's story with tragic qualities, this ending never actually takes place in *Heroides* 18–19. In accordance with the epistolary mode of Ovid's double *Heroides*, these letters can be penned only as long as the hero and heroine are alive; in this way, their love paradoxically survives (if I may be allowed to repeat myself) in 'the eternal now of literature'.[8]

All of the above-mentioned examples contribute, alongside many other texts in antiquity, to notions of love that combine erotic desire with a care for the beloved's person that goes beyond that desire. And, among these examples, which overlap more or less with 'true love' as outlined above, Ovid's Leander and Hero arguably stand out as its perfect embodiment, inasmuch as both are simultaneously loving subjects *and* objects of love – each loves the other equally – and both are *writers*,[9] thus underscoring the very important metapoetic aspect of ancient love literature, to which I shall return below.

---

[8] Thorsen 2013c, 127.
[9] Both also arguably rewrite crucial passages in the Ovidian corpus, which enhances their metapoetic significance; see Thorsen 2018. The metapoetics of love poetry in the case of Ovid has received fresh attention in Oliensis 2019.

Divides in scholarship

Despite examples such as these, the claim that a concept of love of the kind outlined at the outset of this chapter existed in antiquity remains a contentious one. The contentiousness is upheld by a number of divides that mark current scholarship, and which therefore merit specific scrutiny. These divides include that between 1) classical and post-classical conceptions of love; more strictly within classical scholarship, that between 2) studies on love and studies on sexuality; and 3) Attic New/Roman Comedy and Latin love elegy on the one hand and other kinds of ancient literature pivoting on love on the other. While these divides all have their merits, they also have limitations, on which I will focus here.

One of the most fundamental divides in the relevant scholarship concerns the classical and post-classical conceptions of love. For a considerable, influential and vigorous body of research argues that the concept of love as described above was invented only by the troubadours and trobairitz, i.e. male and female singer-songwriters, of twelfth-century Provence. Notably, in this scholarship – and beyond – 'true love'[10] is alternatively labelled 'courtly'[11] and 'romantic', evoking the feudal society of mediaeval *courts*, and the *Romance* languages of the early middle ages. These terms are thus designed to tie the concept of true love to mediaeval France. Moreover, scholarship interprets this love in accordance with the religious world view of the time, by identifying the lover's exaltation of the beloved, who as a rule is already married, and with whom the lover envisages no wedlock or propagation of children, as a 'cult', in which 'woman' has become 'religion'.[12] However, contrary

---

10 Cf. 'véritable amour', Briffault 1945, 144; 'true love', Lyne 1980, e.g. 114, 'true love'; Reddy 2012, *passim*.

11 The term 'courtly love' was invented by Gaston Paris in his study of *Lancelot, ou le Chevalier de la Charrette* (see n. 13 below): 'Dans aucun ouvrage français, autant qu'il me semble, cet amour courtois n'apparaît avant le *Chevalier de la Charrette*', Paris 1883, 519; see also Hult 1996 and Kim 2010; 2012, who sees the choice of this term as a strategy to render the theme of love more scientific and scholarly.

12 Gillet 1941, 22–3 in this longer passage: 'ils [the troubadours] avaient fait une chose extraordinaire ... ils avaient inventé le culte de la femme. Révolution de portée immense! Ces vieux poètes archaïques, que personne ne lit plus ..., travaillèrent pour les siècles, gravèrent dans nos âmes le trait fondamental de notre civilisation ... En calquant les formes de l'amour sur celles du service et de l'hommage chevaleresque, en lui donnant des rites et un langage spéciaux ..., ils opérèrent un changement d'une nouveauté incalculable. C'était une véritable création morale, la plus originale du Moyen Age, *une sorte d'amour entièrement détaché de la génération et de la reproduction de l'espèce*. La femme devint une religion.' My italics, quoted from Briffault 1945, 88. This male-centred interpretation, typical of its time, fails to take into account the women singer-songwriters, the trobairitz, of whom we have more than twenty names preserved, some

to the religion of the Church, the 'woman' as 'religion' includes adulterous sex, though only with the (married) beloved,[13] and only if it is not to the detriment of the beloved's well-being. If sex is impossible or harmful to the beloved, the lover (usually) happily abstains.

Departing from such assumptions, which amount to what I will call the mediaeval model of love, the historian and anthropologist William Reddy makes the following claim, in his book *The Making of Romantic Love: Longing and Sexuality in Europe, South Asia and Japan 900–1200 CE* (2012):

> In a common Western way of feeling, romantic love is paired with sexual desire ... When the beloved returns one's love, and when neither of the two lovers' well-being is threatened by sexual embrace, then love and desire may both be fulfilled without harm. The opposition between love and desire is thus a productive one. This particular dualism is unique to Western conceptions and practices ... Western conception of romantic love was first formulated in the twelfth century CE ... One searches in vain through ancient Greek and Latin literature – from the *Iliad* to the *Aeneid*, from Sappho to Ovid, from Plutarch's account of Antony and Cleopatra's love to the later Greek romances – for any trace of opposition between love and desire ... The originality of the 'courtly love' phenomenon is well known to medievalists. The inventiveness of the trobairitz and troubadours has never been doubted. But scholars have not agreed on the origin and the significance of the twelfth century conception of 'courtly love'.[14]

As is hinted at in Reddy's last sentence in this passage, behind claims such as his[15] lies a massive scholarly discussion that involves many and various arguments, which, despite seriously questioning many of Reddy's claims, nevertheless seems to have made scholarship somewhat reluctant to deal with the concept of love as both erotic and other-oriented in antiquity. It is therefore important to outline some of the most significant contributions to this discussion and show

---

poetry and the music of one song; see e.g. Sankovitch 1999. Since these women poets and composers loved men, in a fashion similar to that of the troubadours, the 'religion' in question should rather have been described inclusively with regard to sex: in other words, as that of 'the beloved', instead of as that of the female sex only. This problem may be regarded as solved, though arguably in a misogynous manner, by the Lacanian theory of desire in which the *femme* is understood as a function which may be occupied by either sex; cf. Janan 2001, Lindheim 2003 and Palmore in this volume.
13 As e.g. in the adulterous story of Geneviève, wife of King Arthur, and his knight Lancelot in *Lancelot, ou le Chevalier de la Charrette* by Chrétien de Troyes (fl. 1165–81) – see n. 11 above – and, more generally, in *De arte honeste amandi* by Andreas Capellanus (fl. late 1180s).
14 Reddy 2012, 1–2.
15 The same idea is expressed even more crudely in e.g. the subheading 'A world without love: The Greco-Roman world and early Christianity' in chapter 3 of Lindberg 2008.

how these are linked to central strands of relevance to this chapter's topic in classical scholarship.

Monumental in this regard are C.S. Lewis' *The Allegory of Love: A Study in the Mediaeval Tradition* (1936) and Denis de Rougemont's *L'amour et l'Occident* (1939; revised in 1956 and again in 1972), which was translated into English under the titles *Passion and Society* (1951, 2nd rev. ed. 1965 and 3rd rev. ed. 1962, UK) and *Love in the Western World* (1940, 2nd rev. ed. 1956 and 1983, US). In his book, Lewis dismissed the relevance of ancient love poets, especially Ovid, for the understanding of the notion of love that emerged in the middle ages and that, according to the trajectory of Lewis' study, was brought to full fruition in the English literature of Edmund Spenser. Thus, the then recent work of scholars such as Wilibald Schrötter (1908) and E.K. Rand (1925), which revealed strong affinities between the love in Ovidian works and that of troubadour literature (a fact which scholarship has continued to confirm),[16] was rejected. Similarly, the book by de Rougemont, which may be regarded as *the* classic treatment of the concept of love in Europe, rehearsed the same trajectory, but following the lines of French literary history more closely, launching true love as a heretical, anti-establishment religion in opposition to that of the Church.[17] Unlike Lewis, de Rougemont did not even mention Ovid, nor the love literature of other ancient poets, in his history of 'love in the Western world'.[18]

---

16 See e.g. Minnis 2001, on the influence of Ovid on the crucial work in mediaeval love literature, the *Roman de la rose*; Clark/Coulson/McKinley 2011 for influences on mediaeval culture more generally; and Kretschmer 2013 for Ovid's influence on mediaeval love poetry.

17 I leave it to future scholarship to gauge the significance of Christian concepts of love for that of the mediaeval model, but would like to add that as long as this kind of love, by being sexual and adulterous, violates some of the most fundamental Christian codes, preliminary observations suggest that the Church played much the same role in relation to love literature in the middle ages as Augustan legislation did in ancient Rome; cf. below and n. 67.

18 In one (UK) English translation of his work, de Rougemont explains in the preface: '... some readers have supposed – and there I may have been to blame – that I regard passionate love as an invention of the twelfth century. Actually, the matter is more complex. At all times and in all places the natural growth of what I call passionate love has been visible. But alike in Greece and Rome and in the East the frenzy of passion was treated as simply a frenzy and nothing more. Not till the twelfth century – the century of Abélard, Saint Bernard, the Troubadours and *Tristan* – and then in Western Europe, did the natural seeds of passion, instead of being destroyed, suddenly begin to be cultivated. The love frenzy was raised to the level of religious wisdom. It was given a symbolic expression that made it acceptable, a dignified form, and a rhetoric that endowed it with standing. Unfortunate love was admitted to be beautiful and good *to the extent it was woeful*. "De tous les maux le mien diffère: il me plaît", wrote Chrestien de Troyes. Delight in the tribulations of love is the novelty I set out from – the "difference" I have sought to account for', de Rougemont 1962, 9.

Lewis' and de Rougemont's omission of ancient poetry as irrelevant to this history did not remain uncriticised. In the decades that followed these publications, scholars such as J.P. Sullivan (1961), Godo Lieberg (1962), Niall Rudd (1981) and Lesley Cahoon (1987) all responded in various ways, pointing to numerous examples of classical concepts of love that seem confoundingly similar to those in mediaeval literature, such as the cult of the beloved in Catullus (esp. Lieberg), Medea's all-consuming passion in Apollonius' *Argonautica* (Rudd) and Ovid's many lovers and beloveds (Sullivan and Cahoon). To this list, the mediaevalist and Latinist Peter Dronke must be added,[19] whose scepticism towards the mediaeval model of love appears grounded in his knowledge of the rich reception of Ovid in that era, as well as in his deep insights into the multifaceted nature of the love that the middle ages thus received:

> ... the middle ages ... knew the *Amores* and the *Heroides* almost equally well [as the *Metamorphoses*]. And what they found in these was far more ... for these works displayed the greatest imaginable range in love of men and women, from the lightest to the most tragic, from flirtation to the utmost bounds of passionate love. No shade of feeling, shallow or profound, is alien to them.[20]

Alongside these responses to the mediaeval model of love, a shift in the understanding of Latin love poetry, and of Ovid in particular,[21] took place in classical scholarship especially from the 1980s onwards. Seminal here was R.O.A.M. Lyne's *The Latin Love Poets: From Catullus to Horace* (so entitled despite ending not with Horace, but Ovid; 1980), which was fairly conservative in its approach to the relationship between the historical reality and the literariness of the genres in question. However, this book was also pioneering, inasmuch as it introduced the concept of 'whole love',[22] which included erotic passion and other-oriented affection in much the same way as the kind of love outlined at the outset of this

---

19 See also Crosland 1947.
20 Dronke 1965 I, 161.
21 Seminal in Ovidian studies are Hinds 1987a and 1987b, Conte 1989, Barchiesi 1986; 1987, and McKeown 1987; 1989; 1998, all preparing the ground for an even richer scholarly *aetas Ovidiana* in the following years, the vastness of which is reflected in the fact that Ovid is the only ancient author to whom as many as five *Oxford Bibliographies Online* articles have thus far been dedicated: Myers 2009, Thorsen 2017, Fratantuono 2017, Tissol 2017 and Fumo 2017. Of these two, Thorsen 2017 and Fumo 2017 are dedicated to 'Ovid's love poetry' and 'Ovid and the Middle Ages' alone.
22 See n. 1 above.

chapter. Lyne found this kind of love to be present in Roman poetry from Catullus onwards.²³

This shift could perhaps have made love a more natural topic to explore *per se* in classical scholarship, were it not for Paul Veyne's publication *L'élégie érotique romaine: l'amour, la poésie et l'Occident* (1983), which was issued in English under the title *Roman Erotic Elegy: Love, Poetry and the West* (1988). For it is indeed tempting to see some connection between Veyne's massively influential study and the scholarship on Latin love poetry that followed, which focused sharply on its artistic sophistication from the point of view of literary theory,²⁴ as well as on gender and power play inspired by feminist perspectives,²⁵ and less on the phenomenon of love *per se*. While valuable in many regards, not least for replacing reductive biographical-historical approaches to elegy with the interpretative sophistication of literary theory, Veyne's study functioned as a Trojan horse of sorts for the outlook on Western literature promoted in de Rougemont's book, to which Veyne's French subtitle explicitly alludes.²⁶ For while Veyne extended the project of de Rougemont by focusing on love in antiquity, and thus in many ways corrected the latter's outline of the history of love in the West, Veyne nevertheless subscribed to the fundamental claim of de Rougemont, in the sense that the love he saw in Latin elegy was not true, but rehearsed, dead and boring.²⁷

This problematic divide between classical and post-classical conceptions of love is furthermore linked to another division more strictly located within classical scholarship itself, namely that between studies on love on the one hand and those on sexuality on the other. For while this scholarship abounds with studies

---

23 '… a profound, systematic, and continuing exploration of a single relationship through poems which relate to and illuminate each other … is not in any ancient poet's manner or nature before Catullus. There is no precedent in ancient literature for Catullus and Lesbia', Lyne 1980, 21.
24 E.g. Veyne 1983; 1988 (see above) and Kennedy 1993, which draws on the French literary theorist Roland Barthes, and especially his *Fragments d'un discours amoureux* (1977), and Miller 2004, which expounds on the genre's historical uniqueness by means of perspectives such as those drawn from Marxism and psychoanalysis.
25 E.g. Greene 1998, which focuses on male-centred aspects of the genres in question, Wyke 2002, which investigates the nature, or rather the male-made *art* of the female beloved in Roman elegy, and James 2003, to which I will return below. Most recently, Spentzou 2013 revisits the genre from the point of view of its cultural context, reaching back to Syme 1939, and McCoskey/Torlone 2014 summarize the *Stand der Forschung* so far, while touching upon the very important homoerotic aspects of this body of literature. For further examples of this vast scholarship I refer to Conte 1994b, 321–66, Gold 2012 and Thorsen 2013a.
26 Veyne 1988, 140–1 also explicitly refers to de Rougemont, though without mentioning his name, as related to his own project; see also Thorsen 2013b, 17.
27 Veyne 1988, 33.

on the latter, those on the former topic are scanty indeed. This situation is without doubt informed by another monumental figure within French theory, namely Michel Foucault, who was also a personal friend of Veyne.[28] The part of Foucault's project that has been most conspicuously relevant for classical scholarship is the two volumes of his four-book *History of Sexuality*[29] entitled *L'usage des plaisirs* (1984, volume 2) and *Le souci de soi* (1984, volume 3). The first of these focuses on sources from ancient Greece and was published in English as *The Uses of Pleasure* (1985a), while the other concentrates on sources in Greek and Latin from the time of imperial Rome and was translated into English as *The Care of the Self* (1985b).

The influence of Foucault, which has mostly been embraced, but also criticized by classicists,[30] is felt almost everywhere in the vast scholarship on ancient sexuality, which, as already mentioned, arguably eclipses the theme of love. So, in a standard reference work such as the *Oxford Classical Dictionary*, there is only one article that sports the word 'love' in its title, and it is paired with 'friendship' in a non-erotic, philosophical (yet affectionate and other-oriented) sense.[31] By comparison, the dictionary includes several articles with the word 'sexuality' and related vocabulary in their titles.[32] Even in the pioneering work of David Konstan,[33] in which he identifies true love (i.e. 'symmetrical and reciprocal') in the genre of the ancient Greek novel, 'sex[ual]' literally comes before 'love' even in the title, which is *Sexual Symmetry: Love in the Novel and Related Genres* (1994).[34] And in the recent vogue of studies on emotions in antiquity, love has remained surprisingly little explored, albeit with exceptions such as *In the Orbit of Love: Affection in Ancient Greece and Rome* (2018), also by Konstan. However, here too

---

28 See Veyne 2008 and 2013. The non-romantic approach to sex-related issues in Rome is upheld in Veyne 2005.
29 Of which only three were published in his lifetime and the final volume, *Les Aveux de la chair*, was published posthumously in 2018.
30 Among more or less critical voices are Richlin 1993; 1998, Goldhill 1995, Larmour/Miller/Platter 1998, Foxhall 1998, Davidson 2001, Halperin 2002, and Detel 2005.
31 *OCD* s.v. 'love and friendship in Greek philosophy'.
32 See e.g. *OCD* s.v. 'sexuality', 'sexuality, textual representation of', 'heterosexuality', 'sex, anal', 'homosexuality', 'homosexuality, female', 'sexual representation, visual', 'prostitution, sacred', 'prostitution, secular male', 'prostitution, secular female', 'pornography', 'incest', etc.
33 Arguably more pioneering still is Konstan's article on Terence's *Eunuchus* as one of the 'origins of erotic subjectivity', which not only has 'love' as the first word in the article title, but also identifies the citizen boy Phaedria's love for the prostitute Thais as 'a harbinger … of a moment in the history of love that found expression in the elegists of the Augustan principate, and, after another transformation, in the mediaeval tradition of courtly love', 1986, 372.
34 Whitmarsh 2018, also on the novel, features 'love' prominently, even in the title of his work.

the phenomenon under scrutiny is explicitly non-erotic and of the kind which may exist between friends and family members.

Finally, our understanding of love in ancient literature is also complicated by the challenges arising from yet another divide in classical scholarship, namely that between Attic New/Roman Comedy and elegy on the one hand and other love literature on the other. The comparison of Attic New/Roman Comedy with elegy has considerable merits and is well explored in scholarship.[35] Even so, comparisons between elegy and other poetic genres may prove equally if not more useful in drawing up a map that more accurately fits the actual landscape of love in ancient literature.

In this landscape, Latin love elegy does certainly stand out. Not only is the genre surprisingly easily defined by a striking unity, represented by one metre (the elegiac couplet), one canon (Gallus, Tibullus, Propertius and Ovid) and one theme (love),[36] it is also one of the most prominent candidates among ancient media for a genre concerned with true love. For love is essential in the life of an elegiac lover, who either makes love to the beloved if he or she is present (and willing) or writes about the agony of not making love to the beloved when he or she is absent (often due to the beloved's rejection of the lover); moreover, the beloved is sometimes married or belongs to someone else, but the lover has no concern for conventional wedlock or children;[37] the lover's only care is love, which governs his or her life, either in the active form of 'love's fighting/soldiering for love' (*militia amoris*),[38] or in the passive form of the lover's inescapable 'love's slavery/slavery of love', (*seruitium amoris*).[39] Either way, the lover is willing to risk everything for the beloved, even life.[40] In fact, in Latin love elegy there is no life outside love.[41]

---

[35] See Gold 2012.
[36] Thorsen 2013b, 4–5. As I argue in Thorsen 2013c, the *Heroides*, including the letters of Leander and Hero, also belong to the genre of Latin love elegy.
[37] The absence of traditional wedlock and children is also a conspicuous feature of the mediaeval concept of love; see n. 12 above.
[38] Sharrock 2013a.
[39] Fulkerson 2013.
[40] E.g. Prop. 1.1; 2.1.47; 2.15.36, Tib. 1.1.59–68; 1.6.27–8.
[41] This is also the deeper message in Ovid's *Remedia amoris*; see Conte 1989, Fulkerson 2004 and Thorsen 2014, 184–93; in terms of the relevance of this insight for the mediaeval model of love, it is highly noticeable that the twelfth-century Chrétien de Troyes, the author of *Lancelot, ou le Chévalier de la Charrette* (see n. 11 and 13 above) lists *Et les comandemanz d'Ovide* as one of his works in the opening of his *Cligés*, which likely refers to a translation in the vernacular of Ovid's *Remedia amoris*; see Zink 1987.

Now, the striking characteristics of this genre have prompted classicists, whose disciplinary instinct is traditionally to assume that 'nothing arises from nothing', to search for its origin via a style of *Quellenforschung* that has been applied for more than a century.[42] This quest has now resulted in the establishment of what may be labelled the 'comedy model'. This model is most prominently expounded by Sharon James in her milestone publication *Learned Girls and Male Persuasion: Gender and Reading in Roman Love Elegy* (2003). This book builds on the century-long hypothesis that Attic New/Roman Comedy is the most important literary precursor of Latin love elegy, but innovatively suggests that, though the two genres share many similarities, the major difference is that whereas the comic *adulescens* ('youth') pays money for his love (if the beloved is a prostitute),[43] the elegiac *amans* ('lover') offers poems to his beloved, who, though they are described in a notoriously fleeting and indefinite manner,[44] are understood (in this model) to evoke much the same category of women as the comic *meretrix* ('prostitute'). James argues that the elegists thus promote a love that is no truer than that of the comic *adulescens*, who uses money rather than words[45] (when he does not resort to violence)[46] to express his interest in the beloved. In fact, the elegist's love may be regarded as crueller, as the lover's goal still is to have sex with the beloved, but he (usually)[47] tries to achieve this in exchange for poems, which are of limited use to the beloved; her highly literary qualities notwithstanding, she still needs cash to sustain her livelihood. From such a woman's point of view, accepting the elegist's love (= poetry) means starving.[48]

James' interpretation of elegiac love as a male poet-lover's means of getting sex for free, while sugar-coating the harsh social reality of working girls in

---

42 See Sharrock and Brecke in this volume for an overview of the relevant scholarship.
43 The beloved may also be a citizen's daughter, but in that case the *adulescens* normally does not express his love by paying her, but by raping her; see Brecke 2020 and Brecke in this volume.
44 See e.g. Wyke 2002, Brecke and my final chapter in this volume.
45 See Sharrock in this volume.
46 See Brecke in this volume.
47 The Latin love elegist and woman Sulpicia, who strongly complicates this interpretation, is explicitly argued out of it by James 2003, 220.
48 James' argument is strikingly similar to that of the prostitute Philochremation ('lover of money') in Aristaenetus' letter 1.14: οὔτε αὐλὸς ἑταίραν οἶδε προτρέπειν οὔτε λύρα τις ἐφέλκεται πόρνας ἀργυρίου χωρίς· κέρδει μόνον δουλεύομεν, οὐ θελγόμεθα μελῳδίαις. τί οὖν μάτην, ὦ νέοι, διαρρήγνυσθε τὰς γνάθους ἐμφυσῶντες τῇ σύριγγι; οὐδὲν ὑμᾶς ὀνήσει τὰ κιθαρίσματα (Arist. 1.14.1–5 Drago, 'You can't win over a hetaira by playing a flute, nor can you attract prostitutes with a lyre if you don't have money. We are slaves only to profit and are not bewitched by melodies', transl. Höschele and Bing). I have yet to see this text referred to in the comedy-elegy scholarship.

Rome,[49] has (at least) two consequences for scholarship. First, this interpretation is very much in line with the idea that true love is a mediaeval phenomenon, in the sense that it largely denies the existence of a concept of true love in Latin love elegy, which is one of the most obvious locales for such ideas in antiquity. Next, James' interpretation has, due to its sheer influence, which has been considerable, driven a wedge between the study of this genre and that of other non-dramatic love literature,[50] making it hard, for example, to assess the relevance of poetry such as Anacreon Fr. 402c: ἐμὲ γὰρ λόγων < ∪ – > εἵνεκα παῖδες ἄν φιλέοιεν / χαρίεντα μέν γ'ἀείδω, χαρίεντα δ' οἶδα λέξαι ('It is for my art that boys should love me: I can sing gracious songs, and I can speak kind words'),[51] or concepts such as Konstan's 'sexual symmetry' between a boy and a girl in the Greek novel.[52]

The homopoetic model of love

Given the circumstances outlined above, ancient literature should arguably be included in the mediaeval model of love, which would thus call for a rebranding. As an alternative term, I would like to suggest the 'homopoetic model of love'. The first part of the coinage 'homopoetic', which evokes the Greek adjective ὁμός, refers to love's ideal of sameness, in the sense that the love experience is envisaged (however unrealized or unrealizable this may be) as 'common' and 'joint', felt and shared equally between the two partners.[53] The next part of the coinage, 'poetic', refers to the medium of most relevance in this context, which is literature that prominently, though not exclusively, takes the form of poetry. Moreover, this common and joint experience is to be understood in terms of equality and reciprocity, both of which may remain only imagined and longed for, and it may or may not encompass sameness of sex. Thus, the model includes heteroerotic and heterosexual kinds of love in antiquity (and beyond) as freely as homoerotic and

---

49 The topic of prostitution, especially its harsher aspects, is of course an important subject *per se*, which has traditionally been unjustly neglected in scholarship.
50 An exception in this regard is Keith 2011a, focusing on another genre with which Latin love elegy shares strong affinities, namely epigram; see also Keith in this volume.
51 See D'Andrea in this volume.
52 See my final chapter in this volume.
53 *LSJ* sv 'ὁμός', 'one and the same, common, joint.'

homosexual ones.⁵⁴ Finally, according to this model, love has no divine cause, no societal purpose and aims for equality in terms of voluntary, affectionate reciprocity.

Consequently, it is not love if the love in question is orchestrated by (usually) an Olympian god as a part of a divine plan. This feature makes the homopoetic model of love less compatible with the grand erotic schemes in the genres of epic and tragedy. This does not mean that these genres cannot accommodate conceptions of love understood as true, such as that of Achilles for Patroclus.⁵⁵ However, while love plays a prominent role in the *Iliad*, with Aphrodite's plot to have Paris seduce – or rape? – Helen as the trigger that eventually launches the Trojan War, we are told at the very outset of the epic that it all happened in order to fulfil the 'will' or 'plan' of Zeus (Διὸς ... βουλή, *Il.* 1.5). The incompatibility of such an outlook on love with the homopoetic model is sharply underscored by Sappho in the preamble, known as Fr. 16 Voigt, in which she relieves us of the uncertainty around whether Paris raped Helen, taking her against her will, or not. For here Sappho uses precisely Helen's love for Paris – which made her sacrifice everything, parents, husband and child – to demonstrate how an object of love, whether a phenomenon or a person, is 'the most beautiful thing on the black earth' (Sappho, Fr. 16.2-3 Voigt, ἐπ[ὶ] γᾶν μέλαι[ν]αν / ἔ]μμεναι κάλλιστον). Likewise, Phaedra's love for her stepson Hippolytus in Euripides' eponymous tragedy is ultimately the maddening result of Aphrodite's double revenge. This revenge is directed both against the Sun god,⁵⁶ whose descendants, including Phaedra, were cursed by Aphrodite because the god exposed her extramarital affair with Ares, and against Artemis, the anti-erotic virgin goddess to whom Hippolytus pledges his allegiance, thus scorning the powers of the goddess of love.⁵⁷ Accordingly, in the genres of epic and tragedy, love is readily applied as an instrument of divinely instilled insanity, personified in the *Iliad* by Ate, the daughter of Zeus (cf. *Il.* 19.91, 'Madness'), usually with death and devastation as its result. By contrast, according to the homopoetic model of love, which we have seen applies to Helen in Sappho Fr. 16 Voigt, only the beloved can be the cause of love.

That said, it should be added that the model does not imply the exclusion of divinities altogether. For a start, the presence and veneration of Aphrodite/Venus

---

54 The model could thus have been called 'bisexual', which, despite being a modern term, makes sense in the context of ancient conceptions of love and desire, as expounded by Cantarella 1992; cf. also e.g. Harrison 2018a and Ingleheart in this volume.
55 See Acosta-Hughes in this volume.
56 Cf. Eur. *Hipp.* 337–41, Ov. *Her.* 4.53–66, and Sen. *Phaedr.* 124–8. See also Armstrong 2006, 62–3.
57 Hom. *Od.* 8.266–366 and Ov. *Ars am.* 2.561–92.

is so deeply embedded within this model that one may talk about a 'cult of love'. This 'cult' is most prominently exemplified by Sappho's hymn to the goddess, known (despite being the poet's only extant complete poem) as Fr. 1 Voigt. Here, Aphrodite divulges, notably as witnessed by Sappho herself, that she fully intends to cure the lovesickness of the poet, who in turn famously bids the goddess, in the imperative, to assist her in her *militia amoris*:[58] σὺ δ' αὔτα / σύμμαχος ἔσσο (Sappho 1.27–8 Voigt, 'and you, yourself, be my fellow-fighter'). Moreover, the non-Olympian god of love, in Greek called Eros (sometimes Erotes, in the plural), and Amor and Cupido in Latin, is a constant presence in the ancient love literature that operates according to the homopoetic model. Again, Sappho splendidly captures the overpowering (λυσιμέλης), paradoxical-state-stirring (γλυκύπικρον), inescapable (ἀμάχανον) and beastly (ὄρπετον) nature of the god and the phenomenon of Love/love all in just one fragment: Ἔρος δηὖτέ μ' ὁ λυσιμέλης δόνει, / γλυκύπικρον ἀμάχανον ὄρπετον (Sappho, Fr. 130 Voigt, 'Once again limb-loosening Love makes me tremble, the bitter-sweet, irresistible creature'). No wonder Love/love is not one but a multitude of emotions, as brilliantly expressed also by Sappho in Fr. 31 Voigt, in which the poetic I is famously struck dumb, burns, goes blind, hears pounding in her ears, sweats, turns greener than grass and is on the verge of death, all at once, at the sight of her beloved, a woman, chatting and laughing in front of a man.

Last but not least is the character of the god and phenomenon of Love/love as 'weaver of stories', again in the brilliant word of Sappho (Fr. 188 Voigt, μυθοπλόκον). This quality, love's loquaciousness and urge to tell tales, underscores the very important metapoetic dimension of love in ancient literature,[59] where the lover may also be seen as represented by the poet, and the beloved by the reader, who together secure the survival of literature and render 'art enduring', *ars longa*.[60] In fact, the ultimate object of love may also be other (most often dead) poets. Indeed, the names of the elegiac *puellae* such as Lesbia (recalling Sappho from Lesbos) and Corinna (the second most famous woman poet in antiquity)

---

58 See above.
59 And not only in antiquity: in fact, love and literature become inseparable in Dante's casting of the famous story of Paolo and Francesca, modelled on historically real persons known personally to the poet, and often heralded as the paramount example of the mediaeval model (it is the painter Ingres' portrayal of the two that decorates the jacket of Reddy 2012). In the *Divine Comedy*, Francesca explains to Dante that it was while reading how Geneviève kissed Lancelot (see n. 13) that Paolo and she fell in love: 'Galeotto fu 'l libro e chi lo scrisse' (*Div. comm.* 5.137, 'Galeotto was that book and the one who wrote it'). Galeotto is the name of the seneschal who acted as a messenger between Lancelot and Geneviève.
60 Cf. e.g. Svenbro 1993 and Nilsson 2009.

may be regarded as hints at the fact that the poets Catullus and Ovid are ultimately in love not with Roman ladies of their own day and age, but with an artifice of eternity that is crafted by words; their own as well as those of other – including women – poets.[61]

Moreover, according to this model, love is not love if its ultimate goal is to uphold the marital institution and secure offspring. This aspect renders the model largely incompatible with the grander schemes of the genres of Attic New/Roman Comedy. However, as it does in the case of Achilles in the *Iliad*, a kind of love that matches the model may also occur in the comic genre.[62] Moreover, the idea of marriage as a sacred union between the lover and beloved is not completely alien to the homopoetic model of love. Roman love poets may for example envisage themselves in relationships with their beloveds that seem almost more binding than normal wedlock, as famously dramatized in Catullus poem 68.[63] Love may indeed be conflated with marriage, as in the Greek novel, but as its token, not its purpose. In a similar fashion, love may result in children, but it is not love if its purpose and motivation is producing them. Indeed, the validity of the homopoetic model of love can perhaps be seen most acutely in poetry based on heterosexual configurations, since even here not only wedlock, but also the question of children remains a difficult issue. Thus, in Tibullus' dream-vision of a life shared with his beloved Delia, he envisages her not with their child, but a *uerna*, a 'slave-child' from his household, in her lap (Tib. 1.5.26), while Propertius refuses outright to engender soldiers for the regime (Prop. 2.7.14) and Ovid's abortion poems (*Am.* 2.13 and 2.14) strongly complicate the relationship between love

---

[61] See also Astrup Sundt in this volume. The double nature of the 'written girl' as an artifice in herself *and* as a tribute to 'writings' – included those of women poets – is captured in Propertius' second book of elegies, where we encounter the phrase *scripta puella* applied to Cynthia (Prop. 2.10.8), cf. Wyke 2002, but also *scripta Corinnae* (2.3.21), the 'writings of Corinna [of Tanagra, the poet]'; see Thorsen 2012a; 2019b. Although these two instances of the word *scripta* (belonging to different grammatical categories) are rarely linked in scholarship, the double metapoetic aspect they represent offers a different perspective on James' line of reasoning about the cruel 'getting sex for free' motivation of the love of the Latin love elegists, since their poetry is not to be unequivocally understood as addressed to the beloved; instead, their writing is a symptom of the beloved's (voluntary or involuntary) absence, and if their poetry does have a motive beyond offering the only alternative activity that the lover is able to resort to when he or she is unable to make love, then this motive is to address posterity, which would explain why the elegist – as a corollary – can offer the beloved eternal fame in verse.
[62] As e.g. in the case of Phaedria's love for the *meretrix* Thais in Terence's *Eunuchus*, which is not destined for wedlock; see n. 33 and Brecke in this volume.
[63] One of the most conjugal interpretations of this poem is found in Lyne 1980, 52–69.

and procreation (and the relevance of these two phenomena to Augustan politics).

Finally, this model posits a kind of love that is pre-eminently voluntary, affectionate and reciprocal.[64] Certainly, Konstan (1994) is quite right when he argues that this kind of love is realised in a sustained manner within one literary genre in antiquity only: that of the Greek novel. Indeed, this genre is marked by configurations of striking symmetry (even if the lovers are of different sexes): usually both are equally active, equally deeply in love (although one girl ends up being kicked so badly by the boy in a fit of jealousy that she faints and is mistaken for dead)[65] and both are also equals in terms of social status (though sometimes from enemy families). However, instead of regarding this novelistic 'sexual symmetry' as exceptional, we may see it as the fulfilment of a drive towards equality that is embedded more generally in the concept of love in ancient literature, even in its homoerotic form. In fact, the reality of asymmetries[66] is something the lover in ancient literature seeks to overturn, or even expressly perceives as less real than the reality in which the lover regards the beloved as on a par with, or even more highly placed than the lover him- or herself.

Three consequences follow from this drive towards reciprocity in the homopoetic model of love: (a) money can't buy you love, (b) violence cannot produce love, and (c) love is potentially revolutionary. The last point is perhaps best illustrated by the Augustan laws against adultery, which not only made it a punishable crime to have extramarital sexual relations with the daughters, wives and widows of Roman citizens,[67] but also prohibited a citizen from manumitting a slave with whom he had fallen in love so that he could marry her.[68] A lover's disregard of the beloved's place in existing hierarchical structures (asymmetries) is

---

64 As pondered on by Whitmarsh 2018, 172–3.
65 Chariton, *Callirhoe* 1.4.
66 Perhaps most conspicuously embodied in the older penetrator/younger penetrated paradigm, which is so strongly associated in scholarship with Greek homosexuality and which has been criticized by Davidson 2001.
67 These laws (*lex Iulia de maritandis ordinibus*; *lex Iulia de adulteriis coercendis*; *lex Iulia theatralis*; *lex Fufia Caninia* and *lex Aelia Sentina*; see Cooley 2013, 'section S') may be regarded as a proof that love of the kind Reddy describes above existed in antiquity. For if desire in the form of sexual appetite was the only urge that was known at a time when slaves and prostitutes were freely available for the gratification of such desire, why would anyone risk exile or worse to have sex with someone for any reason other than love? Cf. also Treggiari 1991; 1996, Cohen 1991.
68 Gardner 1993.

a potential threat to the social order, and the guardians of such an order may impose severe measures to curb its latent dangers for the establishment, such as the Julian laws introduced in Rome from the last decades BCE onwards.[69]

Concluding remarks

I will close this chapter by pointing out two consequences that follow from the homopoetic model of love as a means of drawing a map in scholarship that arguably fits the landscape of ancient love literature more accurately than the models currently in common use. These consequences have to do with love in literature as a research object more generally.

First, the homopoetic model of love privileges the experience of the lover through verbal descriptions and narratives, which aligns love not only with literature itself but also with metapoetics.[70] Next, the model focuses attention on the presence and reality of the beloved, who may be idealized, though not necessarily, and who may be both attractive and intimidating.[71] This focus on the beloved as an imposing, desirable, but also inescapable and sometimes frightening, even repugnant person, who is at the same time the cause and the goal of the lover's love, also highlights the literary qualities of this kind of love and renders it different from love e.g. in philosophy, where the ultimate object may be pleasure (Epicurus) or beauty (Plato).[72]

Both aspects, the description and narrations of the lover's experience and the lover's sustained focus on the person of the beloved, underscore the literary–aesthetic specificity of this model, which therefore includes the term 'poetics': through the god and phenomenon of Love/love which Sappho rightly identifies as a 'weaver of stories', 'you' and 'I'[73] become distinctive literary realities.[74]

---

[69] It is just as likely that these laws were manifestations of a dictator's (i.e. Augustus') need to control all spheres of life, including emotional and sexual relations, as it is that the laws were a reaction to some alleged decadence and lack of moral decency among Romans at the time, as assumed e.g. by Lyne 1980, 8–17. Cf. also Edwards 1993.

[70] And not only in ancient literature; see n. 59 above.

[71] Thus, the concept of 'crystallization', the process which transforms the beloved, however unlovely, into a flawless and unequivocally delightful person in the lover's eyes, in Stendhal 1822 (= 2014), is too reductive to cover the range of perceptions of the beloved in ancient literature.

[72] See Kayachev in this volume.

[73] Or, in third-person narratives, the 'one' and the 'other'.

[74] I pursue the former 'literary reality' further in the last chapter in this volume.

Benjamin Acosta-Hughes
There Falls a Lone Tear: Longing for a Vanished Love – Tracing an Erotic Motif from Homer to Horace

*For Richard Hunter
in friendship and gratitude*

Prelude

The origin of this study came about in tracing Homeric echoes in an epigram of Callimachus: as so often happens, what seemed a fairly straightforward allusion, or better a series of allusions, has evolved into a rather longer enquiry, one still based in Callimachean epigram, but one which has come to encompass a rather broader and more complicated composition with the reiteration of a single *leitmotiv* – the single, or occasional tear.

Longing for Patroclus

In the beautiful economy of Homer's *Iliad,* Book 1 narrates the loss of two symbols of honour, two γέρα, and the origin of the wrath or μῆνις of Achilles. Book 24 opens (*Il.* 24.1–18) with two corpses, and Achilles' visceral, emotional interactions with both.

Λῦτο δ' ἀγών, λαοὶ δὲ θοὰς ἐπὶ νῆας ἕκαστοι
ἐσκίδναντ' ἰέναι. τοὶ μὲν δόρποιο μέδοντο
ὕπνου τε γλυκεροῦ ταρπήμεναι· αὐτὰρ Ἀχιλλεὺς
κλαῖε φίλου ἑτάρου μεμνημένος, οὐδέ μιν ὕπνος
ᾕρει πανδαμάτωρ, ἀλλ' ἐστρέφετ' ἔνθα καὶ ἔνθα   5
Πατρόκλου ποθέων ἀνδροτῆτά τε καὶ μένος ἠΰ,
ἠδ' ὁπόσα τολύπευσε σὺν αὐτῷ καὶ πάθεν ἄλγεα
ἀνδρῶν τε πτολέμους ἀλεγεινά τε κύματα πείρων·
τῶν μιμνησκόμενος θαλερὸν κατὰ δάκρυον εἶβεν,
ἄλλοτ' ἐπὶ πλευρὰς κατακείμενος, ἄλλοτε δ' αὖτε   10
ὕπτιος, ἄλλοτε δὲ πρηνής· τοτὲ δ' ὀρθὸς ἀναστὰς
δινεύεσκ' ἀλύων παρὰ θῖν' ἁλός· οὐδέ μιν ἠὼς
φαινομένη λήθεσκεν ὑπεὶρ ἅλα τ' ἠϊόνας τε.
ἀλλ' ὅ γ' ἐπεὶ ζεύξειεν ὑφ' ἅρμασιν ὠκέας ἵππους,
Ἕκτορα δ' ἕλκεσθαι δησάσκετο δίφρου ὄπισθεν,   15
τρὶς δ' ἐρύσας περὶ σῆμα Μενοιτιάδαο θανόντος

αὖτις ἐνὶ κλισίῃ παυέσκετο, τὸν δέ τ' ἔασκεν
ἐν κόνι ἐκτανύσας προπρηνέα·

The contest broke up, and each group of people scattered to go to their swift ships. They thought of their dinner, and to take pleasure from sweet sleep. But Achilles mourned remembering his dear companion, nor did all-subduing sleep take him, but he turned here and there, longing for Patroclus, his manliness and his great strength, and all the hard things he carried out and suffered with him, making trial of enemies among men and the grievous waves.[1] Remembering these things he shed a thick tear, now lying on his side, now on his back, and now on his front. Then, standing aright, he turned wandering by the shore of the sea. Nor did the dawn upon shining forth over the sea and the beaches escape him. But then he would yoke his swift horses below his car, and bind Hector to be dragged behind his chariot, and when he had dragged him three times around the tomb marker of the dead son of Menoeteus, again he would leave off at his shelter and, unbinding Hector, would leave him prone in the dust.[2]

Achilles' mourning for the dead Patroclus is configured of memory (line 4: φίλου ἑτάρου μεμνημένος), sleeplessness (lines 4-5: οὐδέ μιν ὕπνος / ᾕρει πανδαμάτωρ), longing (line 6: ποθέων) for the physicality of the man (line 6: Πατρόκλου ... ἀνδροτῆτά τε καὶ μένος ἄλγεα), memory again (line 9: τῶν μιμνσκόμενος), the shedding of a thick tear (line 9: θαλερὸν κατὰ δάκρυον εἶβεν), sleeplessness again (line 10: ἄλλοτ' ἐπὶ πλευρὰς κατακείμενος, ἄλλοτε δ' αὖτε), and then wandering until dawn (lines 11-13). The latter, wandering in longing at night, is a classic symptom of longing for one absent (so e.g. Sapph. fr. 96.15–16 V., also *Il.* 2.777–8, here of his own men longing for Achilles). The lone thick tear serves as something of an emblem of the entire mourning experience, as it is both part of the physical present and of the remembered past. While there are many uses of δάκρυον in Homer, the formulaic phrase θαλερὸν δάκρυον 'thick tear', or τέρεν δάκρυον, 'soft tear' is always singular and always represents something of a collective experience. I give a list of these occurrences as an appendix to this study. A particularly vivid parallel occurs in Achilles' mourning speech to Patroclus (*Il.* 19.315-37) where Achilles imagines his own father Peleus in mourning for the loss, literally the 'want', or 'lack' of his son (19.324–5): τέρεν κατὰ δάκρυον εἴβει / χήτει τοιοῦδ' υἷος, 'he sheds a gentle tear, for want of his son'. There are three other occurrences of the phrase θαλερὸν δάκρυον in the *Iliad*, and, notably, it concludes the poignant interchange of Hector and Andromache at the Skaian Gate (*Il.* 6.496: ἄλοχος δὲ φίλη οἰκόνδε βεβήκει / ἐντροπαλιζομένη, θαλερὸν κατὰ

---

[1] Lines 6–9 were athetized by the Alexandrian scholars Aristophanes and Aristarchus. The second zeugma of line 8 is awkward. I would argue though that the authenticity of line 9 gains some support from the parallel image at 19.323. Cf. further MacLeod 1982, *ad loc.*
[2] All translations are my own.

δάκρυ χέουσα, 'his beloved wife went home, ever looking behind her, shedding a thick tear'). Another instance, at *Il.* 24.794, concludes the cremation of Hector; noteworthy too is δάκρυ χέοντες at line 786 in the same book of the laying out of Hector on his pyre. The first occurrence of this phrase describes Thersites following his humiliation by Odysseus at *Il.* 2.266 and is mock-heroic, fittingly of the mock hero Thersites. It is unsurprising that in a poem marked by delicate compositional balances, the single tear in mourning for Patroclus at the opening of *Il.* 24 should be recalled by the single tear in mourning for Hector at the poem's end.

A tear for Heraclitus

Callimachus *Epigr.* 2 Pf. (34 GP) is perhaps the Alexandrian poet's best-known poem in this genre. This is among the most admired of his epigrams, has been studied from a variety of critical perspectives, and has long been a favorite among the poet's readers:[3]

Εἶπέ τις, Ἡράκλειτε, τεὸν μόρον, ἐς δέ με δάκρυ
 ἤγαγεν· ἐμνήσθην δ' ὁσσάκις ἀμφότεροι
ἥλιον ἐν λέσχῃ κατεδύσαμεν. ἀλλὰ σὺ μέν που,
 ξεῖν' Ἁλικαρνησεῦ, τετράπαλαι σποδιή,
αἱ δὲ τεαὶ ζώουσιν ἀηδόνες, ᾗσιν ὁ πάντων   5
 ἁρπακτὴς Ἀΐδης οὐκ ἐπὶ χεῖρα βαλεῖ.

Someone told, Heracleitus, of your death, and this brought a tear to me. I remembered how often we both set the sun to sleep in our conversation. But you somewhere, Halicarnassian friend, are long ago dust. Yet your nightingales live on; upon these Hades, who steals all away, will not set his hand.

In his posthumously published study of this poem, the late G.B. Walsh acutely articulated the very 'modern' delineation of thought processes in this six-line epigram;[4] a conventional epigram type (the *epitaph*) becomes rather only the template for construction of an interior conversation. The poet thinks of his friend, the pleasure of the time they shared, the absence of that association, and the

---

[3] Among recent treatments, see especially Hunter 1992; see also Meyer 2005, 221–2, Walsh 1990, Gutzwiller 1988, 206–8, MacQueen 1982.
[4] Walsh 1990.

friend's memory preserved through his poetry.[5] The framing of the memory is homosocial rather than symposiastic; the memory of distant association, while not tempered with explicit erotic associations, can nonetheless be read as one of pleasure and longing. The overall movement of the poem can be phrased as apostrophe, memory of time spent together, separation, poetry, and then final reference to a destructive deity.[6] The move from external impulse ('someone told me') to internal sensation mirrors earlier Greek lyric (Sappho fr. 31 V., φαίνεταί μοι κῆνος e.g.), as does some of the poem's language of memory and longing. And as with *synaphaea* in the Sapphic stanza, so here the poem's form, in this case the distich, or elegiac couplet, contributes to the poem's progress: present to past in two lines, past to present in two lines, present to future in two lines. In his acutely intelligent 1992 reading of the poem R. Hunter deftly pointed to the possible *Odyssean* parallels of grief quenched only by sunset, reworked here by Callimachus in the association of grief/memory and leisure/sunset. I would suggest another possible Homeric sunset allusion here, the same grief of Achilles for Patroclus at the opening of *Iliad* 24, particularly line 9: τῶν μιμνησκόμενος θαλερὸν κατὰ δάκρυον εἶβεν: the association of memory and the single tear. The allusion grants a further epicizing touch to the epigram's reading: the Homeric features of the poem further shed light on the poet's use of the striking μόρος of the opening line, a term usually reserved for major heroic figures in the *Iliad*. The short poem is thus given epic grandeur, culminating in the image of all-destructive Hades at the end. And its reading turns out to be a complex one: an association of generic epigram types, of two poets (both Callimachus and Heracleitus),[7] and a lexicon of poetic memory.

Typical of the philologist poet, there is a play on Homeric vocabulary in line 3 ἥλιον ἐν λέσχῃ κατεδύσαμεν. As N. Hopkinson well observes,[8] λέσχη is a Homeric *hapax legomenon*, occurring at *Odyssey* 18.327–30 in Melantho's abusive treatment of the beggar Odysseus:

ξεῖνε τάλαν, σύ γέ τις φρένας ἐκπεπαταγμένος ἐσσί,
οὐδ' ἐθέλεις εὕδειν χαλκήϊον ἐς δόμον ἐλθὼν
ἠέ που ἐς λέσχην, ἀλλ' ἐνθάδε πόλλ' ἀγορεύεις
θαρσαλέως πολλοῖσι μετ' ἀνδράσιν

---

[5] For further examples of poets mourning the loss of preceding poets, read Astrup Sundt in this volume.
[6] The final image ὁ πάντων / ἁρπακτὴς Ἀΐδης seems to pre-figure Catullus' 3.13–14: *malae tenebrae / Orci, quae omnia bella deuoratis*. Both are rare, striking poetic images of death.
[7] On the identity of the poet Heraclitus (Strab. 14.2.16 and Diog. Laert. 9.17) see esp. Hunter 1992.
[8] Hopkinson 1988, 249.

Wretched stranger, you are out of your mind, why aren't you willing to go and sleep at the blacksmith's, or at the λέσχη, and there speak boldly among many men?

The scholia to this passage identify the λέσχη as a windowless public place where impoverished men go to sleep, and by extension the conversation that goes on there. With ἥλιον ... κατεδύσαμεν Callimachus plays further with Homeric vocabulary: 'when the sun set' ἦμος ἠέλιος κατέδυ, and 'together with the sun setting' ἅμ' ἠελίῳ καταδύντι, become here rather the 'putting the sun to sleep' as object of the two poets' agency. The epigram that frames longing for the absent friend/poet does so in terms of the two poets' own interests in poetry and poetic memory.

It is worth noting in this context that while the Heracleitus epigram is not overtly erotic, the controversy surrounding its most famous English translation has led it to be frequently classed (and frequently condemned) with Callimachus' homoerotic love poetry. The translation of the epigram that opens 'They told me Heracleitus, they told me you were dead', was penned by William Johnson Cory, Greek master at Eton from 1845–72, who was allegedly dismissed on the grounds of his close relationships with some of his male pupils.[9] The famous English rendition thus acquired an equally famous notoriety.

Longing for a 'lost' poet on a sleepless night

I return to Callimachus *Epigr.* 2 Pf. (34 GP), to consider it from a very different perspective: its Catullan reception. Catullus' poem to his friend Licinius Calvus, poem 50, allows for a very interesting comparative reading.

> Hesterno, Licini, die otiosi
> multum lusimus in meis tabellis,
> ut conuenerat esse delicatos:
> scribens uersiculos uterque nostrum
> ludebat numero modo hoc modo illoc,   5
> reddens mutua per iocum atque uinum.
> atque illinc abii tuo lepore
> incensus, Licini, facetiisque,
> ut nec me miserum cibus iuuaret
> nec somnus tegeret quiete ocellos,   10
> sed toto indomitus furore lecto
> uersarer, cupiens uidere lucem,

---

[9] One of Cory's pupils, Reginald Brett, 2nd Viscount Esher (1852–1930) authored a 1923 book devoted to Cory, entitled *Ionicus*, a reference to Cory's own 2 volume poetry collection *Ionica*.

ut tecum loquerer simulque ut essem.
At defessa labore membra postquam
semimortua lectulo iacebant,   15
hoc, iucunde, tibi poema feci,
ex quo perspiceres meum dolorem.[10]
Nunc audax caue sis, precesque nostras,
Oramus, caue despuas, ocelle,
Ne poenas Nemesis reposcat a te.   20
Est uemens dea: laedere hanc caueto.

Yesterday, Licinius, at leisure we played much in my writing tablets, as we had agreed to be lovely; each of us writing little verses played now with this meter now with that one, giving mutual pleasure with laughter and wine. From there I went away, on fire from your charm, Licinius, and your wit, so that neither was food any help to wretched me, nor did sleep touch my eyes with rest, but overcome with passion I kept tossing about all over the couch, wanting to see the light, that I might speak with you and be together. But after my limbs, half-dead with fatigue, lay exhausted on my little bed, I made this poem for you, from which you might appreciate my suffering. Now beware that you not sniff at my entreaties, or spite them, my love, for fear Nemesis demand payment from you. She's a powerful goddess – take care not to offend her.

I would like to touch first on a couple of similarities of the two poems. The first is the Callimachean phrase ὁσσάκις ἀμφότεροι / ἥλιον ἐν λέσχῃ κατεδύσαμεν. Each element appears reconfigured in Catullus' poem: ἐν λέσχῃ ~ *otiosi*; ὁσσάκις ~ multum; ἥλιον ... κατεδύσαμεν ~ *hesterno ... die*. Each poem characterizes itself as a memory. In each case the memory leads to an emotive response (one much more passionate and effusive in the case of Catullus). In each case the result of remembered pleasure is the composition of a poem (whether or not the referent of Catull. 50.16 is this poem or poem 51). There are a few smaller similarities: line 17 *ex quo perspiceres meum dolorem*, sorrow to be perceived from the composition, and ἐς δέ με δάκρυ. The last vivid image of the epigram, all-consuming Hades, does not appear recalled in Catullus' poem – but may be imitated at Catull. 3.13–14: *malae tenebrae / Orci, quae omnia bella deuoratis*, a differently figured personification of death (and an evocation of death that is also, here through enjambment, metrically remarkable). That one element of an intertext may occur elsewhere than in its more prominent imitation in a later poem is an important conclusion of J. Wills' brilliant 1998 study;[11] the suggestion here would then be that it might occur elsewhere in the same collection of short poems.

---

10 Text of Catullus throughout is the 1958 *OCT* edited by Mynors.
11 Wills 1998, 288; 296.

Then there are the differences. In the Callimachus epigram the association is one both temporally and spatially distant. Catullus presents the reverse: the friend is both close to the poet's recall in time (*hesterno die*) and space (*atque illinc abii ... ut tecum loquerer simulque ut essem*). Catullus 50 is replete with erotic imagery.[12] This is largely absent in the Callimachus epigram, though this epigram came indeed to have a long reception as an erotically-tinged composition.[13] The language of poem 50 is also that of the Roman elite: *conuenerat, reddens mutua* evoke Roman social interchange; even *otiosi* can be understood as reflective of a specifically Roman definition; and thus the surprise effect of line 2, with its whiff of Callimachean composition (*Aetia* fr. 1.21–2, the poet as school-boy). *Lepor, delicatus, iucundus* are terms that can be understood as poetic and at the same time reflective of Roman elite social comportment of the late Republic.[14] In this light, lines 7–8 *tuo lepore / incensus* might be something of a *double-entendre*, as *lepor/lepidus* can be understood as a Latin rendition of the Greek *leptotes*, a poetic term often associated particularly with Callimachus.[15] And while Callimachus' poem is a six-line epigram, Catullus 50 is a poem of 22 lines in phalacean hendecasyllables, a predominant meter of the *Polymetrics* (and also one of the meters of Sappho Book 5). The single tear of the Callimachus epigram and its evocation of distant longing is absent in Catullus' poem, but Catullus' affectionate *ocelle* (line 19) recalls both the image of the eye as 'organ' of longing for what is absent, and also, subtly, the remarkable singular of Callimachus' δάκρυ.

It is worth noting in this context that Callimachus prefigures the Roman poets in his portrayal of the physicality of poetic composition, poetry as *labor*, though with a jocular touch, as in the poet as school-boy at *Aetia* fr. 1.21–2: καὶ γὰρ ὅτ]ε πρ[ώ]τιστον ἐμοῖς ἐπὶ δέλτον ἔθηκα γούνασι]ν, 'when I first put my tablet on my knees'),[16] or Aratus' fine verses as proof of his poetic sleeplessness at *Epigr*. 56 GP (27 Pf.) (3–4: χαίρετε λεπταί / ῥήσιες, Ἀρήτου σύμβολον ἀγρυπνίης, 'farewell fine verses, symbol of Aratus' sleeplessness'). The references to writing, and also to reading, in his poetry lay the groundwork for what was to evolve as the idea of poet *qua* métier among his Roman successors, as well as for the increasingly popular association of poetic composition and night.

---

12 Fitzgerald 1992, 428–30.
13 On William Johnson Cory's rendition of the poem, see Nisbet 2013, 157, 160, 287.
14 Krostenko 2001.
15 See Knox 2007, 157.
16 On this image see Acosta-Hughes/Stephens 2002, 243–4.

Horace's *rara lacrima*

Horace *Odes* 4.1 opens with a famous recreation of Sappho's prayer to Aphrodite (fr. 1 V, the first poem of the first book of the Alexandrian Sappho edition) and an emotional, psychological tension between the *then* of the poet's earlier composition, *Odes* 1–3, and the younger poet, and the return to lyric composition of a now much older poet with *Odes* 4. The outline of this tension frames the poem's first eight stanzas, the temporal distinction of line 3 *non sum qualis eram bonae / sub regno Cinarae* ('I am not such as I was, under Cinara's reign') being then thematically recalled in the eighth stanza (lines 29–32):

> me nec femina nec puer
>   iam nec spes animi credula mutui
> nec certare iuuat mero
>   nec uincire nouis tempora floribus.

> Neither woman nor boy now pleases me, nor the naïve hope of a responding mind, nor to contend with wine, nor to bind my temples with fresh flowers.

Yet this distinction that Horace seeks to make, the distance that he wants to establish, between his younger and older compositional selves is not impenetrable: his unconscious, whether in a wakeful or somnolent state, allows the past to reappear in the present, and the single tear is again the emblem in the following stanza (line 34).

> sed cur heu, Ligurine, cur
>   manat rara meas lacrima per genas?
> cur facunda parum decoro   35
>   inter uerba cadit lingua silentio?
>
> nocturnis ego somniis
>   iam captum teneo, iam uolucrem sequor
> te per gramina Martii
>   campi, te per aquas, dure, uolubilis.   40

> But why, alas, Ligurinus, why does an infrequent tear drip down my cheeks? Why amidst its words does my eloquent tongue fall into a scarcely eloquent silence? In my dreams at night I hold you captive, now in flight I pursue you, in flight through the grasses of the field of Mars, you, harsh one, through the rolling waves.

Again, the lone tear serves as something of an emblem of the entire experience of longing, and it is both part of the physical present and of the remembered past. The lone tear sets in motion a sequence of unconscious experiences, the poet's sudden clumsy inarticulateness, the revival of a long-past love in dream. In sleep the poet-ἐράστης ever pursues his boy-love, and captures him only to lose him. There is no lasting attainment, desire is only replaced by more desire, the last image is one of flight and pursuit through vast space and water in motion.[17]

In composing this study I became intrigued by a possible Callimachean presence at this poem's end, one that I do not believe has received any attention before – although Horace's *Odes*, including 4.1, have been much studied for their Callimachean resonances. As with Callim. *Ep.* 2 Pf. and Catullus 50, this is a Callimachean presence that may not be obvious on a first reading. The Callimachean epigram is one that Horace paraphrases in *Sat.* 1.2.105–10, and may also use to affect the tonal change of *Odes* 1.37 (the *Cleopatra Ode*). Ovid also uses this epigram at *Amores* 2.9.9–10.[18] The epigram in question is Callim. 31 Pf. (1 GP).

Ὡγρευτής, Ἐπίκυδες, ἐν οὔρεσι πάντα λαγωόν
  διφᾷ καὶ πάσης ἴχνια δορκαλίδος
στίβῃ καὶ νιφετῷ κεχρημένος· ἢν δέ τις εἴπῃ
  'τῇ, τόδε βέβληται θηρίον', οὐκ ἔλαβεν
χοὖμὸς ἔρως τοιόσδε· τὰ μὲν φεύγοντα διώκειν
  οἶδε, τὰ δ' ἐν μέσσῳ κείμενα παρπέταται.

A hunter, Epicydes, in the mountains follows every hare and in the tracks of every roe-deer, tracking it in hoar-frost and snow.[19] If someone says 'there lies a beast shot' he does not take it up. And such is my love. It knows to pursue what flees, but what lies in its midst it flies on by.

The parallel imagery of pursuit in the hunt is not surprising, given that this imagery is typical of depictions of pederastic love in both poetry and art, although the division effected by the caesura at line 5 of the epigram and by the caesura in line 38, the second line of the second Aesclepiad, is striking. Metrically Ἐπίκυδες (⏑⏑–⏑) and Ligurine (⏑⏑–⏑) have the same configuration of syllable quantities. While Horace uses Callimachus' winter imagery in another rendition of this epigram, the vision of the hunt in sleep, as the hunt imagined in a distant wintry mountain setting, has a similar effect of creating a change of space, an 'elsewhere'. Βέβληται corresponds to *captum*, παρπέταται both to *uolucrem*, and also, as an image of mobility, to *uolubilis*, both poems concluding with an image of

---

17 My reading of this poem has been much influenced by Aaron Palmore's 2016 dissertation, which pairs Horace *Odes* 4 and the Lacanian conception of desire. For a further development of some of the arguments in this dissertation, see the chapter by Palmore in the present volume.
18 Ov. *Am.* 2.9.9–10: *uenator sequitur fugientia, capta relinquit, / semper et inuentis ulteriora petit.*
19 On the sense of στίβῃ καὶ νιφετῷ κεχρημένος see Marshall 2015.

transient mobility. The tone of the two passages is of course different: Callimachus' Epikydes epigram lacks the sense of personal regret of Horace 4.1,[20] nor is there the sense of temporal distance in 4.1 (then further emphasized in 4.10) of regretful longing for an earlier state. Yet the parallels remain, resulting in an interesting transition in 4.1 itself. The poem thematically moves from heteroerotic in reference and imagery (Cinara, prayer that Venus attend upon Paulus Maximus, where boys and virgins will celebrate her in the dance) to the poet's own invulnerability to woman or boy (line 29: *me nec femina nec puer*) and finally to his *rara lacrima* for one boy of the past (Ligurinus). So too the poem moves from Sappho as model (imitation of Sappho fr. 1 V, evocation of world of public choral dance performance) to Callimachus, to the standard homoerotic image of Love and the Hunt, to one of almost Proustian involuntary memory. The single tear here, as in the opening of *Iliad* 24, recalls a love now 'on the other side', irretrievable, no longer attainable, *uolubilis*.

A final thought. Callimachus *Ep.* 31 (Epikydes) is the parallel to this last stanza of Hor. 4.1 in a particular way: while the Other is alive, the hunt for something that cannot be found is delightful and intellectually engaging. Once the Other is dead, or rendered unrealizable by the passage of time, the hunt is a source of sorrow. The poet's knowledge about the outcome of the hunt decides whether he enjoys it or not.[21]

---

20 Gow-Page *ad loc.*: 'We may perhaps conjecture that he (sc. Epikydes) was a friend who had commented on the fickleness of C's affections ...'. There is no reason to think that Epikydes is the object of the poet's desire.
21 Again, I would like to thank Laura Marshall for discussion on this point.

Peter Astrup Sundt
Orpheus and Sappho as Model Poets: Blurring Greek and Latin Love in *Lament for Bion*, Catullus 51, and Horace *Odes* 1.24

Introduction

Orpheus and Sappho have both played an important role as exemplars of poetic ideals for subsequent poets to emulate and by including them as figures of comparison it may equally be possible to signal a poet's autonomy from these old masters. There are many differences between how the two function as figures of reference in later poems, but they share an important characteristic in that their varied associations with both same-sex and heterosexual love may be reconfigured to suit the particular needs of a later poet. We shall look at three examples, of how this plays out in practice and how the lines between homoerotic and heteroerotic may be drawn less markedly than they at first appear. The first example concerns Orpheus and the anonymous the *Lament for Bion*, the next will investigate the role of Sappho in the case of Catullus, and finally Orpheus will re-emerge in a complex case in Horace.

Starting with the anonymous pastoral *Lament for Bion*, which in virtue of being written by an 'Ausonian' (i.e. Italian) poet composing in Greek acts as a natural bridge between the Greek and Latin poetic traditions, we will continue onto two Latin examples. In the *Lament*, Orpheus' heterosexual love story acts like a destabilising force upon the poem's portrayal of the relationship between the poem's author and the deceased Bion. In a way, the poet surprisingly exploits the homoerotic associations of Orpheus to add to the poem's latent sexual innuendo. In the Sapphic *Catullus* 51, the homoerotic associations of Sappho's poetic *persona* in her model poem (fr. 31) are largely replaced by Catullus' heteroerotic love-triangle between his poetic *persona*, Lesbia, and another man, but where the role-play ultimately carries with it an appropriation of the role of a woman in love with another woman. Finally, in the Asclepiadean *Carm.* 1.24, Horace includes Orpheus' heteroerotic love story in reference to Virgil's grief for the deceased critic Quintilius Varus, effectively casting Quintilius in the role of Eurydice to Virgil's Orpheus, which, much like in the *Lament for Bion* creates homoerotic associations, not in spite of, but through the heteroerotic associations of Orpheus within the poem. Given Virgil's extensive interaction with Orpheus within *his* poetic corpus, Horace's inclusion of this mythic exemplar may be seen as Horace advising Virgil by way of one of his own examples.

Orpheus and pederastic overtones in the *Lament for Bion*

We shall start by looking at the *Lament for Bion*. The author of this anonymous poem, whom I will refer to as the Epitaphist,[1] portrays himself as a student and poetic heir to the pastoral/bucolic poet Bion. This relationship between Bion and the Epitaphist exists in tandem with their respective connections with Orpheus. We shall see that this second set of relationships may be described as an agonistic one, where Bion and the Epitaphist can be described as vying over who gets to be the new Orpheus and who must assume the more passive role of Eurydice. However, the manner in which Orpheus' love story is presented makes it questionable whether it is better to be Orpheus' heir. In this poem, Orpheus' heteroerotic love story with his wife Eurydice plays a prominent part, yet the less famous story of Orpheus as the pederastic lover of the Argonaut Calaïs and Orpheus' associated function as teacher of pederasty among the Thracians (as recounted in the Hellenistic poem *Loves or Beautiful Boys* by Phanocles) may be echoed in the description of Bion and the Epitaphist's relationship.

Though Orpheus was considered by some writers in antiquity to have been an author of poems, it is not productive to look for intertextual allusions to any 'Orphic poems' in the *Lament for Bion*, given that as a mythic poet it was all too easy for poets to ascribe anonymous poems to his name. Without a strictly defined poetic output, Orpheus could act like a poetic exemplar for poets of any genre, and in the *Lament* he becomes a benchmark for bucolic poets. However, as we shall see, his position as such is problematised by his heteroerotic love story, centred on his journey to the Underworld in an attempt to retrieve his wife Eurydice. I will first look at this function of the heteroerotic associations of Orpheus, before turning to look at the function of his less overt homoerotic associations.

Troia has described the *Lament* as:

---

1 I here follow the example of Troia in avoiding the problematic and long term 'Pseudo-Moschus' used in earlier scholarship, see Troia 2016, 3.

[...] a series of agones and agonistic episodes marked by the fictionalisation of the major characters, particularly Bion, who appears in the poem as an archetypal bucolic shepherd-poet and onto whom the settings, themes, and characters from his own poetry are projected.[2]

This agonistic attitude towards the *Lament* is very much in line with more recent approaches to the pastoral tradition in general. Pastoral poetry was long considered primarily in terms of its inherent mixture of urbane complexity and rural simplicity; however, according to Hubbard pastoral poetry should rather be approached as a poetic tradition driven by the desire of novice poets to challenge their predecessors and create a name for themselves within a confined generic framework. Above all this is the case of the subgroup of pastoral poems centered on shepherds, the bucolic:

> The bucolic, more than any other poetic type, is about poetic influence and succession: bucolic poetry by its very nature can exist only as part of an interconnected tradition of poets influencing other poets.[3]

This interconnected tradition is evident e.g. in the *Lament*'s reworking of the earliest surviving poem from the pastoral genre, Theocritus' *Idylls* 1. Like the *Lament*, this poem contains an extended lament for a bucolic shepherd-poet, the mythical Daphnis, and the recurring refrains of both these poems exhort the Muses to take the lead in the lamentation.[4] Similarly, the topos of tradition and poetic influence is central to the *Lament* where the author of the poem openly presents himself as the poetic heir of Bion:

> ... αὐτὰρ ἐγώ τοι
> Αὐσονικᾶς ὀδύνας μέλπω μέλος, οὐ ξένος ᾠδᾶς
> βουκολικᾶς, ἀλλ' ἄντε διδάξαο σεῖο μαθητάς   95
> κλαρονόμος μοίσας τᾶς Δωρίδοσ, ᾇ με γεραίρων
> ἄλλοις μὲν τεὸν ὄλβον ἐμοὶ δ' ἀπέλειπες ἀοιδάν.
>
> (*Lament for Bion*, 93–7)

> But the dirge I sing for you expresses the grief of Italy. I am no stranger to bucolic song: I have inherited that Dorian Muse which you taught your pupils; that was your bequest to me when you left your wealth to others but to me your song.
>
> (trans. Hopkinson)

---

2 Troia 2016, 6.
3 Hubbard 1998, 21.
4 Hubbard 1998, 42.

This open assertion of the author that he claims to be the heir to Bion, and to the tradition that he represents, is a prime example of Hubbard's point about pastoral as a tradition driven by early-career poets challenging their predecessors. Bion and the Epitaphist are both compared with Orpheus within the *Lament for Bion*. Bion is compared with Orpheus at the end of the third stanza of the poem:

> Στρυμόνιοι μύρεσθε παρ' ὕδασιν αἴλινα κύκνοι,
> καὶ γοεροῖς στομάτεσσι μελίσδετε πένθιμον ᾠδάν   15
> †οἵαν ὑμετέροις ποτὶ χείλεσι γῆρας ἀείδει.†
> εἴπατε δ' αὖ κούραις Οἰαγρίσιν, εἴπατε πάσαις
> Βιστονίαις Νύμφαισιν, 'ἀπώλετο Δώριος Ὀρφεύς.'
> ἄρχετε Σικελικαί, τῷ πένθεος ἄρχετε, Μοῖσαι.

(*Lament for Bion*, 14–19)

> You swans of Strymon, cry woe beside your waters; with your lamenting voices sing a dirge such as old age produces from your throats. Say once more to the daughters of Oeagrus, say to all the Nymphs of Bistonia, 'The Dorian Orpheus is dead.'

(trans. Hopkinson)

Troia sees this as a reference to 'his [Orpheus'] role as a legendary, foundational character in the evolution of a specifically bucolic strain of herdsmanly song.'[5] The role of Orpheus in the opening of the poem, where the grief of a number of elements drawn from the natural world precedes that of the swans and nymphs in the third stanza (glades (v. 1), rivers (vs. 1–2), flowers (vs. 4–7) etc.) can be envisaged as drawing up comparisons between Orpheus' supernatural music and Bion's poetic prowess based upon the similar reactions of the natural world to their deaths.[6] Kania sees Orpheus' initial function within the poem as being a paradigmatic figure for the topos of the natural world's mourning for a poet, which he interprets as the defining characteristic of the *Lament's* fictional bucolic world.[7] Whilst the *Lament* avoids any direct reference to a similar case of pathetic fallacy (i.e. the supernatural grief of the natural world in sympathy with a dead person) in the aftermath of Orpheus' own death, the poem nevertheless alludes to such a possibility.[8] Troia notes that the opening stanzas can be seen to draw up comparisons not just between Bion and Orpheus, but also indirectly between Orpheus and the Epitaphist as a display of the 'Epitaphist's own command over

---

5 Troia 2016, 12.
6 Troia 2016, 150.
7 Kania 2012, 668.
8 Kania 2012, 668.

the natural world in the manner of Orpheus'.[9] This can be arguably be seen through the use of imperatives, in that the Epitaphist's song directs the grief of the natural world much as Orpheus is typically depicted as controlling flora, fauna and minerals with his singing.

In the final stanza of the poem, Orpheus reappears as a poetic figure of comparison and this time he is explicitly aligned with both Bion and the Epitaphist:

ἀλλὰ Δίκα κίχε πάντας· ἐγὼ δ' ἐπὶ πένθεϊ τῷδε
δακρυχέων τεὸν οἶτον ὀδύρομαι. εἰ δυνάμαν δέ,   115
ὡς Ὀρφεὺς καταβὰς ποτὶ Τάρταρον, ὥς ποκ' Ὀδυσσεύς,
ὡς πάρος Ἀλκεΐδας, κἠγώ τάχ' ἂν ἐς δόμον ἦλθον
Πλουτέος ὥς κέ σ' ἴδοιμι καί, εἰ Πλουτῇ μελίσδῃ,
ὡς ἂν ἀκουσαίμαν τί μελίσδεαι. ἀλλ' ἄγε Κώρᾳ
Σικελικόν τι λίγαινε καὶ ἁδύ τι βουκολιάζευ·   120
καὶ κείνα Σικελά, καὶ ἐν Αἰτναίαισιν ἔπαιζεν
ᾀόσι, καὶ μέλος οἶδε τὸ Δώριον· οὐκ ἀγέραστος
ἐσσεῖθ' ἁ μολπά, χώς Ὀρφέι πρόσθεν ἔδωκεν
ἁδέα φορμίζοντι παλίσσυτον Εὐρυδίκειαν,
καὶ σέ, Βίων, πέμψει τοῖς ὤρεσιν. εἰ δέ τι κἠγών   125
συρίσδων δυνάμαν, παρὰ Πλουτέι κ' αὐτὸς ἄειδον.

But Justice catches up with every man. Even so, I shed tears at this sad event and lament your death. Had it been possible, I would have gone down to Tartarus and maybe entered the halls of Hades like Orpheus, like Odysseus once did, like Alcides, in order to see you and, if you sing for Pluto, to hear what song it is. But come, play for the Maiden some Sicilian song, some sweet country melody. She too is a Sicilian who used to play on the shores of Etna, and she knows the Dorian mode. Your song will not go unrewarded; just as she once gave back Eurydice to Orpheus for his sweet lyre playing, so she will restore you, Bion, to your hills. And if my piping had any power, I would myself have played for Pluto.

(trans. Hopkinson)

The Epitaphist here imagines what it would be like to visit the Underworld in order to see Bion. He appears almost absorbed into this dream vision when he suddenly exhorts Bion to sing to Persephone in order that Bion might be restored to his hills. Orpheus's act of entering the Underworld (v. 116) is mentioned in addition to Heracles and Odysseus as one of three famous katabasts (vs. 116–17) who together seem to indicate that it could be possible to undertake such a journey. The success of such an endeavour is not certain, as the example of Orpheus may illustrate. Heath has argued that Orpheus failed ultimately in resurrecting his wife Eurydice in all ancient poetic accounts.[10] We might think that the Epitaphist

---

9 Troia 2016, 151.
10 Heath 1994.

consciously alludes to Orpheus' failure in resurrecting Eurydice in order to make him appear a limited poetic exemplar, whose poetic prowess is surpassed by Bion. Unlike Orpheus, Bion would surely be able to resurrect someone (himself) if he tried to, he implies. However, the Epitaphist does not make it clear that Bion is singing in the Underworld, or that he sings to Persephone, whom the poem depicts as the deity responsible for handing over Eurydice. The idea that Bion might be singing to Pluto is at first only floated in a hypothetical mood of uncertainty: εἰ Πλουτῆι μελίσδη (118, 'if you sing to Pluto'), and it appears as if Bion would require the help of the Epitaphist to stir him into singing to Persephone.[11] If he were to sing to Persephone he could take advantage of her Sicilian background by singing something bucolic – Bion is associated with Sicily within the poetic world of the *Epitaph*.[12] Bion, who up until this point in the poem has been given the highest praise is now seen to be limited. Though he might be able to outperform Orpheus his success is dependent upon the help of his poetic heir, the Epitaphist. Not only insomuch as the Epitaphist's *persona* is required to command Bion into action, but also by the fact that (on a metapoetic level) this is a fiction created by the Epitaphist.

It is also possible to see the appearance of Orpheus' *katabasis* as an attempt of the Epitaphist to display his mastery of a character within Bion's own poetry. Bion's *fr.* 6 is a good candidate for a poem concerned with Orpheus. This fragment contains a problematic line printed with daggers by Gow:

μηδὲ λίπης μ'ἀγέραστον, †ἐπὴν χὠ Φοῖβος ἀείδειν
μισθὸν ἔδωκε.† τιμὰ δὲ τὰ πράγματα κρέσσονα ποιεῖ. (vs. 1–2)

Don't leave me unrewarded. Even Phoebus rewards singing, and honour makes things better.
(trans. Hopkinson)

Regardless of how this fragment should be emended, it seems safe to conclude that it speaks about recompense for singing and could well fit with the setting of Orpheus pleading before the gods of the Underworld. Reed (1997) entertains the possibility that Bion's *fr.* 6. did contain the story of Orpheus and notes a possible allusion to it when the word ἀγέραστος appears in the *Lament* at exactly the point where the Epitaphist discussed the likelihood that Persephone would reward

---

[11] Note the imperatives in vv. 119–20: ἄγε ('come on'), λίγαινε ('play'), βουκολιάζευ ('sing bucolically').

[12] Theocritus wrote several poems in Siciliy, and the *Epitaph* makes Sicily central to bucolic song, which can be seen e.g. from the recurring refrain: ἄρχετε Σικελικαί, τῶ πένθεος ἄρχετε, Μοῖσαι ('begin your mourning, Sicilian Muses') see also Troia 2016, 23, n. 50.

Bion for his song (like she did Orpheus): ... οὐκ ἀγέραστος / ἐσσεῖθ'ἁ μολπά ... (vv. 122–3, 'the song would not go unrewarded', trans. Hopkinson).[13] Such an allusion could increase the standing of the Epitaphist in his agon with Bion by demonstrating his ability to manipulate his predecessor's poetic output.

Although this might be the case, there is a problem when the Epitaphist implictly compares himself with Orpheus. Orpheus was used as an example of how the living could visit the Underworld (vs. 115–16), and as the only example of a poet *katabast* he is once more a natural figure of reference for both Bion and the Epitaphist. A problem arises when we realise that the success of Orpheus was limited. This makes the second comparison with the Epitaphist more ambivalent: εἰ δέ τι κἠγών / συρίσδων δυνάμαν, παρὰ Πλουτέι κ' αὐτὸς ἄειδον (vs. 125–6, 'And if my piping had any power, I would myself have played for Pluto', trans. Hopkinson). If the Epitaphist had been able to visit the Underworld and use his poetic powers to attempt to resurrect someone (like Orpheus did), he would have attempted it. This statement is troubling in many ways. Troia notes that this whole visit to the Underworld 'is presented to the reader in the form of a contrary-to-fact condition, implying that the Epitaphist does not view this result as possible'.[14] What was the point of bringing up the spectre of Orpheus' *katabasis* when its end result differed from the Epitaphist's desired goal of helping Bion to ressurect himself? Moreover, if the Epitaphist compares himself with Orpheus, but questions whether his poetic powers are equivalent to those of the Thracian bard, this would make him appear inferior to Bion, who potentially could succeed in the role of Orpheus in the Underworld. Another point worth noticing is that the Epitaphist seems to imagine that Bion's road to rescue is through singing to Persephone, but he ends the poem by saying that if he had been given the opportunity he himself would have sung to the seemingly unmovable Pluto.

This should make it clear that the *Lament*'s recurring use of Orpheus can be seen to inform an agonistic relationship between the Epitaphist and Bion in a way that initially seems to favour the younger poet, but the comparisons with Orpheus and with his heteroerotic love story at the ending of the poem appear to undermine the Epitaphist's position of superiority vis-a-vis his fictionalised poetic predecessor Bion. Neither of these two poets can resurrect themselves and overcome death, but require the help of another, both on an intrapoetic level in order to direct their song to the right divinity, Persephone, as well as on a metapoetic level – by requiring the help of a successor to be remembered. In the former case, even if they could sing to Persephone, their success in resurrecting themselves would not be guaranteed, as

---

[13] Reed 1997, 152.
[14] Troia 2016, 151.

the example of Orpheus' failed katabasis illustrates, and in the latter, their resurrection would only be limited to that of being a memory, or a poem.

We may now look at the way that Orpheus' homoerotic associations may be alluded to within the *Lament*. During the eleventh stanza, the Epitaphist engages in a lengthy *synkrisis* where Bion is placed on an equal footing with the great Homer. At the end of this we learn the following details about Bion:

> καὶ παίδων ἐδίδασκε φιλήματα καὶ τὸν Ἔρωτα
> ἔτρεφεν ἐν κόλποισι καὶ ἤρεθε τὰν Ἀφροδίταν.
>
> (*Lament for Bion*, vs. 83–4)

> ... and taught about the kisses of boys; he kept Love close by him and provoked Aphrodite.
> (trans. Hopkinson)

To teach about the kisses of boys may be seen to refer to the teaching of pederastic practices. Pederasty is an important theme in pastoral/bucolic poetry, and this might well be an allusion to earlier bucolic poems where it plays a part. A possible candidate for this would be Theocritus' *Idyll* 5. Just like the agonistic relationship between Bion and the Epitaphist we encountered in the *Lament*, Theocritus' poem is concerned with the relationship between a poetic mentor and his student, yet it is not a poem of mourning, but a more straightforward poetic agon between the two contestants Comatas and Lacon. The elder Comatas is open about the fact that he has engaged in a pederastic relationship with Lacon, and that this relationship, as is often associated with pederasty, involved teaching Lacon a thing or two other than pederasty:

> ΚΟ. ἀλλ' οὔτι σπεύδω· μέγα δ' ἄχθομαι εἰ τύ με τολμῇς   35
> ὄμμασι τοῖς ὀρθοῖσι ποτιβλέπεν, ὅν ποκ' ἐόντα
> παῖδ' ἔτ' ἐγὼν ἐδίδασκον. ἴδ' ἁ χάρις ἐς τί ποχ' ἕρπει·
> θρέψαι καὶ λυκιδεῖς, θρέψαι κύνας, ὥς τυ φάγωντι.
> ΛΑ. καὶ πόκ' ἐγὼν παρὰ τεῦς τι μαθὼν καλὸν ἢ καὶ ἀκούσας
> μέμναμ, ὦ φθονερὸν τὺ καὶ ἀπρεπὲς ἀνδρίον αὔτως;   40
> ΚΟ. ἁνίκ' ἐπύγιζόν τυ, τὺ δ' ἄλγεες·
>
> (Theoc. *Id.* 5.35–41)

> CO. I'm not in a hurry; but I'm annoyed that you dare to look me in the face, me who used to teach you when you were still a boy. See what a good turn comes to at last: rear wolf cubs, rear dogs, and they'll eat you up.
> LA. And when do I remember ever learning or even hearing anything good from you, you simply envious and foul little fellow?
> CO. When I was buggering you, and you were in pain;
>
> (trans. Hopkinson)

Hubbard sees this exchange as a struggle for poetic independence on the part of Lacon, who claims to have forgotten his relationship with Comatas and resorts to free himself from the role of student by in turn becoming a pederastic lover of boys.[15] Lacon claims to have won the love of not one, but two boys, the latter whom he presented with a gift in return for a kiss:

ΛΑ. ἀλλ' ἐγὼ Εὐμήδευς ἔραμαι μέγα· καὶ γὰρ ὅκ' αὐτῷ
τὰν σύριγγ' ὤρεξα, καλόν τί με κάρτ' ἐφίλησεν.

(Theoc. *Id.* 5.134–5)

LA. But I am much in love with Eumedes; and when I gave him the panpipe he gave me a fine kiss.

(trans. Hopkinson)

The giving of gifts is another common element in pederastic relationships, as is the boyish expression of love that is limited to kisses. In another of Theocritus' *Idylls*, the twelfth, boys compete in a kissing contest. With regards to the pederastic passage from the *Lament* (vs. 83–4) we might imagine that the Epitaphist is referring not to one, but to a number of poems. Theocritus' *Idyll* 5 might merely be hinted at through the mention of παίδων ... φιλήματα 'kisses of boys' (v. 83), just as there might be an allusion to *Idyll* 1 in line 84 since Daphnis angered Aphrodite in the former poem, just as Bion: ἤρεθε τὰν Ἀφροδίταν 'provoked Aphrodite' (84).[16] A more important lesson to learn from *Idyll* 5 is that pederasty is an important ingredient in bucolic poetry and can be intimately tied to the relationship between generations of poets. By alluding to this side of the bucolic tradition in his depiction of Bion, the Epitaphist prepares the reader for his subsequent revelation of being Bion's heir (vs. 93–7). When he reveals this, he does not mention anything about having been involved in a pederastic relationship with Bion, and strictly speaking, he hasn't said that Bion was actively a pederast, merely that he had been a teacher of pederasty: παίδων ἐδίδασκε φιλήματα 'he taught about the kisses of boys' (83).

This role of Bion as pederastic pedagogue is reminiscent of a poem outside the bucolic tradition (the boundaries of which are severely overdrawn by the Epitaphist to encompass e.g. Homer alongside Bion). In Phanocles' elegiac *Loves or Beautiful Boys* Orpheus was presented as a pederastic lover of the Argonaut Calaïs. He appears to have been unsuccessful also in this undertaking, and the

---

15 Hubbard 1998, 33.
16 For the beloved as παῖς, 'child/boy/girl/slave', male and female, see the final chapter by Thorsen.

poem opens with a description of the love-sickness caused by Calaïs (vs. 1–6). The pederastic side of Orpheus isn't limited to his own love-affairs. When he is subsequently killed by a group of Thracian women, their motive is revealed to be the following:

οὕνεκα πρῶτος ἔδειξεν ἐνὶ Θρήκεσσιν ἔρωτας
ἄρρενας, οὐδὲ πόθους ᾔνεσε θηλυτέρων.

(Phanocles Fr. 1.9–10)

>...because he was the first to reveal male loves among the Thracians and did not recommend love of women.
>
> (trans. Burges Watson)

Phanocles makes Orpheus into a teacher of pederasty among the men of Thrace. This position as a teacher of pederasty is much rarer within Greek culture than the relatively common practice of *being* a pederast.[17] I will not argue that the Epitaphist alludes very directly to Phanocles here (the explicit references to Eurydice at the end of the *Epitaph* seem to draw attention away from Orpheus' pederastic side), but the pederastic pedagogy of Orpheus widens the range of associations created by his comparisons with Bion.

By presenting Bion as a teacher of pederasty, and himself as his heir, the Epitaphist raises the possibility that Orpheus' homoerotic, pederastic side also played a part in his function as a bucolic poetic exemplar within the *Lament*. This point is never made explicit, but at least we have Phanocles' description of Orpheus as pederastic teacher and lover, unlike the line of argument by Kania concerning Orpheus' connection with the pathetic fallacy, which relied upon the existence of a now lost poem.

There is one final way in which the homoerotic/pederastic associations of Orpheus may be evoked within the *Lament*, albeit almost in reverse as it can be seen from the references to his heteroerotic associations. As we have seen, in the final stanza the Epitaphist expressed his desire to have been able to perform a *katabasis* in order to see Bion in the Underworld and guide him to rescue himself back to life. The poem's final lines then described the Epitaphist's intention to have acted like Orpheus himself and to have attempted to bring Bion back to life, if this had been a possibility. Though the main effect of this was to destabilise the relative poetic standing between Bion, the Epitaphist and Orpheus, the positioning of the Epitaphist in the role of Orpheus also adds to his pederastic connection

---

[17] For an overview of the wide occurences of pederasty in ancient Greek society see Davidson 2008.

with Bion. By adopting the role of Orpheus, failed as it may be, the Epitaphist effectively forces the role of Eurydice upon Bion. As the object for his *katabasis*, Bion assumes the character of the Epitaphist's beloved. In a slightly similar way, the earlier reference to Bion's assumption of the role of Orpheus, albeit possibly a more successful version of him, creates the possibility of seeing the Epitaphist as a kind of Eurydice, but with a reversal of the positions of Orpheus and Eurydice in the myth, with Orpheus (Bion) being deceased and Eurydice (the Epitaphist) remaining alive. This alternation between playing the role of a feminised object for desire and an active agent can be seen as a kind of homoerotic agonism, albeit a less explicit one than the agon we saw between Comatas and Lacon in *Idylls* 5. In this rather surprising manner, the homoerotic associations of Orpheus may be glimpsed through his heteroerotic associations within the *Lament*. Such a link may be even more relevant when we later look at Horace's *Carm.* 1.24.

Gender- and sexual reorientation in Catullus 51: Catullus appropriating Sappho fr. 31 Voigt

From having looked at the way that both Orpheus' heteroerotic and homoerotic associations may be used to strengthen the homoerotic overtones of the relationship between the Epitaphists and Bion in the *Lament*, we will now take a look at a poem where the homoerotic associations of Sappho are used as a parallel for a heteroerotic relationship. However, in this case too, a male poet's linking of himself with a poetic exemplar can be seen to encompass homoerotic overtones, albeit arguably to a lesser degree and in a slightly different way to what the Epitaphist did in the *Lament*.

One of the most famous poems in the Catullan corpus is the repurposing of Sappho 31 Voigt in Catullus 51:

> Ille mi par esse deo uidetur
> ille, si fas est, superare diuos
> qui sedens aduersus identidem te
>   spectat et audit
>
> 5   dulce ridentem, misero quod omnis
>   eripit sensus mihi: nam simul te,
>   Lesbia, aspexi, nihil est super mi
>   ...
>   lingua sed torpet, tenuis sub artus
> 10 flamma demanat, sonitu suopte

> tintinant aures, gemina teguntur
>   lumina nocte.
>
> otium, Catulle, tibi molestum est:
> otio exsultas nimiumque gestis:
> 15   otium et reges prius et beatas
>   perdidit urbes.

> He seems to me to be equal to a god, he, if it may be, seems to surpass the very gods, who sitting opposite you again and again gazes at you and hears you sweetly laughing. Such a thing takes away all my senses, alas! for whenever I see you, Lesbia, at once no [sound of voice] remains [within my mouth], but my tongue falters, a subtle flame steals down through my limbs, my ears ring with inward humming, my eyes are shrouded in twofold night. Idleness, Catullus, does you harm, you riot in your idleness and wanton too much. Idleness ere now has ruined both kings and wealthy cities.
>
> (trans. Cornish *et al.*)

In this poem Catullus focuses upon his poetic *persona's* emotional reaction to seeing Lesbia talking with another man and subsequently reminding himself that too much *otium* idleness is ruinous to him. Sappho, the real life poet imitated in this translation, is also invoked in Catullus' pet-name for his beloved, Lesbia, which may have been chosen for the literary associations she provided, but erotic associations may also have been important.[18] Like the mythic exemplar of the preceding poem in the collection (Achilles), Sappho was famous for having had erotic relationships with both men and with women.[19] Though she today is most famous for her homoerotic relationships, examples of her supposed relationships with men include the youth Phaon, who is named as an object of her love in Ov. *Her.* 15 and she is pursued by the poets Anacreon (anachronistically) and Alcaeus in Hermesianax' *Leontion* fr. 7 Powell. In a different context, Catullus could have drawn upon Sappho to allude to her lesbianism just as much as to her heterosexual relationships, yet this seems hard to reconcile with his inclusion of himself as a literary *persona* within Catullus 51, though it may be possible to think of the Catullan speaker as not only being feminised by replacing the role of a woman poet's *persona*, but also as being partially 'lesbianised'. Even so, the theme of

---

[18] Gram provides a useful summary of the various connotations behind the name Lesbia, ranging from Sappho as Muse and Sappho's beauty to negative associations with hetaeras famous for fellatio. He argues in favour of a conscious ambiguity in this choice of appellation, see Gram 2019.

[19] Thorsen points out the vacillation between homoerotic and heteroerotic objects of love in Sappho fr. 16 Voigt as well as in Ovid's *Heroides* 15, see Thorsen 2019c, 252–3.

homoerotic desire may still play a minor part in the poem given that the associations between gender-roles and sexuality in Catullus 51 are fairly complex.

In Catullus' recasting of a poem by Sappho, he partially assumes the position of Sappho's poetic *persona*.[20] Sappho fr. 31 Voigt describes a seeming love-triangle between a man and a woman who both desire the same woman, and where the speaker, Sappho's poetic *persona*, is a jealous observer providing an internal monologue. In Catullus 51 the roles are redistributed so that the speaker becomes a man, Catullus' poetic *persona* (named in v. 13), whilst the other characters remain in their traditional genders. By naming the desired woman Lesbia, Catullus also widens the poem's connections with Sappho, who may act as a model for comparison for his beloved, as well as for the poem's speaker. Holzberg has seen Catullus' overall strategy in adopting Sappho as a figure of reference within his poems as a veritable splitting-up of Sappho into a positive side attached to himself that embodies Sappho as a poetic ideal, and a negative side attached to Lesbia that hints at Sappho's unbridled eroticism and association with *hetaerae* as conceived within the ancient pseudo-biographical tradition.[21] In his interpretation of Lesbia's connections with Sappho, Lesbia is compared with the elegiac *puellae* of Roman Love Elegy, and like them belongs to the world of the lascivious, beautiful, and sophisticated hetaerae, but unlike the *docta* Cynthia of Propertius, she is less explicitly described as an inspiration for Catullus' poetry nor as a woman of great poetic acumen.[22] Holzberg argues that Lesbia is the only woman for Catullus' poetic *persona* and that the unnamed *puellae* associated with him in Catullus 32 and 42 should be understood as synonymous with her.[23] He puts great emphasis upon her active role in sex, which deviates from the Roman ideals of feminine passivity, in particular her possible penchant for fellatio.[24] The links between the nickname *Lesbia* and fellatio were already noted by Wirshbo.[25] In contrast, Catullus' poetic *persona* mimicks Sappho's heightened emotionality, her thematic predilection for writing epithalamia and poems about her close relatives, particularly her brothers, and he directly alludes to Sappho's poetry at key

---

20 See Skinner's discussion of Catullus' manipulation of a female literary voice in terms of semiotics and Foucalt's theories about sexuality, Skinner 1997, 131.
21 Holzberg 2001. For an introduction into the ancient pseudo-biographical tradition of Sappho as an unbridled hetaera, see Thorsen 2019b, 34–43.
22 Holzberg 2001, 33.
23 Holzberg 2001, 32.
24 Holzberg 2001, 34–5, 40.
25 Wirshbo 1980.

moments within his poetic corpus, notably at Catullus 11, also composed in sapphic stanzas.[26] In this latter poem, based upon a possible allusion to Sappho fr. 105c Voigt in the final stanza's reversal of sex-roles, where Catullus' *persona* describes feeling like a flower that is mercilessly ploughed down (Catullus 11.22–4), Miller notes that: ' … at least in a figurative sense, [Catullus] portrays himself as deflowered by the phallus of *mascula Lesbia*.'[27]

Holzberg's interpretation of Lesbia's name as a reflection of the overly erotic, negative side of the ancient reception of Sappho does not appear to be explicitly linked with Catullus 51, though there may be traces of this there as well. In Catullus' poem, like its Sapphic original, the desired woman remains the only active agent in her conversation with the unnamed man. In some small way this can make her more masculine in comparison with the feminised Catullan speaker. However, Greene has noted that Catullus puts greater emphasis upon the role of the unnamed man in the poem than Sappho did, who acts as a contrasting model of emotional composure and masculinity.[28] In this regard, Lesbia's masculinity appears only as secondary, and her entirely unerotic actions in the poem dissuade further from any allusion to Sappho's associations with active eroticism. Thorsen has noted how the pseudo-biographical tradition of Sappho contains several examples of a different erotic role, where 'Sappho appears not so much as a promiscuous female in the sexual sense, as an attractive object of the (literary) rivalry of male poets.'[29] In labelling the desired woman in the poem *Lesbia*, Catullus may have been following in this tradition by effectively turning Sappho from speaker in Sappho fr. 31 Voigt to an object of affection of at least one poet, the Catullan speaker. Instead of considering the other man in the poem as the future husband of Lesbia, which Holzberg dissuades us from doing, since what he, perhaps too reductively, sees as her *hetaera*-status would make this an impossibility, it is just as possible to think of him as a rival poet, vying for the affections of Lesbia as well for the poetic heritage of the poet Sappho.

In dealing with the role of Sappho as both a poetic model figure and as a model for his desired Lesbia in Catullus 51, Catullus arguably avoids most of the homoerotic associations attached to Sappho even in translating a poem with clear homoerotic overtones. By recasting the roles of the poem and reversing the sexual dynamics, the Catullan speaker becomes feminised, and plays out the part

---

26 Holzberg 2001, 36–9.
27 Miller 1993, 193.
28 Greene 1999, 3–7.
29 Thorsen 2019b, 36.

of the Sapphic speaker. Though as a man he cannot in reality embody the homoerotic sexual dynamic of Sappho fr. 31 Voigt, within the poem's fictional world he may nevertheless play the part of not just a woman poet but also of a woman in love with another woman.

Homoerotic overtones through Orpheus and Eurydice in Horace Odes 1.24

We will finally look at another instance where Orpheus' heteroerotic love story is referred in a way that invites homoerotic overtones in its reflection of a relationship between two men, the poet Virgil and the critic Quintilius Varus. In the first book of his *Odes* Horace writes a striking poem of lament and of possible consolation addressed to Virgil who laments the death of Quintilius (*Carm.* 1.24):

> Quis desiderio sit pudor aut modus
> tam cari capitis? praecipe lugubris
> cantus, Melpomene, cui liquidam pater
>   uocem cum cithara dedit.
>
> 5   ergo Quintilium perpetuus sopor
> urget; cui Pudor et Iustitiae soror
> incorrupta Fides nudaque Veritas
>   quando ullum inueniet parem?
>
> multis ille bonis flebilis occidit,
> 10 nulli flebilior quam tibi, Vergili.
> tu frustra pius, heu, non ita creditum
>   poscis Quintilium deos.
>
> quid? si Threicio blandius Orpheo
> auditam moderere arboribus fidem,
> 15 num uanae redeat sanguis imagini,
>   quam uirga semel horrida
>
> non lenis precibus fata recludere
> nigro conpulerit Mercurius gregi?
> durum: sed leuius fit patientia
> 20 quidquid corrigere est nefas.

What restraint, what limit can there be to our sense of loss for one so beloved? Teach me a song of mourning, Melpomene, for our Father has given you a clear-toned voice and the lyre to accompany it. So then, sleep without end lies heavy on Quintilius. Modesty, and incorruptible Good Faith (sister of Justice), and naked Truth – when will they find his equal? Many a good man weeps at his death, and none weeps more than you, Vergil. You beg the gods to restore Quintilius, pleading that he was not entrusted to them on such terms; but your piety is all in vain. What if you could play more charmingly than Thracian Orpheus the lyre that was once heeded by the trees? Would blood return to the empty wraith once Mercury, who is never soft-hearted enough to open the gates of death in response to prayers, has driven it with his dreaded staff to join the dusky herd? It is hard. But endurance can make lighter what no one is allowed to put right.

(trans. Rudd)

This poem stands at a slight remove from the situation of lament we witnessed in the *Lament*. Horace does not present himself as the leading mourner for Quintilius, but instead addresses Virgil, whom he places in that position. This is despite the fact that Horace also may have known Quintilius and have had a personal stake in mourning his passing as he is one of our main sources for what we know of Quintilius. Quintilius appears in Horace's later *Ars Poetica* as a contemporary example of a good critic: *Quintilio siquid recitares: 'corrige, sodes, / hoc' aiebat 'et hoc'* ... (*Ars P*. 438–9, 'If you ever read aught to Quintilius, he would say: "Pray correct this and this"', trans. Fairclough). This passage is filled with legal language, positioning a would-be-poet as defendant against the judgment, or perhaps, the prosecution of the critic Quintilius: *si defendere delictum quam uertere malles...* (*Ars P*. 442, 'If you preferred defending your mistake to amending it...,' trans. Fairclough). The critic is here hailed almost in the same way as the elder Cato's definition of a Roman orator: *Sit ergo nobis orator quem constituimus is qui a M. Catone finitur uir bonus dicendi peritus*, (Quint. *Inst*. 12.1.1, 'Let us base ourselves upon that an orator is he who is defined by M. Cato as a good man skilled in speaking', trans. Russell). In the *Ars P*. (445–6) the description runs: *Vir bonus et prudens uersus reprehendet inertis, / culpabit duros* ... ('An honest and sensible man will censure lifeless lines, he will find fault with harsh ones', trans. Fairclough) and he is even portrayed with a word connected with the office of censor: *arguet ambigue dictum, mutanda notabit* ... (*Ars P*. 449, 'he will force you to flood the obscure with light, will convict the doubtful phrase', trans. Fairclough).[30] The legalistic language used to describe the literary critic's profession in the *Ars* is reminiscent of the virtues represented by the goddesses mentioned in connection with Quintilius in *Carm*. 1.24: *Pudor* – Modesty, *Justitia* – Justice, *Fides* – Trustworthiness and *Veritas* – Truth.

---

30 Brink comments on another part of the *Ars P*. that the verb notare can be associated with the censor's black mark, the *nota*, see Brink 1971, 232.

We know little else about Quintilius other than this praise for his just literary criticism. His role as a superb critic among the Augustan poets (*multis...bonis* 9) may be considered as part of the reason for Virgil's particular sorrow (*nulli flebilior quam tibi* 10). However, I will argue that it is possible to read this emphasis upon Virgil's relationship with Quintilius as something more than literary affection and friendship.

Orpheus plays a central role in Horace's depiction of the relationship between Virgil and Quintilius, and he clearly attaches Virgil to Orpheus, who was a recurring character within his poems (appearing in all three of his poetry collections). In comparing Virgil's situation with that of Orpheus, Horace draws on the most common version of Orpheus' story in literature – his search for his lost wife Eurydice. Virgil's own version of this story in the *Georgics* is echoed quite directly in the ode, at least at one point.[31] Just like Mercury is *non lenis precibus* (*Carm.*1.24. 17, 'never soft-hearted ... in response to prayers', trans. Rudd), so too is Pluto described: ... *Manisque adiit regemque tremendum / nesciaque humanis precibus mansuescere corda* (*G.* 4.469–70, 'and made his way to the land of the dead with its fearful king and hearts no human prayers can soften', trans. Fairclough).

In Virgil's version there is a large emphasis upon the *furor* – madness, or sexual desire – that drove Orpheus into looking back and losing Eurydice, on the very point of retrieving her. Her final words upon vanishing forever make this clear: *illa 'quis et me' inquit 'miseram et te perdidit, Orpheu / quis tantus furor? ...* (*G.* 4.494–5, 'She cried: "What madness, Orpheus, what dreadful madness has brought disaster alike upon you and me, poor soul?"', trans. Fairclough). Eurydice is blameless, and can in many ways be described as exhibiting the opposite quality of *furor* – namely *pudor* 'restraint'. Similarly, this was one of the qualities attached to Quintilius (*Carm.* 1.24.6), emphatically positioned first in his 'catalogue of virtues'. It also appears in the opening line, and is given added force through repetition. Khan has suggested that Horace may deliberately have reprimanded Virgil for his comparative lack of *pudor*:

> ... in his 'outweeping' others to whom the death of Quintilius brought grief, [Virgil] transgressed the limits of pudor ... Horace may well be hinting that Virgil does not possess to a sufficient degree a quality so obvious in the man whose death he mourns![32]

Orpheus too is noted for his lack of restraint in grieving. When he mourned for Eurydice after his failed *katabasis*, Virgil lets Orpheus mourn for a full seven months:

---

31 Thom notes that the 'tone and the details ... mirrors that of Vergil', see Thom 1996, 119.
32 Khan 1999, 76.

> septem illum totos perhibent ex ordine mensis
> rupe sub aëria deserti ad Strymonis undam
> fleuisse ...
>
> (G. 4.507–9)

Of him they tell that for seven whole months day after day beneath a lofty crag beside lonely Strymon's stream he wept.

(trans. Fairclough)

In this way Horace may draw upon Virgil's own depiction of Orpheus in order to convey a point about moderation in grief, effectively using Virgil to teach Virgil to dry his tears. In order to do so, he explicitly links Virgil with Orpheus' supreme poetic abilities in the penultimate stanza within the context of a hypothetical *katabasis* on Virgil's part. This sounds very much like the situation of the Epitaphist considering the possibility of a similar venture in the *Lament for Bion*. There we saw how the reference to Orpheus' *katabasis* could imply overtones of Orpheus' homoerotic associations in the Epitaphist's and Bion's suggested imitation of his attempt to rescue his beloved. If Horace is placing Virgil in the role of Orpheus, then by taking on the likeness of Eurydice, or at least her equivalent position as desired object for an attempted *katabasis*, Quintilius assumes a role in their relationship that goes above and beyond that of a friend and certainly that of the critic's professional relationship. Putnam also noted how the opening of *Carm.* 1.24 alludes to Catullus 96 wherein Catullus tries to console his friend Calvus on the death of his wife Quintilia, whose name 'slides easily into Quintilius'.[33] If Horace is evoking this other poem at this instance, then we have an added emphasis upon the femine positioning of Quintilius vis-à-vis the active Virgil. Hinting towards a homoerotic relationship between the two may not least explain why Virgil is depicted as excessively grieving and why he mourns Quintilius more than anyone else, more even than any family members.

Conclusion

We have here seen how the homoerotic associations of Orpheus surprisingly could be hinted at through two poems, the Epitaphist's *Lament for Bion* and Horace's *Carm.* 1.24 where male mourners of another man may consider to act like

---

[33] Putnam 1992, 124.

Orpheus in his most famous heteroerotic venture, i.e. his failed *katabasis* to rescue his wife Eurydice. This association between male couples and Orpheus and Eurydice may be stable, as in the case of *Carm.* 1.24 where only the poet Virgil can be mapped easily onto the poet Orpheus, or it may vacillate between who assumes what role in what may be described as a case of homoerotic agonism, as in the relationship constructed between the Epitaphist and Bion in the *Lament*. Surprisingly, we found that the heteroerotic side of Orpheus far from pointing away from the homoretic overtones in these poems actually added to them. This situation may be contrasted with the comparatively less ambiguous linking to one side only of Sappho's sexual orientations in Catullus 51. In that poem, we saw how the homoerotic love-triangle of Sappho's model poem (fr. 31 Voigt) was reapplied onto a heteroerotic love-triangle, but still retained trace elements of the lesbian love of Sappho's poetic *persona* in Catullus' appropriation of her position within the poem.

Alison Sharrock
Amans et Egens and *Exclusus Amator*: The Connection (or not) between Comedy and Elegy

The question this paper seeks to address is as follows: how similar are Roman comedy and Latin love elegy and, in particular, how similar are the love stories they tell? It is an old question, especially in its manifestation as the 'origins of Latin love elegy', in which comedy has frequently been regarded as one of the parents of the younger genre, even if perhaps an illegitimate one.[1] By 'illegitimate', I allude to the perception among some early scholars that the important relationship is between the elegists and Greek new comedy, with Plautus and Terence as the embarrassing intermediary. The statement of Leo[2] that the elegists 'preferred any other reading matter to the comedies of Plautus', and that any similarities must go back to a common source, is typical of the disparaging attitude towards Roman comedy and the preference for Greek over Roman 'origins'. But why does elegy need a parent at all? Classical scholarship has been so obsessed with the question, I suggest, originally because (a) Quellenforschung was a driving force across the board, (b) a number of factors, including Romanticism and (I suspect) the association between Latin and early education, conspired with ancient commentators themselves to create a huge burden of 'anxiety of influence' regarding the relationship between Greek and Roman literature, which means that there is a far stronger drive to 'find where' Roman literature 'came from' than is the case for any genre of Greek literature, at least before the Roman period, and therefore (c) it was felt that this remarkable flowering of a particular form of poetic self-expression needs to be 'explained' by means of poetic ancestry.

My argument in this paper is that the two genres, particularly the two types of lover, are more different than is often thought, and that elegy does not in any organic sense derive from comedy, nor is the comic lover in general a strong model for his elegiac counterpart, except insofar as they both belong to a wider nexus of erotic discourse. Connections between the two figures and genres are better thought of in terms of intertextuality, in the broad sense that all texts exist within a network of other texts.[3] In arguing against the existence of any strong,

---
[1] Day 1938, 85–101 is an example of pro-Greek, anti-Roman prejudice in this regard.
[2] Quoted in Barsby 1996, 135.
[3] Barthes' lesson that we learn to say 'I love you' because it has been said before is particularly apposite here.

organic connection between comedy and elegy, then, I do not mean to deny the existence of interactions between the two genres. Indeed, I have been concerned elsewhere to argue for the intertextual mainstreaming of Roman comedy, especially Terence.[4] My goal is rather to celebrate the uniqueness of each genre, in particular as regards the nature of the love it espouses. In doing so, I am also driven by a desire to oppose the notion that 'origin' is of itself explanatory.[5]

In making such a case, I am aligning myself with the conclusions put forward by Georg Luck (1959/69) and John Barsby (1996), although both scholars frame the question in terms of sources and influence, whereas I am more concerned with what the differences between the two genres can tell us about each type of lover. Luck follows a balanced account of the Greek elegiac and general Hellenistic background to Roman love elegy with four pages on the relationship with comedy, which touch on points I am making.[6] He says, first, that 'many scholars still maintain that it is impossible to understand the role of the lover and poet in the Latin elegy without a previous study of Terence and Plautus'. Crucially, he sees the controversy as concerning 'the very essence of elegiac poetry' and maintains that 'the influence of Menander, Plautus and Terence can be disregarded, at least in the case of Tibullus and Propertius; [and] that there is no evidence which would force us to derive one literary *genus* from the other.' Like many scholars then and now, he is inclined to make the comic plays more similar to each other than they actually are, but nonetheless he draws the crucial point that 'the inevitable happy ending of these plays is contrary to the very nature of the elegiac love-affair' (44). While acknowledging that some stock characters from comedy also appear in elegy, he says that 'they play such a subordinated role that they have hardly any influence on the course of the love-affair'. (A point not often sufficiently recognised is that they occur in other genres also, including oratory and declamation.) Barsby offers a measured analysis of potential specific interactions between poems in Ovid's *Amores* and plays of Roman comedy (an analysis which benefits from his deep knowledge of both genres and is less inclined than many to oversimplify comedy), which he finds wanting at any degree of specificity. Barsby is reacting to Griffin (1985) and Yardley (1987a), who make what Barsby describes (136) as 'bold' claims for the possibility that the elegists

---

[4] Sharrock 2009, and 2013b. For a connection between Ovid and Terence, see the chapter by Brecke in the present volume.

[5] An argument against the idea of organic growth of elegy out of new comedy is that the connection between genres is least strong in Propertius and strongest in Ovid, especially in his later erotodidactic works. The comic connection might therefore be better seen as a development within elegy, rather than relating to the origins of elegy.

[6] Luck 1969, originally published 1959, 43–6.

might be directly influenced by Roman comedy. On that side of the fence, the commentaries of Booth (1991) and McKeown (1989, and 1998) make many references to 'comic influence'.[7] A return to this old chestnut seems particularly timely, because recent publications have staked a claim for the importance of comedy for elegy in the strongest terms. James confidently states that 'Roman love elegy everywhere shows its roots in New Comedy' (2012a, 254).[8] Nuanced, but nonetheless giving more credence to the comic parent than I would support, are statements in several chapters in the *Cambridge Companion to Latin Love Elegy* (2013), in which Bessone, Fulkerson, and Piazzi repeat the standard history,[9] although I would strongly support the judgement of Bessone that 'all the work of comparison with previous poetic experiences has rendered more evident the decisive transformation achieved by Latin elegy'.[10]

A major element in the debate over the 'origins of Latin love elegy' is where this first-person emotional expression and introspective interiority comes from.[11] The grief of love is a major element in elegy, so much so that some poems explicitly bathe in the pleasure of pain.[12] It exists in comedy, but is very limited, with

---

[7] For further examples of the koine, see also Day 1938, ch. 5, Hubbard 2001, 51–2, Keith 2008, 103–4, Heyworth 2007, 455.

[8] James's account of comic plots is more nuanced than many, but still inclined to fudge them closer together than I would regard as accurate. Her case here is in keeping with her argument in James 2003, that stresses a real, economic environment for elegy, in which the beloved is straightforwardly an independent prostitute.

[9] I too repeated something of the standard account, in a paper about Terentian intertextuality (2013b), saying (61): 'It is generally accepted that to some extent the world of Roman comedy functions as an ancestor of Augustan elegy in the creation of the 'demi-monde' society which it is deemed to depict.'

[10] Bessone 2013, 41. Piazzi 2013 acknowledges the range of genres intertextually involved with elegy, but the features she regards as coming from comedy ('in particular with regard to specific figures like the young man in love and the temptress', 224) do not seem particularly apposite to me. Moreover, her claim (236) that '[b]oth the youthful lover of comedy and the elegiac poet assume reckless and scandalous behaviour as a result of amorous passion' could apply to almost any love literature.

[11] Miller 2004, 4 seems to me to come to the right conclusion, although his concession is, in the argument of this paper, unnecessary: 'The themes and dramatic situations exploited in the elegist's relation to his *domina* may have already been explored by the figure of comedy's *iuuenis* [AS: comedy actually prefers the term *adulescens*] in his subjection to the *meretrix* [AS: but there is very little in comedy that looks like *seruitium amoris*] and his conflict with the *senex*. Nonetheless, the unique position of the first-person speaking subject in elegy, its constitution as the site of contradiction and aporia, of temporal complexity and personal depth, remain unprecedented.'

[12] See for example Ov. *Am.* 2.19 and Prop. 3.8.

Plautine lovers showing us very little of their interior sufferings.[13] Some scholars have suggested, however, that in some passages of Terence not only can we see the beginnings of the kind of first-person expression of emotion and psychological pain, but even that these passages may be significant 'ancestors' for elegy. It is particularly in the person of the older brother, Phaedria, in Terence' *Eunuchus* that this new representation of interiority has been identified.[14] It is, I believe, quite right to point to a Terentian development, expanding the capabilities of Roman comic drama, and also to grant Terence his rightful place within the intertextual network of ancient Greek and Roman love poetry. I contend, however, that the extent of psychological expression within the comic corpus is far too small to justify claims of ancestry.

Let us take a look at each of my programmatic descriptions of the comic and elegiac lovers, to consider the extent to which they fit, and whether they have implications for the other genre.

It was Segal[15] who coined the description *amans et egens* as encapsulating the situation of the lover in Roman comedy, privileging the kind of plot in which a rather dopey young man desires a prostitute but lacks the necessary funds to pay for access. With the help of (usually) his clever slave, the lover will cheat someone, often his father, of the necessary money and will thus achieve access. Such an account fits particularly well to one of Plautus' best and funniest plays, *Pseudolus*, while it works well also for *Bacchides, Epidicus, Mostellaria*, but not very well for any of the other 17 plays, nor for any of the plays of Terence.[16] The fact that the 'classic' *amans et egens* is relatively rare does not stop the figure from being programmatic, as we will see further below, but it is nonetheless worth being aware of the extent to which the core character is only one among many manifestations of the lover in comedy. It is also worth looking at the Plautine line to which Segal was referring (implicitly). The phrase itself, without the connective but for programmatic purposes conveniently placed in an opening line, comes in fact from a highly non-typical lover, Toxilus in *Persa*.[17]

---

13 Nice examples of the comic expression of erotic 'grief' can be seen from the Calidorus of *Pseud.* or the Charinus of *Merc.*, both in the opening scenes.
14 Konstan 1995, 131–40, Barsby 1999a, Sharrock 2009; 2013b.
15 Segal 1987, 15 and 57, including the connective on both occasions. The reference here is to the second edition, the first edition having been published in 1968.
16 The plots of Roman comedy, while undoubtedly generic and inclined to play with stereotypes, are in fact more varied than is often assumed. See Sharrock 2009 8, 97.
17 See Sharrock 2016, including 105, n. 34, where I also discuss reference to the phrase *amans et egens* occurring in *Pseud.* 273, in the form *amatur atque egetur*.

> TO. Qui amans egens ingressus est princeps in Amoris uias
> superauit aerumnis suis aerumnas Hercul<e>i.
> nam cum leone, cum excetra, cum ceruo, cum apro Aetolico,
> cum auibus Stymphalicis, cum Antaeo deluctari mauelim
> quam cum Amore: ita fio miser quaerendo argento mutuo   5
> nec quicquam nisi 'non est' sciunt mihi respondere quos rogo.
>
> (Plaut. *Pers.* 1–6)

> TOXILUS: He who as a lover and needy has entered first onto the paths of Love has surpassed with his labours the labours of Hercules. For with the lion, with the snake, with the deer, with the Aetolian boar, with the birds of Stamphyla, with Antaeus I would prefer to wrestle, rather than with Love. So I am made miserable seeking for a loan and those whom I ask have nothing to say except 'nothing'.

Toxilus is unique in being a lover who seeks to buy the freedom of his prostitute-slave beloved, but is *himself a slave*. His (absent) master might be expected to play the 'father' role, but in fact he never appears. A friend-slave from another household, Sagaristio, attempts to play the 'clever slave' role and cheats his own master of the necessary money by means of a trick, but the eponymous trick of the play, the one which enables the purchase of the beloved (it involves passing a virgin off as a person for sale, then staging a coup based on her citizen status) is arranged by Toxilus himself together with the virgin's father, a free parasite called Saturio. In its immediate context, moreover, the designation *amans egens* hardly fits the stereotype of the resourceless *adolescens*, since he launches immediately into delusions of Herculean grandeur. Toxilus is unusual also in being the only comic lover ever to speak nastily to his beloved.[18]

What makes the description programmatic beyond its immediate situation, despite the relative paucity of clear cases and the unusual expression of the lover in *Persa*, is that being 'in love' and 'in need' does accurately reflect the situation of all comic lovers whose story is not heading for marriage, precisely because *they know they need to pay*. They may occasionally seek credit, but they never (other than for momentary rhetorical purposes) claim that they should get the girl purely because of mutual affection or their own good qualities. In particular, they don't try to persuade the girl in this way. Indeed, rarely are they trying to persuade the *girl* at all – they are trying to persuade others to allow them access to the girl. By contrast, elegiac lovers are utterly focused on persuading the girl, by their loyalty, *bene facta*, and especially their poetry. This will be discussed further below.

---

[18] Discussed in Sharrock 2016.

To turn now to the elegiac designation of a lover: the *exclusus amator* certainly does stand powerfully as programmatic for elegy, being able to conjure up and capture in a nutshell the elegiac situation in anything from a whole poem to a few words. As well as the three canonical examples, Prop. 1.16, Tib. 1.2, and Ov. *Am.* 1.6, there are many allusions to the nexus of imagery around the door.[19] The closed door of elegy and the topos of the locked-out lover, singing his programmatic song paraclausithyron on the doorstep in an attempt (at least nominally) to achieve entry to the beloved, draws on an existing literary scenario but develops it into euphemistic meditation on desire and a powerful metaphor not only for the subjective experience of rejection and but also for the equally subjective feeling of loss of control for the lover, who thus becomes 'slave' to his beloved (thereby linking it to the other great elegiac metaphor, *seruitium amoris*[20]). The topos derives its details from epigram much more than from comedy, but it is worth pausing for a moment to consider what is and what is not Comic in the literary history of the image.

Just as the *amans et egens* takes its terminology from a highly atypical example of the type, so too the phrase *exclusus amator* derives not from elegy at all, but from the parody of lovers and love poetry towards the end of the fourth book of Lucretius' *De Rerum Natura*.[21]

> at lacrimans exclusus amator limina saepe
> floribus et sertis operit postisque superbos
> unguit amaracino et foribus miser oscula figit
>
> (Lucr. 4.1177–9)
>
> But the weeping locked-out lover often covers the threshold with flowers and garlands and anoints the arrogant doorposts with marjoram and pitifully fastens kisses on the doors.

The imagined moment of this exclusion is that the beloved is not in the arms of another but involved in her toilette, such that if the lover were indeed granted entry he would run a mile.[22] Elsewhere in the same extended passage, Lucretius

---

19 It is near-impossible to talk about elegy without discussion of the paraclausithyron. See Copley 1956, Cairns 1975, Pucci 1978. Debrohun 2003, chapter 3, gives an excellent account of the importance of the locked-out lover for understanding the nature of elegy.
20 See McCarthy 1998. Fulkerson 2013 gives an excellent account of *seruitium amoris* in elegy, rightly pointing to this as an elegiac innovation (190), though her comment (191) about connections between elegiac and comic plots seems overstated to me.
21 See also Piazzi 2013, 225.
22 See Brown 1987, 297–8. Ovid plays with this idea in both *Ars am.* and *Rem. am.*, though Brown argues that Lucretius is less 'overtly misogynistic' than Ovid and other later poets.

parodies the use of pet names to disguise faults in the beloved, a habit on which Ovid riffs in both directions in his erotodidactic poetry,[23] but which has little or no purchase on either straight elegy or comedy. Be that as it may, the Lucretian *exclusus amator* seems so strongly redolent of elegy that scholars have felt the need to make a link. Piazzi, for example, says (2013, 225): 'it is likely that Lucretius means to make fun of Catullus' concept of an all-consuming love … But it is probable that Lucretius is also thinking of the young lovers of Latin comedy in their Greek setting'. The link with comedy, however, is tenuous. The primary butt of Lucretius' attack specifically on the *exclusus* must be something in the tradition of Hellenistic epigram,[24] perhaps including Roman poems in that tradition, though not Catullus. Piazzi's stress is on the foolish idealisation of the beloved, as well as the behaviour outside the closed door, but neither of these is much developed in comedy.[25]

What is there in comedy in the way of locked-out lovers? Doors generally are of great importance in Graeco-Roman drama. New and Roman comedy are conventionally staged with two or occasionally three houses in front of which the action takes place, the movements in and out of the house enacting the structure of the play and often heralded by a squeaking door.[26] There is, moreover, a stock 'doorman' scene, going back to Greek old comedy. This general importance of the door, however, is not reflected in any close association with the elegiac paraclausithyron. There is only one passage in extant Roman and Greek new comedy[27] which involves a lover singing outside his beloved's door in the hopes of meeting her. That is the delightful opening scene in Plautus' *Curculio*, when the young lover Phaedromus, accompanied by his slave Palinurus, arrives before dawn to 'bring breakfast to Venus' (71–3).[28]

---

23 *Ars am.* 2.657–62, *Rem. am.* 323–30.
24 Piazzi 2013, 236: 'together with epigram, comedy is the genre that has most often been considered "parent" of the elegy.'
25 It is true that comic lovers idealise their beloved, but no more so than in any other erotic discourse. Indeed, comic lovers spend remarkably little time (either in monologue or in dialogue) expanding unrealistically on the charms of the beloved.
26 See Sharrock 2008, n. 15.
27 Barsby 1996, n. 27 describes the first fragment of Menander's *Misoumenos* as a paraclausithyron, although with 'no striking similarities to *Am.* 1.6'. I would not count it as a paraclausithyron at all. The house is the lover's own and he is master of it. He has not been locked out and is not pleading for entry. What he is doing is to bewail his situation to an attendant slave and the audience. The scene has more in common with that between Agamemnon and his attendant in Euripides *Iphigenia in Aulis* 1–163 than with the epigrammatic and elegiac paraclausithyron.
28 I have discussed this passage in Sharrock 2008, where further bibliography may be found.

Phaedromus' goal is to tempt from the house an old slave woman (who has some control over entrance and exit but who is not the owner of the brothel), with the promise of wine, to persuade her to enable the exit through the door and onto the stage of his beloved, a quasi-prostitute (i.e., under the control of a pimp but still a virgin) who will (inevitably) turn out to be freeborn and therefore become his wife. Although Phaedromus has a lovely 'song to the door', which almost certainly does have some degree of intertextual relationship with the great elegiac door poems, even my very brief description should make it clear how different the situation is from that of elegy. Crucially, Phaedromus' wishes are reciprocated. Although there are examples in elegy where *puellae* are encouraged to 'cheat the guard' (for example, Tib. 1.2.15–18), and blame for the exclusion is sometimes concentrated on either the physical door or the eponymous doorman, nonetheless the underlying drive in the elegiac paraclausithyron is emotional exclusion of the lover. This is not a problem for Phaedromus. Moreover, Phaedromus is not trying to get into the house, but to arrange for the beloved to come out – or rather, first, for a comic old woman to come out.[29] This means 'out' into the public arena of the stage, thus enabling the progress of the plot. There is great play in the scene with the dramatic convention of the creaking door, including mildly obscene hints on how to make the door open silently (e.g. *Curc.* 94). When Ovid, in his great paraclausithyron poem, teases with the possibility of a noisily opening door, he is, I suggest, alluding explicitly to the dramatic convention to which Plautus also alludes, but which is not particular to erotic situations.

> fallimur, an uerso sonuerunt cardine postes
>   raucaque concussae signa dedere fores?
> fallimur: impulsa est animoso ianua uento.
>   ei mihi, quam longe spem tulit aura meam!
>
> (Ov. *Am.* 1.6.49–52)

> Am I deceived, or did the doorposts make a noise as the hinge was turned, and did the shaken doors give their raucous indication? I am deceived: the door was driven by the lively wind. Alas, how far the breeze bore my hope!

This play with a comic motif may be part of the intertextual broadening of the relationship between comedy and elegy which Ovid initiates in the *Amores* and develops considerably in the erotodidactic poems, but in the context of this poem it does as much to express the differences as the connections between the two

---

29 Perhaps the closest parallel in elegy, though without the intermediary, is Calliope's instruction to Propertius that he should sing in such a way that a lover *per te clausas sciat excantare puellas*, 3.3.49.

situations. Plautus' girl, Planesium, is eventually brought out and has a brief scene of mutual love with Phaedromus, until the door really does make a noise, heralding the entrance of the *leno* Cappadox, Planesium's master.

The scene between these lovers can act as an example of how comic love relates to and differs from elegiac. Phaedromus feels himself divine (*sum deus*, 167) in enjoying the love of his Venus (193), which very occasionally elegiac lovers also experience (Prop. 2.15.39–40, Ov. *Am.* 2.5.51-2), but it is a topos far older than either genre, perhaps its most powerful early expression being that of Sappho (φαίνεταί μοι κῆνος ἴσος θέοισιν, 'he seems to be to be like a god', fr. 31.1 LP). Planesium reciprocates Phaedromus' desires. She calls on him to embrace her[30] to which the lover replies *hoc etiam est quam ob rem cupiam uiuere* ('it is for this that I want to live', 172), but 'her master prohibits it'. Planesium responds with typical comic repetition combined with a promise of eternal devotion: (... *Prohibet? nec prohibere quit / nec prohibebit, nisi mors meum animum aps te abalienauerit.* 'prohibits it? He can't prohibit it and he won't prohibit it, unless death takes away my soul from you', *Curc.* 173–4). Here we have mutual love which our knowledge of comic plots tells us will end in marriage. There is nothing unreasonably self-deceiving about the love of this young couple, nothing in the manner of Lucretius' diatribe, except perhaps a hint in the comic commentary kept up, at the same time, by the slave Palinurus, who wants to save his master from too much love.

> enim uero nequeo durare quin ego erum accusem meum:
> nam bonum est pauxillum amare sane, insane non bonum est;
> uerum totum insanum amare, hoc est - quod meus erus facit.
>
> (Plaut. *Curc.* 175-7)

> Indeed I can't stop myself from accusing my master: for it is a good thing to be a bit in love in a healthy way, but it is not good to be insanely in love; indeed the whole 'insane love' thing, that is – what my master is doing.

Phaedromus does not respond directly but rather expatiates on his choice for this love as being better than any wealth or kingdom.

> sibi sua habeant regna reges, sibi diuitias diuites,
> sibi honores, sibi uirtutes, sibi pugnas, sibi proelia:
> dum mi abstineant inuidere, sibi quisque habeant quod suom est.
>
> (Plaut. *Curc.* 178-80)

---

30 *Curc.* 172, *tene me, amplectere ergo*: as commonly in comedy the stage directions come in the dialogue.

> Let the kings keep their kingdoms, the wealthy their wealth, their honours, virtues, fights, battles: as long as they don't envy me, everyone can keep what is his.

Although comically expressed, the sentiment is not far from that of Tibullus' programmatic opening *diuitias alius fuluo sibi congerat auro* ('let another heap up for himself riches in yellow gold', 1.1). Tibullus' poem, however, develops the idea not so much in terms of the value of his relationship over any other form of blessing (as does Phaedromus), but rather as a statement about lifestyle and poetics, in which nothing erotic appears until line 46, and even then it is only a generalised one among many blessings of this chosen lifestyle: *et dominam tenero continuisse sinu* ... ('to have held a mistress in tender embrace').

Two final points about the *Curculio* scene which are relevant for their specificity to comedy: the lovers are surrounded by other characters, and their love is directed towards marriage.

But before we leave the subject of the door, there is another small group of passages that must be considered. There are very few broken doors in either comedy or elegy, but there are one or two cases which make it look as though a broken door might be programmatic. There is no sign in Menander of anything resembling the paraclausithyron, but there is a passage which looks at first sight as though breaking down the door to get at the desired prostitute is appropriate comic behaviour. This is when, early in *Dyskolos*, the helper Chaireas suggests getting drunk and burning down doors as the right behaviour to help a friend in love with a prostitute, whereas if it's a case of a citizen girl he would work towards a properly respectable marriage (*Dysk.* 57–68).[31] This broken door is a matter of violence against the property of the pimp, with none of the metaphorical or emotional overtones which characterise elegiac entry.[32] Chaireas' plan is followed by Aeschinus in the immediate back-story to Terence's *Adelphoi*, when he uses this direct technique to get hold of the prostitute who is the object of his brother's interest – but that is more or less the sum total of the *exclusus amator* in comedy. Other attacks on the house in extant comedy are not directly erotic at all. The soldier Thraso threatens to attack the prostitute's house in Terence's *Eunuchus*, but that isn't to get access to the beloved. It is to regain the bargaining counter, the girl who has been given to Thais by the soldier as a present (and is the victim of rape by the disguised 'eunuch' who is the present provided by Thraso's rival Phaedria). In Plautus *Bacchides* 925–78, the military attack on the house which

---

[31] See Carey 2013, 174 for this type of scene as belonging also to court speeches.
[32] See also the pimp in Menander's *Kolax* E236–7 (new Loeb), where he fears that the rather aggressive lover might kidnap the girl in question and that he would have to go to law to get her back.

is an obstacle to the affair is all a big metaphorical game of 'Ulysses' (the clever slave, Chrysalus) against 'Troy'. The house is that of the lover's father, not the beloved or her keeper, and is a matter of extracting the money needed to pay for the girl, not the girl herself.

If the locked-out lover has nothing to do with comedy, does the broken door have anything to do with elegy? Tibullus picks up something which might look similar to Chaireas' Menandrian programme, in a passage on the love-behaviour appropriate to youth.

> nunc leuis est tractanda uenus, dum frangere postes
>   non pudet et rixas inseruisse iuuat.
> hic ego dux milesque bonus: uos, signa tubaeque,   75
>   ite procul, cupidis uulnera ferte uiris,
> ferte et opes: ego conposito securus aceruo
>   dites despiciam despiciamque famem.
>
> (Tib. 1.1.73–8)

Now is the time for engaging in light sex, while it is not shameful to break down doors and it is pleasing to get involved in fights. Here I am a general and a good soldier: away with you, standards and trumpets, take your wounds to greedy men, and take them wealth: may I, secure on the heap which I have gathered, look down on wealth as I look down on hunger.

I have quoted the couplets following the broken doors, which constitute the end of 1.1, because the context shows the elegiac-metaphorical nature of the kind of battling involved here. This is not the place to go into details about the problems of erotic violence in elegy, merely to point out the slippage between brawling and sex which finds its most explicit expression in Propertius' *dulcis ... rixa* (3.8.1).[33] At a primary level, Tib. 1.1.73 almost certainly does allude to the kind of damage to property associated in a range of genres with young men, too much alcohol, and sexual desire.[34] In its context, it may also include a hint at rape, rare within elegy, but it is in any case far removed from the relationship with the door which will develop in the very next poem.

Not only in these two opening poems of Tibullus, but throughout the elegiac corpus, a crucial element of the door is that it is more metaphorical than real. The closed door of elegy stands for the erotic psychology of the lover, his weakness and loss of autarky, the grief of exclusion, and the attempt at (emotional and sexual) entry by persuasion – rather than by payment or violent forcible entry. Propertius, in his (provisional) farewell to Cynthia and elegy (3.25), gestures at the

---

[33] See James 2012b, Frederick 2012, 431–6, Bowditch 2012, 130–1, Fredrick 1997.
[34] See Keith 2011a, 44–8, Baker 2000, 82–3, Cairns 1979, 158–9, 166–9.

paraclausithyron (and at other elegiac topoi) with the explicit statement that however angry he was as an elegist, he nonetheless never used violence: *nec tamen irata ianua fracta manu* ('but the door was never broken by my angry hand', 3.25.10). This is why rape[35] has almost no role in pure elegy. It appears only in the form of the lover's worry that his beloved it might be having a nightmare about being raped (Prop. 1.3.30), or in unspoken fantasy or subsumed into wider sexual violence.[36] While from certain points of view it may be important not to make a strict distinction between the actual performance of rape and various threats and fantasies of sexual violence, for understanding the nature of the elegiac lover's self-representation it is a necessary distinction. It's only in the *Ars*, which is in a number of ways closer to comedy, that there is any suggestion that rape might be a suitable strategy.[37] By contrast, in comedy rape plays a substantial role, but only in preparation for marriage.[38] Prostitutes are never raped in comedy.

It is true that both Plautus' *Curculio* and Tibullus 1.2 apostrophise the door. Here is Phaedromus first:

> PH. pessuli, heus pessuli, uos saluto lubens,
> uos amo, uos uolo, uos peto atque opsecro,
> gerite amanti mihi morem, amoenissumi,
> fite caussa mea ludii barbari,   150
> sussilite, opsecro, et mittite istanc foras
> quae mihi misero amanti ebibit sanguinem.
> hoc uide ut dormiunt pessuli pessumi
> nec mea gratia commouent se ocius!
>
> (Plaut. *Curc.* 147–54)

> PHAEDROMUS: Bolts, hey you bolts, I'm very pleased to greet you, I love you, I want you, I seek you and I beg you, be accommodating to me as a lover, most delightful ones, become barbarian stageplayers for my sake, jump up, I beseech you, and send that woman outside, who drinks the blood of me, a poor lover. Look how the wretched bolts are sleeping and won't move themselves quicker for my sake!

And here is Tibullus:

> ianua difficilis domini te uerberet imber,
>   te Iouis imperio fulmina missa petant.

---

35 Or at least '*rape* rape', as the students described in Liveley 2012, 544 call it.
36 See Liveley 2012, and James 2012b.
37 See the outrageous *Ars am.* 1.669–78.
38 This topos is shared with declamation.

> ianua, iam pateas uni mihi uicta querellis,
>   neu furtim uerso cardine aperta sones.
>
> (Tib. 1.2.7–10)

> Door of a difficult master, may the rain beat you, may thunderbolts sent at the command of Jupiter seek you out. Door, now please would you open just for me, conquered by my complaints, and don't make any noise as you open with the hinge turned furtively.

Unsurprisingly, the style of the two forms of address is significantly different. It might look as though Tibullus' reference to the need for the door to open quietly could be an allusion to Plautus, but I think it is more likely that it is a commonplace[39] – which is itself another form of intertextuality. Be that as it may, the crucial difference between the two scenes is the position of the speaker. Phaedromus' position has been discussed above; Tibullus' may perhaps best be thought of as a development of the couplet from his previous (opening) poem:

> me retinent uinctum formosae uincla puellae,   55
>   et sedeo duras ianitor ante fores.
>
> (Tib. 1.1.55–62)

> The chains of a beautiful girl hold me bound, and I sit as a doorman in front of hard doors.

That is, he is held by his devotion to the beloved, her exclusion of him, and the genre of elegy. In all, then, I would suggest that neither programmatic statement, *amans et egens* and *exclusus amator*, has any significant purchase on the other genre, beyond koine (general erotic intertextuality) and occasional moments of possible allusion.

I have referred above several times to marriage and to payment, which I offer as crucial differences between comic and elegiac love. The next stage is to explore in slightly more detail the extent of those differences and exceptions to them. It is impossible to address this awkward nexus surrounding the love relationship in the Roman world without facing the question of the socio-legal status of the beloved, which, moreover, is of itself another site of generic difference. In essence, the socio-legal status of the beloved is vague in elegy, but very precise in comedy and often crucial to the plot.[40] There is a strong connection between love and marriage in

---

39 For doors open quietly in elegy, see Tib. 1.2.20, 1.8. 59–62, 2.1.75, Prop. 4.5.73–4, Ov. *Am.* 1.6.7–8, 3.1.51–4.
40 Miller 2004, 61–8 gives a good account of the impossibility of settling the elegiac question: 'an either/or solution to this problem is simply not available without mutilating the text.'

comedy.⁴¹ All six plays of Terence involve a love marriage, and, perhaps more surprisingly, around half of the plays of Plautus. By contrast, elegy is not directed towards marriage. This last statement needs to be nuanced, in that the language of marriage does indeed feature in the elegiac relationship, for example in the famous words of Propertius that Cynthia is *semper amica mihi, semper et uxor* (1.6.36). The desired long-term relationship sometimes expressed by the elegists⁴² may look somewhat like marriage, given that permanent cohabitation has no immediate resonance in Roman culture. But while these moments draw on some of the language and imagery of marriage, they avoid its legal and socio-political structures. I offer two reasons for this avoidance which have nothing to do with biographical criticism and everything to do with the nature of elegiac love poetry. The first is that when, as in many comedies, marriage is the telos of the work of literature, any obstacles to it must inevitably be short-lived, with the marriage achieved at the end and everyone living 'happily ever after'. Marriage belongs to a heavily plot-directed and goal-directed form such as the individual play. It can sit only very awkwardly with the fuzzy logic of elegiac quasi-narrative, broken up into the individual poems whose narrative relationship with each other is complex and vague.⁴³ The second reason why marriage is not the telos of the elegiac relationship, I suggest, is that an overwhelming value in the elegiac erotic economy is persuasion. While I would argue for a greater connection between love and marriage in Roman literature and culture than is sometimes acknowledged, nonetheless the fact that Roman women have very little choice about marriage, in theory and largely in practice, means that a genre whose whole purpose is to persuade a woman to make a choice is not well suited to a marital telos.

In comedy, by contrast, the lover knows exactly what he is up against and is after. If it's a citizen girl (known or unknown), it's marriage. If it's a prostitute, it is access, usually with little thought for the question of how long that should last, but he knows perfectly well that he will have to pay, by fair means or foul. As regards the elegiac lover, it is not at all clear to us and in some sense not even clear to the lover what he is after, but whatever it is, it is not marriage, and he does not expect to have to pay.

---

41 Even James 2012a, 261 acknowledges that marriage is a generic goal of new comedy, 'so its complete erasure in elegy is a significant difference between the two genres'.
42 See for example Tibullus' rural fantasy at 1.5.19–34, or his pious hope for lifelong devotion: *nos, Delia, amoris / exemplum cana simus uterque coma* ('let us, Delia, be a model of love, both of us with white hair', 1.6.85–6), cf. Thorsen's final chapter in this volume, n. 37.
43 On elegiac narrative, see Liveley/Salzman-Mitchell 2008, Liveley 2012, and Janan 2012, 375–6.

Griffin (1985, 117) claims that the comic lover 'is naturally out to get what he wants without paying for it', but this is misleading. Even the example he quotes, Ter. *Hec.* 67–70, speaks of *quam minimo pretio* ('as cheaply as possible', 69), not no cost at all. More importantly, in no play of either Plautus or Terence does a lover achieve access to a prostitute without either direct payment or a trick which substitutes for it (or both).[44] While no doubt they would like to pay less, and they do sometimes beg for credit (Argyrippus in *Asin.*, Calidorus in *Pseud.*) the *adulescentes'* awareness of the nature of the deal, so to speak, may be seen in responses such as that of even the inexperienced lover Pistoclerus in *Bacchides*:

> PI. uiscus merus uostrast blanditia. BA. quid iam? PI. quia enim intellego,   50
> duae unum expetitis palumbem, peri, harundo alas uerberat.
> non ego istuc facinus mihi, mulier, conducibile esse arbitror.
> BA. qui, amabo? PI. quia, Bacchis, Bacchas metuo et bacchanal tuom.
> BA. quid est? quid metuis? ne tibi lectus malitiam apud me suadeat?
> PI. magis inlectum tuom quam lectum metuo. mala tu es bestia.   55
> nam huic aetati non conducit, mulier, latebrosus locus.
>
> (Plaut. *Bacch.* 50–6)

PISTOCLERUS: Your flattery is pure birdlime. BACCHIS: What you mean? PISTOCLERUS: Because I know very well that you two are attacking one pigeon. I'm done for, the twig is beating my wings. I don't think that this deed, woman, is profitable for me. BACCHIS: Why, sweetie? PISTOCLERUS: Because, Bacchis, I fear bacchants and your bacchanal. BACCHIS: What is it? What are you afraid of? That the bed at my place might suggest some naughtiness to you? PISTOCLERUS: I fear your charm more than your bed. You're a bad beast. Your shady spot is not profitable to my age, woman.

For the elegiac lover, the means of access is persuasion – and persuasion directly of the beloved, not of an owner or other intermediary. This is crucial to the nature of elegiac love and fundamentally different from comic love: the elegiac lover's

---

44 Of the 21 plays of Plautus, irrelevant for this purpose are *Amph.*, *Capt.*, and *Stich.*, while *Vid.* is too fragmentary for us to tell, but is almost certainly directed towards marriage. Other plays where the main goal is marriage do sometimes include questions of dowry, for example *Aul.* and *Trin.*, but this is not the point. All remaining plays involve some sort of payment for sexual access, often by means of a trick. The only partial exceptions are *Cas.*, where the love object is already owned by the *senex* who is competing with his son for access to her (in fact, there turns out to be a recognition plot in the background, so the eponymous Casina is recognised and married to the young man), and *Mil.*, where the beloved is kidnapped (with her connivance) from the soldier, who had kidnapped her in the first place (against her will). Of the plays of Terence, only *An.* does not include payment of a prostitute (it includes no true prostitute at all). In *Ad.*, the prostitute-beloved is kidnapped by Aeschinus on his brother's behalf, but no-one imagines that this does not have to be paid for eventually.

goal is to persuade his beloved to want to receive him and to reciprocate his love. There may be various nuances or even duplicities involved here, but the underlying telos of the love-plot and the very raison d'être of love elegy as a type of literature is to try to make the *puella* respond lovingly. Propertius' bitter complaint expresses the matter in a couplet:[45]

> munera quanta dedi uel qualia carmina feci!
>   illa tamen numquam ferrea dixit 'Amo.'

(Prop. 2.8.11–12)

> What gifts I gave or what poems I made, but she, iron-hearted, never said 'I love you'.

There is certainly a concern about expensive gifts in elegy, characteristically vaguer than the explicitly monetary payments commonly required by comedy, and gifts are indeed sometimes given by elegiac lovers, but typically the problem is not that the elegiac lover is out of funds through which he may pay, rather that paying does not fit in with his conception of what elegiac love is. Ovid is explicit about this in *Am.* 1. 10, a poem which plays with the diatribe against greed while making claims for mutuality in elegiac love (which perhaps may not be in keeping with Roman reality).[46]

> quae Venus ex aequo uentura est grata duobus,
>   altera cur illam uendit et alter emit?
> cur mihi sit damno, tibi sit lucrosa uoluptas,
>   quam socio motu femina uirque ferunt?

(Ov. *Am.* 1.10.33–6)

> That love which comes welcome to both equally, why should the female one sell it and the male one buy it? Why should pleasure, which woman and man bring together by their common movement, be a source of financial loss to me, but gain to you?

After luxuries are denigrated in standard moral fashion, the good services of a *pauper* are presented as a preferable alternative (57–8), while the poet's own art is presented as the best *dos* (dowry) of all (59–60, 'dowry' of course belongs to

---

45 There are difficulties over the text of this poem and the position, or even authenticity, of these lines, but for our purposes all that matters is that the couplet expresses the elegiac goal and its failure. See Heyworth 2007, 143–6.
46 See also Thorsen's final chapter in this volume.

the discourse of marriage), as it is able to confer *fama perennis* (62).[47] In typical Ovidian fashion, the final couplet changes the stakes:

> nec dare, sed pretium posci dedignor et odi;
> quod nego poscenti, desine uelle, dabo.
>
> (Ov. *Am.* 1.10.63–4)

> It is not giving, but being asked to pay that I disdain and hate; what I refuse when asked, stop wanting, and I'll give.

A good place to see the goal of elegiac love as amatory persuasion is when Propertius has (unusually) actually succeeded in persuading his *puella* to choose to accept his love.

> Hic erit: hic iurata manet; rumpantur iniqui!
> uicimus: assiduas non tulit illa preces.
> falsa licet cupidus deponat gaudia Liuor:
> destitit ire nouas Cynthia nostra uias.   30
> illi carus ego, et per me carissima Roma
> dicitur, et sine me dulcia regna negat.
>
> (Prop. 1.8b.27–32)

> She'll be here: she is staying here as she swore; let my enemies burst! I've conquered: she did not bear continual prayers. Let desirous Jealousy put aside false joys: my Cynthia has stopped going on new paths. I am called dear by her, and through me Rome is dearest, and she denies that any kingdoms are sweet without me.

And the way he has done this is equally crucial to the elegiac programme:

> hanc ego non auro, non Indis flectere conchis,
> sed potui blandi carminis obsequio.
>
> (Prop. 1.8.39–40)

> I have been able to persuade her not by gold, nor by Indian pearls, but by the service of flattering song.

However illusory the choice exercised by the elegiac woman might be, whether because of underlying economic necessity or because she is wholly a creation of the poet,[48] if our goal is to describe accurately the nature of elegiac love, then this

---

[47] Prop. 3.13 is another poem which partakes in the diatribe against monetary remuneration in erotic matters. Here it is clear that the connection between money and sex is not just for prostitutes, but also potentially in adulterous relationships (see especially 9–12).
[48] James 2003, esp. 20–9 and Wyke 2002.

representation of choice is crucial. No comic woman has the degree of self-determination presented in poems such as Propertius 1.8. If it is a question of marriage, sometimes she has no choice, especially if she is a rape victim, but she is never opposed to the idea – or rather, she has never given any opportunity to express any opposition. It is true that she may sometimes be in love with the young man and desirous to marry him, although this attitude generally only seems to be available to her if she is an unrecognised citizen.[49] But we never see any efforts on the part of the young man to win her love.[50] By contrast, the main purpose of elegy is to persuade the beloved. In the case of a prostitute-beloved, some comic women express themselves as loving the *adulescens* (especially if he has freed her or is likely to do so, e.g. *Mostell.*, *Pers.*), while others are merely pawns in the hands of those who trade in female bodies. What we do not see is any comic woman needing to be coaxed into accepting the hero as her lover. Partial exceptions could be Thais in *Eunuchus* or Phronesium in *Truculentus*, but even these women are both massively constrained by the plot. Thais persuades Phaedria to let his rival have primary access to her for a few days, so that she can secure his gift, the unrecognised citizen girl whom Thais hopes to restore to her family. Phronesium does play one man off against another to increase her income (the only significant example of this in Roman comedy, despite popular misconceptions), but she too is unable to decide whom to love based on personal choice.

Then there is the question of the 'stock characters'. Most commonly discussed among the comedy characters stepping into the world of elegy are various slave-figures,[51] the soldier-rival,[52] and the *lena* who attempts to persuade the elegiac beloved to receive rich lovers in place of the poet. This last character has been the subject of much attention, because it is extensively treated in two

---

[49] Selenium in *Cistellaria* is a good example, as is Planesium in *Curculio*. It has been well noted by Konstan 1994, 146–7, that women who will become brides in comedy rarely get an opportunity to consent or otherwise, but that quasi-prostitutes occasionally do so. It should be noted that they only ever express pleasure and desire, not opposition.

[50] The nearest I can find to a comic example of a girl who needs to be persuaded to marriage comes from Menander. In the highly fragmentary *Misoumenos*, a girl is taken captive in war and comes into the possession of a soldier, who falls in love with her. She rejects him because she believes that he has killed her brother. Eventually she is discovered by her father and married to the soldier, although how the issue with the brother was resolved is unclear. While this is a rare example of a woman in comedy being allowed to express an opinion, it appears to be a case of misunderstanding rather than any emotional plot-development.

[51] But note how poor is the connection, for example, between the eunuch Bagoas in *Am.* 2.2 and 2.3, and the one example of the eunuch in Roman comedy, which is in Terence's eponymous play. Barsby 1996, 144–6.

[52] Also effectively debunked by Barsby 1996, 146–8.

poems, Prop. 4.5 and *Am*. 1.8.⁵³ I do not doubt that the reader is meant to see the Comic games at work in *Am*. 1.8,⁵⁴ although the particular relevance of comedy, as opposed to the generality of low genres, to the other *lena*-poems seems less convincing. Barsby is right to argue that the only scene in Roman comedy to show any significant degree of correspondence with the elegiac poems is in Plautus' *Mostellaria*,⁵⁵ when the slave-attendant Scapha is overheard by the lover Philolaches as she advises the beloved Philematium (whom he has just freed) not to rely on the long-term devotion of one lover. Although the situation of eavesdropping is distinctly comic, Barsby argues that specific connection between the two scenes is limited. I would add, not only that Scapha is not a *lena*, just an attendant,⁵⁶ but also that very little of the extensive scene involves advice on how to deceive men.⁵⁷

As Myers rightly points out,⁵⁸ the elegiac *lenae* 'participate in the ancient Greek and Roman tradition of invective against old women and women in general; she is bibulous, mercenary, and dangerously magical, a witch. Parallels may be found in epigram, comedy, satire, and oratory.' This is true: what is not often noted, however, is that a different subset of elements from misogynistic diatribe is at work in comedy and in elegy. In particular, there is nothing in comedy which imputes magical powers to older women. Leaena in Plautus' *Curculio* may drink too much, but she is not a witch. It is no doubt right to be aware of the background of Roman door magic in the scene,⁵⁹ but it does not seem to have anything to do with Leaena. She is also not a *lena*.

Indeed, I would go so far as to say that the *lena* is a rare figure in comedy.⁶⁰ I would take issue with Myers' otherwise excellent account of the elegiac *lena*

---

53 The 'bawd' appears also in Tib. 1.5.47–8 and 2.6.43–54.
54 The double doors of *Am*. 1.8.22 are particularly telling in this regard.
55 Barsby 1996, 138–40. McKeown 1989, 198–9 overstates the connection with Plaut. *Mostell.*, but rightly points out that 'Plautus' scenario was probably conventional' and that 'Ovid may have been influenced at least substantially by Herodas' first mimiamb as by Comedy'.
56 In the *dramatis personae* she is described as *ancilla*. Philolaches, as an insult, aside while he is eavesdropping, may call her *uitilena*, although the text is corrupt (213). He does call her *lena* (*non uideor uidisse lenam callidiorem ullam alteras*, 270, still eavesdropping) later, but this is clearly metaphorical. Scapha has no control over Philematium, who threatens her with beating (209–10).
57 Barsby 1996, 140: 'very little overlap between the arguments of Plautus' bawd and Ovid's'.
58 Myers 1996, 6, and 9 n. 57 on the connection of magical and erotic powers.
59 Debrohun 2003, 126 gives a good account of the importance of doors and other thresholds in Roman culture, including their magical significance.
60 In comedy, it is the male version who is more common, on which see Griffin 1985, 114.

when she joins in the obsession with comic origins for elegy, saying 'the appearance of the procuratress in the elegies of all three poets may indeed constitute a programmatic acknowledgement of the literary indebtedness of Latin erotic elegy to comedy.'[61] Myers points particularly to Plautus' *Mostellaria* and *Asinaria*,[62] but I would suggest that claims for close association between elegiac and comic *lenae* are overstated. The only significant character in the entirety of Plautus and Terence who is designated *lena* is Cleareta in Plautus' *Asinaria*, who is the mother as well as the manager of the beloved Philaenium. She, however, is not at all similar to the elegiac *lenae*, most of her interaction being with the young men who are her customers. There is a scene between Cleareta and Philaenium (*As.* 504–44), in which the *lena*-mother is angry because her daughter wants to receive Argyrippus without payment. Emphasis in the scene is heavily on financial need and filial duty.

Although neither is called *lena*, there is also the case of the prostitute-mothers in Plautus' *Cistellaria*, who manage their daughters as prostitutes. One of these (who does not appear) is actually a foster-mother, who had received the female romantic lead Selenium as a baby after she was exposed (therefore she is a quasi-prostitute who will eventually marry her lover). The other mother, possibly called Syra, has a scene with her own prostitute-daughter and Selenium, in which the misogynistic motif of excessive drinking plays its comic role, together with a strong sense of financial need. Apart from these cases, there is no significant *lena*.[63] There are slave-attendants, like Scapha in *Mostellaria*, and more mature prostitute-advisers, like Syra in Terence' *Hecyra*, who advise the female romantic leads to make as much money as they can and not to be too sentimental. While this clearly has affinities with the advice of Acanthis and Dipsas, it is not specific or exclusive. In all, therefore, it seems to me that there is not enough in comedy to suggest that the elegiac *lena* in any sense derives from that genre.

Another major difference between the situation of the comic and the elegiac lover, which is not just a feature of the difference of medium, is the wider context within which they operate. The comic lover is usually dependent on parents and, in a different sense, on a clever and helpful slave (occasionally parasite). Of the

---

61 Myers 1996, 3.
62 Myers 1996: the *lena* character is 'collided with that of the old nurse or maid … or even mother', across a range of genres, including epigram and mime.
63 There is a mother in Plaut. *Mil.* who is described by Palaestrio *seruus* in the prologue as *lenae, matri mulieris* (110, the word having been used also in 108). It is through her agency that the eponymous soldier was able to get to know the female lead, Philocomasium, but he took her away *clam matrem* (111), while the mother also works with Palaestrio and Pleusicles *adulescens* to free Philocomasium from the soldier.

21 plays of Plautus sufficiently extant to make judgement possible, the vast majority situate a youthful male lead within a family context, while they all contain at least one slave who plays a more or less significant role in the plot. The largest group of plays put their male romantic lead into a clear domestic situation, with at least one parent: *Asin., Aul., Bacch., Cas., Epid., Merc., Mostell., Poen., Pseud., Trin., Truc., Vid.* Three plays, *Cist., Curc.*, and *Rud.*, depend for their telos on the domestic position of the beloved (she finds her parents in *Cist.* and *Rud.*, her brother in *Curc.*). Although the young man's father does not play a significant role, they are directed towards marriage, which is a family matter. *Amphitruo* is a special case, but its 'lover' (Jupiter) and his 'rival' (the eponymous Theban general) have clear socio-political positions. *Stichus* is a different kind of special case, but again firmly based within normal social relations (two daughters are married to two brothers who have gone abroad to seek their fortunes, but in their absence the father of the girls wants them to remarry). A third special case, *Captiui*, the only Plautine play with no female roles, also has an active father. Different again is *Men.*, in which the love plot (such as it is) is subordinate to the mistaken identity of the twins, but again the socio-legal position of the *adulescentes* is crucial to the plot. *Pers.*, as explained above, is bizarre in having a lover who legally has no father, being a slave, but as such he nonetheless has a(n unfortunate) clear socio-legal position, while the legal status of the parasite's daughter is important to the plot. That means only *Mil.*, a play in which the male romantic lead, Pleusicles (who is not at all *egens*), does not have family directly appearing, but even he achieves his goal not only with the help of the magnificent slave Palaestrio, but also through the good offices of a classic *senex lepidus*, Periplectomenus, who happens to be the neighbour of the rival soldier – and also a friend of Pleusicles' father. In all the plays of Terence, the male lead has at least one parent who plays a significant role, plus at least one slave or parasite who helps, more or less effectively, in the management of the affair. The comic lover, therefore, exists very much within a wider context, with his love being directed towards situations which are entirely recognisable within the wider context: marriage, of course, is a legal entity which is the bedrock of society, while a paid relationship with a prostitute is a well-recognised, if somewhat less respectable, feature of that society.

The elegiac lover, by contrast, seems to be largely independent and considerably alone.[64] Ovid makes very brief reference to 'either parent' at 1.3.10, but this

---

[64] James 2012a, acknowledges that the elegiac lover operates free of family constraints. In explanation of the fact that elegy is not directed towards marriage, she suggests that elegy is situated at an earlier stage in a young man's life, which seems to me inconsistent with the relationship of both types of lover with family and society. The comic lover is sometimes very young

is part of the topos of ancestral 'poverty', which plays an extensive (and poetological) role in the self-presentation of the equestrian elegists. McKeown *ad loc.* gives parallels for the topos, both in elegy and in the wider discourse of thrift as a Roman virtue. I suggest, however, that he is misleading in the claim that Ovid is 'exploiting Comic typology' here. The *durus pater* of comedy is not generally obsessed with thrift,[65] but rather with not paying for prostitutes, while there is no example in comedy of a thrifty mother, or indeed one who is otherwise *dura*. McKeown is on stronger ground when he suggests that 'for the emphasis here on control exerted by both parents, one may perhaps compare [Theoc.] 8.15f. and Verg. *Ecl.* 3.33f.'. It seems to me that the pastoral phrase is by far the most active here. Otherwise, apart from the generalised references to ancestors, guarantors of Roman status and of genteel poverty, the love elegists seem largely to exist independently of family members. On the other hand, there are in all three elegiac collections various 'friends', including fellow-poets, other elite Romans climbing the slippery pole, up to and including major political figures such as Maecenas and Messala. I have argued elsewhere, apropos Propertius, that the involvement of real Romans in the elegiac world forms part of its construction of the reality effect.[66] These characters constitute part of the way the poetry insinuates itself into the contemporary society – something which comedy does almost not at all.

My argument in this paper has been that elegiac love is very different from comic love, being much less socially recognisable and sanctioned. It is in the erotodidactic poems that Ovid's games with comedy are developed, although, even here, vagueness about the socio-legal status of the beloved is maintained,[67] with the only clear indicator continuing to be that the elegiac relationship is not directed towards marriage (*non legis iussu lectum uenistis in unum*, 'you haven't come into one bed on the orders of the law', *Ars am.* 2.157). What is much more explicit is the manipulative nature of elegiac love. As a flatterer, cheater, and manipulator, however, Ovid's trainee lover does not take the comic *amans et egens* as his model: the character from comedy who is implicitly offered to him as an

---

indeed (for example, the younger brother in Terence' *Eunuchus*), while the elegiac lover is more of an ageless *iuuenis*. Indeed, James's example of the comic lover talking to his father and the elegiac lover talking to his friends and patrons seems to support my impression of their relative ages.

65 The one who is obsessed in this way, Menedemus in Terence' *Haut.*, is not at all *durus* with regard to his son, but rather with himself. He positively wants to pay for his son's affair, which in any case conveniently turns into a marriage.

66 Sharrock 2000.

67 Gibson 1998.

exemplum to follow might, rather, be the clever slave who drives the deceptive and manipulative plot of comedy.[68] There is also, less comfortably, a clear Comic allusion in the *partes* which Ovid instructs his pupil, *fac ... agas* (i.e., he must 'play the part' ordered by his mistress, *Ars am.* 2.198). He must mould every aspect of his behaviour and (apparent) opinions to those of the beloved (*Ars am.* 2.199–202), in language which closely evokes that of the parasite Gnatho in Terence' *Eunuchus* 250–3, expounding a programme for manipulating rich patrons. If Ovid exploits potential connections with comedy more extensively in the didactic poems, it is in such a way as in fact to move *away* from the elegiac norm into something much more socially recognisable, not to mention more manipulative and self-serving.

---

[68] James 2012a and Fulkerson 2013, 190–2 both suggest a possible connection between the comic clever slave and the elegiac lover.

Iris Brecke
Rape and Violence in Terence's *Eunuchus* and Ovid's Love Elegies

Introduction

This paper argues that the controversial rape scene in Terence's *Eunuchus* has a particularly rich reception in Ovid's love elegies,[1] predominantly in passages depicting sexualized violence.[2] In the following, the function of the presence of Terence will be analysed by identifying allusions to the play in Ovid and tracing common patterns between its highly shocking rape scene and some of Ovid's most famous stories of rape and violence against women; the rape of the Sabine women in *Ars amatoria* 1.89–134, Ilia's rape by Mars in *Amores* 3.6, Oenone's rape by Apollo in *Heroides* 5, and the poet-lover's violent attack on the *puella* in *Amores* 1.7.[3]

The theme of rape and sexual violence is prominent in both the Roman elegiac genre and the preceding comic tradition.[4] In New Comedy, the rape of young girls that in the end turn out to be citizen daughters and consequently eligible for marriage with their rapist – always a young citizen man – is so common that it

---

[1] The genres of Latin love elegy and New Comedy have traditionally been seen as closely connected within the Classics, see e.g. Leo 1895, Jacoby 1905, Day 1938, Yardley 1972 (on Plautus' *Asinaria* in Propertius); 1987b, Griffin 1985, Konstan 1986 (on Terence's *Eunuchus* in particular), Barsby 1996, James 1998; 2006; 2012a; 2016, Piazzi 2013, 236–7, Sharrock 2013b, 61–3.
[2] My paper is based on a talk at the conference 'Greek and Roman literature: the erotic connection' (Oxford, June 11. 2016). James 2016, published later that year, also treats the connection between the first book of the *Ars amatoria* and the *Eunuchus*, pointing to several of the same allusions that I do. Some of the argument overlaps with Brecke 2020, which does not treat *Am.* 3.6 and 1.7.
[3] The thematic organisation of the paper does not follow the traditional chronological order of the works, which might be fictional, as internal allusions suggests that all works might have been re-worked by Ovid for a revised edition at around 2 CE. See Thorsen 2014, 9–38 (25–29 in particular).
[4] Examples of the theme of violence against the *puella* in elegy are e.g. Tib. 1.1.73-4, 1.6.73-4, 1.10.53–66, Prop. 2.5.21–6, 2.15.17–20, 4.5.31, Ov. *Am.* 1.7, 2.5.45–6, *Ars am.* 2.169–72, 3.567–70. In addition, there are several depictions of violence and rape in the mythological and legendary sphere; the rape of Ilia in Ov. *Am.* 3.6, the Sabine rape at Ov. *Ars am.* 1.89–134, Achilles' rape of Deidamia at Ov. *Ars am.* 1.689–704 and Oenone's rape by Apollo at Ov. *Her.* 5.140–6 are examples of such rape descriptions.

https://doi.org/10.1515/9783110633030-006

might be regarded as a stock motif of the genre.⁵ In Roman comedy, rape is by far a more dominant feature in Terence than in Plautus. In four of Terence's six plays, rape occurs directly as part of the storyline and leads the action towards its conventional denouement, and one further comedy tells of a rape in the parent generation that leads to the marriage between the daughter of the rape victim and a citizen man of the younger generation. In the Plautine corpus, four of the 20 surviving plays include an act of rape as a part of the story line.⁶ In addition, two of the Terentian rapes are described as particularly violent (in the *Hecyra* and the *Eunuchus*). In the later Latin elegiac genre rape and sexualized violence against women are also recurring issues, or in the words of James, 'rape is part of a pattern of violence toward women in elegy, a subject most visible in Ovid'.⁷ The theme of rape and violence against the beloved object in love elegy is often seen as a trait that is inherited from comedy, and thus as connecting the two genres.⁸

However, rape in the comic genre has a specific function as a pretext for marriage, and the rape of a comic *uirgo* conventionally ends with the recognition of her as a citizen and a legitimate marriage union between her and the rapist, and in many cases the birth of a legitimate citizen child.⁹ This is the conventional goal of the comedies in which this motif occurs, so that when the audience heard that a *uirgo* had been raped, they would probably expect that she would turn out to be of citizen status and married off to her rapist towards the end of the play. This would be seen as a fortunate outcome, and the girl would often 'marry up' into a well-off family, which further contributed to the positive reception of the rape. Thus, the main plot line of New Comedy is in the end perfectly in line with traditional Roman values and norms.¹⁰ Traditional lifestyle choices, including marrying and having children, stand in contrast to Ovid's anti-marital elegiac universe,¹¹ and he was indeed deemed to be immoral and a threat to traditional

---

5 Rape in New Comedy has been a point of focus in research the last decades. See e.g. Pierce 1997, Rosivach 1998, Omitowoju 2002, 135–233 (rape in Menander), James 1998, Konstan/Raval 2008, 55–62. On rape in antiquity in general, see Deacy/Pierce 1997.
6 I here base myself on the rapes defined as 'consummated rapes' in Leisner-Jensen 2002. Here, four instances of rape in the Plautine corpus (*Aulularia*, *Cistellaria*, *Epidicus*, *Truculentus*), and four in Terence (*Andria*, *Eunuchus*, *Hecyra*, *Adelphoe*), are treated. In addition, there is talk of a rape in Terence's *Phormio*, which facilitates the marriage between the victim's daughter and a young citizen man.
7 James 2012b, 549.
8 See e.g. McKeown 1989, *ad* Ov. *Am*. 1.7.
9 The use of the term *uirgo* indicates citizen status within the comedy convention, see Watson 1983.
10 See Barsby 1999b, 242–3.
11 On the nature of elegiac love, see Thorsen 2013b, 2–4.

values promoted by Augustus: his *Ars amatoria* was probably at least partially the cause for his relegation to Tomis in 8 CE.[12] As will be demonstrated throughout this paper, despite the clear differences between Latin Love Elegy and the preceding comic genre when it comes to the different function of issues such as rape and marriage, Ovid incorporates aspects of Terence's most unconventional rape scene into his own descriptions of sexualized violence.

The *Eunuchus*: rape at the centre of the action

The rape of the comic *uirgo* Pamphila by the young citizen man Chaerea in *Eunuchus* is one of the most widely discussed scenes in the New Comic corpus,[13] and understandably so. The depiction of the violent rape is highly shocking to modern readers and must have stood out even in in the second century BCE, as it differs in many ways from the conventional rape plot line of the comic genre. There are several factors that separate the scene from the conventional comic rapes. Most striking is perhaps the description of the perpetrator's use of violence, and the time and place of the deed. Conventionally, the comic rapes had taken place prior to the action of the play, often after dark, outside, at a religious festival, and it was typically a spur-of-the-moment action conducted by a young man overcome by lust and too much wine. These factors all serve as explanations or excuses for the young man's actions, and simultaneously to free the victim or her family from blame, by offering a reason for why a citizen girl was unprotected and available for a young man to rape, and by highlighting the fact that she was in fact raped and not seduced. Thus, the rapes within the genre are not usually morally problematized, and the conventional denouement of such plots with the marriage between rapist and victim was considered a happy outcome for both parties.

However, in the *Eunuchus*, the rape follows a rather different plot line. The *adulescens* Chaerea sees the girl Pamphila in the street in the middle of the day

---

[12] Ovid was relegated to Tomis (modern Constanza in Romania) on the Black Sea by emperor Augustus in 8 or 9 CE due to *duo crimina, carmen et error* (Ov. *Tr.* 2.207, 'two crimes, a poem and a blunder'). In the opening of *Tristia* 2, it becomes evident that the poem is the *Ars amatoria*: *carmina fecerunt ut me moresque notaret / iam pridem demi iussa Caesar ab Arte meos* (Ov. *Tr.* 2.7–8 'verse caused Caesar to brand me and my ways by commanding that my "Art" be forthwith taken away'). Ovid was charged with being an *obsceni doctor adulterii* (Ov. *Tr.* 2.212, 'a teacher of obscene adultery'). My text for *Tristia* 2 is Ingleheart 2010a.
[13] See e.g. James 1998; 2016, Christenson 2013.

whilst being taken to the *meretrix* Thais as a present from the boastful solider Thraso, and immediately falls in love with her and decides that he must have her. He turns to the family slave Parmeno, and asks for his aid:

> CHAEREA: nunc, Parmeno, ostendes te qui uir sies.
> scis te mihi saepe pollicitum esse 'Chaerea, aliquid inueni
> modo quod ames; in ea re utilitatem ego faciam ut cognoscas meam'.
>
> (Ter. *Eun*. 307–9)

> CHAEREA: Now, Parmeno, you shall show what sort of man you are ... you often made me a promise: 'Chaerea, just find someone to love, and I'll make you aware how useful I can be in that regard.'[14]

Chaerea has no idea who the girl is, but Parmeno has already heard Thais tell the story about how a girl was abducted as a child, given to Thais' mother and brought up as her sister, and knows that her soldier-lover has now bought the very same girl as a gift for her, without any knowledge of her background story. He warns Chaerea that it will be impossible for him to obtain her, but the latter refuses to back off. What is more, Parmeno is on this day supposed to bring Thais a slave girl and a eunuch, gifts from Chaerea's older brother Phaedria who is competing with Thraso for Thais' attention. Chaerea expresses how jealous he is of the eunuch, who will get to live under the same roof as the girl as a fellow slave,[15] whereupon Parmeno suggests a way for Chaerea to become just as lucky:

> PARMENO: tu illis fruare commodis quibus tu illum dicebas modo:
> cibum una capias adsis tangas ludas propter dormias.
>
> (Ter. *Eun*. 372–3)

> PARMENO: You could enjoy the benefits which you were just saying would be his—eat with her, live with her, touch her, play with her, sleep next to her.

The suggestion is for Chaerea to disguise himself as the eunuch, and let himself be delivered to Thais' house. Chaerea takes the advice, enters the house, and rapes the girl as soon as Thais goes out. The audience learns about the rape when Chaerea brags to a friend about it, expressing how exceedingly happy he is that everything has turned out just the way he wanted. There are no explanations or

---

14 My text for the *Eunuchus* is Barsby 1999b, for Ovid I use Hollis 2009 [1977] for *Ars amatoria* 1, McKeown 1987 for *Amores*, and Knox 1995 for the *Heroides*. All translations are from the Loeb Classical Library, with modifications, unless otherwise stated.
15 Pamphila is really a citizen girl, a fact that Chaerea does not yet know.

circumstances that can excuse the rape other than the perpetrator's own motivation for doing it, i.e. that he did it for love, and furthermore, that he was inspired by a painting of Jupiter's rape of Danaë (575–606).

Later we hear from Pythias, a maid in Thais' house, and from Thais herself, that the rape was particularly violent, and that the perpetrator had torn the girl's clothes and hair, and that the she was left crying and silenced by fear:

> PYTHIAS: quin etiam insuper scelus, postquam ludificatust uirginem
> uestem omnem miserae discidit, tum ipsam capillo conscidit.
>
> (Ter. *Eun.* 645–6)

> PYTHIAS: Why, on top of it all, after he'd had his fun and games with the poor girl, the villain ripped her whole dress and tore her hair.

> PYTHIAS: ego illum nescio
> qui fuerit; hoc quod fecit, res ipsa indicat.
> uirgo ipsa lacrumat neque, quom rogites, quid sit audet dicere.
>
> (Ter. *Eun.* 657–9)

> PYTHIAS: I don't know who he was, but what he did is clear from the facts. The girl is crying and doesn't dare say what happened when you ask her.

> THAIS: ... non tu istuc mihi dictura aperte's quidquid est?
> uirgo conscissa ueste lacrumans opticet;
>
> (Ter. *Eun.* 819–20)

> THAIS: ... Won't you tell me in plain words what is going on? The girl's dress is torn, she's weeping, and she won't say a word.

This is one of the most explicit depictions of rape within the Roman comedy corpus: it is at the centre of the action,[16] conducted after the divine *exemplum* of Jupiter's rape of Danaë, described in some detail, and crucial for the action of the play. It might also be said to be the most problematized case of rape in comedy: through the maid Pythias, Terence lets the audience know that the rape was conducted with particular violence, and furthermore, reveals the girl's reaction to it, i.e. that she is scared, and that she is crying and unable to tell anyone about what

---

[16] The description of it is placed almost exactly in the middle of the play, see Germany 2016, 1.

has happened to her. Pythias is furious and eager to take revenge on behalf of the girl, and threatens to attack the perpetrator physically.

The description of the girl as a victim of violence, her reaction to the violent rape, and how infuriated the action has left one of the other (female) characters, help to underscore the problematic aspect of the action and the harsh consequences of rape for the victim in an unconventional manner. However, the play takes a traditional turn towards the end of the action, when the girl is recognized as a citizen and promised in marriage to her rapist. This even seems to calm Pythias, and we never hear more about Pamphila and how she feels about her own situation. Nevertheless, as will be argued in what follows, similar elements to those detected in this unconventional and explicit depiction of a rape are incorporated into the rape narratives in Ovid's elegiac works.

Ars amatoria 1.89–134: an Ovidian rape-marriage plot?

When Ovid chooses the theatre as the scene for the rape of the Sabine women in his depiction of it in the *Ars amatoria*, it is a deliberate altering of the established tradition of the aetiological history of Rome. The theatre is not the conventional setting for the legendary rape,[17] an incident that is crucial for the city's foundational legend and the means by which the founding father secured the growth of the city that evolved into an empire. The rape is also the story of the first Roman wives and the origin of the institution of Roman marriage. At the time when Ovid wrote the *Ars amatoria*, it had recently been reinforced by the Augustan legislation to improve the reduced marriage and fertility rate among the elite classes and to confront what was allegedly perceived as an increased sexual licence and a lack of respect for Roman traditions.[18] It is therefore more than puzzling that Ovid lets the story serve as an example for the search for an elegiac *puella*. One of the main issues is that it adds to the controversy concerning the status of the *puella*: Ovid apparently claims in the opening of the *Ars amatoria* that he is not

---

17 According to the tradition, the rape took place at the first celebration of the *Consualia*, and the entertainment was horseracing, not theatrical plays. On the connection between the rape of the Sabine women and the *Consualia*, see e.g. Ogilvie 1965, 66–70. Ovid mentions this festival and its traditional venue at *Fast.* 3.197–200.
18 See e.g. Eder 2005, 28

referring to Roman wives or girls of citizen status,[19] yet the Sabine women serve as the ultimate symbol of such females.[20]

The interlude on the Sabine Rape is introduced by Ovid's *praeceptor amoris*, as he is instructing young men about suitable locations to find a mistress. He gives an account of the legendary rape to demonstrate how the theatre, ever since the time of Romulus and the first Romans, has been the best and most fertile place to search:

> sed tu praecipue curuis uenare theatris;
>   haec loca sunt uoto fertiliora tuo.
> illic inuenies quod ames, quod ludere possis,
>   quodque semel tangas, quodque tenere uelis.
>
> (Ov. *Ars am.* 1.89–92)
>
> primus sollicitos fecisti, Romule, ludos,
>   cum iuuit uiduos rapta Sabina uiros.
>
> (Ov. *Ars am.* 1.101–2)

But specially do your hunting in the round theatres: more bountifully do these repay your vows. There will you find an object for passion or for deception, something to taste but once, or to keep, if so you wish.

You first, Romulus, disturbed the games, when the rape of Sabine women consoled the wifeless men.

Ovid's audience would notice this change of setting, and it is one of several factors that separates it from Livy's account of the same story.[21] However, the choice of the theatre is hardly a coincidence: lines 91–2 bear a prominent textual resemblance to lines 308–9 of the *Eunuchus*, where Chaerea reminds Parmeno of his earlier promise to help him if he were to fall in love: *Chaerea, aliquid inueni / modo quod ames* (Ter. *Eun.* 308–9).[22] In the play, Parmeno subsequently assumes a role strikingly similar to the one of the *praeceptor*, and gives advice to the *adulescens* to use in his pursuit for the girl. The use of the neuter pronoun *quod* stands out in both texts,[23]

---

19 See Ov. *Ars am.* 1.31–4, quoted below.
20 On the blurred status of the *puella* throughout Ovid's love elegies, see Gibson 1998; 2009 [2003] and the chapter by Sharrock and the last chapter by Thorsen in this volume.
21 On the differences between Livy and Ovid's account of the Sabine rape, see Hemker 1985.
22 James also points to the similarity between lines 91–2 of the *Ars* and 308–9 and 372–3 of the *Eunuchus*. See James 2016, 88–9.
23 The neuter pronoun as object for *amare* is previously found in Plautus (*Epidicus* 653), and in Lucretius (4.1061); see also the chapter by Ingleheart in this volume.

and the allusion is further marked by Ovid's phrase *quod ludere possis, / quodque semel tangas*, which picks up Parmeno's line 373 *cibum una capias adsis tangas ludas propter dormias*; likewise at 372, the comic slave lists the advantages, *commodis* (Ter. *Eun.* 372) of living in Thais' house disguised as a eunuch, the word recalls Ov. *Ars am.* 1.131–2 on the *commoda* given to the men by Romulus: *Romule, militibus scisti dare commoda solus: / haec mihi si dederis commoda, miles ero*, 'Ah, Romulus, only you knew how to bestow bounty on your warriors; if you would bestow such bounty upon me, I will be a warrior').[24] In Terence *tangas* and *ludas* possess the same meaning and the same erotic undertone as in the Ovidian line. It appears that Ovid, in rating the theatre as the best place to find a *puella*, draws the reader's attention to the theatre not only as a setting suitable for flirting, but on a metaliterary and generic level as well.

Ovid introduces the story of the Sabine rape as an example of how to execute a successful hunt, with the use of *uenare* in line 89. The interlude on the rape extends over lines 101–34, describing how Romulus' men sit amongst the theatre audience, stare at the women, each marking out the one he wants, thinking carefully about it, before they unexpectedly jump up, on the sign of their leader, and like predators attack the women, now termed *uirginibus* in line 116. Panic breaks loose, and the women, the prey, try to flee the attackers in a terrified state before they are captured and carried off:

> ut fugiunt aquilas, timidissima turba, columbae
>   ut fugit inuisos agna nouella lupos,
> sic illae timuere uiros sine more ruentes;
>   constitit in nulla qui fuit ante color.
> nam timor unus erat, facies non una timoris:
>   pars laniat crines, pars sine mente sedet;
> altera maesta silet, frustra uocat altera matrem;
>   haec queritur, stupet haec; haec manet, illa fugit.
> ducuntur raptae, genialis praeda, puellae,
>   et potuit multas ipse decere timor.
> siqua repugnarat nimium comitemque negarat,
>   sublatum cupido uir tulit ipse sinu
> atque ita 'quid teneros lacrimis corrumpis ocellos?
>   quod matri pater est, hoc tibi' dixit 'ero'.
>
> (Ov. *Ars am.* 1.117–29)

---

[24] The similar use of *commodum* in the *Ars amatoria* and *Eunuchus* is pointed out in James 2016. In Terence's *Hecyra*, the *meretrix* Bacchis similarly says that she has brought her previous lover Pamphilus *commodas res* (Ter. *Hec.* 817), after she has aided him by securing his marriage to his wife, whom he loves. Interestingly, she assumes a role similar to the role of the *praeceptor* (Ter. *Hec.* 816–20).

As doves, most timorous of birds, flee from the eagles, as the weanling lamb from the hated wolf, so feared they the men rushing wildly on them; in none remained her former colour. For their fear was one, but not one was the appearance of their fear: some tear their hair, some sit crazed; one is silent in dismay, one calls in vain upon her mother; this one bewails, that one is struck dumb; this one remains, that one flees. The captured women are led off, spoil for the marriage-couch, and to many their very fear had power to lend grace. If any struggled overmuch and resisted her mate, up-borne on his eager breast he carried her off himself, saying: 'Why do you spoil those tender eyes with tears? What your sire was to your mother that will I be to you.'

The way Ovid lets the men gaze at the women and 'mark with their eyes' their desired girl, *respiciunt, oculisque notant sibi quisque puellam / quam uelit, et tacito pectore multa mouent* (Ov. *Ars am.* 1.109–10, 'They look about them, and each notes with his glance the woman he desires, and they brood much in their secret hearts'), stands in opposition to Livy's version of the story, where chance decides which girl each man ends up with.[25] In this way, the story fits Ovid's own programme better: in Livy's account, it is arbitrary which girl each man ends up with, whereas in Ovid's erotodidactic work, the individual man's lust for a specific girl is the point of focus.[26] In the context of the Terentian allusion in the interlude, it also mirrors Chaerea's constant gazing at Pamphila, and his focus on the sight of her, as he is chasing after her. He is first angry for having lost sight of her, *illam a conspectu amisi meo* (Ter. *Eun.* 293, 'I've lost sight of her'), then he looks for her again after having been held up by an old relative of his father, *huc respicio ad uirginem* (Ter. *Eun.* 342, 'I looked this way for the girl'). Finally, when he has managed to blend in with Thais' slaves and is left alone with the girl, he sneaks a last glance at her from behind a fan that he is holding, immediately before the rape: *ego limis specto / sic per flabellum clanculum* (Ter. *Eun.* 601-2, 'I looked at her sideways through the fan, like this').

In Chaerea's description of the rape, we learn that Pamphila had fallen asleep, but later also that there must have been a fight or some resistance on the girl's part, as her dress and hair are torn. We also learn the she was traumatized by the rape, and reacted with fright, silence and tears, much as Ovid describes the first reaction of the Sabine women. Finally, the rape is described as a brutal attack on a weaker party, just like a predator's attack on helpless prey. It is worth noting that Terence uses a similar motif at line 118, when Thais accuses Pythias

---

25 Liv. 1.9.11. The exception is a few girls that were considered particularly attractive and therefore handpicked for the leading men.
26 See also Hollis 2009 [1977], *ad loc.*

of having let the wolf watch over the lamb: *scelesta, ouem lupo commisti* (Ter. *Eun.* 832, 'You wretch, entrusting a lamb to the proverbial wolf').

Ovid's use of the Sabine Rape as *exemplum* is an obvious paradox considering the context, and so are the allusions to the rape of a comic *uirgo*, a stock character of the genre and always a citizen girl.[27] The Sabine women were the first legal wives of Rome, and the mythological rape constitutes the origin of the Roman marriage institution itself. This stands in sharp contrast to the anti-marital programme of Ovid, and the violence described in the episode, i.e. the seizing and abduction of the women, does not fit well with the elegiac notion of *exorare puellam* (Ov. *Ars am.* 1.37, 'to win the girl'), introduced just a few lines earlier. The Sabine women have much more in common with the *uirgo* in comedy than with the elegiac *puella*, something which is also highlighted by the reference to them as *uirginibus* in line 116. Ovid seems here to highlight the tension between *uirgo* and *puella*, and make it into a play with the status of the elegiac mistress.

Labate, treating the paradoxical *exemplum* of the Sabine rape in the *Ars amatoria*,[28] discusses the function of the representation of the Sabine rape in the opening, and stresses the point that the ultimate goal, to find women, is the same for Romulus' men and Ovid's pupils, who will frequent theatres to find them and single out the most attractive ones. He argues that the Sabine rape presents an *exemplum* which acts as an anti-*exemplum*, as Romulus' method is *sine arte* and more suited to the pre-civilized world and too simplistic and direct for the more refined world of Augustan Rome. Ovid's pupils will hunt for women in the theatres and find the most attractive ones, but they will use *ars*, symbolised by the 'artistic' procedures of *exorare*, and a love that is free from the primitive ways of Romulus' soldiers.[29] I would here like to draw attention to a further aspect of the paradox that lies in both Ovid's exploitation of the Sabine Rape and the allusions to the Terentian rape plot; in addition to the methods used, the end goal for both Romulus and the comic plot, i.e. marriage and procreation, contrasts with the Ovidian programme. For an elegiac lover, marriage is something that should be avoided, rather than sought after, and the anti-*exemplum,* in addition to applying to the methods used by Romulus' men, also applies to the fact that the Sabine Rape is the foundation of the marriage institution. It might be that Ovid, in his anti-marital programme, through the paradoxical *exemplum*, also points to brutal and outdated aspects of the patriarchal marriage institution, recently reinforced

---

[27] The term *uirgo* denotes a young girl of citizen status in the comic genre. See Watson 1983 for full discussion.
[28] Labate 2006, 193–215.
[29] Labate 2006, 213–15.

by legislation, and its opposition to his own elegiac notion of love. The paradox is further strengthened by the allusions to the rape in the *Eunuchus*, one of the most brutal rape-marriage plot in the comic corpus known to us.

Amores 3.6: rape, marriage and suicide?

Another rape closely linked to the foundation of Rome and the Sabine Rape is the rape of Ilia, described in *Amores* 3.6. After her rape by Mars, the Vestal virgin gave birth to Romulus and Remus, and she is thus a significant character in the legendary history of the City and the divine lineage of the emperor. In addition to being a part of the same story line, the portrayal of Ilia in *Amores* 3.6 is also, as it will be shown in what follows, textually linked to the interlude on the rape of the Sabine women in the *Ars amatoria* and thus in a chain of intertextual succession to the rape scene in the *Eunuchus*.

In *Amores* 3.6, the young poet-lover addresses a flooded river and asks it to let him pass, in order to get to his mistress. Rivers ought to aid young men in love, he states, as rivers too know what it is to love. He goes on to list rivers that have fallen for women, and lingers on the river Anio, who was charmed by Ilia when she was wandering near his shores after her rape by Mars:

> nec te praetereo, qui per caua saxa uolutans
>   Tiburis Argei pomifera arua rigas,
> Ilia cui placuit, quamuis erat horrida cultu,
>   ungue notata comas, ungue notata genas.
> illa gemens patruique nefas delictaque Martis,
>   errabat nudo per loca sola pede.
> hanc Anien rapidis animosus uidit ab undis
>   raucaque de mediis sustulit ora uadis
> atque ita 'quid nostras' dixit 'teris anxia ripas,
>   Ilia, ab Idaeo Laumedonte genus?
> quo cultus abiere tui? quid sola uagaris,
>   uitta nec euinctas impedit alba comas?
> quid fles et madidos lacrimis corrumpis ocellos
>   pectoraque insana plangis aperta manu?

(*Ov. Am.* 3.6.45–58)

Nor do I pass you by, stream tumbling over the hollowed rocks and moisting the fruit-bearing acres of Argive Tibur, you whom Ilia charmed, ill kept though she appeared, with hair that showed the nail, and cheeks that showed the nail. Bemoaning the crime of her uncle and the wrongs of Mars, with unshod feet she wandered through lone places. Her did eager Anio behold, looking forth from his sweeping floods, and reared from amid the wave his

> hoarse-toned mouth, and 'Why do you anxiously,' thus he spoke, 'tread my shores, O Ilia, blood of Idaean Laomedon? Where have your comely raiment gone? Why are you abroad alone, with no white fillet to keep your hair bound up? Why are you weeping, and staining thine eyes with dropping tears? And why do you lay open and beat your breast with maddened hand? ... '

The ending of line 57 here is exactly the same as the end of line 129 in the first book of the *Ars amatoria*, where Ovid is depicting a Roman carrying off a Sabine woman, while he asks her why she is crying: *atque ita 'quid teneros lacrimis corrumpis ocellos?'*[30] The question is of course rhetorical, and the Roman goes on to explain that he will be to her what her father is to her mother, i.e. a husband. Hence, there is no reason to cry, as the outcome will be fortunate, and she will lead a good and suitable Roman life with all the proper rights.[31] Similarly, the outcome of Ilia's rape will be fortunate, and the river tells Ilia to put away her fear and be his wife.

In both the case of Ilia and the Sabine women, the outcome of the events will be fortunate from a larger, legendary perspective. Ilia will give birth to Romulus, who founds Rome and secures its growth by the rape of the Sabine women. This is however not the focus in Ovid's account of either of the legends. Ilia, similar to the Sabine women, is depicted as scared and in tears. She is described as having scratched cheeks and torn hair, and laments the wrongs done to her by her uncle. When Anio suggests that she marries him, she tries to flee him three times, but is stopped by his waves, and eventually she gives up as her fear takes away her power to resist. Ovid's focus is on the violence that lies in rape, the visible signs of a fight and the traumatic state in which it leaves the victim.

After a speech where she laments the loss of her virginity, *o utinam mea lecta forent patrioque sepulchro / condita, cum poterant uirginis ossa legi!* (Ov. Am. 3.6.73–4, 'Oh, would that my bones had been gathered and laid away in the tomb of my fathers when they yet could be gathered as the bones of a virgin!'), and being called to marriage, she gives in to Anio and throws herself into the river, an event that can be read both as a second rape as they forge a marriage union, and possibly as a suicide:

> hactenus, et uestem tumidis praetendit ocellis
> atque ita se in rapidas perdita misit aquas;
> supposuisse manus ad pectora lubricus amnis
> dicitur et socii iura dedisse tori.
>
> (Ov. Am. 3.6.79–82)

---

[30] I am grateful to Thea S. Thorsen for pointing out this allusion to me.
[31] According to Livy, the Sabine women were promised full citizen rights and that their children would be legitimate citizens. Liv. 1.9.11.

Thus far, and she held her cloak before her tumid eyes, gave up all hope, and so threw herself into the rushing waters. The smooth-gliding stream, they say, laid his hands to her breast and bore her up, and shared with her the rights of the wedded couch.

Ovid also refers to the rape of Ilia in *Amores* 3.4, where he states that a husband who is upset by an adulterous wife, is too *rusticus*, and not sufficiently acquainted with the manners of the city where the sons of Mars were born *non sine crimine*, i.e. rape. It is hard to read this as anything else than a provocation considering the Augustan laws on marriage and sexuality, especially as the poem is followed by the detailed depiction of Ilia's harsh fate shortly after, stripped of all signs of grandeur and honour. This use of *crimen* as equivalent to rape also lends an interesting flavour to the introduction to the *Ars amatoria*, lines 31–4:

> este procul, uittae tenues, insigne pudoris,
> quaeque tegis medios instita longa pedes:
> nos Venerem tutam concessaque furta canemus
> inque meo nullam carmine crimen erit.
>
> (Ov. *Ars am.* 1.31–4)

> Keep far away, you slender fillets, emblems of modesty, and the long skirt that hides the feet in its folds. Of safe love-making do I sing, and permitted secrecy, and in my verse shall be no wrong-doing.

The *uitta* is a characteristic of Roman matrons, and were also worn by unmarried freeborn women,[32] and the apparent meaning here is that respectable Roman women are not included in the *Ars amatoria*, and that no crime, i.e. breaking of the Augustan laws, will occur. However, the verses gain a double meaning in light of Ovid's earlier pointing to the *crimen* that lies at the foundation of Rome with the rape of Ilia.[33] Furthermore, he shortly after this statement follows up with a paradoxical and violent depiction of the Sabine rape, with its allusions to the violent rape of a citizen girl in the *Eunuchus*. It is evident that the rape of Ilia and the rape of the Sabine women, in addition to being part of the same story ultimately leading up to the rule of Augustus, are also tied together on the textual level by Ovid, with the same problematizing focus on the link between rape, marriage and Roman tradition, and what really constitutes a *crimen*.

---

32 Hollis 2009 [1977], *ad loc.*
33 It is worth noting that Ilia is not wearing her *uitta*, the visible sign of her status, in *Am.* 3.6. This might be compared to the fact that Ovid asks the *uitta* to stay away from his *Ars amatoria* at line 1.31, quoted above.

Heroides 5: wife versus *puella*

Another legendary or mythological rape showing similar traits is found in *Heroides* 5, written in the name of the abandoned Oenone and addressed to her run-away husband Paris. It contains the only story of her alleged rape by Apollo, who in return gave her the art of medicine and the ability to heal. The graphic description of it has shocked readers and editors to such an extent that Merkel and others with him have deleted the lines 140–5, and it has traditionally received little scholarly attention.[34] The account of the rape is uniquely explicit, and Oenone herself gives an account of how she struggled against her rapist, tore his hair and scratched his face:

> ille meae spolium uirginitatis habet,
>   id quoque luctando. rupi tamen ungue capillos,
>   oraque sunt digitis aspera facta meis.
> nec pretium stupri gemmas aurumque poposci:
>   turpiter ingenuum munera corpus emunt.
> ipse ratus dignam medicas mihi tradidit artes
>   admisitque meas ad sua dona manus.

(Ov. *Her.* 5.140–6)

> He took the spoils of my virginity, and that too by a fight, Yet I tore hair with my nail, and wounded face with my fingers. And I did not ask for precious stones and gold as price for the rape: It is shameful to purchase a free-born body. He deemed me worthy and gave me the gift of healing, and taught to my hands his own gift.[35]

The focus is also here on the fact that the rape happened with a struggle, and the possible interpretation that Oenone fought back by attacking her perpetrator's face and hair.[36] If the Latin text is interpreted in this manner, it happens in a way very similar to the way that the Pythias of the *Eunuchus* threatens to attack the

---

34 See, however, Casali 1992; 1997. As Knox 1995, I treat lines 140–5 as Ovid's invention. See Knox 1995, *ad loc*. Jacobson 1974, 185–94, also argues for the authenticity of the lines. Thorsen (forthcoming a) is a recent contribution to the debate, which supports the authenticity of the lines.

35 The translation is my own. As Thea S. Thorsen has correctly pointed out to me, the Latin text does not say whose fingers tore whose cheeks or hair. I have taken this into account in my translation.

36 The text is on this point intriguingly open for interpretation, as Oenone also might be talking about her own hair and cheeks, to show her grief over her rape by Apollo through self-harm; see Thorsen (forthcoming a). Either way, it is clear that there was a fight between rapist and victim, cf. line 141, *id quoque luctando*.

rapist Chaerea (*Eun.* 647–8, see below), and parallels another Ovidian situation, that is the lover-poet of Ovid's *Amores* 1.7 and his wish that his *puella* had fought back when he attacked her, a theme treated below. In *Heroides* 5, the description of the fight serves a particular function, even though the context seems at first puzzling: Oenone is reminding Paris how she has remained *casta* for him even though she often had the opportunity not to, whereas Helen will not be faithful to him, as she has been unfaithful so many times before. The distinction seems to be that in Oenone's view, she herself remained *casta*, even after the rape and the loss of her virginity to Apollo, whereas Helen has not remained so after the loss of her virginity and her alleged rapes. The proof of Oenone's chastity seems to lie in the fact that she fought, and that it was definitely involuntary. Helen on the other hand, from Oenone's point of view, must have made herself available, since she has been raped so many times.

Knox notes in his commentary that Ovid repeats the first half of line 131, *uim licet appelles* ('you may call it violence'), in the first book of the *Ars amatoria*, line 673. In this passage, Ovid describes how girls might struggle and say no, when they really mean yes. In the description of her own rape, Oenone makes it clear that she did not welcome Apollo's actions, as she explicitly stated that it happened with a fight: she truly meant no. As Knox concludes, Oenone's view is that Paris has found a faithless mistress in Helen, whereas she herself was a faithful wife.[37] Helen, in Oenone's view, welcomes men's approaches, while she herself remains *casta*.

In this poem, the tension between marriage and elegiac love is pointed out. Ovid, in Oenone's voice, draws a line between the *puella* represented by Helen, and a chaste woman and wife, represented by herself (though she simultaneously tries to cast herself as a type of *puella*, a *digna puella*),[38] and the line is rape. This idea can be compared with the fact that in the comedy genre, a *uirgo* is still called *uirgo* after having been raped, as in the *Eunuchus*, where it is presented as obvious that the *uirgo* Pamphila has been raped and is not really a 'virgin' anymore in the modern sense of the word, as the perpetrator brags about the deed.[39] Oenone also stresses that she did not ask for gifts as compensation from Apollo, which would be more similar to the financial transactions of the *meretrix*. The

---

[37] See Knox 1995, 165, *ad* lines 133–46.
[38] Cf. *at manet Oenone fallenti casta marito* (Ov. *Her.* 5.133, 'But Oenone remains chaste, false though her husband prove' and *et potes et merui: dignae miserere puellae!* (Ov. *Her.* 5.155, 'You can bestow it, and I have merited—have pity on a deserving girl!') I am grateful to Thea S. Thorsen for pointing this out to me.
[39] E.g. at Ter. *Eun.* 659. At Ter. *Ad.* 728, we are told that a *uirgo* has given birth.

meretrix is the opposite of the chaste and 'proper' woman, which Oenone professes to be.⁴⁰

It is clear that Ovid's Oenone contrasts herself with the type of *puella* that Helen represents, by stating that she herself did not give in to suitors, but was raped, which is often the fate of *uirgines* (cf. the vestal virgin Ilia, the Sabine women, the first Roman wives, and the comic *uirgines*). This is highlighted by the use of the Roman legal term *stuprum*, or improper intercourse, in line 143, which is defined as a crime in the Augustan law, and can only be committed with or against 'proper' women of high status, herself included (whereas Helen is not).⁴¹ However, Paris will not be moved by her letter, as he now belongs to the elegiac universe, and with Helen instead of his wife.⁴² Like the comic rapes and the rapes in Ovid's legendary universe, the rape of Oenone also had the potential of a fortunate outcome, as this is how, according to Ovid, she gained the ability to heal her beloved Paris. However, she refuses to do so and in the end commits suicide.⁴³ This fits well with Ovid's overall focus on the harsh fates and dangers faced by 'proper', high-status women, as opposed to their role in the larger, legendary picture.

Amores 1.7: violence, rape and status

The last Ovidian case that will be treated is not a rape, but rather a case of what might be termed sexualized violence: *Amores* 1.7 is a well-known and much discussed case of violence against the *puella* in the elegiac corpus, where Ovid as

---

40 This passage too contains a link to the comic genre, and its two diametrical opposed objects for love, the *meretrix* and the *uirgo*. Knox 1995 compares line 143, *nec pretium stupri gemmas aurumque poposci*, with line 286 in Plautus' *Mostellaria*: *amator meretricis mores sibi emit auro et purpura* (Plaut. Mostell. 286, 'a lover buys a prostitute's favors with jewelry and purple-dyed clothes'). My text for Plautus is Lindsay 1903.

41 See Csillag 1976, 179–80. One would not talk about the rape of e.g. one's own slave, and women living in concubinage and prostitutes by profession were not included among the women who could be involved in stuprum, see Csillag 1976, 181. It is not all clear how freedwomen prostitutes stood with regards to freeborn women's right to freedom from rape, but there is little surviving legal or literary evidence for the prosecution of rape of a Roman prostitute, even if she were to fall under the definition 'free'. See Strong 2016, 15 and McGinn 1998, 326–37 for discussion. Even though Oenone, Helen and Paris are not Romans, they must be read in a Roman context as characters in Ovid's Roman elegiac universe.

42 On the separation between Oenone as a pastoral character and Helen as object for Paris' elegiac love, see Lindheim 2000, 96–101. See also Fulkerson 2005, 58–65. See Drinkwater 2015 for Oenone as a manipulator of pastoral, elegy and epic to win back Paris.

43 Cf. e.g. Lycoph. *Alex.* 57–68, Parth. *Amat. narr.* 4, Apollod. *Bibl.* 3.12.6, Conon, *Narr.* 23.

the poet-lover laments how he has violently attacked his beloved. The poem presents an anomalous case of violence within Ovid's works and the elegiac genre overall. In the genre in general, the lover usually only considers, discusses or fantasizes about the possibility of conducting violence against the *puella*, whereas the poet-lover in *Amores* 1.7 contends that he has physically attacked his girl.[44] Actual violence presents a line of action that is more common for the comedy genre, where violence conducted against the beloved, i.e. rape (and other violence in connection with the rape) is an important way of driving the action forwards towards the conventional denouement of the plot. In Ovid, however, violence and rape are primarily described as conducted against women in the legendary and mythological sphere rather than the *puella*, and the victims thus stand in contrast to her, as already discussed in the cases above.

However, the *idea* of conducting violence against the beloved object is a recurring motif in Augustan elegy, and is commonly seen as general trait of the genre that is inherited from New Comedy, where the theme is particularly frequent.[45] McKeown links *Amores* 1.7 to Menander's *Perikeiromene*, as the plot of the play focuses on a lover who feels remorse after having attacked his mistress and cut off her hair.[46] Nevertheless, as Barsby points out, the situation in Ovid's poem is different from the one in Menander's play, where the focus is on the cutting off of a woman's hair rather than a more violent assault, and there are indeed no close parallels between *Amores* 1.7 and the extant lines of the play.[47] What is more, Barsby sees no close parallel between *Amores* 1.7 and *any* comic play.[48] The tone in *Amores* 1.7, i.e. the focus on remorse for having done violence against someone that one professes to love, does in fact differ very much from conventional comedy, where violence against women in most cases goes unproblematized, and in the case of rape, is 'expunged' by the marriage between perpetrator and victim. Nevertheless, I would argue that it is still fruitful to go further in pursuing some traits that the poem shares with the *Eunuchus*,[49] in light of the connection that can be traced between this play and Ovid's elegiac depictions of rape.

---

[44] Burkowski 2012, 113. See my n. 4 for passages depicting the possibility of conducting violence against the *puella*.
[45] See McKeown 1989, *ad loc*.
[46] McKeown 1989, *ad loc*.
[47] Barsby 1996, 149.
[48] See Barsby 1996, 149 and note 54.
[49] McKeown lists Ter. *Eun*. 646 among the possible parallel situations in New Comedy, see McKeown 1989, 162.

In the opening of the poem, Ovid blames his hands for their horrendous deed towards his mistress, and we learn that it has taken the form of an attack on her hair, cheeks and clothes:

> nonne satis fuerat timidae inclamasse puellae
>   nec nimium rigidas intonuisse minas
> aut tunicam a summa diducere turpiter ora
>   ad mediam (mediae zona tulisset opem)?
> at nunc sustinui raptis a fronte capillis
>   ferreus ingenuas ungue notare genas.
>
> (Ov. *Am.* 1.7.45–50)

> Were it not enough to have cried out at the frightened girl, without the too hard threats I thundered? Or to have shamed her by tearing apart her gown from top to middle? – her girdle would have come to the rescue there. But, as it was, I could endure to rend cruelly the hair from her brow and mark with my nail her free-born cheeks.

Ovid also focuses upon the *puella*'s reaction to his violence, namely that she is silenced by fear and crying:

> quis mihi non 'demens', quis non mihi 'barbare' dixit ?
>   ipsa nihil: pauido est lingua retenta metu.
> sed taciti fecere tamen conuicia uultus;
>   egit me lacrimis ore silente reum.
>
> (Ov. *Am.* 1.7.19–23)

> Who did not say to me: 'Madman!' who did not say: 'Barbarian!' Herself said nothing; her tongue was kept from it by trembling fear. But her face, for all her silence, uttered reproaches none the less; tears charged me with my crime, though her lips were dumb.

Even though this is not a case of rape, but rather what we might define as 'partner violence', the girl is described in the same manner as the rape victim in the *Eunuchus* and Ovid's legendary rape victims. She bears the marks of the fight, cries, and is silenced by fear. This is also highlighted by the comparison with the mythological rape victim Cassandra in line 17–18: *sic, nisi uittatis quod erat, Cassandra, capillis, / procubuit templo, casta Minerua tuo.* (Ov. *Am.* 1.7.17–18, 'thus was Cassandra – except that fillets bound her hair – when down she sank at your shrine, O chaste Minerva'). The situation very much parallels the situation in Terence's comedy, and all the signs of the rape of Pamphila: the torn hair and dress, the shock and trauma, tears, silence, and fear.

A major difference between the situation in *Amores* 1.7 and in the *Eunuchus* is the attitude of the perpetrator. Chaerea is exceedingly happy and content with his deed and the result of it, while the lover-poet shows remorse when faced with his girlfriend's tears, and uses several examples to illustrate the injustice of the action. He even wishes that his mistress would take revenge and attack him in a similar manner– much like Oenone fought her perpetrator (cf. *Her.* 5.141–2) – to match his actions:

> at tu ne dubita (minuet uindicta dolorem)
>   protinus in uultus unguibus ire meos,
> nec nostris oculis nec nostris parce capillis;
>
> (Ov. *Am.* 1.7.63–5)

> But you, stay not – for your vengeance will lessen my grief – from straight assailing my features with your nails. Spare neither my eyes nor yet my hair.

The feeling of guilt shown by the poet-lover contrasts with Chaerea's reaction and the conventions of comedy in general. The poet-lover's longing for the girl's vengeance can, however, be said to be mirrored by the anger shown by Thais' servant Pythias, and her wish to take revenge and attack Chaerea's hair and eyes with her nails:

> PYTHIAS: qui nunc si detur mihi,
> ut ego unguibus facile illi in oculos inuolem uenefico!
>
> (Ter. *Eun.* 647–8)

> Pythias: If I get my hands on him, I can't wait to fly at his face with my nails, the poisonous wretch!

> PYTHIAS: conseruam! uix me contineo quin inuolem in
> capillum, monstrum.
>
> (Ter. *Eun.* 859–60)

> Pythias: A fellow slave! I can scarcely restrain myself from flying at your hair, you monster!

In the last quotation, Pythias and Thais have just met Chaerea on the street after the rape, and he is still dressed up as a eunuch and pretending to be a slave, and status is an issue, as Chaerea is confronted by Pythias with the fact that he has raped a *uirgo*, a citizen girl. He claims that he thought that she was a *conserua*, a fellow slave, as he at the time of the rape was unaware of her status. Thais tells Pythias to get lost, but Pythias on her side answers in an ironic manner, and the meaning of these somewhat puzzling lines seems to be that she cannot see any problem with an attack on Chaerea, as he is himself claiming to be a slave in Thais' house:

> PYTHIAS: quid ita? uero debeam,
> credo, isti quicquam furcifero si id fecerim,
> praesertim quom se seruom fateatur tuom.
>
> (Ter. *Eun.* 861–3)

> Pythias: What do you mean? I'm scarcely going to be held liable if I do anything to this rascal, especially as he's claiming to be your slave.

The paradox lies in that as long as Chaerea claims to be a slave, he is without legal rights and Pythias' physical attack on him would be unproblematic, and even more so as he has raped a girl of citizen status.[50] Ovid proposes a similar paradox when he places himself in the role of the slave when he asks with what right he has hit his *domina* at line 30,[51] since he would be punished for hitting the least of the *Quirites*: *an, si pulsassem minimum de plebe Quiritem, / plecterer, in dominam ius mihi maius erit?* (Ov. *Am.* 1.7.29–30, 'What! if I had struck the least of the Quirites among the crowd, should I be punished – and should my right over my mistress be greater?') The poet places himself in the role of the *seruus*, as a *seruus amoris* for his *puella*, his *domina*, and compares his situation with the punishment he would receive for violating another citizen, and asks whether there is any real difference. In the *Eunuchus*, the rape of Pamphila ceases to be problematic when her status is revealed to Chaerea, who then resumes his proper role as a male citizen and offers to marry her, and thus brings about a fortunate outcome for the rape. In Ovid's elegiac universe, the status of the *puella* remains blurred: marriage is out of the picture, and within the bounds of the poem, he remains, as he claimed to be at the opening of the poem, a criminal.

Conclusion

In the New Comic genre, rape is closely connected to status, and comic rape victims almost always turns out to be citizen daughters. The function of rape of the comic *uirgo* is to act as a pretext for marriage, and in the end to mark the *adulescens*' entrance into a traditional and appropriate way of life, with a legitimate citizen wife and legitimate citizen offspring. In this way, comic rapes are unproblematic, as the outcome is considered to be fortunate for all parties. The comic rape-marriage plot line is in fact perfectly in line with the legendary origin

---

50 See Barsby 1999b, *ad loc.*
51 Cf. also *ingenuas ... genas*, free-born cheeks, at line 50, which adds to the question of the status of the *puella*.

of the Roman marriage institution itself, and in the end, this is also the case in the *Eunuchus*. On the other hand, the rape here is described as excessively violent, focusing on the physical and emotional reactions of the victim, and thus stands out among the comic rapes; this, I would argue, creates a tension in the text, between the brutality and violence of rape, and the fortunate outcome that rapes have within the genre (and the Roman tradition in general). It seems to me that Ovid picks up on this tension, and connects the Terentian rape-marriage plot pattern to his elegiac rapes to create a similar effect in his texts, highlighting the brutality that is imminent in the Roman legend.

In the Roman context, rape also denotes status, as *stuprum* was primarily defined as the violation of *uirgines* and widows, i.e. women of citizen status.[52] The Sabine women are the ultimate symbol for chaste, high-status Roman wives and citizen daughters, and the Vestal Virgin Ilia would be a a model for the same category; rape of such women would definitely be defined as *stuprum* within the Roman context. Rape linked to high status and 'chastity' is also in play in Oenone's letter, as she uses her violent rape to prove how she has remained *casta* and to contrast herself to Helen, explicitly pointing out that it was *stuprum* at line 143. *Amores* 1.7 is the only example of actual violence against the *puella*, and status is very much an issue through the poem: if she is the lover's *domina*, and he is thus her slave (through the key elegiac image of *seruitium amoris*),[53] why should his violence against her not count as a crime? There is no solution to the situation, and no fortunate outcome: marriage is out of the question, and the girl refuses to fight back (which actually might have made *her* the criminal instead, for attacking the body of a citizen, just as Pythias cannot legally attack the rapist in the *Eunuchus* due to his citizen status). In Terence, I believe, Ovid finds a Roman context for problematizing the issue of women's status and violence, and the forced aspect of Roman marriage, which had traditionally originated in rape.

---

[52] See Csillag 1976, 179–80 for the formulation.
[53] For the image of *seruitium amoris*, see e.g. Murgatroyd 1981, Fulkerson 2013.

Boris Kayachev
Love and Poetry in Virgil's Sixth Eclogue: A Platonic Perspective

Love is manifestly a central topic in Virgil's sixth eclogue. Its importance is already adumbrated in the proem, by suggesting that love is what drives readers to read poetry (*Ecl.* 6.10), and it repeatedly resurfaces in the song of Silenus, which takes up most of the eclogue (*Ecl.* 6.31–81): having started with the creation of the world (*Ecl.* 6.31–40), it alludes to the erotic tales of Hercules' beloved boy Hylas who was abducted by nymphs (*Ecl.* 6.43–4), Pasiphae's passion for a bull (*Ecl.* 6.44–60), Hippomenes' winning over of Atalanta with the help of golden apples (*Ecl.* 6.61), Scylla's love for Minos which made her betray her own father (*Ecl.* 6.74–7), and Tereus' lust for his sister-in-law Philomela whom he raped, in revenge for which he was served his own son for dinner (*Ecl.* 6.78–81); a place of pride is accorded to an account of the poetic initiation of the Latin love elegist Cornelius Gallus by the Muses, Apollo and Linus (*Ecl.* 6.64–73). I propose to argue that the notion of love implied in the eclogue has affinities with both the Epicurean and the Platonic concepts of love as the aspiration for either the pleasurable (Epicurus) or the beautiful (Plato). Virgil follows Lucretius in casting love as the driving force of poetic composition, but understands the essence of this process along Platonic lines: Gallus' ascent to the top of Helicon is akin to the philosopher's ascent to the form of beauty. According to my reading of the eclogue, for Virgil poetry must be rooted in the knowledge of ontological reality.

The song of Silenus (*Ecl.* 6.31–81)

A remarkable feature of the song of Silenus is the large amount of pointed lexical repetitions.[1] I shall focus on several such 'key words' that can help us better to grasp the internal logical structure of the concept of love in the eclogue.[2] The word *amor* occurs in the song of Silenus only once (*Pasiphaen niuei solatur amore iuuenci*, *Ecl.* 6.46, 'he comforts Pasiphae in her passion for a snow-white bull')[3] and is thus of little help. The next relevant entry is *errare*; it will not contribute

---

1 See esp. Elder 1961, 114; cf. von Albrecht 2001, 162 and 165.
2 Cf. Davis 2011, who makes a similar argument about the importance of the Epicurean concept of love for the sixth eclogue.
3 All translations are my own, unless indicated otherwise.

much to my analysis of the concept at present, but it is a good illustration of how several contexts of the same word inform its meaning in each other. It is obvious that in the *Eclogues* the stem has erotic connotations:⁴ *ut me malus abstulit* error (*Ecl.* 8.41, 'a cruel madness snatched me away') is a 'translation with paronomasia'⁵ of Theocritus' ὡς ἐς βαθὺν ἅλατ' ἔρωτα (*Id.* 3.42, 'she leapt into the depths of passion'). Here *error* does not just evoke, but in a sense actually means, ἔρως, in the same way as *cura* in *tua cura Lycoris* (*Ecl.* 10.22, 'your pining, Lycoris'), through association with Theocritus' ἁ δέ τυ κώρα (*Id.* 1.82, 'the girl [in search for] you'), comes to mean 'beloved girl'.⁶ Likewise, I suggest, *errare* can be considered a transliteration of ἐρᾶν ('to love'), almost.⁷ This meaning would be particularly suitable in *tu nunc in montibus erras* (*Ecl.* 6.52, 'you now wander in the mountains'), addressed to Pasiphae in love with a bull. The bull, in his turn, wanders following a cow (*errabunda bouis uestigia*, *Ecl.* 6.58, 'the wandering steps of the bull'). When used of Gallus (*errantem Permessi ad flumina Gallum*, *Ecl.* 6.64, 'Gallus wandering at the stream of Permessus'), the verb implies not only that he is thought of, after Hesiod's manner, as a shepherd, but also that he is an elegiac lover. Finally, the wandering animals in *Ecl.* 6.40 (*errent animalia [per] montis*, 'animals roam in the mountains') may appear merely idle at first sight, but in the light of the other contexts (note esp. *Ecl.* 6.52) it is difficult not to imagine that they, too, wander not without a purpose, but in search of a partner.

The verb *capere* has only two contexts in the song of Silenus, but it deserves attention because it is used in the suggestive phrase *captus amore*, applied to the reader in the prologue (*Ecl.* 6.10, 'taken over by love'). In a finite form it occurs in *Ecl.* 6.47 *dementia cepit* ('madness took [you] over'), a phrase that expresses basically the same idea as *captus amore* (*dementia* is 'love passion').⁸ The other oc-

---

4 Cf. Davis 2011, 50.
5 O'Hara 1996, 63, though he does not consider this particular case; but he mentions the *cura* / κώρα example.
6 For more about the beloved as girl, see the last chapter by Thorsen.
7 Perhaps the clearest example of the wordplay is found in Ov. *Ars am.* 3.436 *errat et in nulla sede moratur amor*: on the one hand, *in nulla sede moratur* is a periphrasis for *errat*, whilst, on the other, it etymologises *amor* as *a-mor(a)*, 'that which never pauses' (a similar pun seems to be at play in *Ecl.* 2.68 *quis enim modus adsit amori?* – there can be no limit [*modus*] for love [*a-mor*], for it would be a contradiction in terms); accordingly, ἔρως is 'what *errat*'.
8 The same phrase occurs in *G.* 4.488 *dementia cepit amantem*, where Virgil seems to be etymologising *amans* as *amens* (= *demens*); cf. Plaut. *Merc.* 83. It is also used in *Ecl.* 2.69, a context that, as I shall be arguing shortly, is relevant to the sixth eclogue. For love as divinely instilled madness, see the Introduction by Thorsen.

currence is, like that in the prologue, a passive participle, used in the same syntactical construction (*Ecl.* 6.59 *herba captum*, 'attracted by grass'). Another recurrent word is *sequi*, which has four contexts. Although it does not have obvious erotic connotations, this verb comes closest to expressing the basic idea of the concept of love. Twice it is applied to Pasiphae's bull pursuing a cow (*Ecl.* 6.55 *aliquam in magno sequitur grege*, 'he follows some cow out of the big herd'; *Ecl.* 6.59 *armenta secutum*, 'following the cattle'). In a third context it is used even more explicitly (if in a negative statement) of Proetus' daughters not seeking intercourse with cattle (*Ecl.* 6.49–50 *non ... secuta / concubitus*). The fourth and last context is puzzling, as it is not clear in what sense 'fame follows Scylla' (*Ecl.* 6.74 *quam fama secuta est*).[9] The full implications of *sequi* become apparent if one takes into account a gnomic priamel in the second eclogue where the verb describes the relation that constitutes the essence of 'love':

> torua leaena lupum sequitur, lupus ipse capellam,
> florentem cytisum sequitur lasciua capella,
> te Corydon, o Alexi: trahit sua quemque uoluptas.
>
> (Verg. *Ecl.* 6.63–5)

> The fierce lioness goes after the wolf, the wolf himself after the goat, the frisky goat goes after the tree medick in bloom, Corydon after you, Alexis: everyone is dragged by their own pleasure.

This passage implies more than just a superficial analogy between human passion and different kinds of desire in the natural world: the concluding maxim, an echo of Lucretian *quo ducit quemque uoluptas* (2.258, 'where pleasure drives each one'), conflated with Lucr. 2.261 *sua cuique uoluntas*, 'one's own will', expresses in fact a core Epicurean tenet. As is observed by Fowler, this is a pointed allusion: whereas the Lucretian context implies 'that *voluntas* is manifested in two phenomena, both the pursuit of the immediately pleasurable and its avoidance',[10] in Virgil 'the pleasure of love has a less benign side and paradoxically drags us all unwilling'.[11] In such a context *sequi* functions as a close equivalent of διώκειν in its technical sense of 'pursuing (pleasure or good)'; this connotation seems also to be present, if less manifestly, in the uses of *sequi* in the sixth eclogue. As is easy to see, *capere* conveys the same idea of attraction to the pleasurable (in particular, we may link *Ecl.* 6.59 *herba captum* with *Ecl.* 2.64 *cytisum sequitur*). Finally, I

---

9 For possible interpretations, see Coleman 1977, 199.
10 Fowler 2002b, 326.
11 Fowler 2002b, 325.

suggest that *ducere*, another recurrent 'key word', belongs to the same semantic field (note *ducit* at Lucr. 2.258 above, cf. 2.172 *deducit dux uitae dia uoluptas*, 'divine pleasure, the guide of life, leads [men]': attraction to the pleasurable as a fundamental principle of life). In the clearest possible way this connotation is brought out in the context speaking of Pasiphae's bull being led by cows (*Ecl.* 6.59–60 *aut herba captum uiridi aut armenta secutum / perducant aliquae stabula ad Gortynia uaccae*, 'perhaps some heifers will bring him, either attracted by green grass or following the herd, to the stables of Gortyn'), where (*per*)*ducere* is closely associated with both *capere* and *sequi*. But one has to infer it also in two closely interrelated uses of *ducere* in the scene of Gallus' initiation: being both a poet and a lover, Gallus is led up the hills by a Muse (*Ecl.* 6.65 *Aonas in montis ut duxerit una sororum*, 'how one of the sisters led [him] up the Aonian mountains'); conversely, Hesiod brings down from the hills ash-trees captivated by the beauty of his song (*Ecl.* 6.71 *cantando rigidas deducere montibus ornos*, 'to bring down stiff ash-trees from the mountains by singing'). The poet is led by the Muses and in turn leads the audience, just as the bull both attracts Pasiphae and in turn is attracted by lush grass and cows.

The idea of a certain analogy between poetic inspiration and sexual desire is more explicit in a programmatic passage in the *Georgics* (3.284–94), a passage clearly related to the sixth eclogue[12] (note *G.* 3.285 *capti amore*, reminiscent of *captus amore*[13]). As has been observed in connection with the *Georgics* passage, the idea that the poet is driven by love, analogous if not exactly identical to sexual desire, appears derived in Virgil from Lucretius.[14] In Lucretius, the most striking expression of this idea is produced by the pointed repetition of a phrase speaking of Venus' impact on the animal world (Lucr. 1.19 *omnibus incutiens blandum per pectora amorem*, 'instilling pleasant love into everyone's hearts') in reference to the force that urges the poet to compose (Lucr. 1.924–5 *incussit suauem mi in pectus amorem / Musarum*, '[ambition] instilled into my heart sweet love for the Muses').[15] Similarly the seminal aretalogical definition of Venus as *hominum diuumque uoluptas* (Lucr. 1.1, 'the pleasure of men and gods') is later transferred to Calliope: *requies hominum diuumque uoluptas* (Lucr. 6.94, 'the relaxation of men and the pleasure of gods'). Particularly relevant is a third case of such an internal

---

12 See esp. Davis 2011, 41.
13 Cf. e.g. Thomas 1988, 96.
14 See Gale 1991, 421, and Gale 2000, 191–2; cf. Rumpf 1996, 258–62. On Lucretius' presence in the *Eclogues*, see in general: Giesecke 2000, 31–58, Breed 2000, Van Sickle 2000, Lipka 2001, 65–80, Hardie 2006.
15 See Gale 1994, 146 and 213 n. 26.

echo: Lucretius speaks of following Epicurus (Lucr. 3.3–6 *te sequor ... non ita certandi cupidus quam propter amorem / quod te imitari aueo*, 'I follow you, not so much wishing to compete as for the sake of love, because I want to imitate you') in terms that recall the description of Venus' power in the proem (Lucr. 1.15–16 *ita capta lepore / te sequitur cupide quo quamque inducere pergis*, 'every animal, attracted by your charm, eagerly follows you wherever you aim to lead them'). Just as in *Ecl.* 6.59–60, in Lucr. 1.15–16 all the three 'key words' are found together: *capere*, *sequi*, and *ducere*; and all three express here in the clearest possible way the idea of pursuing pleasure.[16] Lucr. 3.3 *te sequor* is intended specifically to recall 1.16 *te sequitur*, and this internal self-reference hits at the very core of Lucretius' poetics: Lucretius follows Epicurus (that is, preaches Epicureanism) because this gives him pleasure, precisely as 'following Venus' gives pleasure to all creatures. As Gale puts it, Lucretius 'evaluates poetry (or, more precisely, his own, Epicurean poetry) not merely as a pleasure, but as a pleasure worthy to be chosen (ἡδονὴ αἱρετή), since it is one that will result in greater pleasure in the long run'.[17] This is the essence of Lucretius' concept of poetry to which Virgil alludes in the sixth eclogue with the emphatic use of *capere*, *sequi*, and *ducere*; yet although Virgil adopts Lucretius' basic analogy between 'inspiration' (the urge to compose poetry) and 'love' (for Lucretius, sexual instinct), there are significant differences between the two. First, the *Eclogues* are not Epicurean poetry,[18] at least not explicitly, and therefore, though reading (or composing) them may be pleasurable, this will not 'result in greater pleasure in the long run'. Second, examples of erotic passion that are given in the song of Silenus are profoundly unlike the picture of the serene sexual pleasure enjoyed by animals that Lucretius makes a model for describing his own experience as a poet; on the contrary, they fall precisely in the category of the pathological infatuation criticised by Lucretius (4.1030–1287) in contrast to the wholesome sexual instinct.

---

16 Cf. Gale 1994, 148–50, who rightly links the passage with Lucr. 2.172 and 258 (quoted above) and explains the connection with Lucretius' poetics.
17 Gale 1994, 149.
18 This may be a debatable point, but there seem to be reasons to suppose that Virgil rather shared Philodemus' view that poetry, 'insofar as it is poetry, does not benefit its readers' (Sider 1997, 31).

The prelude (*Ecl.* 6.13–30)

The lively prelude introducing the song of Silenus – the only dramatic scene of the eclogue – is not usually considered programmatically important.[19] Coleman, however, has interestingly suggested that Virgil's choice of Silenus as the main voice to be heard in the eclogue may have been influenced by Alcibiades' famous comparison of Socrates to statuettes of σιληνοί in Plato's *Symposium*.[20] I propose to argue that the parallels between the *Symposium* and the eclogue are more numerous and that the dialogue is of crucial importance for understanding Virgil's poetics.[21]

To begin with, love is a central issue in the eclogue, and, of course, love is the subject of Plato's dialogue in general and of Socrates' speech in particular (e.g. 201d τὸν δὲ λόγον τὸν περὶ τοῦ Ἔρωτος, 'the speech about Eros'). On the formal level, the elaborate 'Chinese box' narrative structure of the sixth eclogue is similar to that of the *Symposium*. In the eclogue Tityrus (or Virgil himself?) retells a song sung by Silenus, which turns out to be originally a composition by Apollo that apparently has only reached Silenus through a number of intermediaries.[22] In the *Symposium* the events and speeches of the banquet are narrated by Apollodorus who was not present there himself but learnt the story from Aristodemus; moreover, the most important of the speeches told at the banquet, that by Socrates, is a repeat of what he had heard from Diotima. It has often been observed that Plato's use of indirect narration is not just a decorative literary device, but reflects his views on the nature of philosophical discourse. Likewise the complex narrative strategy employed in the eclogue seems to be intended to comment on the nature of poetic tradition.

Before considering the philosophical content of the *Symposium*, I wish to point out a number of details in Plato's representation of the banquet that find correspondences in the scene introducing the song of Silenus. None of these parallels can admittedly count as a certain allusion, but taken together they build a

---

[19] Cf. recently Paraskeviotis 2014.
[20] Coleman 1977, 179; note also Davis 2011, 45 n. 18, who, however, sees no more than just 'a playful analogy between the Silenus-figure and the Socrates represented in Alcibiades' speech'.
[21] Cf. in general Van Sickle 2000 and Pilipović 2013, on the presence in the *Eclogues* of Plato's *Phaedrus*. On the *Symposium* as a subtext of the Nisus and Euryalus episode in *Aeneid* 9, see Makowsky 1989 and Wardy 2007. Cf. further Peraki-Kyriakidou 2003, 164–6, on Virgil's use of Plato's *Ion* in the *Georgics*.
[22] I take 82 *omnia quae* as summing up the preceding themes rather than introducing a new one; cf. Cucchiarelli 2012, 370. Contrast Knox 1990, 185–93.

case for believing that in the sixth eclogue Virgil engages with Plato's *Symposium*. In his commentary Coleman observes, on 16 *serta*, that 'garlands were often worn at drinking parties; e.g. Pl. *Symp*. 212e (Alcibiades' entry)';[23] I would take this comparison a step further: in a sense like Chromis and Mnasyllos who bind Silenus with garlands fallen from his head (*Ecl*. 6.19 *iniciunt ipsis ex uincula sertis*, 'they put on him ties made out of garlands'), Alcibiades wreathes with his own garlands first Agathon and then Socrates (213e αὐτὸν λαβόντα τῶν ταινιῶν ἀναδεῖν τὸν Σωκράτη, 'taking headbands, he wreathed Socrates': though *uincula* renders the idea of δεῖν rather than ἀναδεῖν). A similar case of 'mistranslation' is arguably found in Silenus' plea to unbind him (*Ecl*. 6.24 *soluite me, pueri*, 'untie me, guys') that sounds not unlike Agathon's order to take off Alcibiades' shoes (213b ὑπολύετε, παῖδες, Ἀλκιβιάδην, 'boys, untie Alcibiades' shoes': again, *soluite* would correspond to the unprefixed λύετε rather than ὑπολύετε). A more direct point of contact is created by Silenus' promise that his capturers will hear the song they want (*Ecl*. 6.25 *carmina quae uultis cognoscite*, 'hear the songs you wish'), which evokes the symposiastic convention that the audience can order the topic of the speech (e.g. 214c ἐπιτάξαι Σωκράτει ὅτι ἂν βούλῃ, καὶ τοῦτον τῷ ἐπὶ δεξιὰ καὶ οὕτω τοὺς ἄλλους, 'he should order Socrates whatever topic he chooses, and Socrates to the one on his right, and the others likewise'). Another detail that adds to producing the atmosphere of a banquet is Silenus' massive cup (*Ecl*. 6.17 *grauis ... cantharus*), which can be compared with the one Socrates is found drinking from on the next morning (223c πίνειν ἐκ φιάλης μεγάλης, 'to drink from a large bowl'). A more specific parallel is that both the banquet of Plato's *Symposium* and the capturing of Silenus in the eclogue were preceded by heavy drinking on the day before: in the dialogue Pausanias and Aristophanes complain of a hangover (176a πάνυ χαλεπῶς ἔχω ὑπὸ τοῦ χθὲς πότου, 'I'm rather unwell from yesterday's drinking', 176b καὶ γὰρ αὐτός εἰμι τῶν χθὲς βεβαπτισμένων, 'I'm myself one of those who were soaked yesterday'), in the eclogue Silenus is found intoxicated with 'yesterday's Bacchus' (*Ecl*. 6.15 *inflatum hesterno uenas, ut semper, Iaccho*, 'his vein swollen, as always, with yesterday's Bacchus'). However, despite having drunk heavily on the day before, Silenus seems to be in a perfect condition to perform a song, while Socrates is famous for staying sober no matter how much he drinks (220a Σωκράτη μεθύοντα οὐδεὶς πώποτε ἑώρακεν ἀνθρώπων, 'no man has ever seen Socrates drunk'). There are also other parallels between Silenus and Alcibiades' portrait of Socrates. Silenus charms with his song the whole natural world, both animate and inanimate, like Orpheus (27–30); Alcibiades compares Socrates with Marsyas who charmed (215c ἐκήλει) listeners with his flute,

---

[23] Coleman 1977, 179.

for Socrates' speeches have the same effect on everyone who hears them (215d ἐκπεπληγμένοι ἐσμὲν καὶ κατεχόμεθα, 'we are astonished and captivated'). Silenus is said to have often deluded Chromis and Mnasyllos with a promise of a song (*Ecl.* 6.18–19 *saepe senex spe carminis ambo / luserat*, 'the old man has often deceived the two with a promise of a song'); Alcibiades tells a story about how Socrates constantly stirred his (and others') hopes for an erotic relationship, only to deceive them (222b οὐκ ἐμὲ μόνον ταῦτα πεποίηκεν, ἀλλὰ ... καὶ ἄλλους πάνυ πολλούς, οὓς οὗτος ἐξαπατῶν ὡς ἐραστὴς παιδικὰ μᾶλλον αὐτὸς καθίσταται ἀντ' ἐραστοῦ, 'he has done this not just to me, but to very many others, whom he tricked by pretending to be a lover, only to turn into a beloved instead of a lover').[24]

If the setting of Silenus' song is indeed modelled on that of the *Symposium*, and the figure of Silenus himself on that of Socrates, one can expect that the philosophical content of the dialogue may also be reflected in the eclogue. For the moment I confine myself to one basic observation. As we have seen, in the song of Silenus it is possible to discern, expressed in Lucretius' words, the Epicurean notion of love as the pursuit of the pleasurable.[25] The Platonic concept of love as expounded in the speech of Socrates is similar, except that it has a different end. For Plato, love is the aspiration for the good (not the pleasurable): 205d πᾶσα ἡ τῶν ἀγαθῶν ἐπιθυμία καὶ τοῦ εὐδαιμονεῖν ὁ μέγιστός τε καὶ δολερὸς ἔρως ('all desire of good things and the greatest and painful longing for happiness'). Both pleasure, for Epicurus, and good, for Plato, are the things that constitute happiness (εὐδαιμονία). Both philosophers are aware that this pursuit of one's own supreme good can be misguided, and hold that it is the main aim of philosophy to direct it. Such a conflation of two analogous but irreconcilable models would be very close to a typically Virgilian procedure that is often described as 'remythologisation'. As Gale explains, the *Georgics* feature many passages where 'language suggestive of Lucretius' rationalizing approach to natural phenomena is combined with allusion to other texts which offer mythological accounts of the same phenomena', with the implication 'that the different world-views embodied in the various intertexts have equal validity; that their accounts of reality are

---

[24] Cf. further Kayachev 2015, where I suggest that Alcibiades' portrayal of Socrates may also have left traces in the tenth eclogue: the picture of Lycoris walking barefoot through hoarfrost (10.49 *a, tibi ne teneras glacies secet aspera plantas*) may be intended to evoke Socrates who always went barefoot, even at a particularly cold moment during the Potidaea expedition (220b καὶ ποτε ὄντος πάγου οἵου δεινοτάτου ... ἀνυπόδητος δὲ διὰ τοῦ κρυστάλλου ῥᾷον ἐπορεύετο ἢ οἱ ἄλλοι ὑποδεδεμένοι).

[25] Of course, Epicurus does not call it 'love' in the strict sense, reserving this term (*eros*) for personal erotic attraction; but Lucretius does use *amor* in that meaning (e.g. at 1.19), though admittedly not terminologically.

equally plausible, if incompatible with each other'.²⁶ I believe a similar strategy is at work in the sixth eclogue. It is a well-known fact that Epicurean philosophy originated and developed in stark opposition to Platonism; and Lucretius is no exception, for, as has been argued by De Lacy, his poem manifests a profound, if implicit and polemical, concern with Plato's works.²⁷ If I am right that in the sixth eclogue Virgil confronts Lucretius' Epicurean concept of the pursuit of the pleasurable with the Platonic concept of the pursuit of the good, this can be viewed as a case of, so to speak, 'replatonisation'; which, of course, does not have to mean that thus Virgil unconditionally subscribes to Platonism.²⁸

The initiation scene (*Ecl.* 6.64–73)

The account of Gallus' encounter with the Muses has received much speculation.²⁹ The central question raised by it, however, is quite simple: what does Virgil say about Gallus as a poet? The usual answer is that Virgil pictures Gallus progressing from erotic to aetiological poetry.³⁰ The only scholar to question this reading was Ross, who argued it 'impossible that Virgil ... could have meant the Permessus to represent 'subjective love elegy' opposed to Helicon and Hesiodic-

---

26 Gale 2000, 116.
27 De Lacy 1983, 291: 'The world view that Lucretius so eloquently proclaims in *De Rerum Natura* is at almost every point antithetical to Platonism, and often the antithesis is so precise that passages in *Nat.* can be paired with passages from the *Dialogues*. ... An examination of the evidence ... suggests very strongly that Lucretius did indeed have a first-hand knowledge of Plato's writings and that he not only rejected Platonism but even derived anti-Platonic arguments from the *Dialogues*, thus turning Plato against himself'.
28 Note for comparison that in his epigrams Philodemus, Virgil's mentor in Epicureanism, freely 'alludes to ideas and anecdotes associated with other philosophers, such as Socrates, Aristotle, and Polemon' (Sider 1997, 38). Also, the prominent presence of Gallus, generally considered the inventor of the erotic genre of lament par excellence in erotic elegy, is also at jar with a notion that Virgil should subscribe in a straightforward manner to philosophical programmes of 'happiness'.
29 It is commonly assumed that Virgil is faithfully reproducing a scene from a poem by Gallus where the latter described his own initiation. I believe that rather the reverse is true: if there was in Gallus' poetry an explicit account of his initiation at all, Virgil's version is likely to be as different from its model as possible. The scene is without doubt a response to Gallus, and we would have been in a better position to understand it had his poetry survived; but it is Virgil's response, and one can expect it to make sense within the internal logic of the eclogue.
30 See e.g. Clausen 1994, 200. Cf. e.g. Hollis 2007, 231.

Callimachean aetiological poetry',[31] taking Gallus' ascent instead as an homage to his previous poetic accomplishments rather than a way of initiation into a new kind of poetry. Ross's argument from topography may not be unassailable, but his real reason for rejecting this scholastic opposition of erotic and aetiological poetry lies in the fundamental insight that Gallus' main achievement was the 'idea that all poetry arises from a single source ... and, whatever forms it may take, never departs from a single demonstrable tradition'.[32]

I have argued that by using verbs *sequi* and *capere* to express the idea of attraction to whatever is the object of one's desire Virgil evokes the Epicurean concept of the pursuit of the pleasurable, but at the same time also the Platonic concept of the pursuit of the good. I have also suggested that *ducere* is another way of expressing the same notion; however, in the light of Plato's *Symposium* this assertion can be modified. While the idea that, so as to achieve pure pleasure uncontaminated with pain, one's desire for the pleasurable needs to be controlled by reason is quite Epicurean, Plato puts a much more specific emphasis on the need for a right kind of guidance to direct one's aspiration for the good, if it is to lead to real happiness that consists in the knowledge of the form of beauty. In his report of Diotima's account, Socrates distinguishes between two classes of people aspiring to the good with their souls (as opposed to a third class of people who aspire to the good with their bodies): those who lack proper guidance and therefore end up acquiring what is only a relative good (209a–e), and those who pursue the supreme good following the right method (210a–212a).[33] This method has two distinctive features: first, it requires a guide to direct one's pursuit of the good (210a ἡγῆται ὁ ἡγούμενος, 'the guide guides', c ἀγαγεῖν, 'to lead', e παιδαγωγηθῇ, 'is instructed', 211c ὑπ' ἄλλου ἄγεσθαι, 'is led by another'); second, it is a way of gradual ascent (211b ἐπανιών, 'going upwards', c ἐπανιέναι, ὥσπερ ἐπαναβασμοῖς χρώμενον, 'to ascend, as if by a staircase'). By contrast, the progress of those seeking the good without a method is erratic (209b ζητεῖ ... περιιών, 'he searches wandering around') and stops at whatever good they come first upon (ἐντύχῃ).[34] The scene of Gallus' initiation, I suggest, alludes to this Platonic model of two ways of pursuing the good. At first Gallus wanders (*Ecl.* 6.64 *errantem*) by the banks of the Permessus, like those of the second class in Socrates'

---

[31] Ross 1975, 33.
[32] Ross 1975, 37.
[33] I base my (extremely simplified) account on the excellent analysis of the dialogue in Sheffield 2006.
[34] See Sheffield 2006, 138–9; note especially his remark on περιιών: 'although the word is not always used in a derogatory sense, it is so used in the dialogues, particularly when paired with ἐντύχῃ'.

account; Socrates actually includes poets in this category (209d), and, *qua* merely erotic poet, Gallus belongs there. But later he is led by a Muse (*Ecl.* 6.65 *duxerit*) up to the top of Helicon where he is introduced to *Phoebi chorus* (*Ecl.* 6.66), the supreme embodiment of the idea of poetry, as it were; in that he resembles those constituting the latter class, namely philosophers, who are able to ascend to the knowledge of the form of beauty. Thus at first sight my reading of the initiation scene may appear to support the standard interpretation postulating a qualitative change in Gallus' poetry. Yet one must remember that the two ways of pursuing the good described by Socrates are both, *ex hypothesi*, manifestations of the same phenomenon of love. Hence, in terms of the *Symposium*, it is wrong to say that Gallus abandons love poetry; on the contrary, what Gallus' ascent should symbolise according to the logic of the Platonic subtext is rather the opposite, namely that he comes to a deeper understanding, and fulfilment, of love.

I wish to illustrate this claim by suggesting an allusion to Moschus' *Runaway Eros*.[35] The words with which Linus gives Hesiod's panpipe to Gallus (*Ecl.* 6.69 *hos tibi dant calamos, en accipe, Musae*, 'the Muses give you these reeds – take them!') arguably evoke Eros' offer of his bow and arrows (*Runaway Eros* 28 λάβε ταῦτα· χαρίζομαι ὅσσα μοι ὅπλα, 'take these: I gift you all my weapons', where Greek λάβε ~ Latin *accipe*, and Greek χαρίζομαι ~ Latin *dant*). By contrast, in the two main models for the initiation scene, Hesiod's *Theogony* and Theocritus' *Thalysia*, the giving of a symbolic gift is only reported by the narrator, but is not announced by the giver (*Theog.* 30–1, Theoc. 7.128–9). In both models it is a staff (σκῆπτρον 'staff' in Hesiod, λαγωβόλον 'shepherd's staff' in Theocritus), not a musical instrument as in Virgil, that is given. Here we have another parallel: like the panpipe in Virgil (*calami*), in Moschus Eros' arrows are referred to as 'reeds' (*Runaway Eros* 21 κάλαμοι); what is more, both contexts describe in comparable terms their previous application: the panpipe given to Gallus used to be played upon by Hesiod (*Ecl.* 6.70 *quibus ille solebat* ... 'with which he used [to charm trees]'), the arrows offered by Eros used to be shot at Aphrodite herself (*Runaway Eros* 21 τοῖς πολλάκι κἀμὲ τιτρώσκει, 'with which he often wounds even me': Greek πολλάκι ~ Latin *solebat*). An additional confirmation of Virgil's interest in this passage of Moschus can be found in the third eclogue where Damoetas accuses Menalcas of having broken Daphnis' bow and arrows – *calamos* (*Ecl.* 3.13) – that he had been given as a present. Coleman misleadingly comments that '*calamos* is frequently used by synecdoche for *sagittas*',[36] but Clausen is right to point

---

35 The *Runaway Eros* seems to have been quite popular in antiquity: see Czapla 2006, 74–6; this suggests that Virgil would have been familiar with it.
36 Coleman 1977, 111.

out that this is the first such usage in Latin poetry.[37] In fact, the use of κάλαμοι for 'arrows' does not seem to be widespread in Greek poetry either: Moschus may well have been the model for *Ecl.* 3.13, since it is not just the metonymical use of κάλαμοι / *calami* that the two texts share, but also the motif of gift-giving. If so, on the level of allusion Daphnis' bow and arrows turn out to be, as it were, a present from Eros; indeed, the motif of breaking both bow and arrows (*Ecl.* 3.12–13 *arcum / fregisti et calamos*, 'you broke the bow and arrows') may be derived from another context concerned with Eros, a passage in Apollonius' *Argonautica* where Aphrodite tells of a threat she once made to her son that she would break his bow and arrows (*Argon.* 3.96 αὐτοῖσιν τόξοισι δυσηχέας ἆξαι ὀιστούς, 'to break the sorrow-bringing arrows along with the bow').

If my argument that the initiation scene engages with both Plato's *Symposium* and Moschus' *Runaway Eros* is valid, what does it mean that Gallus receives not just Hesiod's, but actually Eros', κάλαμοι? In Platonic terms this means that, like Socrates, Gallus becomes an expert in 'erotics' (cf. 177d οὐδέν φημι ἄλλο ἐπίστασθαι ἢ τὰ ἐρωτικά, 'I claim to know nothing else but erotics'), thus fulfilling, rather than abandoning, what he began while wandering at the banks of the Permessus. It has often been argued that in his lost poetry Gallus may have cast himself in the role of Acontius from Callimachus' *Aetia*.[38] In particular, Morgan has made an ingenious suggestion that the use of *dicere* and *legere* at the beginning of the tenth eclogue (*Ecl.* 10.2–3 *pauca meo Gallo, sed quae legat ipsa Lycoris, / carmina sunt dicenda*, 'a few songs, but such as Lycoris would read, are to be sung by Gallus') may allude – following an example in Gallus' own poetry – to Acontius' throwing (*deicere*, which can stand for both *dicere* and *de-icere*) an apple inscribed with an oath and Cydippe's picking it up (*legere*) and reading the oath.[39] The same pun may be present in the proem of the sixth eclogue, where Virgil is instructed to *deductum dicere carmen* (*Ecl.* 6.5, 'to sing a delicate song') and hopes that the reader *captus amore leget* (*Ecl.* 6.10). This wordplay (especially on *deicere*) reveals the poetological metaphor that is at the core of the Acontius and Cydippe episode in the *Aetia*: writing (love) poetry as shooting arrows (of love). The tenor and the vehicle are brought together in the image of the inscribed apple, which can be seen as both a missile and a piece of poetry. On one level of meaning the reason why Eros can teach Acontius this stratagem (*Aet.* fr. 67.1 αὐτὸς Ἔρως ἐδίδαξεν Ἀκόντιον, 'Eros himself taught Acontius') is that he himself

---

37 Clausen 1994, 96.
38 See most conveniently Rosen/Farrell 1986.
39 Morgan 1995, 83. For the story of Acontius and Cydippe, who picked up the apple, see the chapter by Thorsen.

is an archer *par excellence*;⁴⁰ but on a deeper level the reason seems to lie in the idea of Eros as a teacher of poetry, an idea proclaimed in a famous Euripidean fragment, to which Callimachus apparently alludes (fr. 663): ποιητὴν δ' ἄρα / Ἔρως διδάσκει, κἂν ἄμουσος ᾖ τὸ πρίν ('Eros can teach a man to be a poet, even if he was unrefined before').⁴¹ Similarly, according to my argument, when Gallus is given κάλαμοι, he, on the one hand, is thus initiated as a poet, while, on the other, becomes an archer, both poetry and archery being means of inspiring love.

The prologue (*Ecl.* 6.1–12)

How is the centrality of love as a poetic principle to be reconciled with Apollo's prominence in the eclogue? It is Apollo, after all, who appears as the supreme poetic authority both in the prologue (*Ecl.* 6.3 *Cynthius* and 11 *Phoebo*) and in the initiation scene (*Ecl.* 6.66 *Phoebi chorus* and 73 *Apollo*): in the former Apollo guides Virgil's development as a poet, by defining what sort of poetry he is to write and ensuring its success; in the latter it is likewise Apollo who, by proxy, gives Gallus recognition as a poet and suggests a particular topic for him to write a poem on. In the sixth eclogue, I suggest, Apollo's authority is subordinate to that of Eros.

The idea that Apollo is a poet by virtue of being a lover can be traced back to Plato's *Symposium*, to a passage in Agathon's speech where Eros is praised as the teacher of all arts (196d–197b).⁴² First Agathon states, quoting Euripides, that Eros can teach anybody to be a poet and therefore must be a poet himself, since one cannot teach others what one does not know oneself:

> ποιητὴς ὁ θεὸς σοφὸς οὕτως ὥστε καὶ ἄλλον ποιῆσαι· πᾶς γοῦν ποιητὴς γίγνεται, 'κἂν ἄμουσος ᾖ τὸ πρίν', οὗ ἂν Ἔρως ἅψηται. ᾧ δὴ πρέπει ἡμᾶς μαρτυρίῳ χρῆσθαι, ὅτι ποιητὴς ὁ Ἔρως ἀγαθὸς ἐν κεφαλαίῳ πᾶσαν ποίησιν τὴν κατὰ μουσικήν· ἃ γάρ τις ἢ μὴ ἔχει ἢ μὴ οἶδεν, οὔτ' ἂν ἑτέρῳ δοίη οὔτ' ἂν ἄλλον διδάξειεν.
>
> (Pl. *Symp.* 196e)

---

40 Of course, Acontius is an archer (or a javelin-man) too, by virtue of his name, and in fact he had wounded many men even before he was taught by Eros (fr. 69 and 70); apparently the point is that until he fell in love with Cydippe, he could not (or just had no need to) direct his darts at a specific person.
41 Callim. *Aet.* fr. 67.3 οὐ γὰρ ὅγ' ἔσκε πολύκροτος may be hinting at Euripides' ἄμουσος.
42 On the connection between Agathon's and Socrates' concepts of love, see Sheffield 2006, 208–9.

The god is a skilful poet, so that he is also able to make another person a poet too. At any rate, at his touch every man becomes a poet 'though formerly unvisited by the Muse'. This we can properly take as evidence that Love is a skilful creator in virtually every form of artistic creation; for no one could give or teach another something which he does not possess or know himself.

(Transl. Howatson 2008, 30–1, adapted.)

Then he extrapolates this principle to other arts, whilst also making a more serious claim that Eros does not just teach ordinary artisans, but actually inspired the inventors of every single art:

ἀλλὰ τὴν τῶν τεχνῶν δημιουργίαν οὐκ ἴσμεν, ὅτι οὗ μὲν ἂν ὁ θεὸς οὗτος διδάσκαλος γένηται, ἐλλόγιμος καὶ φανὸς ἀπέβη, οὗ δ' ἂν Ἔρως μὴ ἐφάψηται, σκοτεινός; τοξικήν γε μὴν καὶ ἰατρικὴν καὶ μαντικὴν Ἀπόλλων ἀνηῦρεν ἐπιθυμίας καὶ ἔρωτος ἡγεμονεύσαντος, ὥστε καὶ οὗτος Ἔρωτος ἂν εἴη μαθητής, καὶ Μοῦσαι μουσικῆς (and so on).

(Pl. *Symp.* 197a–b)

Do we not know that in the practice of a craft any man who has this god for a teacher will turn out to be brilliant and famous, while the man untouched by Love will remain obscure? Similarly it was under the guidance of love and desire that Apollo discovered archery and medicine and divination, so that he too can be called a pupil of Love, and likewise the Muses in the arts...

(Transl. Howatson 2008, 31, adapted.)

In mythological terms this is, for the sixth eclogue, a more or less plausible construal of the relation between what can be labelled an Apolline and an Erotic poetics: if Apollo is a poet only by virtue of being a lover, his poetic authority is necessarily subordinate to that of Eros. But what is the essence of these two poetics in conceptual terms? Apollo, who offers specific advice on how to write poetry, can probably be seen as the embodiment of τέχνη, or *ars*, with its rules. By analogy, Eros may stand for *ingenium*, or inspiration; what would this mean?

The meaning of love as a poetological concept in the sixth eclogue is to be understood, I suggest, along Platonic lines. A comprehensive discussion of such a Platonising poetics would require a much broader perspective and involve a much wider range of poetic and technical texts; what I can offer here is just some basic ideas. As I have pointed out earlier, the sixth eclogue features two conceptual structures related to the notion of love that find parallels in the treatment of love in Plato's *Symposium*. One point of structural similarity is that both texts construct the concept of love as the aspiration to something that one wants. The other is that in both of them this aspiration potentially (and desirably) involves progress to a better understanding (and hence, a fuller achievement) of what one really aspires to. In Plato the object of one's love is defined as the good and the beautiful,⁴³ and in aspiring to this object one has gradually to transfer one's attention from particular good and beautiful things (which are only relatively good and beautiful) to the form of beauty, the knowledge of which constitutes one's supreme good (εὐδαιμονία). The question is how this scheme can be applied to a poetics.

In Plato's account a link to poetry can be found in a characteristic feature of those who aspire for the good with their souls (rather than bodies): they produce 'speeches' (λόγοι) that in some way express their understanding of the good (209b–c εὐπορεῖ λόγων περὶ ἀρετῆς καὶ περὶ οἷον χρὴ εἶναι τὸν ἄνδρα τὸν ἀγαθὸν καὶ ἃ ἐπιτηδεύειν, 'he is abundant in speeches about excellence and on what a good man should be like and what he should do', 210c τίκτειν λόγους τοιούτους καὶ ζητεῖν οἵτινες ποιήσουσι βελτίους τοὺς νέους, 'to produce such speeches and to seek out those that improve young men').⁴⁴ In respect to these speeches the difference between those who aspire to the good without a method and those who do so methodically lies in that the former believe, erroneously, that they already possess the knowledge of the good and therefore are precluded from any further progress, whereas the latter realise that the understanding of the good expressed in their speeches is only of a provisional character and therefore are able gradually to ascend, by improving their speeches, to the knowledge of the supreme good. Thus, though this is not the point Plato wants to emphasise since speeches play only a technical role in the ascent, the latter are bound to produce, at least at the higher levels of their ascent, better speeches than the former. What is important for the present argument is that Plato considers poets such as Homer and Hesiod among those who produce speeches in the mistaken belief that they possess the knowledge of the good (209d). Plato may have held that those who pursue the good following the right method would not compose poetry at all; but if they should, *a fortiori* they must eventually be able to produce better poems, as a class of λόγοι, than those who are not making the ascent. To highlight the parallelism with the sixth eclogue, in both Plato and (according to my argument) Virgil the production of speeches or poems is governed by love, or, to put it another way, it is a characteristic manifestation of love. As in Plato speeches are delivered by both types of lovers, aspiring to the good either with a method or without one, so, it can be assumed, in Virgil the point is that not all poets ascend, like Gallus, to the top of Helicon, but only – for the lack of a better term – metaphysical poets.

---

43 On the relation of the two concepts, see Sheffield 2006, 94–9; they are deeply interrelated, though not exactly identical, and here I use them, for the sake of simplicity, more or less interchangeably.
44 On the role of λόγοι in Plato's argument, see Sheffield 2006, 121–4.

Can this claim for a certain philosophical expertise made by Virgil be taken to some extent literally, or should it be understood merely as a figure of speech? Again, this is a question that cannot be discussed here in full; yet I wish to suggest a possible way in which Virgil's claim could make sense as a serious statement. What, then, does it mean for the poet to possess the knowledge of the form of beauty, or at least to aspire to such knowledge? Aristotle's famous remark on the difference between poetry and history in *Poetics* 9 may be suggestive of a possible answer: φιλοσοφώτερον καὶ σπουδαιότερον ποίησις ἱστορίας ἐστίν· ἡ μὲν γὰρ ποίησις μᾶλλον τὰ καθόλου, ἡ δ' ἱστορία τὰ καθ' ἕκαστον λέγει (1451b, 'poetry is more philosophical and more serious that history: for poetry conveys more what is general, history what is particular'). Halliwell's comments on the passage are worth quoting at some length:

> the principle of generality or typicality which Poetics 9 sketches means that the events of a dramatic poem should exhibit a higher level of intelligibility, particularly causal intelligibility, than is usually to be found in life. ... it is not immediately to life that the poet must turn for his material, but to an imagined world ... in which the underlying designs of causality, so often obscured in the world as we encounter it, will be made manifest.[45]

The ability to discern 'the underlying designs of causality' by turning 'to an imagined world' that Aristotle attributes to the poet (in contrast to the historian) can be seen, I suggest, precisely as a manifestation of the poet's deeper knowledge of, or at least interest in, the beautiful, since it is (the form of) beauty that is the ultimate principle of unity and intelligibility in both the ideal and the real world. It is true that Aristotle is speaking specifically of the plot of a dramatic poem rather than of every possible constituent of poetry;[46] but arguably the 'principle of generality or typicality' can be extrapolated, *mutatis mutandis*, to other constituents as well. The extended application of this principle can perhaps be best formulated in terms of mimesis. As Halliwell makes clear, Plato's dialogues feature two competing notions of mimesis, manifested in 'a radical divergence between his attempts to arrogate the language of mimesis for philosophy's relation to metaphysical truth, and his condemnation of the specious and meretricious status of works of artistic mimesis'.[47] To put it in an extremely simplified way, mimesis can have as its object either the ideal or the real world: for Plato, philosophy engages in mimesis of the former type, arts in that of the latter. But for Aristotle such a radical opposition is no more valid, for, to use Halliwell's apt wording once more,

---

[45] Halliwell 1986, 135.
[46] For a detailed discussion, see Heath 1991 and Armstrong 1998.
[47] Halliwell 1986, 120.

he 'has come round to regarding poetry from an angle which endows it with at least something of the force which Plato has speculatively attributed to philosophical mimesis in his late work: the capacity to enlarge understanding and to direct the mind from particulars to objects of higher significance'.[48] This capacity must obviously be rooted in the poet himself, that is he must, to return to the imagery of Plato's *Symposium*, already have made the ascent to the form of beauty, or at least be actively engaged in it; for it is precisely by learning to grasp abstract beauty in beautiful particulars that the ascent is effected. In other words, the poet ought to be in love and to exercise his love – that is, his aspiration to the good and the beautiful – in a right way. And for Virgil, the reader needs to be *captus amore* too.

This account of what I have labeled the Erotic poetics provides a plausible explanation for its precedence over the Apolline poetics: it seems right to assume, first, that the rules of art (Apollo) are founded in the knowledge of the beautiful (Eros) and, second, that although they do express a to a certain degree generalised understanding of the beautiful, there always will be a higher level of generalisation in the ascent to the form of beauty for which no rules exist (either because no rules have yet been found, or because rules cannot adequately formulate the knowledge of beauty at that level of abstraction). If that is what Virgil says, how then is the famous allusion to the *Aetia* prologue to be understood? As Farrell has rightly insisted, 'there is no reason to think that Callimacheanism in Latin poetry was a Vergilian innovation', and since 'Callimachus had been so important in Latin poetry during the two decades that preceded the *Eclogues*', there would be no point in 'Vergil's merely parroting the *Aetia* prologue'.[49] Should we think that in the sixth eclogue Virgil is criticising Callimachus for making Apollo the supreme poetic authority?

I have argued elsewhere that Apollo's admonition in the *Aetia* prologue is intended to evoke the instructions of Parmenides' Goddess.[50] Callimachus is to follow the untrodden path (*Aet.* fr. 1.25–6 τὰ μὴ πατέουσιν ἅμαξαι / τὰ στείβειν, 'to walk paths untrodden by carriages'), not for the sake of originality, but because it is the only way that leads to true knowledge and hence genuine excellence in poetry (cf. Parm. fr. 1.27 ἀπ' ἀνθρώπων ἐκτὸς πάτου, 'away from men's path'). He thus aligns himself with metaphysical philosophers, whereas casting his critics (*Aet.* fr. 1.2 νήιδες) in the category of those βροτοὶ εἰδότες οὐδέν (Parm. fr. 6.4, 'mortals knowing nothing') who enquire into the phenomenal world about

---

48 Halliwell 1986, 136.
49 Farrell 1991, 294.
50 Kayachev 2012, 31.

which no firm knowledge can be obtained. Whether or not Virgil recognised the allusion to Parmenides, one way or another he must have grasped its implication, namely that for Callimachus poetry needs to be grounded in the knowledge of ontological reality (however one construes the relation between poetry and such knowledge). By subjecting the authority of Apollo to that of Eros, Virgil is therefore not contesting, but asserting this essential point of Callimachus' poetics, which could easily be misunderstood or even lost.[51]

Conclusion

Needless to say, my argument has left many questions unanswered or even not touched upon. It is one such question that I now wish briefly to address by way of conclusion: what part did Gallus play in formulating the poetics that Virgil expounds in the sixth eclogue? Certainty is impossible here; but one relevant observation can be made. Whether or not Gallus himself used the Platonic image of the ascent to the form of beauty as a model to describe the process of poetic composition, the idea that poetry is derived from above seems to have played an important role in his oeuvre. This is the implication of the Qaṣr Ibrîm fragment, which presents the Muses, rather than Gallus himself, as the real author of his poetry (6): *fecerunt carmina Musae* ('the Muses composed the poems'). It has been suggested that this or some related context in Gallus' poetry may lurk behind the Virgilian initiation scene in which Gallus receives from the Muses an instrument for composing songs (rather than songs themselves).[52] But the Gallan image of songs being received in a ready form from the Muses may be reflected in the sixth eclogue in a more direct, though implicit, manner. As has often been pointed out,

---

[51] Cf. the recent discussion of Platonic subtexts in the *Aetia* prologue by Acosta-Hughes/Stephens 2012, 31–47. In respect of the prologue's content and its concerns with philosophy they have come to a conclusion comparable, though not exactly identical, to mine (p. 43–4): 'The injunction to judge poetry by *technê* was scarcely a novel idea even in Plato, let alone for Callimachus in the early third century BC. Therefore, what has for a generation been the scholarly consensus, namely, that Callimachus asserts the priority of *technê* over inspiration, is in need of some re-evaluation. Callimachus' Prologue is not a banal affirmation of the value of *technê* so much as a reclamation project that seeks to reestablish an older relationship of *technê* and inspiration to *sophia*, or poetry that seeks to reclaim its former position in society. ... The rules, therefore, are not the whole story: the poet must achieve and should be judged for what Callimachus calls by the time-honored name of *sophia*'.
[52] See e.g. Lieberg 1987, 542.

the epithet *deductum* that defines *carmen* in line 5 may imply, apart from rendering Callimachus' λεπταλέην, also a more literal meaning of the verb *deducere*, especially in view of its literal use in the same eclogue (*Ecl.* 6.71 *cantando rigidas deducere montibus ornos*, 'to bring down stiff ash-trees from the mountains by singing') and in a related poetological context in the *Georgics* (3.11 *Aonio rediens deducam uertice Musas*, 'as I return, I will bring the Muses down from the Aonian peak').[53] Taken literally, *deductum carmen* would mean 'a song brought down': in mythological terms, a song derived from the Muses; in philosophical terms, a song deduced from the knowledge of the form of beauty.

---

53 See e.g. Henkel 2009, 266. Cf. further Álvarez Hernández 2014, who interestingly argues that a third meaning is also at play ('subdued, reduced', therefore 'humble').

Paola D'Andrea
Longum Bibebat Amorem: Virgilian Adaptation of Sympotic Poetry

Introduction

The present essay intends to make a small contribution to the subject of 'generic enrichment' that has been questioning many of the established tenets of the study of Classical literature.[1] It does so through the proposal of a new comparative framework inviting a reassessment of the genre of Virgil's *Aeneid* in light of its engagement with archaic Greek lyric poetry.[2] Specifically, its focus is devoted to the Dido-and-Aeneas episode (Book 1–4) as a recasting of elements harking

---

[1] This critical attitude has been defined in its scope and purpose by Stephen J. Harrison, as an approach that explores 'the way in which generically identifiable texts gain literary depth and texture from detailed confrontation with, and consequent inclusion of elements from, texts which appear to belong to other literary genres'. The pivotal premise underlying the entire argument is that 'works, in particular genres, can incorporate elements of a different or opposing genre' according to the 'principle of incorporating elements form a different, "guest" genre while retaining the overall framework of the primary, "host" genre'. It is thanks to the resulting osmotic process that 'one genre confronts, includes and gains from another' Harrison 2007, 1–21.

[2] As for the definition of 'literary genre', this treatment largely draws on the notion of 'a discursive form capable of constructing a coherent model of the world in its own image', providing 'a language, that is, a lexicon and style, but ... also a system of the imagination and a grammar of things' Conte 1994a, 132. Metaphorically speaking, genre is the 'software' of potential and actual texts, a cell that encapsulates, within its nucleus, a normative code containing directions and orientations that can concretely, although not necessarily, materialise into actual texts. Its conventional nature is defined in the terms of a 'statutory identity', which articulates across an extensive system of devices: tropes, themes, subject matters, motifs, images. Amongst these markers, metre plays a privileged role, in Conte's theorisation, as the most immediately recognisable indicator of a generic discourse, and as such, a decisive, sufficient criterion for establishing generic fields of competence. Metre is the only aspect in which this contribution takes a cautionary distance from Conte, on the grounds that archaic Greek lyric displays a wide range of metrical choices that not always respect a one-to-one matching of form and content. However, Conte himself grants a constitutional flexibility to his notion of genre, in which boundaries are drawn along dotted, rather than continuous, lines, and each constituent is 'susceptible to transformation' Conte 1994a, 40. The bibliography in this field is vast and, even within Conte's scholarly output, not limited to a single work: see at least Conte 1986; 2007, Conte/Most 1996. For an updated, revisionist take on his operative formulation see Lee 2016, who has recently preferred the label of 'script conditions' to the conventional one of genre, in keeping with recent achievements of cognitive theory.

https://doi.org/10.1515/9783110633030-008

back to the discursive tradition of sympotic poetry – a tradition that is regarded here as mostly belonging to early Greek lyric.[3]

As such, this work builds upon emerging trends in recent scholarship emphasising the enrichment that arises from the connection between different sets of polarities in Classical texts, i.e. Greek and Roman, hetero- and homoerotic. It will hopefully promote further reflection on the universal scope of the theme of love, in its ability to bridge gaps and facilitate lines of continuity through time. This potential is exemplified at its best by the display of tropes from Greek lyric emerging in the poetic construction of the ill-fated love between Dido and Aeneas. A reconsideration of the ways in which the lyric aesthetics of sympotic narration affect the epic narrative of the *Aeneid* will unmask the fluidity that lies at the core of two poetical traditions that, though separate in time, place and context, are already textualized as parts of the same continuum.[4]

Epic and lyric in the Dido-episode

The main argument put forward here can be formulated as follows: the first and fourth books of the *Aeneid* can be viewed as a consistently lyric unit, where the Dido-and-Aeneas episode derives some of its shape from the deployment of a figurative phraseology and range of situations that belong, unequivocally, to the domain of archaic Greek lyric.

---

[3] The adjective 'lyric' is used, and should be taken, throughout this paper, in the broadest sense as concerning, somewhat *uia negatiua,* poems, pieces of poetry or single verse utterances of relatively short length belonging neither to the epic nor to the dramatic genre: that is, including e.g. elegy. In making this claim, I am fully aware that the broader questions of the ultimate 'essence' of Greek lyric poetry and its literary systematisation, are by no means beyond ambiguity and controversy. One needs to think about the issues surrounding the role of elegy within, or beyond, the corpus of lyric genres, not to mention the debate on the applicability of the dividing line between monodic and choral destination. On these burning issues see, for example, Rutherford 2010, Bowie 1986, Davies 1988. Without tackling the intricate questions relating to the controversial status of the lyric genre in ancient Greek poetry, I limit myself to inserting a necessary preliminary caveat: the distinctions that will be proposed below (i.e. elegy, sympotic, love poetry) do not refer to any conclusive taxonomy, but serve rather as a set of working categories allowing for a remapping of the *Aeneid*'s defining features.

[4] The terms 'sympotic' and 'convivial' are alternatively used, throughout this paper, as referring to the same poetic tradition featuring commensal indoor activities. However, far from being a univocal concept, the tradition of sympotic/convivial poetry often crosses path with other 'labels' applied to the lyric production, e.g. elegiac, erotic, political. Cf. Cazzato/Obbink/Prodi 2016.

The conception of love that we normally think of as characteristic of the Latin erotic elegy of Virgil's contemporaries Tibullus and Propertius, as the fruit of free choice and reciprocal availability, against and beyond the norms of social consolidation, is already fully at play in Greek lyric verse, both archaic and Hellenistic.[5] This intersectional area is created by a fundamental convergence of properties that crucially pivot on a shift from a homoerotic to a heterosexual slant. In other words, the imagery and motifs displayed in Latin love poetry, and which articulate the narrative of the heterosexual couple, not only in the Latin elegists, but also in the case of Dido and Aeneas, are deeply embedded within the horizon of the pederastic couple of the Greek lyric tradition.[6] In this context, a younger partner (ἐρώμενος) is the object of affection of an adult, experienced lover (ἐραστής) within the broader context of an educative mission that takes place, most eminently, though not exclusively, in the highly ritualised framework of the symposion.[7]

The development of the passionate love story of Dido and Aeneas, together with its unhappy ending, has been predominantly interpreted as endorsing the dichotomy 'male' vs. 'female'. The first term denotes devotion to duty and civic deeds (Aeneas), whereas the latter denotes inclination to emotion and unconstrained passion (Dido), preluding the disastrous outcomes of such conditions. According to this separation of prerogatives, the male pole lines up with restraint and order, representing the rational and fully functional side of society, whereas the female sphere is constitutionally subject to emotional impulses, embodying an aspect of danger for the community. This has been one of the strongest, and most deeply encrusted underlayers of Western worldviews across the centuries.[8]

The idea of a lyric intertext in the *Aeneid* has loosely surfaced at several moments in Virgil's scholarship, but has emerged, as a line of inquiry in its own right, most conspicuously from the end of the 1980s. Francis Cairns (1989) was

---

5 A detailed illustration of Roman love elegy as foregrounding the ideal of 'love for love's sake' is in Thorsen 2013b. Calame 1999 identifies the requirements of the lyric love affair within the framework of a relationship alien from the aspects of stability and duration, which are instead typically ratified by the wedding-epilogue in other genres (e.g. comedy, see below).
6 The affinity between the elegiac genre and the Dido-and-Aeneas episode in Virgil's epic is underscored by the fact that in *Heroides* 7, Ovid recasts Dido as an elegiac poet-lover (cf. *Her.* 7.183–4) and Aeneas as an elegiac scoundrel, *scelerate*, cf. *Her.* 7.133).
7 On the major issues of ancient Greek attitudes towards homosexuality, see two ground-breaking, although opposed, views in Dover 1978 and Davidson 2007.
8 On the opposition between Dido and Aeneas: Monti 1981, Feeney 1983, Privitera 1996, Morton Braund 1998, Nuttal 1998, Binder 2000, Ghiselli 2004, Fratantuono 2007, James 2012c, Totola 2012.

one of the first exponents to test this hypothesis, through a series of parallels that have revealed a distinctively lyric texture at play in the poem, to be interpreted as part of the 'varied literary heritage, which … ranged far beyond earlier epic', eclectically employed in adherence to Hellenistic tenets.[9] What acquires relevance, in Cairns' interpretation, is that the role of Greek lyric repertoire in the *Aeneid* seems intrinsically marked in terms of gender, since its influence becomes manifest as a distinct trait of female characterisation. However, the significance of such underlying lyric conventions is acknowledged as unique to the figure of Lavinia, in which the model of Sappho plays a predominant part in the portrayal of virginal attitudes. In Cairns' view, the acknowledgement of heterogeneous substrata in Virgil's epic structure excludes the possibility of contemplating Sappho amongst the sources of Dido's profile, on the grounds of homoerotic aspects that were incompatible with the cultural-ideological milieu in which Virgil operated. The sympotic situation stimulating the erotic entanglement at Carthage is indeed acknowledged by Cairns as an aspect absent from the original epic repertoire, but is regarded, however, as a specific pattern of Roman erotic elegy. This interpretive stance frames the discussion within a much more suitable genre displaying a heterosexual slant, but rejects, perhaps too aprioristically, the possibility of Sappho as a 'lyric analogue', on the ground of the fact that 'she was given to falling in love with young girls'.[10]

The hypothesis of a lyric undertone in Virgil's presentation of the love-affair in Carthage has been fully endorsed, for the first time, by Alexander E.W. Hall (2011), who has pointed to the Aeneas-and-Dido episode as a springboard for investigating the ways in which 'Aeneas, in both his actions and his words, frames his relationship to Dido in lyric terms'.[11] This vector of research is proposed on the basis of a conceptual framework that, in line with Claude Calame's theorisation (1999), displays the portrayal of a temporary erotic attachment, leading neither to a regular marriage nor to a permanent family connection.

On the textual level, specific passages can be interpreted as 'markers' testifying to a process of lyric incorporation at work in the *Aeneid*. Scholarly attention has been paid (particularly, albeit not exclusively) to Book 6, in which strong clues can be spotted in the last meeting between Aeneas and Dido's shade in the Underworld. In this regard, for example, the hero's confession *inuitus, regina, tuo de litore cessi* (*Aen.* 6.460 'Unwilling, Queen, did I depart from your shore') is crafted as a multiple allusion. It is not only (famously) an echo of Catullus' elegiac

---

9 Cairns 1989, 129.
10 Cairns 1989, 137.
11 Hall 2011, 620.

Coma Berenices: *inuita, o regina, tuo de uertice cessi* (Catull. 66.39, 'Unwilling, Queen, did I depart from your head') and perhaps to the lost Callimachean original; but it was also, in all probability, modelled upon the lamentation of the departing girl in Sappho: Ψάπφ' ἦ μάν σ' ἀέκοισ' ἀπυλιμπάνω (Sappho Fr. 94.5 LP, 'Unwillingly, Sappho, do I leave you behind').[12] This borrowing carries with itself a switch in gender. Indeed, using Sappho's words, a male protagonist (Aeneas) appropriates a traditionally feminine 'script' to address his former lover. This gender-disjunction entailed in the re-usage of the same apostrophe acquires further relevance in light of a further circumstance: namely, that the words in question are used, in the original Sapphic context, to express a likely 'Sapphic' (i.e. same-sex) attraction, whereas in Virgil they display a heterosexual orientation.

What emerges from a reading of current contributions on the subject is that intertextual knots and allusive signals often take the shape of triangulations involving different characters and authorial personae. Uncovering these stratified layers of lyric reception in Virgil entails as a consequence a number of repercussions and complexities, in particular in terms of gender.

On these grounds, the conclusion of Hall's article sounds like a call for a thorough examination: 'What is needed ... is a comprehensive study of Virgil's references to Sappho and the lyric poets, in the *Aeneid* specifically but also in his works generally'.[13]

The first systematic answer to this fundamental question is to be found in a contribution by Stephen Harrison (2019), who has offered an analysis of the ways in which the model of Sappho is refigured in all the three major works of Virgil. For the first time, an all-encompassing scholarly focus points to the acknowledgement that 'echoes of Sappho are more widespread ... than scholars have generally allowed'.[14]

Notwithstanding, the issue of lyric in the *Aeneid* is still far from being addressed in its full scope. Of course, this cannot be the aim of this chapter, which intends rather to supplement the conceptual framing so far set out, with the addition of some further preliminary steps.

---

12 On the (debated) intertextuality with Catullus see Griffith 1995, whereas the implications of the Sapphic allusions are discussed by Acosta-Hughes, 2008.
13 Hall 2011, 631.
14 Harrison 2019, 149.

A lyric symposion at Carthage?

In the first book of the *Aeneid*, the royal banquet at Carthage provides the scene for the first-person narration by and about Aeneas. As is well-known, two units of action are incorporated in the same storytelling format: on the one hand, the destruction of Troy (Book 2), on the other one, the subsequent trials and peregrinations of the Trojan survivors at sea (Book 3). Displayed, as can be argued, as a 'preview' preluding the outburst of passion between Dido and Aeneas, this articulation of sequences is not fortuitous, but rather reflects a specific pattern: that is, the framework of sympotic poetry as one of the privileged settings of Greek lyric.[15]

The convivial gathering acquires relevance, in the Greek poetic tradition, for the decisive role that it plays in delineating a pathway for an alternative version of love. As already mentioned, this is a horizon in which love is conceived per se, neither stemming from, nor leading to, the institutional framework of marriage.

The salient requisites of this alternative idea of love are deeply embedded within the highly ritualised environment of the all-male, or prevalently all-male, symposion.[16] In this context, the erotic experience takes shape in the specific format of the pederastic couple, within the interaction between a young boy (ἐρώμενος) and an older lover (ἐραστής) who is in charge of his education and cultural refinement. The adult partner undertakes thus a formative mission, in

---

15 Perhaps the most privileged setting, according to some scholars. One of them was certainly Rossi, who claimed that '[t]he history of lyric is the history of the symposion' (transl. mine of the Italian: 'la storia della lirica è la storia del simposio') Rossi 1983, 41. By the same author, see also 1971. On the allegedly intrinsic link between lyric poetry and symposion, see also Vetta 1983, Gentili, 1984, Lissaragué 1990, Murray 1990. The latter scholar claims that 'archaic poetry in almost all its aspects ... was developed within the symposion – first by poets who were themselves full members of the sympotic group (Alcaeus, Sappho) and later by professional symposiast poets like Anacreon' Murray 1990, 264. For an introductory overview of the multivalent aspects of the symposion, see recently Hobden 2013 and also Henderson 2000, as well as note 17 below.

16 As for the assumption of gender exclusivity in sympotic activities, the issue is still in doubt and far from being established. Indeed, the standard view of an all-male symposion has been challenged by evidence (literary texts, but above all vase painting) testifying to instances of women participating in drinking events. The possibility of female companionship is suggested by the role of the *hetairai*, a term whose translation oscillates from 'entertainers', 'courtesans', 'concubines' to 'prostitutes'. The status of these women, as well as the degree of their association to male symposiasts, is still a matter of speculation, the picture being complicated by the fact that a pedagogical function was often credited to their role. Also on the basis of this evidence, Bowie 2016 has recently argued that Sappho's poems became part of the artistic programme of allegedly male symposia in the classical period.

which intimacy and togetherness unfold as the consequence of a sentimental education (παιδεία), which entails a psychological involvement as well as an ethical commitment.[17] Such an idea is fully lyric, and is expressed in the form of programmatic intention in Theognis: σοὶ δ' ἐγὼ εὖ φρονέων ὑποθήσομαι, οἷά περ αὐτός, Κύρν', ἀπὸ τῶν ἀγαθῶν παῖς ἔτ' ἐὼν ἔμαθον. (Thgn. 27–8, 'Wishing you well, Cyrnus, I will teach you the things that I myself learned from the best of men when I was still a boy'). To narrow the focus on the cluster of love and education in lyric poetry, the formative role of *eros* fully emerges in Sappho's prevalently accepted characterisation as a 'schoolmistress', and certainly in Theognis (to the point that the latter was considered a didactic poet).[18] As is well-known, this concept of love as a set of attitudes and actions revolving around a pedagogic practice finds a female counterpart in the instructing role played by Sappho in her θίασος ('band').[19]

Such a formative experience takes place in the name of a convergence of interests among the members of the same group, according to a process of gender homologation which emblematises the first vehicle of close comradeship. The experience of love is aimed at cementing the group through the promotion of solidarity and fidelity as its leading values. Like affinity and cohesion, however, elements of reluctance stem from this very same pattern. When this happens, as it tends to do, courtship translates into a veritable pursuit of a partner who, because of his young age, can easily change his mind or forget. Hopes and expectations are therefore left to moments of invocation, or indeed prayer, to be addressed to the deputed gods – Eros and/or Aphrodite – or to the lover himself.

When requited, love is reciprocated in the name of a shared path of growth and feelings, which implies an arduous journey involving compromise and mutual support. This is possible only in the environments that promote such key values and behaviours: namely, the predominantly mono-gender milieu of the θίασος and the symposion.

The convivial venue carves out an enclosed universe where individuality and subjectivity take full scope, and the 'speaking I' finds the apt space to ascertain,

---

17 On the educational function of the symposion see the aforementioned Calame 1999, in particular the section entitled 'The Propaedeutic Practices of the *symposium*', 93–100. See also Nagy 1996, Aloni 1998.
18 However, the role of Sappho as a teacher and headmistress of a female school community still presents some dubious aspects, on which see Yatromanolakis 2007, Elisei 2010. Specifically on Theognis see, amongst the others, Lewis 1985, Cantarella/Lear 2008.
19 The term θίασος refers here to the religious-didactic institutions devoted to the training and accomplishment of young girls before entering the marital status, as in the famous example of the all-female community led by Sappho in the island of Lesbos. (Cf. Yatromanolakis 2007).

alternatively, the effects of passion (when talking of love) or the ruinous effects of military conflict (when talking about war), while fuelling the audience with *exempla* and exhortations to valour.

At this point, I would argue that something similar is happening at Dido's banquet. The scene has long been explained on the basis of its Homeric models. First and most notably, the articulation of the Carthaginian episodes evokes *Odyssey* Book 8, where Odysseus lands incognito at Scheria to be welcomed later as a guest at the court of king Alcinous. Virgil's Homeric allusion is not limited to circumstantial factors but includes the bipartite structure of the inset flashback as a whole.[20] As already mentioned, Aeneas' account constitutes a sort of diptych, insofar as it combines together two macro-episodes: the destruction of Troy, in Book 2, and the *nostos*, in Book 3. The choice of this patterning on Virgil's part has been interpreted as a deliberate reference to the large-scale analepsis in *Odyssey* Book 8, where the song of Demodocus (*Od.* 8.482–566) is immediately followed by Odysseus' narration of his misfortunes across the sea.[21]

However, as I argue, it is possible to look at the same section of the *Aeneid* using a lyric lens: a lens that is not arbitrarily applied from outside the text, so to speak, but is suggested by the very context which is displayed in the same text.[22] What happens, in a nutshell, is this: Aeneas' subjective experience and individual emotions take centre stage in a first-person assertion. In the meantime, Dido falls in love, as in a sort of side effect, while cups keep circulating amongst the drinking company: *longum bibebat amorem* (*Aen.* 1.749). This arrangement of sequences in Virgil is an innovative element not seen in the Homeric model, where Nausicaa's admiration for Odysseus is not the direct consequence of Odysseus' narration or of the sympotic framework in which the latter takes place. By staging the 'zero hour' for the inception of love within the conventions of lyric poetry, the *Aeneid* offers a recasting of roles. On the one hand, Aeneas, who is posited, diegetically, as the agent, is not only responsible for the delivery of a highly instructive tale about human knowledge and experience, but is also the pursuing ἐραστής of the lyric tradition. On the other hand, Dido can be identified as the listening, pursued ἐρώμενος.

The first important consequence of this can be formulated as follows: Book 2 and 3 of the *Aeneid* must be looked at in light of their pragmatic grounding, that

---

20 Williams 1963, Hunter 2018.
21 On this topic see especially Heinze 1915, Otis 1976, Barchiesi 1984, Papanghelis 1999, Hexter 2010.
22 For an updated development of this analytical tool, indeed capable of wider application, see Budelmann/Philips 2018.

is, as an instantiation of poetic performance.[23] The context of the banquet at Carthage acquires relevance not only because it provides the occasion for a composition-in-performance, but also because it triggers a feeling of love. As the next-in-line singer after the professional bard Iopas, Aeneas is requested to give an oral account of his own military deeds and subsequent misfortunes at sea. True to the pragmatic code of the symposion, explicit requests for performance, along with suggestion for the subject-matter, come to the improviser from the public itself.[24] In our case it is Dido, the mistress of ceremonies and patroness of the event, who appeals to Aeneas' role as eyewitness by summoning him to tell his own version of the story. Indeed, the topic is already more than famous, as the hero himself realised a few moments before in Juno's temple, where he found himself facing the images of the Trojan cycle (*Aen.* 1.446–95). The character of Aeneas references the figure of the symposiast who is aware of a rich and varied flux of tales around, but more importantly *about*, himself, and is now asked to adapt his performance to the occasion, and to the expectations of his own external audience.

The notion of audience comes into play on multiple levels. In Jakobsonian terms, Aeneas is the message sender who knows well that the content he is about to produce will reach a diversified range of addressees.[25] Within the restricted audience gathered at the reception, Dido takes centre stage as the hostess and explicit requester, followed by the Trojan and Carthaginian peers who participate in the banquet. In keeping with the compositional technique of sympotic poetry, Aeneas employs poetic licence as a creative performer who arranges his material in adherence to convivial venue and purposes, with an eye towards the concrete performance requirements, as well as to the assumptions and evocations that may pre-orient his audience's response. The fact that Aeneas frames the myth of the fall of Troy as a *carmen conuiuale* in adherence to the rules of behaviour and group values established within the sympotic setting, bears important consequences with relation to the collective reception of the message. Indeed, his creative intervention draws the opportunity for Aeneas to speak to the community gathered at the banquet. Here Aeneas displays his talents as a poet but also as a political leader who is perfectly aware that this is an occasion on which communal relationships are forged for the sake of survival. The banquet, in fact, repre-

---

23 Gentili 1990.
24 An example of this practice is, emblematically, in Horace *Carm.* 1.27.
25 For the sake of terminology, the concepts of 'audience' and 'addressees' are derived here from the pragmatic theory of language. See Jakobson 1987, and Austin 1975².

sents the initiatic prelude to an – albeit temporary – common life. Dido's goodwill, however already assured by the queen herself before the feast (*Urbem quam statuo uestra est* ... / *Tros Tyriusque mihi nullo discrimine agetur*, *Aen.* 1.573–4, 'The city I am founding is yours ... I shall not make distinction between Trojans and Tyrians') is crucial for political concord. Indeed, the two peoples that are united for the occasion, the Carthaginians and the Trojan exiles, are going to share their paths thanks to the union between their chieftains, although for a limited portion of time.

The concept of community entails a further level in Aeneas' sphere of interests, in consideration of the fact that the Trojans of today are meant to become the Romans of tomorrow. Besides the Trojan-Carthaginian alliance, which concerns him for the immediate future – an alliance that, let us remind, is insubstantial within the schemes of capital-H history – Aeneas is speaking to the men who are still available to follow him in the mission of founding Rome. These men need to process what they have endured up to that moment and to regain their courage for what remains to be done. After seven years at sea, Aeneas finds in Carthage the conviviality of a truly sympotic setting, which enables him to comment on the margin of what he has endured up to that moment. This circumstance represents a *rite de passage* that allows the Trojans' leader to digest the trauma of exile and loss, and to get ready for the challenges that are still in store in Italy. Aeneas' tale shows an eminently lyric-elegiac flavour in its immediate outcomes: indeed, it is a tale of glory and heroism in defeat that triggers the feeling of love in Dido.

The symposion carves out a mundane and highly ritualised dimension in which Aeneas takes his turn in an ongoing poetic context. What he produces is, truly, a *carmen conuiuale* in which he engages, upon request, with the shaping of a literary tradition on a plotline (the *Ilioupersis*) that has closely and directly concerned him. Here lies the unprecedented novelty of Virgil's incorporation of a lyric mode into the epic fabric of his poem: cast anew as a poetic, speaking I, Aeneas assumes centre stage and exclusive focus, becoming 'the thematic centre of gravity' of the narration, while intervening in a fluidly circulating tradition that counts himself amongst its protagonists. As can be argued, the autobiographical pose, along with the self-reflecting orientation of Aeneas' tale, signposts an incursion into the lyric field on Virgil's part. The latter observation is corroborated in light of the metaliterary stance that is blended into this further facet of the hero's characterisation.[26] As already noted, Aeneas-the-political-leader accepts the invitation to tell his story as the occasion for a self-conscious reflection of his past hardship, with the trail of psychological and strategic advantages that this

---

26 On *Aeneid* 3 and its transactions with metapoetic subjects, see Gasti 2010.

opportunity has in store for him and his people. However, in his newly cast role as a poet, Aeneas is offered the opportunity to make his own contribution on a widely known narrative tradition. He does so by producing a piece of poetry that inserts an exclusively subjective viewpoint, as well as a pathetically loaded revisionist take, on a highly mainstream topic: in other words, realigning, improving, variating in compliance with the dos and don'ts of Alexandrian poetics.

What said up to now can be substantiated by a further consideration. Upon closer examination, the very fact of falling in love, in the *Aeneid*, grows out of the sympotic moment itself, at the end of which the queen finds herself irremediably struck by desire. The erotic/persuasive function of Aeneas' emotionally involving account is acknowledged by Dido herself, when she remembers with her sister Anna *quae bella exhausta canebat* (*Aen.* 4.14, 'what wars, long endured, did he sing!'). The central contention here is that the display of sympotic tropes, as it unfolds in the Dido-and-Aeneas encounter, as well as in the erotic relationship that immediately follows, shows an inherent connection with the themes of poetry and feasting, a connection that is a prevalent common denominator in Greek lyric poetry.

That Virgil knew his Greek lyric poetry well is a standard, as well as a thoroughly documented tenet in scholarship nowadays. In the late Republican age (ca. 80–30 BCE), this tradition came to be canonised and widely exploited in Rome as a fully codified literary genre, which had shifted, throughout the *longue durée* of the Hellenistic period, from a largely oral tradition to a predominantly written erudite transmission.[27] This transition was the outcome of a systematic work of scholarly compilation and editorial commentary, resulting from the joint contribution of philologists and librarians based mainly, though not exclusively, at Alexandria.[28] The tradition of sympotic poetry fully entered this process of canonisation, which resulted in enhancing the authority and status of earlier Greek lyric as a model for future authors.[29] In Virgil's own time, the impact of convivial poetry from Greece was as such as to exert a formative influence: sympotic anthologies and verse collections were widely circulating in Rome and formed a substantial part of the educational curriculum.[30] Set texts of the so-called Greek lyric canon, usually referred to as 'the nine lyric poets', were available in Rome

---

27 To my knowledge, the most recent contribution in this area comes from Currie/Rutherford 2020. See also, amongst the others, Acosta-Hughes 2010, Williams 1998, Fraser 1972.
28 As Barchiesi aptly remarks, this process of canonisation was 'dependent on a world of letters based on critics, wide readership, book trade, anthologies and schools, something that came into existence ... in the centuries between Isocrates and Meleager' Barchiesi 2009, 319.
29 Nagy 2004.
30 Cribiore 2001, Barbantani 2009.

for didactic usage in editions with comprehensive introductions and detailed commentaries made by earlier Greek philologists with all probability between the third and the second centuries BCE.³¹

The need for self-positioning with relation not only to the literary landscape of their own time, but also to the exemplary models of an earlier, by-gone age, was felt as an essential requirement by Virgil and his poetic generation. Suffice it to recall that in the same years his friend Horace was casting himself as the Roman successor of archaic Greek lyric, claiming to be the first who adapted Greek lyric verses to Latin poetry. A forerunner of this trend was, of course, Catullus, whose proposal of a 'new poetry' played a pioneering role in experimenting with metres and models.³²

Positing that the function of orality is fully at work in Aeneas' tale offers thus a new reading key to the two books as a properly lyric unity within the epic scope of the poem as a whole. As this article contends, the link between epic and lyric has hardly been so clearly displayed anywhere else in ancient literature.

The process of giving into erotic inebriation, on Dido's part, is textualized by Virgil as an act of 'liquid' absorption, on both the sensory and emotional level, again: *longumque bibebat amorem* (*Aen.* 1.749). The contemplation of the object of love consists, primarily, of an act of listening. It is the very act of reciting aloud, on the part of Aeneas, that triggers the process of falling in love – an emotional process that is accompanied, as well as seconded in its development, by wine-drinking. Within this dynamic, according to which poetic composition proceeds in tandem with affective involvement, wine-drinking and *eros* are interconnected as the two sides of the same coin. The imagery of drinking and falling in love as two complementary actions, in which the intoxication of feelings goes hand in

---

31 However, scholarly output on Greek lyric did not come to a halt in the late Hellenistic period. The production of editions and supporting material extended well into and beyond Virgil's time. Suffice it to mention that some of the most important scholiasts (such as Didymus Chalcenterus, Theon and Aristonicus of Alexandria) whose contributions still survive in the indirect tradition, were contemporary with Virgil (or slightly earlier). Under the umbrella of the established canonical nine we find traditionally Alcman, Sappho, Alcaeus, Anacreon, Stesichorus, Ibycus, Simonides, Bacchylides and Pindar. On comments and philological editions see Irigoin 2003. The *locus classicus* remains of course Pfeiffer 1968.

32 For Virgil's self-positioning with relation to his lyrical predecessors see more recently Andrisano 2007. For Horace's self-fashioning as the inventor of Latin lyrics, see *Odes* 1.1, 3.30 and 4.3.23: in the latter, the poet introduces his lines as consecrated in the role as *Romanae fidicen lyrae* ('minstrel of the Roman lyre'). Monographic focus can be found in Pasquali 1920, Feeney, D.C. 1993, Paschalis/Putnam 2002. More recently, Hullinger 2016 has proposed his own philological *lectio* for Anacreon Fr. 417 in a reading that includes, as a supporting argument, Horace's later reception of the same fragment in the *Odes*.

hand (sip to sip, we may want to say), with the effects of wine is fully lyric and finds exhaustive expression in Anacreon, whose name was, already in Virgil's time, proverbially associated with the metaphorical trio of the Muses, Wine and Love (*AP.* 7.27.9–10). The role of wine as the fuel of erotic inebriation is consecrated, in Anacreon's lines, by means of expressions such as μεθύων ἔρωτι (*PMGF* 376, 'drunk with love'), ἔρωτα πίνων (*PMGF* 450, 'drinking love'), or direct invitations such as ἀλλὰ πρόπινε ῥαδινοὺς ὦ φίλε, μηρούς (*PMGF* 407, 'Come, pledge me, dear boy, your slender thighs').

The connection between love and poetry as the two poles of a circuit that unrelentingly feeds on itself is a quintessentially lyric trope. To quote again from Anacreon: ἐμὲ γὰρ λόγων < ∪ – > εἵνεκα παῖδες ἄν φιλέοιεν / χαρίεντα μέν γ' ἀ-είδω, χαρίεντα δ' οἶδα λέξαι (*PMGF* 402c, 'It is for my art that boys should love me: I can sing gracious songs, and I can tell kind words'). This gesture of self-promotion on the part of the lyric I fits a customary scheme in Greek lyric poetry, according to which poetic lines aptly represent the means of seduction.[33]

The symposion triggers the narrative act and sets out what is to become the main object of the narration, i.e. the love story, on a macro level. The convivial

---

33 On the *Nachleben* of this topic in Western poetry see at least Rosenmeyer 1992. The correspondence, on the lexical level, between the Virgilian *iunctura* (*longum bibebat amorem*) and the precedent set by Anacreon ἔρωτα πίνων was already noticed by Servius, who in one of his glossae hinted at its source (*sic Anacreon*), as well as its function, as a sympotic marker (*adlusit ad conuiuium*). The semantic potential embedded in this phraseology is explored by Lyne, who detects 'the idea of a love potion' behind it. In the scholar's view, this interpretation is corroborated by the subsequent text of the *Aeneid* itself, where the association is made explicit by the term *uenenum* (*Aen.* 1.688). In Lyne's words, describing Dido's falling in love as an act of poisoning casts a retrospective light on the banquet scene: 'what better way to administer it than in the sip of wine that Dido takes?'. It is therefore '(the) context (that) heightens our awareness of the literal value of *bibo*'. In reviewing Lyne's contribution, Maria Luisa Delvigo acknowledges the relevance of the sympotic context, but inserts a caveat, along with a different interpretation: 'it is unlikely that the poison is in the cup: at ll.1, 686 f., Venus had explicitly referred to hugs and kisses as the occasion on which Cupid-Ascanius would administer his fire and poison to Dido... If a relationship must be drawn between the metaphor *bibere amorem* and the convivial context, I would acknowledge that in the antiphrastic meaning of *bibere*: the queen, who had limited herself to inaugurating the ritual symposion by touching the cup slightly, now drinks love, whereas all the others drink wine'. (Transl. mine of the Italian: 'che il veleno stia nella coppa è poco probabile: Venere, ai versi 1, 686s., indicava esplicitamente negli abbracci e nei baci l'occasione in cui Cupido-Ascanio avrebbe potuto somministrare alla sventurata regina il suo fuoco e il suo veleno... Ma se un rapporto tra la metafora *bibere amorem* e il contesto conviviale c'è, io lo vedrei piuttosto in un valore quasi antifrastico di *bibere*: la regina (che si era limitata a inaugurare ritualmente il simposio sfiorando appena a fior di labbra la coppa, 1. 737) beve amore, mentre gli altri bevono vino'). See Lyne 1989, Delvigo 1995.

context carves out a field for an emotional encounter, while building up the preliminary requirements for the ripening of a sentimental empathy that will soon translate into romantic passion.

The relations between the *Aeneid* and Greek lyric poetry can emerge through the identification of intertextual knots and plot parallels, but also through recognition of similarities in the shaping of key characters. In this regard, an analysis of the ways in which life trajectories are shaped, in the characterisation of both Aeneas and Dido, shows some typical features of authorial patterning from archaic Greek lyric poetry.

Aeneas as exiled lyric poet?

At the outset of the poem Aeneas's identity conflates and blurs the roles of refugee and poet. Aeneas' status as an exile and an outsider mirrors the traditional (albeit highly fictionalised) biography of a number of Greek lyric poets: Theognis, Alcaeus, Bacchylides, even Sappho.[34] The theme of exile marks a recurring trait in lyric poets' traditional biography, to the point of becoming a clearly recognisable hallmark of the status as poet in Western popular imagination (one need only think of Ovid and Dante).[35]

Aeneas' poetic account at Dido's court harks back to the literary pedigree of an exiled poet. As the future founder of Rome takes on the role as the *poeta loquens*, the model of Solon emerges as an especially significant facet of his profile. As the archetypal lawgiver and political leader, Aeneas speaks of and to his people while ascertaining the ruinous effects of military conflict, with the aim of re-inspiring, at the same time, his followers with *exempla* and exhortations to acts of valour. A textual marker alluding to this reconfiguration can possibly be detected in the verbal utterances denoting Aeneas' reaction to the promising developments seemingly in store for Carthage: *o fortunati, quorum iam moenia surgunt* (*Aen.* 1.437, 'Lucky the ones whose walls are already rising') and again *o terque quaterque beati, / quis ante ora patrum Troiae sub moenibus altis / contigit oppetere* (*Aen.* 1.94–6, 'O three and four time blessed, those whose fate was to fall before their fathers' altars under the high walls of Troy'). The hero's words, in which civic virtues are celebrated in the topos of the *makarismos*, seem to re-echo

---

34 Lefkowitz 2012, Kivilo 2010.
35 Ingleheart 2011.

somewhat Solon: ὄλβιος, ᾧ παῖδές τε φίλοι καὶ μώνυχες ἵπποι καὶ κύνες ἀγρευταὶ καὶ ξένος ἀλλοδαπός (Fr. 23 W, 'Lucky the one who has boys to love, strong horses and hunting dogs, and a guest from far away lands'). In the mouth of Aeneas, figuratively speaking, the idea of a 'foreign guest' can be interpreted as a potentiality of Solon's text that materialises, in Virgil's poem, with all the potential for a ruinous outcome, and as such more suitable for the code of epic. The hypothesis is supported by scholarly insights that have shed light on the affinity between elegy and lyric, stressing the flexibility of the archaic genre system as a whole. This argument is repeated here, just as a way of moving forward from the potential impasse of metric evidence, i.e. the use of the elegiac couplet in Solon, which, according to a well-established view, cannot be counted as properly lyric.

In his profile as an exiled leader, the model of Solon evokes Herodotus' *Histories*, where the Athenian lawgiver is immortalised in the attempt to persuade an Oriental monarch with a narrative account which itself carries a cautionary tale on the unpredictability of human fortune (Hdt. 1.6–95). The case in point here is the encounter with Croesus at the royal palace of Sardis, which is textualised, precisely at the beginning of Herodotus' work, in a setting of hospitality and shared conviviality linked to Solon's visit to Lydia.[36] This framework builds the basis for an oral storytelling on the part of the guest: namely, the inset tales of Tellus, Cleobis and Biton, whom Solon celebrates as paradigmatic heroes of Athenian civic virtues. The moralising content of this narrative will emerge, in its full meaning, at a later point, when the city of Sardis will collapse from the culmination of its splendour.[37]

In alluding to the Herodotean account, Virgil accommodates in the figure of Aeneas salient aspects that already emerged as distinctive features in the portrayal of Solon, especially in his role as a foreign and illustrious visitor addressing

---

[36] In Herodotus, the so-called 'Lydian account' occupies first position on the macrotextual level, placed as it is in Book 1 (out of nine). Also in Virgil, Lydia provides the setting at the very beginning of the poem, as a geographically marked signpost. *Pace Herodotus et al.*, after founding Athens in its democratic constitution, Solo embarked upon a ten-year journey across the Mediterranean, visiting the Middle East. If Virgil, as it is argued here, is alluding to Herodotus in the narrative patterning of Aeneas' exilic trajectory, he offers an opposite treatment of temporality, by inverting the 'before' and the 'after': Aeneas *first* experiences exile, and *then* founds his new homeland.

[37] This epilogue encapsulates, retrospectively, a tragic fate for Croesus, in the Sophoclean sense of a retributory reverse of fortune from a position of perceived invulnerability. By the same token, also Dido is doomed, her *hamartia* consisting on a blinding passion, which she believes sufficient to hubristically prevent Aeneas from his destiny. On Herodotus and tragedy see Griffin 2006, Said 2002.

a representative of an exotic and supposedly decadent culture. This contributes to establishing Aeneas' authority as an inspirational, instructive source of knowledge: the *Ilioupersis* of Book 2 contains a warning, for Dido, about how cities easily collapse, and therefore about the importance of committing to her public duties.

In Herodotus, characterisation revolves around a polarised pair: Solon embodies balance of judgement and sense of measure, whereas Croesus emblematises, by contrast, excess and luxury quintessentially relating to Eastern cultural values. In the Virgilian recasting, the identification with Solon does not concern Aeneas exclusively, but partially extends to Dido, as the leader of a civic body, with her noble birth and status put at risk by enmities and conspiracies.

Drawing an intersectional area between Dido and Aeneas, the model of Solon shows that the two characters are much closer than they seem *prima facie*, and perhaps suitable erotic partners. In terms of political leadership, both of them are charismatic leaders of their respective peoples. In the case of Dido, this function is fully and officially acknowledged on both the civic and legal level, and finds as such a correlative, in the economy of the symposion, in the role that the queen plays as the symposiarch.

This dynamic of appropriation reveals a second layer, in which another 'big name' from archaic lyric surfaces as deeply embedded, this time, in the characterisation of Dido, namely Sappho. As the pivotal agent presiding over Aeneas' sentimental re-education, the queen plays an essential role in paving the way for the hero's re-conversion to the rules of collective society, and is destined to pay the highest price for a relationship that qualifies, in the end, as nothing else than a transitory connection. In making Aeneas accustomed, again, to the experience of married life, and to the patterns of societal transactions more in general, Dido fulfils a formative role that, albeit temporary, is crucial in light of the prospective teleology of the poem. The romantic affair implies a didactic aspect insofar as Dido offers a propaedeutic training, thanks to which Aeneas regains familiarity with the dos and don'ts pertaining to interaction with the other sex, preparing the way for the marriage with Lavinia in Italy. This function is anticipated in Venus' appearance to Aeneas in the outskirts of Carthage, under the guise of an incognito huntress (*Aen.* 1.314–418): apart from providing strategic information, the goddess sets out to instil a source of erotic temptation, which makes him receptive to Dido's likely re-awakened sexual interest.[38]

---

[38] The erotic undercurrents of the Venus-and-Aeneas meeting have received considerable scholarly attention, also in light of its recasting the role of Aphrodite seducing Anchises in the eponymous *Homeric Hymn*. Cf. Harrison 2007, 92–5, with bibliography.

The pedagogic role played by Dido emerges in the continuum joining together Venus, who prepares the way for Dido's intermediate function, and Lavinia as the ultimate destination. Love teacher and abandoned lover are two of the most eminent facets of Sappho's persona, casting Dido as an analogue of the *magistra amoris* in a context that sees Aeneas as her apprentice in matters of love.

The experience of love, with its concomitant turmoil, is textualised in the Dido episode as the result of a triangulation taking place in a vividly constructed communicative situation, where a duo stands in the foreground, to become the object of admiration on the part of a silent observer. The patterning that joins together Aeneas and Ascanius (i.e. Cupid in disguise) at the end of Book 1, sitting close by in a pose that suggests close affection, as the focal point of Dido's gaze and increasing involvement, is a sophisticated recasting of the scenario of Sappho's Fr. 31 LP. The mediating link is of course Catullus 51, which played a pivotal role in paving the way for later Augustan poets to engage with Greek lyric.[39] Virgil's allusion seems to channel a typically Hellenistic twist, insofar as Venus and Cupid are directly involved as *dramatis personae* in the *Aeneid*, and no longer invoked as sources of help, as in Sappho's Fr. 1 LP, in which Venus is entreated as an operating power in the name of the help she has provided in the past. Halfway between a conflation and follow-up of Sappho's lines, Virgil's adaptation offers the textual conditions for the divine assistance to materialise in the present tense of the narrative action, by playing an active, albeit destructive, role in triggering the love entanglement.

This last example illustrates how a lyric tradition encoding homoerotic longing is reforged in a heterosexual context that features, nonetheless, the subjective experience of a female ego. A central aspect in this reconfiguration consists in the display of the same symptoms fitting the diagnosis of love sickness, as a consequence of an exposure to love that has mobilised both aural and visual perception.

In this multivalent role-playing, Dido and Aeneas are cast in roles as ἐρώμενος and ἐραστής that are inherent to the lyric homoerotic couple. Such a prismatic, interchangeable relationship, which has been just defined amongst four poles (Sappho-Dido-Solon-Aeneas) has radically new consequences for our own understanding of the concepts of masculinity and femininity in the poem. The exchange of prerogatives between masters and pupils, supported by engagement with lyric models, creates an ongoing optical illusion, by virtue of which the notions of male and female end up being interchangeable in the poem.

---

39 Yatromanolakis 2007.

This reprocessing of Greek lyric features has unprecedented consequences for the ways that define, and in which we perceive, as readers today, the gender roles in their relationship. The question of gender in the *Aeneid* can thus be reset into a new framework, in which prerogatives become shifting and negotiable, far from complying with the stereotypical boundaries male vs. female, which have shaped across the centuries our reception of Dido and Aeneas as irreducibly opposite.

The banquet scene qualifies as a moment in which Virgil opts for a re-engagement with, and reworking of, the sympotic poetic discourse. Love and poetry between Aeneas and Dido seem to go hand in hand, and indeed to flow from the same spring, within a precisely defined, as well as highly formalised setting, that is, the context of the convivial elite gathering.

By combining the lyric mode with an epic framework, the *Aeneid* qualifies, once again, as a work that questions the boundaries of the epic genre, while continuing to challenge our most established assumptions as scholars and readers.

Conclusion

The preliminary evidence presented above points to the existence of a further implied meaning in the *Aeneid*, which unfolds in adherence to the framework of sympotic poetry in the Greek lyric tradition.

These realignments extend beyond the first third of the *Aeneid* and serve the purpose of illuminating the role that occasionality plays, if and when textualized, in Virgil's lines. Commensality and its implications in the convivial scenes of the *Aeneid* is an aspect on which scholarship has remained relatively silent, to my knowledge, so far. The acknowledgement of a sympotic framework at the beginning of the *Aeneid* has repercussions well after the portions of text in which this framework first appears. Further on, the reader encounters aspects that are characteristics not only of the epic genre, but also of the Greek sympotic domain: e.g. key tropes connected to the sphere of hospitality or to the setting of ritual gatherings, such as exchange of gifts and reciprocal praise. In one compelling case, these elements provide the background, as well as the framework, of a narrative enunciation. In Book 8, the local king Evander welcomes the Trojans at Pallanteum on a day of national festivity, which is celebrated with the ritual recounting of the tale of Hercules and Cacus. Once again, as in the Dido episode, conviviality paves the way for a narrative incursion into the past. (Tangentially, it should be noticed that this time the argument seems to offer further support to the idea of a homoerotic attachment later to develop between Aeneas and Pallas, which has been put forward as an implicit dimension embedded, if only subliminally, in Virgil's text).[40] As long since recognised, each of the episodes displayed in the *Aeneid* is crucial to the very structure of the work on a general narrative level. Hence, the necessity of an examination of their engagement with Greek lyric poetry, which can lead to an even more comprehensive evaluation of the poem as whole. Based on a syncretism of topoi, motifs and semantic chains between two parallel traditions, i.e. the epic and the lyric, the *Aeneid* has contributed to channelling, through the textual medium, notions of affection and desire that were unparalleled, up to that moment, and destined to shape the imagery of Western writers and readers alike for centuries to come.[41]

This chapter has pointed to some of the interpretive gains that can be derived from the acknowledgment of a sympotic framework in *Aeneid* 1–4. Preliminary results of these initial examinations of Virgil's poem have shed light on a certain number of specific texts of relevance within the corpus of Greek lyric poetry.

As demonstrated, the literary constraints and reading expectations that the acknowledgement of this lyric patterning assumes, filter pervasively through the fabric of Virgil's text, revolving around the domain of a first-person expression of a subjective viewpoint on a likely subjective experience.

Concomitantly, the contribution has added to the issue of the poem's literary pedigree, participating in a scholarly debate organically dominated, as it was and still partly is, by the values of heroic epic and, consequently, by the Homeric model. By establishing how characterisations and the significance of central figures in the *Aeneid* emerge in the apparent clash between the ethos of the epic genre and the ethos of the lyric genre, this paper hopefully adds a 'further voice' to the scholarly chorus claiming that 'Homer is not the first and only one'. Examinations carried out in this chapter point to a constellation of correspondences between Greek lyric poetry and the opening section of the *Aeneid*. These connections include a number of textual tropes (rhetorical, grammatical and conceptual relations), but also plot patterns that are not congruous with, or explainable on the basis of, the Homeric model alone. This cluster of elements has been readdressed from the so far unexplored perspective provided by the occasional nature and pragmatic setting of the passages in question. On the basis of these criteria, the first-person tale of Aeneas can be read, for example, as an illustration of an

---

40 The first proponent of this reading has been Putnam (1985, 1995 repr.). Amongst the critics who have responded sceptically to this argument, Harrison (1991) emphasises the quasi-filial relation linking Aeneas to Pallas, denying the possibility of any underlying erotic implication.
41 On this see, amongst the others, Kallendorf 2015, Thomas 1999; 2001, Cox 2011, Grandsen 1996.

epic appropriation of the sympotic poetic tradition. Once acknowledged, the lyric character of Aeneas' narrative points to early Greek lyric poetry as its implied model. When viewed in this light, Books 1–4 of the *Aeneid* can be seen as a sympotic unit, the result of a process of intergeneric osmosis that leaves the characters suspended, as they are, between private and public – one may want to say between lyric and epic, borrowing from the jargon of literary genres.

As argued, there is ground to support the hypothesis that the recasting of Greek lyric units into the *Aeneid*'s hexameters goes well beyond the instances so far highlighted. A reappraisal against the background of Greek lyric models leads to unprecedented consequences for our understanding of the poem as a whole. This chapter also supports the broader argument that links the Roman conception of heterosexual love to Greek homoerotic precedents. In this respect, it has offered supplementary evidence for a complex and entwined relationship between two poetic traditions that, albeit apparently opposed and concurrent, share nonetheless common ground in their foundational and conceptual aspects. What becomes of crucial importance in resetting the boundaries of genres and gender in the *Aeneid*, is that the lyric tradition coming to prominence here is the expression of homoerotic approaches to sexuality. This model has potential for debunking the strictly heteroerotic Homeric tradition. In contrast with mainstream interpretations, the core argument offered here corroborates the scholarly trend to the 'heterosexual tradition of homoerotic poetry', subscribing to the recognition of a conversion in terms of gender tropes that entailed, among its consequences, a shift from homoerotic to heterosexual frames. Wherefore, the use of a new lens is urged: whenever non-conjugal love becomes a source of anguish and misery, as quintessentially in, though not limited to, Latin poetry, the question legitimately arises whether Greek homoerotic poetry is 'around the corner', so to speak. Pointing to a model as yet under-investigated in its totality, this new approach provides an unprecedented key to understanding the compelling ways in which the clash between genre and gender is textualized in Graeco-Roman literature. Taken as a whole, this study has provided fresh insight into one of the most frequently analysed (and adapted) works in Western literature, by contributing to a direction of scholarship challenging assumptions and stereotypes in literary criticism, both Virgilian and more broadly Classical.[42]

---

[42] I offer my deepest thanks first to Thea Selliaas Thorsen, for constantly encouraging me to follow this direction of research. I am also most grateful to Stephen Harrison, Nicola Gardini and Enrico Emanuele Prodi for providing me with invaluable advice and reading suggestions at different moments of the writing, as well as with crucial editorial comments.

Alison Keith
Philodemus and the Augustan Poets

The 'Augustan' Latin poets wrote over the course of the long span of the first Roman emperor's reign and in a variety of different genres: two died within a decade of Augustus' receipt of his honorific cognomen, conferred by a vote of the Senate on 13 January 27 BCE (Virgil and Tibullus, both d. 19 BCE), and a third soon after (Propertius, d. after 16 BCE). Horace lingered until 8 BCE, the year when his friend and patron Maecenas (another Augustan poet, whose work survives only in exiguous fragments) predeceased him. Only Ovid (d. 16/17 CE) outlived the irascible prince (d. 14 CE). Other potential candidates for discussion here – Gallus, Varius, and the rest of the poets mentioned by the extant Augustans – are known to us almost solely by name since their poetry has largely been lost. This chapter focuses on the amatory poetry of Horace, Propertius and Ovid, in an investigation of the reception in Augustan lyric and elegy of the erotic epigrams of their elder contemporary Philodemus, Syrian epigrammatist and Epicurean teacher (b. *c.* 110 BCE; d. before 30 BCE).

Philodemus lived and taught on the Bay of Naples from about 70 BCE to the end of his life, apparently in the patronage of Julius Caesar's father-in-law, L. Calpurnius Piso Caesoninus (cf. *Epigr.* 27 Sider [= *Anth. Pal.* 11.44 = 23 GP]).[1] Literary and documentary evidence confirms his personal acquaintance with Virgil, and the connection suggests that he also knew Maecenas, Augustus' friend and a generous patron of the arts, and the poet Horace, a long-time student of Epicurean philosophy (Hor. *Sat.* 1.5.39–44, 1.6.54–62).[2] Indeed, the first Greek amatory poet

---

1 On Philodemus' life and epigrams, see Sider 1997, from which I cite text and translation of the epigrams.
2 Ongoing excavations at the Villa of the Papyri in Herculaneum have yielded over 1100 charred papyrus rolls, of which Philodemus is the author of the greatest number. Three papyrus fragments are of particular interest to students of Virgil, because they document him as one of the four addressees of at least three of the ten books in Philodemus' *On Vices* (*PHerc.* 253 fr. 12.4, title unknown; *PHerc.* 1082.11.3, 'On Flattery'; *PHerc. Paris* 2, 'On Calumny'). Dated to the middle of the first century BCE, the books consistently address the four friends in the same order (*PHerc. Paris* 2): ὦ Πλώτιε καὶ Οὐά|ρ[ι]ε καὶ Οὐεργ[ί]λιε καὶ Κοιντ[ί]λιε. ('O Plotius and Varius, Virgil and Quintilius'.) On the subscriptions, see Gigante/Capasso 1989, Gigante 2004, 92–5, Blank 2019. On Horace's play with the order of the addressees in Philodemus' subscriptions, see Armstrong 2014, 98–100.

named in Horace's oeuvre is Philodemus, who is cited at the end of *Sermones* 1.2, published *c.* 35 BCE (*Sat.* 1.2.116–24):³

>   ... tument tibi cum inguina, num si
> ancilla aut uerna est praesto puer, impetus in quem
> continuo fiat, malis tentigine rumpi?
> non ego: namque parabilem amo Venerem facilemque.
> illam 'post paulo', 'sed pluris', 'si exierit uir'   120
> Gallis, hanc Philodemus ait sibi quae neque magno
> stet pretio neque cunctetur cum est iussa uenire.
> candida rectaque sit, munda hactenus ut neque longa
> nec magis alba uelit quam dat natura uideri.

> When your loins swell, if a maid or a house-born slave-boy is present on whom an immediate assault can be made, would you prefer to burst with lust? Not me: for I like sex ready and easy. That girl who says 'a little later', 'but for more money', 'if my husband's gone out' – Philodemus says she's for the Galli; he says his type is the kind who doesn't cost a great price, nor delay when she's bidden to come. Let her have a good complexion, good posture, and be neat but without wanting to seem taller or paler than nature granted her.

The utilitarian view of sex here attributed to Philodemus is consistent not only with his reputation as a prominent teacher of Epicurean philosophy on the Bay of Naples from 70 – 40 BCE (Cic. *Fin.* 2.119), but also with Horace's predilection for articulating Epicurean ethical positions in his poetry (c.f., e.g., *Epist.* 1.4.12–16).⁴ While it may be counter-intuitive to find popular poetic expression of such a utilitarian view of sex as Horace here credits to Philodemus, Cicero bears witness in the mid-50s BCE to the vogue that Philodemus' epigrams enjoyed at Rome (Cic. *Pis.* 70):⁵

> Est autem hic de quo loquor non philosophia solum sed etiam ceteris studiis quae fere ceteros Epicureos neglegere dicunt perpolitus; poema porro facit ita festiuum, ita concinnum, ita elegans, nihil ut fieri possit argutius... Rogatus inuitatus coactus ita multa ad istum de isto quoque scripsit ut omnis hominis libidines, omnia stupra, omnia cenarum genera conuiuiorumque, adulteria denique eius delicatissimis uersibus expresserit...

---

3 I cite the text of Horace from Klingner 1982; translations are my own unless otherwise indicated. On *Sat.* 1.2, see Fraenkel 1957, 78–86, Rudd 1966, 9–35, Baldwin 1970, Lefèvre 1975, Brown 1993, 100–14, Gigante 1993, Gibson 2007, 19–42, Gowers 2012, 86–118, Armstrong 2014, 119–23, Yona 2018, 106–19.

4 On Horace's Epicureanism, see Fraenkel 1957, 254–6, 319–20, Nisbet/Hubbard 1970, 376–7. On Epicurean philosophy in Horace's *Sermones*, see Armstrong 2014, Yona 2018.

5 I cite the text of *In Pisonem* from Nisbet 1961; the translation that of Sider 1997. On this passage, cf. Asconius *ad loc.*; and see further Nisbet 1961, appendices 3 and 4, Gigante 1983, 35–53, Sider 1997, 5–18.

Now the Greek of whom I speak is polished not only in philosophy but also in other accomplishments which Epicureans are said commonly to neglect; he furthermore composes poetry so witty, neat, and elegant, that nothing could be cleverer... In response to request, invitation, pressure, he wrote reams of verse to Piso and about Piso, sketching to the life in lines of perfect finish all his lusts and immoralities, all his varied dinners and banquets, all his adulteries...

In their own erotic verses, Horace, Propertius and Ovid reveal many debts to the amatory epigrams composed by Philodemus and here denounced by Cicero.

Horace

Even before Horace names Philodemus at the end of *Sermones* 1.2, he has earlier alluded to one of his amatory epigrams (*Sat.* 1.2.90–4):

> ... ne corporis optima Lyncei   90
> contemplere oculis, Hypsaea caecior illa,
> quae mala sunt, spectes. 'o crus, o bracchia' uerum
> depugis, nasuta, breui latere ac pede longo est.

Do not contemplate the perfections of the body with the eyes of Lynceus, while turning a blinder eye on the blemishes than Hypsaea. 'O what a leg! O what arms!' But she is thin in the buttocks, has a large nose, a short waist and huge foot.

The breathless praise of a woman's physical features that Horace parodies in line 92 (*o crus, o bracchia*) is derived from Philodemus' *Epigram* 12 Sider (= *Anth. Pal.* 5.132 = 12 GP):[6]

> ὦ ποδός, ὦ κνήμης, ὦ τῶν (ἀπόλωλα δικαίως)
>   μηρῶν, ὦ γλουτῶν, ὦ κτενός, ὦ λαγόνων,
> ὦ ὤμοιν, ὦ μαστῶν, ὦ τοῦ ῥαδινοῖο τραχήλου,
>   ὦ χειρῶν, ὦ ταῶν (μαίνομαι) ὀμματίων,
> ὦ κακοτεχνοτάτου κινήματος, ὦ περιάλλων
>   γλωττισμῶν, ὦ τῶν (θῦέ με) φωναρίων·
> εἰ δ' Ὀπικὴ καὶ Φλῶρα καὶ οὐκ ᾄδουσα τὰ Σαπφοῦς,
>   καὶ Περσεὺς Ἰνδῆς ἠράσατ' Ἀνδρομέδης.

---

[6] On Horace's allusion to *Anth. Pal.* 5.132 (= Phld. *Epigr.* 12 Sider) here, see Wright 1921, 168, Cautadella 1950, Gigante 1993, Hunter 2006, 113–14.

O foot, O leg, O (I'm done for) those thighs, O buttocks, O bush, O flanks, O shoulders, O breasts, O delicate neck, O hands, O (madness!) those eyes, O wickedly skilful walk, O fabulous kisses, O (slay me!) her speech. But if Flora is Oscan and does not sing Sappho's verses, Perseus too fell in love with Indian Andromeda.

Scholars have noted the contradiction between the erotic obsession enunciated in Philodemus' carnal epigram detailing the physical attributes of his Oscan mistress Flora and the Epicurean view of love that Horace ascribes to him in the second satire (quoted above, *Sat.* 1.2.121–2).[7] Indeed Sider (1997, 104) draws attention to 'the dynamic point of the poem' precisely as its enactment of 'the great difficulty if not impossibility of a man's maintaining his *sangfroid* – perhaps more specifically his Epicurean *ataraxia* – in the contemplation of a beautiful woman'. Horace thereby juxtaposes Philodemus' potentially contradictory teaching of Epicurean principle about erotic ethics with his epigrammatic expression of erotic obsession to piquant effect.

It has also been suggested that in the lines where Horace names Philodemus and describes the prevarications of the expensive *meretrix* and the adulterous *matrona* (quoted above, *Sat.* 1.2.120), he quotes from a third epigram by Philodemus, no longer extant.[8] Without evidence the suggestion cannot be confirmed, but other scholars have drawn attention to the similarity of the sentiment expressed in these lines (*Sat.* 1.2.121–2) to that of yet another epigram by Philodemus (*Epigr.* 22 Sider = *Anth. Pal.* 5.126 = 25 GP):[9]

> πέντε δίδωσιν ἑνὸς τῇ δεῖνα ὁ δεῖνα τάλαντα
>   καὶ βινεῖ φρίσσων καί, μὰ τόν, οὐδὲ καλήν·
> πέντε δ' ἐγὼ δραχμὰς τῶν δώδεκα Λυσιανάσσῃ,
>   καὶ βινῶ πρὸς τῷ κρείσσονα καὶ φανερῶς.
> Πάντως ἤτοι ἐγὼ φρένας οὐκ ἔχω ἢ τό γε λοιπὸν
>   τοὺς κείνου πελέκει διῒ διδύμους ἀφελεῖν.

Mr. X gives Mrs. Y five talents for one favor, and he screws, shivering with fear, one who is, what's more, God knows, no beauty. I give five – drachmas – to Lysianassa for the twelve favours, and what's more, I screw a finer woman, and openly. Assuredly, either I'm crazy or, after all this, he should have his balls cut off with a knife.

The suggestion that this epigram is also a model for Horace, at this point in the satire, is especially appealing because the Latin poet continues with the reflection that

---

[7] Sider 1997, 104, Harrison 2007, 94.
[8] Cautadella 1950, Gigante 1993, Hunter 2006, 113–14.
[9] Wright 1921, Yona 2018, 115–16.

such a woman (i.e., the prostitute implied by Horace's verb *stet* in line 122)¹⁰ will not occasion the risk of surprise by an angry husband (Hor. *Sat.* 1.2.125–7):

> haec ubi supposuit dextro corpus mihi laeuom
> Ilia et Egeria est; do nomen quodlibet illi.
> Nec uereor, ne, dum futuo, uir rure recurrat ...

> This woman, when she has placed her left side beneath my right, is an Ilia and Egeria to me; I give her any name I want. Nor do I fear lest, while I'm fucking, her husband return from the countryside

In addition to the thematic overlap between Horaces' lines and Philodemus' epigram 22 Sider, commentators point to lexical overlap, in the low register of both poets' descriptions of sex (βινεῖ, Phld. *Epigr.* 22.2; βινῶ, 22.4; *futuo*, Hor. *Sat.* 1.2.127), as well as to the speakers' avoidance of the fear engendered by an adulterous relationship (φρίσσων, Phld. *Epigr.* 22.2; *uereor*, Hor. *Sat.* 1.2.127) in the Epicurean choice of sex with a prostitute.

Richard Hunter (2006, 113–14) has also observed that by naming Philodemus in this context, Horace activates the etymology of his model's name – 'lover of the people' – in order 'to reinforce the message' of his satire. In this, he also follows the example of Philodemus, who does the same in one of his other epigrams (Phld. *Epigr.* 10 Sider = *Anth. Pal.* 5.115 = 6 GP):

> ἠράσθην Δημοῦς Παφίης γένος· οὐ μέγα θαῦμα·
>   καὶ Σαμίης Δημοῦς δεύτερον· οὐχὶ μέγα·
> καὶ πάλιν Ὑσιακῆς Δημοῦς τρίτον· οὐκέτι ταῦτα
>   παίγνια· καὶ Δημοῦς τέτρατον Ἀργολίδος.
> Αὐταί που Μοῖραί με κατωνόμασαν Φιλόδημον,
>   ὡς αἰεὶ Δημοῦς θερμὸς ἔχοι με πόθος.

> I fell in love with Demo from Paphos; no great surprise. And, second, with Demo from Samos; no big deal. And again, and third, with Demo from Hysiai—this is no longer a joke— and fourth with Demo from Argos. It must have been the Moirai themselves who named me Philo-demos, so that burning passion for a Demo would always take hold of me.

Sider (1997, 99) comments on the expectation engendered by the name *Demo* (< Greek δῆμος, the 'common people') that a woman so named will sleep with

---

10 Cf. Hor. *Sat.* 1.2.30, *olenti in fornice stantem* [sc. *meretricem*]. For *sto* in the sense of 'stand at the price of', i.e. verging on *prosto*, 'stand forth for sale', see *OLD* s.v. 23; cf. Gowers 2012, 115, *ad* Hor. *Sat.* 1.2.122.

many men,[11] and it has been recognized that the Latin elegists deploy the name *Lais* (from Greek λαός, 'men, people') to similar effect.[12] Philodemus' joke that he has slept with many Demos ups the ante, however, not only by turning the etymological tables from the prostitute's name to his own, but also by scoring an Epicurean philosophical point.[13]

Such a concentrated nexus of allusions to Philodemus' amatory epigrams as we find here at the end of *Sermones* 1.2 underlines the impact on Horace not only of his elder contemporary's famous epigrams but also of his philosophical teaching, and already in the Latin poet's own earliest poetic undertakings. Nor should it be surprising that, after sounding Philodemus' poetic and philosophical importance to his own literary and ethical designs so insistently here at the outset of his first book of *Sermones*, Horace repeatedly draws on Philodemus' epigrams and Epicurean wisdom in his articulation of lyric themes in the *Carmina* of the 20s BCE, begun perhaps a decade after Philodemus' death. Indeed, we can see Horace's continuing dialogue with Philodemus' erotic ideals, inflected through his Epicurean philosophical commitments, in an ode addressed to an Albius (generally agreed to be the elegist Tibullus)[14] towards the end of the first book of his *Carmina* (*Carm.* 1.33):

> Albi, ne doleas plus nimio memor
> immitis Glycerae neu miserabilis
> decantes elegos, cur tibi iunior
>   laesa praeniteat fide,
> insignem tenui fronte Lycorida
> Cyri torret amor, Cyrus in asperam
> declinat Pholoen; sed prius Apulis
>   iungentur capreae lupis,
> quam turpi Pholoe peccet adultero.
> Sic uisum Veneri, cui placet inparis
> formas atque animos sub iuga aenea
>   saeuo mittere cum ioco.
> Ipsum me melior cum peteret Venus,
> grata detinuit compede Myrtale
> libertina, fretis acrior Hadriae
>   curuantis Calabros sinus.

---

11 Sider (1997, 99) cites Meleager (*Anth. Pal.* 5.197, 172, 173) and Antipater (*Anth. Pal.* 6.175), as well as Philodemus (*Anth. Pal.* 12.173), for the same joke on the meaning of Demo; and (*id.*, 100) Archilochus 207W2, for the play on δῆμος as 'prostitute'.
12 Hinds 1987b, 5; cf. Prop. 2.6.1–2, Ov. *Am.* 1.5.12 (*multis Lais amata uiris*).
13 Sider 1997, 99.
14 Nisbet/Hubbard 1970, 368; *contra* Mayer 2012, 201–2.

Albius, do not indulge in excessive grief, remembering harsh Glycera, nor persistently utter mournful lamentations because she has broken her faith and prefers a younger lover to you. A passion for Cyrus inspires Lycoris, remarkable for her slender forehead; but Cyrus turns away towards harsh Pholoe; yet she-goats will be united with Apulian wolves before Pholoe will stoop to so base a lover. Thus it has seemed good to Venus, who delights in cruel mirth, to subject to her bronze yoke ill-matched forms and minds. When a more eligible beauty wooed me, the freedwoman Myrtale, more passionate than the waves of the Adriatic, which forms the Calabrian bays, entangled me with pleasing fetters.

The poem rehearses amatory sentiments familiar from Sappho (1.21–4), Moschus (6), and Callimachus (*Epigr.* 31.5–6),[15] but ostentatiously rejected by Epicurus and his followers, including Philodemus in his epigrams 10, 12, and 22 Sider (all quoted above), and, as we have seen, by the younger poet of *Sermones* 1.2. Horace's rejection of Tibullan elegy in the *Odes* thus seems to be predicated, at least in part, on its unEpicurean obsession with a specific love-object – we may compare Lucretius' similar disdain for the obsessive lover in his diatribe against love at the end of the fourth book of *De Rerum Natura* (4.1030–287). The lyric poet's espousal at the ode's conclusion of a relationship with a woman of lower status, the freedwoman Myrtale, coheres not only with Epicurean dogma but also with his own poetic past.

But it is in the second book of *Carmina* that Horace develops most fully the Epicurean profile of his lyric *persona*, and he does so precisely by drawing on Philodemus' erotic epigrams. In *Carmen* 2.4, for example, Horace adapts amatory material from a variety of Philodemean models (*Carm.* 2.4):[16]

> Ne sit ancillae tibi amor pudori,
> Xanthis Phoceu, prius insolentem
> serua Briseis niueo colore
>   mouit Achillem;
> mouit Aiacem Telamone natum   5
> forma captiuae dominum Tecmessae;
> arsit Atrides medio in triumpho
>   uirgine rapta,
> barbarae postquam cecidere turmae
> Thessalo uictore et ademptus Hector   10
> tradidit fessis leuiora tolli
>   Pergama Grais.
> Nescias an te generum beati
> Phyllidis flauae decorent parentes :

---

15 Nisbet/Hubbard 1970, 369–70.
16 On *Carm.* 2.4, see Cairns 1977, Nisbet/Hubbard 1978, 66–77, Gagliardi 1995, Höschele 2011, 27–9, Kovacs 2015, Harrison 2017, 74–82.

regium certe genus et penates   15
    maeret iniquos.
crede non illam tibi de scelesta
plebe dilectam, neque sic fidelem,
sic lucro auersam potuisse nasci
    matre pudenda.   20
bracchia et uoltum teretesque suras
integer laudo: fuge suspicari,
cuius octauum trepidauit aetas
    claudere lustrum.

Lest love for a lady's maid shame you, Xanthias Phoceus, [let me remind you that] the slave Briseis once charmed arrogant Achilles with her snow white complexion; captive Tecmessa's beauty charmed her master, Telamon's son, Ajax; the son of Atreus blazed, in the midst of his triumph, with love for the ravished maiden, Cassandra, after the barbarian troops fell before the Thessalian conqueror, and the loss of Hector left Pergamum the easier to plunder for the exhausted Greeks. You cannot know whether blonde Phyllis' noble parents would be an honour to you as their son-in-law: unquestionably of royal lineage, she grieves at the unkindness of her household gods. Believe that she has not been singled out by you from the worthless crowd, nor that one so loyal, so unmercenary could be born of a disreputable mother. Heart-whole, I praise her arms and face and well-turned ankles: flee any suspicion of one whose age is on the verge of closing his fortieth year.

Nisbet and Hubbard note, in connection with *niueo colore* in line 3, that the adjective 'is pointed after *serua*, as one expects slaves to have a dusky complexion' and that therefore 'in love a dark skin sometimes needed apology', and among other examples of epigrammatists apologizing for a dark-complexioned love they cite Philodemus' *Anth. Pal.* 5.121.1–2 (Phld. *Epigr.* 17 Sider = 8 GP):

μικκὴ καὶ μελανεῦσα Φιλαίνιον, ἀλλὰ σελίνων
    οὐλοτέρη καὶ μνοῦ χρῶτα τερεινοτέρη
καὶ κεστοῦ φωνεῦσα μαγώτερα καὶ παρέχουσα
    πάντα καὶ αἰτῆσαι πολλάκι φειδομένη.
Τοιαύτην στέργοιμι Φιλαίνιον ἄχρις ἂν εὕρω   5
    ἄλλην, ὦ χρθσέη Κύπρι, τελειοτέρην.

Small and dark is Philainion, but with hair curlier than celery and skin tenderer than down; and with a voice sexier than Aphrodite's she offers her all, often forgetting to set a price. May I love such a Philainion until, golden Aphrodite, I find another, more perfect one.

We may compare as well Andromeda in the last line of Philodemus' *Epigram* 12 Sider (cited above, 12.8). Of course, this is hardly unique either to Philodemus or to Greek epigram,[17] but taken in conjunction with the intertextual matrix of other Philodemean erotic echoes that close the ode, the suggestion grows more compelling. For in the final stanza, Horace's praise of Phyllis' 'arms, face and well-turned ankles' (*bracchia et uoltum teretesque suras*, *Carm.* 2.4.21) again recalls Philodemus' *Epigram* 12 Sider, though as in *Sermones* 1.2 Horace's restrained quotation of the epigram contrasts with what Nisbet and Hubbard characterize as the 'febrile exclamations' of the Greek epigrammatist.[18]

Also Philodemean in flavour is the implication of Horace's swift aging in the verb *trepidauit* (*Carm.* 2.4.23), which Nisbet and Hubbard translate as 'has hustled', and of which they observe that 'the word suggests fret as well as speed'.[19] Taking into account the numerous other reminiscences of Philodemus in *Carm.* 2.4, they suggest that Horace here recalls Philodemus' *Epigram* 5.3–4 Sider (*Anth. Pal.* 5.112 = 18 GP):

ἠράσθην. τίς δ'οὐχί; κεκώμακα. τί δ' ἀμύητος
κώμων; ἀλλ' ἐμάνην ἐκ τίνος; Οὐχὶ θεοῦ;
ἐρρίφθω, πολιὴ γὰρ ἐπείγεται ἀντὶ μελαίνης
θρὶξ ἤδη, συνετῆς ἄγγελος ἡλικίης.
καὶ παίζειν ὅτε καιρός, ἐπαίξαμεν· ἡνίκα καὶ νῦν   5
οὐκέτι, λωϊτέρης φροντίδος ἁψόμεθα.

I fell in love. Who hasn't? I revelled. Who isn't an initiate of revels? But whose fault is it I went mad? A god's, isn't it? Let it go, for already grey hair rushes in to take the place of black— grey hair, the proclaimer of the age of wisdom. And when it was right to play, we played; and since it is right no longer, we shall lay hold of loftier thoughts.

This is an attractive suggestion, since the final lines of the ode rework in addition the opening of a fourth Philodemean epigram, in which Philodemus 'equates the end of a phase in his life with the end of a paragraph on a papyrus scroll'[20] (Phld. *Epigr.* 4 Sider = *Anth. Pal.* 11.41.1 = 17 GP):

---

17 Cf. Lucr. 4.1160, *nigra melichrus est*; Verg. *Ecl.* 2.16–18, 10.38–9, the latter spoken in the voice of the neoteric elegist Gallus: *quid tum, si fuscus Amyntas; / sed nigrae uiolae sunt et uaccinia nigra*.
18 On Horace's debt to Philodemus' epigram *Anth. Pal.* 5.132 in *Carm.* 2.4, see Nisbet/Hubbard 1978, 67–8, quotation at 68; cf. Harrison 2017, 75–6 and 81–2. On Philodemus' epigram see, in addition to Sider 1997, 72–8, Griffiths 1970 and Giangrande 1973.
19 Nisbet/Hubbard 1978, 76; cf. Harrison (2017, 82), who translates the verb 'has hastened'.
20 Höschele 2011, 29. Griffiths 1970, 37–8, followed by Nisbet/Hubbard 1978, 77, has interpreted the epigram as closural; cf. Sider 1997, 74.

ἑπτὰ τριηκόντεσσιν ἐπέρχονται λυκάβαντες,
  ἤδη μοι βιότου σχιζόμεναι σελίδες·
ἤδη καὶ λευκαί με κατασπείρουσιν ἔθειραι,
  Ξανθίππη, συνετῆς ἄγγελοι ἡλικίης,
ἀλλ' ἔτι μοι ψαλμός τε λάλος κῶμοί τε μέλονται   5
  καὶ πῦρ ἀπλήστῳ τύφετ' ἐνὶ κραδίῃ·
αὐτὴν ἀλλὰ τάχιστα κορωνίδα γράψατε, Μοῦσαι,
  ταύτης ἡμετέρης, δεσπότιδες, μανίης.

Seven years are coming up on thirty; papyrus columns of my life now being torn off; now too, Xanthippe, white hairs besprinkle me, announcing the age of intelligence; but the harp's voice and revels are still a concern to me, and a fire smoulders in my insatiable heart. Inscribe her immediately as the koronis, Mistress Muses, of this my madness.

Nisbet and Hubbard see Horace representing 'the mannered learning of [Philodemus'] archaic λυκάβαντες' (*Epigr.* 4.1 Sider) 'by the solemn reference to [Roman] *lustra*', here eight censorial *quinquennia*, which bring Horace to the age of 40. Horace may even gesture towards the paramount importance of Philodemean models for this ode in the etymologizing collocation *plebe dilectam* at the beginning of line 18, which Regina Höschele has interpreted as a Latin gloss on the name of Philodemus, like the etymological play on his name activated by Horace, in *Sermones* 1.2.121–2, or, indeed, by Philodemus himself, in *Epigram* 10.5–6 Sider.[21]

Horace continues to draw on Philodemean erotics in the poem that follows (*Carm.* 2.5), which reworks Philodemus' *Epigram* 16 Sider (*Anth. Pal.* 5.124 = 10 GP). Several generations of critics have well discussed Horace's aemulative program in this ode.[22] From his first word (*nondum*) he signals his debt to Philodemus' epigram, which similarly begins with οὔπω, and both poems then continue, in their openings, with parallel structures (*nondum*, Hor. *Carm.* 2.5.2; οὐδὲ, Phld. *Epigr.* 16.1 Sider). Both poems characterize the onset of puberty in the erotic object by reference to the purple colour of ripe grapes (Hor. *C.* 2.5.9–12; Phld. *Epigr.* 16.1–2), while the Erotes' swift arrows (Phld. *Epigr.* 16.3 Sider) will recur a few poems later in Horace's second lyric book, in the form of a fierce Cupid likewise cruelly sharpening his arrows on a bloody whetstone (*Carm.* 2.8.13–16: *ridet hoc, inquam, Venus ipsa, rident / simplices Nymphae ferus et Cupido / semper ardentis acuens sagittas / cote cruenta*, 'Venus herself, I say, smiles at this; the good-natured Nymphs smile, and fierce Cupid, constantly sharpening his burning arrows on a

---

[21] Höschele 2011, 28.
[22] On *Carm.* 2.5, see Nisbet/Hubbard 1978, 77–93, MacLeod 1983, 98–9, Sutherland 1997, Höschele 2011, Harrison 2017, 85.

blood-stained whetstone'). Moreover, as Höschele has observed (2011, 30), 'the movement from Horace's "not any more" (in *Carm.* 2.4) to Lalage's "not yet, but soon" (in *Carm.* 2.5)' echoes the movement of the two Philodemean epigrams evoked at the end and beginning, respectively, of the Latin poet's successive odes. Horace's intertextual juxtaposition of Philodemean epigrams draws a thematic connection between them, and, she suggests, may even reflect their relationship 'in the original edition of Philodemus' *epigrammata*, which Horace possibly had at his disposal'.[23]

Be that as it may, it is possible to draw together some firmer conclusions about Horace's debt to Philodemus' erotic epigrams before turning from Horace to Latin elegy. The brevity of Philodemus' epigrams is an especially significant model for Horace's short *Odes* 2.4 and 2.5, where we have seen that the epigrammatist's influence is particularly strong. As we have seen, moreover, Horace invokes Philodemus' epigrammatic erotics from the outset of his poetic career and, in so doing, he sketches his own amatory *persona* within the Epicurean ethical framework that David Sider and others have seen as a structural feature of so many of Philodemus' amatory epigrams. It is highly likely that Horace knew Philodemus personally, for he moved in literary and philosophical circles that overlapped with Philodemus' own; and linguistic, thematic, and ethical debts to Philodemus' philosophical writings, as well as to the full range of his epigrams, have been traced throughout his literary corpus by scholars from David Armstrong and Marcello Gigante to Kirk Freudenburg and Sergio Yona.[24] Horace's intertextual play with Philodemus' erotic epigrams in the *Odes* should be ascribed not only to his Epicurean commitments, moreover, but also to his interest in the work of his literary contemporaries, such as Varius and Virgil, who introduced him to Maecenas (Hor. *Sat.* 1.6.54–5); Quintilius, the astute critic of the *Ars poetica* (438–44); and Philodemus himself. This is a very different background, however, from that of Horace's younger contemporaries, the elegists Propertius, Tibullus and Ovid, to whom we now turn.

Propertius

Propertius' wide-ranging interest in Greek epigram has been well established by such scholars as Paolo Fedeli, Joan Booth and Francis Cairns, who have plotted

---

23 Höschele 2011, 30.
24 See, e.g., Armstrong 1993; 2004; 2014, Freudenburg 1993, 139–50, Gigante 1993, Yona 2018.

in detail his debts both general and specific to a variety of epigrammatists.[25] It is especially striking to find Propertius working with Philodemean epigram already in his first book of elegies, before his formal invitation to join Maecenas' broadly Epicurean circle of poets, his literary *clientela*.[26] Indeed, Propertius' interest in Hellenistic epigram is particularly evident in his first book, as we might expect from the programmatic allusion to an epigram by Meleager (*Anth. Pal.* 12.101) that opens his introductory elegy (Prop. 1.1.1–4).[27] Elegy 1.3 offers an especially appealing example of Propertius' dense intertextual engagement with Greek epigram, as he alludes to epigrams by Callimachus and Philodemus in the course of the poem's forty-six lines, drawing specifically on the latter in his description of the moonlight waking his sleeping mistress (Prop. 1.3.27–33):

> et quotiens raro duxti suspiria motu,
>   obstupui uano credulous auspicio,
> ne qua tibi insolitos portarent uisa timores,
>   neue quis inuitam cogeret esse suam :
> donec diuersas praecurrens luna fenestras,
>   luna moraturis sedula luminibus,
> compositos leuibus radiis patefecit ocellos.

And as often as you drew breath with a slight motion, I stood transfixed, believing the vain omen, lest some dreams brought you unaccustomed fears or someone compelled you to be his against your will: until the moon, the officious moon with her light disposed to linger, rushing by the open window, opened your sleeping eyes with her rays.

Propertius' dynamic moon does what Philodemus invites her Greek avatar Selene to do in *Epigram* 14 Sider (*Anth. Pal.* 5.123 = 9 GP):

> νυκτερινὴ δίκερως φιλοπάννυχε φαῖνε, Σελήνη,
>   φαῖνε δι' εὐτρήτων βαλλομένη θυρίδων·
> αὔγαζε χρυσέην Καλλίστιον. ἐς τὰ φιλεύντων
>   ἔργα κατοπτεύειν οὐ φθόνος ἀθανάτῃ.
> ὀλβίζεις καὶ τήνδε καὶ ἡμέας, οἶδα, Σελήνη·
>   καὶ γὰρ σὴν ψυχὴν ἔφλεγεν Ἐνδυμίων.

---

25 Cairns 1979, 2011; Fedeli 1980a; 1980b; 1985; 2005, Fedeli/Dimundo/Ceccarelli 2015, Booth 2001a; 2001b; 2011.
26 On Maecenas' Epicurean commitments, see André 1967, 15ff.; rejected by Lyne 1997, 114ff.; accepted (without enthusiasm) by Nisbet/Rudd 2004, 346–7; assumed by Cairns 2006, 295–319.
27 On Propertius' debt to Meleager in elegy 1.1, see Fedeli 1980a, 62–7, *ad loc.*, Booth 2001a, and Höschele 2011.

> Shine, o nocturnal bicornate lover of allnight revelry, Selene; pass through the latticed windows and shine. Illumine golden Kallistion. There is no ill-will directed towards your immortal self when you gaze down upon the actions of lovers. You count both her and me happy, I know, Selene; for your soul too was inflamed by Endymion.

The Latin elegist's description of the moon shining 'through the window' confirms the allusion to the Greek epigrammatist, while his moon's 'lingering light' evokes Philodemus' repeated request to Selene to 'illumine' his beloved in her rays (Prop. 1.3.31–2).[28]

Despite the Propertian lover's caution, his sleeping mistress awakens when the moon's rays shine through the window on to her face. The Latin elegist thus adapts the erotic context of Philodemus' epigram to the elegiac situation of the lover's return, in order to illustrate not the idealized beauty of the sleeping courtesan but the lover's cool reception by his angry mistress.[29] Propertius has therefore been seen as elaborating the static scenario of his epigrammatic model into a dynamic elegiac drama, expanding the vignette of the Philodemean original into the developing elegiac plot of his first collection and marking his generic debt to epigram.[30] In some respects, moreover, he has reversed the postulates of Philodemus' epigram: while both the Philodemean and Propertian lovers have come for sex and admire their sleeping mistresses by the light of the moon as a prelude to the erotic action, Philodemus' epigram ends before the sex begins while Cynthia's awakening by the moonlight derails the Propertian lover's plans as his *puella* reproaches him for coming late to her, from another woman's bed (Prop. 1.3.34–46). Cynthia's angry denunciation of her unfaithful lover implies her metatextual familiarity with the Philodemean epigram, as if Propertius were coming to her from Kallistion's bed, turning Propertius' literary admiration for Philodemus' Kallistion into his admiration for a rival *puella*.

Both David Sider and Paolo Fedeli, in his commentary on Propertius' second book of elegies, also see this Philodemean epigram (14 Sider) underlying Propertius' reference to the naked lovemaking of Endymion and Selene in a later Propertian elegy (Prop. 2.15.15–16): *nudus et Endymion Phoebi cepisse sororem / dicitur et nudae concubuisse deae* ('Nude Endymion is said to have captivated Phoebus' sister, and to have lain with the nude goddess'). Indeed, it is tempting to interpret

---

[28] On the allusion, see Fedeli 1980a, 32 *ad* Prop. 1.3.31–3, Sider 1997, 113–14, Booth 2001b; 2011.
[29] For a complementary assessment of the effect of reading Propertius through Philodemus, and vice versa, see Booth 2001b.
[30] On the relationship of Latin elegy to Hellenistic epigram, see Ramsby 2007, Keith 2011a, Piazzi 2013, 226–7. On the relationship of elegy to new comedy, see James 2012a.

the Alexandrian footnote *dicitur* (16) as referring specifically to Philodemus' contemporary epigram, since there are several references to the pair's love affair preserved in the *Palatine Anthology*.³¹ But the main impetus for seeing Propertius as reworking Philodemean erotics in this elegy surely lies in the makarismos of its opening couplets (Prop. 2.15.1–4, 9–10):

> O me felicem! O nox mihi candida! Et o tu
>   lectule deliciis facte beate meis !
> Quam multa apposita narramus uerba lucerna,
>   quantaque sublato lumine rixa fuit! ...
> quam uario amplexu mutamus bracchia! Quantum
>   oscula sunt labris nostra morata tuis!   10

> Oh lucky me! Oh wonderful night for me! And oh you little bed made lucky by my delight! How many words did we speak by lamplight, and how great a lover's quarrel when we laid the light aside! ... What various embraces we exchanged! How long my kisses lingered on your lips!

Propertius audibly signals his debt to Philodemus' *Epigram* 12 Sider (quoted above), in the threefold repetition of '*o*' in his opening line, which recuperates Philodemus' threefold repetition of omega in his opening line.³² Propertius then moves on to anaphora of *quam* and *quanta* in the succeeding couplets (3–4, 9–10), and away from the unvarying repetition of omega that makes Philodemus' epigram so memorable. The allusion is nonetheless secure, because in addition to the audible imitation of the makarismos in the opening couplet, this is one of a precious few elegies in the Propertian corpus to celebrate the lover's amatory success; and that is surely the context of Philodemus' epigram as well. Moreover, Philodemus' epigram was also perhaps calculated to interest his Italian readers because of the Latin name of his mistress, which he himself comments on in his observation that the Oscan Flora could not recite Sappho's Greek verses (*Epigr.* 12.7 Sider, quoted above). How piquant, then, that Propertius' *puella* bears a recondite Greek name, Cynthia, that allies her with the presiding deity of Virgil's sixth eclogue, Apollo 'Cynthius' (Verg. *Ecl.* 6.3); sings Aeolian, possibly Sapphic, lyric; and composes poetry that rivals that of the Greek poetess Corinna (Prop. 2.3.19–22):

---

31 Meleager, *Anth. Pal.* 5.165.6; Leontidas, *Anth. Pal.* 16.357.1; *Anth. Pal.* 6.58.1–2, 16.337.1; cf. Ov. *Am.* 1.13.43, *Ars am.* 3.83, *Tr.* 2.299. On Selene and Endymion in classical literature, see Pecere 1972.
32 Fedeli 2005, 442.

> et quantum Aeolio cum temptat carmina plectro,
> par Aganippeae ludere docta lyrae; 20
> et sua cum antiquae committit scripta Corinnae,
> carmina † quae quiuis † non non putat aequa suis.

... as much as [I like her] when she tries out songs on the Aeolian plectrum, her skill a match for Aganippe's lyre; and when she sets her own against ancient Corinna's writings, and thinks Corinna's not up to her own.

Propertius' literate and learned Greek-speaking Cynthia is thus the exact opposite of Philodemus' unlettered Oscan Flora.[33]

Elsewhere in his first book of elegies, Propertius also seems to draw on Philodemus' *Epigram* 16 Sider in crafting his account of the superiority of the genre of elegy over that of epic. The elegy, addressed to the epic poet Ponticus, warns Propertius' friend to flee seductive elegy (Prop. 1.9.27–30), just as Philodemus urges unlucky lovers to flee the immature Lysidike (Phld. *Epigr*. 16.5 Sider, quoted above). Earlier in the elegy, moreover, Propertius reworks two Philodemean images – of love's smouldering fire (Phld. *Epigr*. 1 Sider) in conjunction with the prediction of the fire to come (*Epigram* 16.6 Sider) – in assessing Ponticus' capitulation to erotic obsession (Prop. 1.9.17–18): *necdum etiam palles, uero nec tangeris igni: / haec est uenturi prima fauilla mali*, 'Nor are you even pale yet; Nor, indeed, are you burned by fire: this is the first spark of the evil to come'). Nor would it be out of place for Propertius to rework epigrammatic motifs in his statement of elegiac superiority over epic, since the genres of elegy and epigram are closely associated in the tradition of Latin erotic verse at least from Catullus, who himself adapts Philodemus' *Epigram* 1 Sider in his poem 85: *odi et amo. Quare id faciam, fortasse requiris? / nescio, sed fieri sentio et excrucior* ('I hate and I love. How can I do that, perhaps you ask? I don't know, but I feel it happening and it tortures me').[34] Propertius has been seen as recasting the same Philodemean couplet (*Epigr*. 1.3–4 Sider: ὦ ψυχή, φλέξει σε· ταὸ δ' ἐκ τίνος ἢ πότε καὶ πῶς / οὐκ οἶδα· γνώμη, δύσμορε, τυφομένη, 'The reasons why or whence or how I don't know; but you will know, ill-fated, that you are burning') in his elegy 2.4 (9–10): *quippe ubi nec causas nec apertos cernimus ictus, / unde tamen ueniant tot mala caeca uia est* ('indeed where we discern neither the reasons nor the blows openly, the way that so many evils nevertheless come is blind').[35]

---

[33] Further reflection on the literary resonances of Philodemus' Flora in Newlands 2016.
[34] On Catullus' knowledge of Philodemus and his poetry, see Sider 1997, 23–4. On the relationship between Latin elegy and Hellenistic epigram, see Keith 2011a.
[35] Sider 1997, 64, citing Jacobs, Fedeli 2005, 167 *ad loc.*

Of paramount interest, however, is Propertius' sustained exploration of the theme of Philodemus' *Epigram* 5 Sider (quoted above), the rejection of erotic revels for the teachings of philosophy, in his elegy 3.5 (lines 19–20, 23–5, 45–6):[36]

me iuuat in prima coluisse Helicona iuuenta	
Musarumque choris impliciusse manus ...	20
atque ubi iam Venerem grauis interceperit aetas,	23
sparserit et nigras alba senecta comas,	
tum mihi naturae libeat perdiscere mores,	
...	...
an ficta in miseras descendit fabula gentis,	45
et timor haud ultra quam rogus esse potest.	

It pleases me to have cultivated Helicon in my first youth and inserted my hands into the Muses' choruses ... but when heavy age has already interrupted love and white old age sprinkled my black hair with grey, then may it please me to learn the ways of nature ... Or has a fictional tale come down to wretched mortals, and can there be no fear beyond the pyre?

The natural philosophical themes of the verses intervening between lines 25 and 45 include the rising and setting of the moon, the course of the constellations of Boötes and the Pleiades, and the causes of the winds, rainbows, earthquakes and seasons (3.5.26–38), after which Propertius rehearses the myths of the underworld (3.5.39–44). It is these latter myths that are interrogated, from what looks like an Epicurean perspective, in 3.5.45–6. The combination of Philodemean erotics and Epicurean philosophy in these lines is unusual for Propertius and underlines his combinatorial allusion to Philodemus' epigram and the Epicurean themes developed by Lucretius (especially in *DRN* 3) and Virgil at the end of *Georgics* 2 (475–82).[37] The convergence of Epicurean themes and intertexts in Propertius' elegy 3.5 recalls Horace's repeated recourse to both in the construction of his own amatory *persona*, and marks an emphatic break with the elegist's customary

---

[36] Sider (1997, 79) follows Tait (1941, 79–81) and Jakoby (1905, 99n3) in seeing Philodemus' influence on Propertius here. Fedeli (2005, 188–9) rejects this view and identifies Virgil (*G.* 2.475–82) as Propertius' primary model; in this he is followed by Heslin (2018, 245–51). Heyworth and Morwood (2010, 139–43) do not mention Philodemus, but identify allusions to Lucretius and Virgil throughout the passage, and suggest that Varius' lost *De Morte* 'might have been a more significant intertext' (143). Cairns 2006, 346, notes the Epicurean phrasing.

[37] Kayachev 2013, 413–17, interprets the elegy as feigning the adoption of Philodemus' persona in the *Epigrams* as an 'imperfect Epicurean'. Heslin 2018, 45–51, focuses on the interplay with Virgil's *Georgics*.

poetics, which insistently reject philosophy in favour of love.[38] It is therefore tempting to see the influence of Horace too here at the end of Propertius' so-called 'Roman Elegies', the opening five elegies of his third collection, which have long been read as engaging with Horace's lyric collection.[39]

Ovid

It is to Ovid that the honour of having penned the best known adaptation of Philodemean erotic epigram in Latin love poetry goes, in his opening book of *Amores* (*Am.* 1.5.17–24):[40]

> ut stetit ante oculos posito uelamine nostros,
>   in toto nusquam corpore menda fuit.
> quos umeros, quales uidi tetigique lacertos!
>   Forma papillarum quam fuit apta premi!   20
> quam castigato planus sub pectore uenter!
>   quantum et quale latus! quam iuuenale femur!
> singula quid referam? nil non laudabile uidi,
>   et nudam pressi corpus ad usque meum.

When she stood before my eyes with her clothing laid aside, there was no blemish on her whole body. What shoulders, what arms did I see and touch! How fit for being caressed was the shape of her breasts! How smooth her belly beneath her tight chest! How long and beautiful her flank! How youthful her thigh! Why go into details? I saw nothing not praiseworthy, and I pressed her nude body along the length of mine.

Strikingly, Ovid's reworking of Philodemus' famous epigram (12 Sider) is mediated by Propertius' adaptation of the same epigram in his elegy 2.15. For Ovid eschews Philodemus' repetition of '*o*' in favour of a Propertian succession of relative and correlative pronouns (*quos, quales, quam, quantum, quam, quid*). This may either imply that Ovid came to Philodemus through Propertius, i.e. through Latin erotic elegy rather than Greek epigram or Epicurean philosophy, or simply

---

38 Cf. Prop. 3.21.25–6, where the Propertian poet-lover proposes to immerse himself in the philosophical study of Plato or Epicurus in order both to cure the lover of his infatuation (*remedia amoris*) and to allow the poet to disengage from elegiac compositional practices: see Keith 2008, 111–12, 157–8.
39 Nethercut 1970.
40 McKeown 1989, 116–17, Courtney 1990, Sider 1997, 104, Newlands 2016.

signal his awareness of the epigrammatic origins of the elegiac genre. In his recasting of both Philodemus' Greek epigram and Propertius' Latin elegy, moreover, Ovid has amplified the representation (and the success) of his lover's carnal appetites, by setting the scene at midday (and so doing away with Propertius' play of darkness and lamplight) and by actually achieving erotic communion with his mistress (which is superfluous to Philodemus' epigram), and markedly early in his elegiac collection. I have argued elsewhere that Ovid is the most carnal of the Latin elegists, and here we can see Ovid responding precisely to the carnal erotics on display in Philodemus' epigram.[41] Scholars have argued that Ovid may also have borrowed the Andromeda exemplum for his dismissal of skin colour as an index of low status and/or foreignness (Ov. *Ars am.* 2.643–4: *nec suus Andromedae color est obiectus ab illo / mobilis in gemino cui pede pinna fuit*, 'Nor was her complexion a reproach to Andromeda by that man who had feathers on each foot') directly from the concluding couplet of Philodemus' famous epigram (12.7–8 Sider, quoted above).[42] Yet, Ovid is not blind to Philodemus' aestheticization of erotic desire in this epigram: his elegiac mistress' fair complexion (*candida colla*, *Am.* 1.5.10) reflects the lucidity (*candor*) of his elegiac poetry.[43]

Just as Ovid stages his carnal embrace of elegiac poetics by reference to Philodemean erotic epigram, so too he dramatizes his disavowal of elegiac composition by reference to another, equally explicit, epigram of Philodemus (*Epigr.* 19 Sider = *Anth. Pal.* 11.30):

ὁ πρὶν ἐγὼ καὶ πέντε καὶ ἐννέα, νῦν, Ἀφροδίτη,
  ἓν μόλις ἐκ πρώτης νυκτὸς ἐς ἠέλιον.
Οἴμοιμοῖ καὶ τοῦτο κατὰ βραχύ, πολλάκι δ' ἤδη
  ἡμιθανὲς θνῄσκει τοῦτο τὸ Τερμέριον.
ὦ Γῆρας Γῆρας, τί ποθ' ὕστερον ἢν ἀφίκηαι   5
  ποιήσεις, ὅτε νῦν ὧδε μαραινόμεθα;

I, earlier capable of five or nine times, now, Aphrodite, with difficulty (manage only) one from sunset to sunrise. Oh my! And this for just a short time; and often already half-dead, this little rammer dies. Old Age, Old Age, what will you manage if ever you arrive, since we now so waste away?

---

41 Keith 1999.
42 Courtney 1990, Knox 1995, 287 *ad Her.* 15.35–6, Newlands 2016, 120–1.
43 For *candidus* in the sense of fair-skinned, see *OLD* s.v. 5; in the sense of literary clarity or lucidity, see *OLD* s.v. 9. For *candor* in the sense of fairness of complexion, see *OLD* s.v. 3; in the sense of authorial clarity or lucidity, see *OLD* s.v. 5. On the elegiac *puella* as the embodiment of Ovidian poetics, see Wyke 1989, Keith 1994; 2012, 297–9.

Philodemus offers a condensation of the problem of impotence, both sexual and poetic, which the Ovidian poet-lover elaborates in *Amores* 3.7.[44] Ovid expands the first couplet in the poet-lover's self-congratulatory reflection on his earlier amatory prowess (Ov. *Am.* 3.7.23–6):

> at nuper bis flaua Chlide, ter candida Pitho,
>   ter Libas officio continuata meo est;
> exigere a nobis angusta nocte Corinnam
>   me memini numeros sustinuisse nouem.

> But recently I satisfied blonde Chlide twice with my attentions, fair Pitho and Libas three times; I remember Corinna asking, and me supplying, nine measures in one short night!

Like Catullus, who promises Ipsitilla 'nine continuous fucks' (*nouem continuas fututiones*, 32.8) in what looks like an earlier aemulative riposte to Philodemus,[45] Ovid retains the epigrammatist's number games, but he ups the ante from five to eight (two plus three plus three) in addition to the Greek poet's other nine, and he boasts of the number of his conquests (four) as well as his sexual stamina. Like Philodemus (and unlike Catullus), however, he sets his erotic success in the past (Ov. *Am.* 3.7.65–6): *nostra tamen iacuere uelut praemortua membra / turpiter hesterna languidiora rosa* ('yet my member lay shamefully as if already dead, drooping more than yesterday's rose'). Ovid's *praemortua membra* echoes Philodemus' 'half-dead Rammer' (ἡμιθανὲς θνῄσκει τοῦτο τὸ Τερμέριον, *Epigr.* 19.4 Sider), though in an aestheticized image that shows the Latin poet disavowing the crudity of Greek epigram in his more elevated verse. But Ovid too figures impotence as death (Philodemus' θνῄσκει), earlier in the elegy (*Am.* 3.7.15–16: *truncus iners iacui, species et inutile pondus, / et non exactum corpus an umbra forem*, 'I lay like a dead tree-trunk, a mere spectacle, a useless weight and it was unclear whether I was body or ghost'). And like Philodemus (*Epigr.* 19.5–6 Sider), Ovid asks what old age will hold for the elegiac lover whose youth has already failed him (*Am.* 3.7.17–18: *quae mihi uentura est, siquidem uentura, senectus, / cum desit numeris ipsa iuuenta suis?* 'What old age will come to me, if indeed it will come, when my youth fails its own measures?'). Ovid also picks up the Philodemean image of wasting away in old age (*Epigr.* 19.6 Sider) in his wry observation that this girl's practiced touch could rejuvenate the proverbial old men of classical myth, Nestor or Tithonos (*Am.* 3.7.41–2: *illius ad tactum Pylius iuuenescere possit / Tithonosque annis fortior esse suis*, 'at her touch the Pylian could be made young again and

---

[44] Keith 1994, 38.
[45] Thomson 1997, 288.

Tithonos become stronger than his years'). Ovid adduces mythological comparanda here in the same way that Philodemus does in *Epigram* 12.7–8 Sider. It would be all the more interesting to know, therefore, just where, in Philodemus' original collection, *Epigram* 19 Sider was placed, as it could shed light on Ovid's models for narrative progression in the arrangement of his *Amores*.[46]

Ovid's debt to Philodemean erotic epigram extends considerably beyond that of either Propertius or Tibullus, or even of both combined.[47] Like Propertius (and similarly to Horace in *Carm.* 2.4 and 2.5), Ovid's interest in Philodemus' epigrams comes to the fore in relatively short elegies, which employ the same metre as his epigrammatist model. Indeed, all three poets evince a concern for both brevity of form and a focus on erotic content in the allusions to Philodemus' epigram we have traced in this chapter. But as the two examples of Ovidian adaptations of Philodemean epigrams that we have considered in depth suggest, Ovid shows no interest in the Epicurean framework in which (Sider argues) Philodemus' erotic epigrams were set, and this is a striking departure from Horace's reception of Philodemus' erotic epigrams and even, on strategic occasions, Propertius'. It may, however, be consistent with Tibullus' relative lack of interest in Philodemean erotics.[48] For in spite of Horace's repeated invitations (*Carm.* 1.33, *Epist.* 1.4) to Tibullus to reject the theme of amatory obsession conventional to elegy and embrace the instrumental sexuality of Epicurean erotics on display in Philodemus' epigrams, Tibullus eschews extended treatment of Philodemean epigram. Nor can Tibullus' indifference to Philodemus' erotic epigrams be explained as indifference to the genre of epigram, for Francis Cairns and Robert Maltby, among others, have documented his

---

46 Cf. the concluding sequence of Propertius' third book, elegies 3.21–5, with Keith 2008, 110–13 and 2013, 110–11.

47 Cf. Ov. *Am.* 1.5.25 *cetera quis nescit?*, with Phld. *Epigr.* 7.6 Sider λειπόμενα; *Am.* 1.8.2–4, *est quaedam nomine Dipsas anus ...*, with Phld. *Epigr.* 6.3–4 Sider; *Am.* 2.4.45 *me tangit serior aetas*, with Phld. *Epigr.* 9 Sider (an older woman is still sexy); *Am.* 2.19.3–4 with Phld. *Epigr.* 11.6 Sider; for the difficult choice between two women (Phld. *Epigr.* 11.6 Sider), cf. *Am.* 2.10 and 3.1. Also indebted to Philodem. *Epigr.* 11.5–6 are Ov. *Am.* 2.9.9–10, 2.19.1–2, 3.4.17–18, 25–6: see Sider 1997, 103. Ov. *Am.* 3.13 is the only Latin elegy to feature a wife; cf. Philodem. *Epigr.* 7.5 (and 6.8). On Ovid's interest in Greek epigram, see also Höschele 2010, Keith 2011a; 2011b, Hines 2014, Newlands 2016.

48 On Tibullus' debts to Philodemus, see Sider 1997, 253, 'Index of the More Important Passages' s.v. Of the three cited in Sider 1997, the most substantial are Tib. 1.2.33-4 *parcite luminibus ... celari uult sua furta Venus* (alluding to Philodem. *Epigr.* 7 Sider: see Sider 1997, 85–6), and Tib. 1.5.39 *Venus deseruit* (alluding to Philodem. *Epigr.* 19.1–2 Sider: see Sider 1997, 129). On Tibullus' interest in Hellenistic Greek epigram, see Maltby 2002, 45, 57, 59–60, and 66; Philodemus does not appear in his Index Nominum.

extensive debt to epigrammatic models.⁴⁹ It is possible, of course, that in the cleavage between the poetic concerns of Horace and Propertius, on the one hand, and Tibullus and Ovid, on the other, we see a difference in the literary emphases of the writers associated with Maecenas and Messalla. But it may also be that as Latin elegy gained in literary prestige, its practitioners exhibited a newly confident literary authority independent of contemporary Greek epigrammatic models and that the traditional poles of influence were even reversed. Indeed, it has recently been suggested that the Greek epigrammatist Rufinus imitates Ovidian elegy rather than the other way around.⁵⁰

---

49 Cairns 1979, Maltby 2002; 2011.
50 Hines 2014; cf. Höschele 2010.

Aaron Palmore
Love and Politics in Horace's *Odes* 4.10

This chapter explores Horace's *Odes* 4.10 from a political angle informed by psychoanalysis. *Odes* 4.10, one of Horace's shortest compositions, is a homoerotic poem that appears in a collection that seems to focus largely on Augustus' achievements. Building upon the work of the psychoanalyst Jacques Lacan, I offer a theoretical basis for understanding the unity of *Odes* 4 through the rubric of desire, which can manifest itself not only in love but also in politics and poetry.[1] *Odes* 4.10 is a valuable case study in this regard, as Horace swaps in Ligurinus (an erotic interest) for Augustus (a political interest) around the key word *incolumis*, 'unharmed'. Horace uses this word only twice in *Odes* 4, once of Augustus (*Carm.* 4.5.27, *incolumi Caesare*, 'with Caesar unharmed') and once of Ligurinus' cheeks (*Carm.* 4.10.8, Ligurinus' *incolumes genae,* 'unharmed cheeks'). This intratextual resonance links the political and the erotic, ultimately suggesting an ideological connection between the language of *Odes* 4.10 and the portrayal of Augustus as a powerful youth (*puer*).[2] Using this perspective, we can further understand the coherence of *Odes* 4, and especially the place of *Odes* 4.10 within it as a link in the collection's trajectory of desire.

I have structured this contribution to move from the philological to the theoretical and back again. The overall structure of *Odes* 4 is an important element of my argument, and so I begin with the structure of the whole book. Since *Odes* 4.10 has often been dismissed as a mere variation on Greek epigram, I then establish the originality of *Odes* 4.10 as a poem worth considering more closely. A close reading of *Odes* 4.10 follows, in which I explore the ways that the poem reaches out to other moments in the collection through its prosody and structural patterns. I then advance some strictly theoretical points, and finally synthesize these threads to suggest that *Odes* 4.10, a short and apparently insignificant poem, is an important intervention in the collection's fusion of political and erotic desire.

---

[1] As Porter/Buchan 2004, 14 put it, 'Lacan in one sense merely points us to phenomena that we might otherwise overlook.' I have made my best attempt to put psychoanalysis in service of my interpretation rather than allow theory to eclipse Horace. For psychoanalytic approaches to Classics more generally, see, e.g., Janan 1994, Janan 2001, Miller 2004, Porter/Buchan 2004, and Oliensis 2009. Alvares 2012 offers a brief but intriguing first step to considering desire in the ancient novel through a Lacanian lens. Gunderson 2015 offers a new approach to Plautus (and comedy more generally) through Lacan.

[2] For the idea of intratextuality more broadly, see most recently Harrison/Frangoulidis/Papanghelis 2018.

The structure of *Odes* 4

Horace published *Odes* 4 around 13 BCE.[3] Suetonius' early testimony for Augustus 'forcing' (*coegerit*) Horace to write several encomiastic poems in the collection was deeply informative for how *Odes* 4 was read in the twentieth century. Scholars sometimes imagined a top-down literary propaganda campaign administered by Augustus, and *Odes* 4 was part of this campaign.[4] The fifteen poems of *Odes* 4, though, move through all sorts of themes aside from praise for Augustus, including love, poetry, and reputation.

In Fraenkel's view, *Odes* 4 is the pinnacle of Augustan poetic book construction: 'no other book shows so refined an arrangement as the last book of Horace's odes.'[5] It is worth considering just what this arrangement might be and how it informs the way that we read the poems. The most common view is to see the book as a set of five triads. Fraenkel proposed this structure, but only really addressed the central triad of 4.7–4.9.[6] Putnam fixed this arrangement more particularly by structuring his 1986 monograph around five triads and concluding each section with discussions of how the poems in parallel positions resonate with one another. In this reading, we will anticipate and find, for example, interesting echoes among 4.1, 4.4, 4.7, 4.10, and 4.13, each of which is the first poem in its respective triad. The triadic structure has since often been understood as an intrinsic feature of the collection.[7]

Most criticism of the triadic structure happens implicitly by opting for another arrangement. Fraenkel himself considered some poems individually and

---

[3] For the dating of *Odes* 4, see most recently Thomas 2011, 5–7, Fedeli/Ciccarelli 2008, 13–16.
[4] This is especially apparent in Dahlmann 1958, La Penna 1963 and Doblhofer 1966; the position was effectively countered by White 1993, who resituated the critical conversation around Augustan literary propaganda to show that, in fact, this conversation is a post-Renaissance development with little historical basis.
[5] Fraenkel 1957, 410; this work in general is the starting point for most discussions in English and German of *Odes* 4. An interesting witness to the state of the field prior to Fraenkel is Norberg 1952; while I doubt many readers familiar with *Odes* 4 would learn anything new from it, consider the fact that it was possible for Norberg to write a short article that covered the entire poetry book. Others, such as Syme 1939 and Wili 1948, had considered *Odes* 4 mostly within the context of other projects rather than for itself.
[6] Fraenkel 1957, 426. Dettmer 1983, 486 keeps this central triad of 4.7-4.9 but sees the rest of the book working differently.
[7] For example, Lowrie 1997, 327 n. 20 on *Odes* 4.4–4.6: 'these poems belong together'. Thomas 2011, 216 describes simply 'the poems of the triad 10–12', though he elsewhere calls attention to Porter 1975, who notes the relationship of 4.11–13 to 1.23–5.

others in pairs, suggesting the limitations of reading the collection systematically in triads.⁸ Most readers tend to view 4.10 especially as something of an oddity: even if it finds a place within a structure, it is usually an uncomfortable fit. Fraenkel considered 4.10 alongside 4.13, Putnam reads it as part of his 4.10–4.12 triad, Johnson reads 4.10–4.13 as a set (under the heading of 'Songs of Mo(u)rning'), Porter reads it together with a group that includes the poems in Johnson's chapter along with 4.1 and 4.7, and Sage sees a strong relationship among 4.8, 4.9, and 4.10.⁹

In what follows, I amplify a less appreciated pentadic structure of the collection (1–5, 6–10 and 11–15). Thomas has already noted that the 'traces of a pentadic system' are present in the development of 4.4 and 4.5 and 4.14 and 4.15, which move from Drusus and Tiberius (respectively) to Augustus.¹⁰ The similarities between the Augustan panegyrics of 4.5 and 4.15 have often been noted.¹¹ The two poems share Augustus as an addressee, and both emphasize his role as protector (*custos*) of the state (*optime Romulae / custos gentis*, 'best protector of the

---

8 Syndikus 1973 discusses the poems individually in sequence with no larger grouping. Putnam 1986 does the same, although he includes the divisions into triads (thus a single chapter is on 1–3, another on 4–6, etc.). Johnson 2004 is idiosyncratically organized: 1 and 2; 3 and 6; 7; 8 and 9; then the rest of the poems individually and in order, with subheadings for 4–5, 10–13, and 14–15. Johnson 2004, xx defends the structure of his book, describing it as a necessary complication. Although this might preserve the 'chiastic structure' that Johnson sees in the collection, it is a result of his reading strategy as much as it is a result of the text itself. Johnson's monograph thus depends upon deciding what certain poems are about and placing them in a certain context with other poems that are about the same thing. In my view, this is exactly what *Odes* 4 resists in its structural and thematic mélange.
9 Fraenkel 1957, Putnam 1986, Johnson 2004, Sage 1994.
10 Thomas 2011, 7. Dahlmann 1958, 344–5 also hints at the pentadic structure but does not explore it; Putnam 1986, 320 toys with the idea of pentads and interlocking decades (e.g., 1 and 10, 2 and 11, etc. through 6 and 15).
11 e.g., Dahlmann 1958, Fraenkel 1957, 431–2; and, more recently, the comment of Thomas 2011, 7 that 'it is hard not to perceive in the close parallelism between the pairings 4.4/5 (Drusus/Augustus) and 4.14/15 (Tiberius/Augustus) the traces of a pentadic system—which would then create an interesting relationship in the juxtaposition of 4.9/4.10.' Although my focus here is primarily on the relationship among 4.5, 4.10, and 4.15, I will take up the question of the relationship of 4.9 to 4.10 elsewhere. Dettmer 1983, 488, in her second of two structures that interlock in *Odes* 4, draws a line from 4.4 to 4.14 and from 4.5 (grouped with 4.6) to 4.15; she discusses the relationship of 4.5 to 4.15 more thoroughly on 506–7, that of 4.4 to 4.14 on 507–8, and 4.4 to 4.5 most extensively on 508–12. See also Norberg 1952, 102–7, Williams 1968, 162–6, Becker 1963, 173–4, Ludwig 1961, 6.

family of Romulus', *Carm.* 4.5.1–2; *custode rerum Caesare*, 'with Caesar as protector of things', *Carm.* 4.15.17).[12] The poems also share a similar structure, as each moves from a first half that enumerates Augustus' accomplishments to a second half that emphasizes the peace and prosperity that follow as a result. These two poems, however, also have an important difference. In 4.5, Rome is the mother seeking her offspring (*ut mater iuuenem ... sic desideriis icta fidelibus / quaerit patria Caesarem, Carm.* 4.5.9–16). Here desire is already politicized, as it is mother Rome struck by 'faithful desires' (*desideriis fidelibus*) who seeks Augustus. In 4.15, the prospect of Augustus' return and the realization of his agenda have consumed and eradicated desire. At the poem's end, which envisions a future world of perfectly organized family units singing together the praises of Rome's past, it is not only Horace who fades into anonymity in the crowd, it is also the very idea of the individual subject.[13]

The triadic structure sets 4.10 in quite a different context than the pentadic one. In the triadic structure, we expect 4.10 to be a beginning rather than an ending. The pentadic approach works for the first and third pentads so well that it prompts significant questions about the middle pentad in retrospect. As the concluding poem of the central pentad, *Odes* 4.10 occupies an important place in the collection. The middle pentad, in its thematic elements, seems to reverse course: 4.1–4.5 and 4.11–4.15 have erotic beginnings and political endings, whereas 4.6–4.10 has a socio-political beginning and erotic ending. The snaking path through the erotic and the political works in both a cyclical and linear fashion, but also introduces juxtapositions that seem out of harmony. Psychoanalytic literary criticism becomes a valuable tool here to solve the problem of the apparent thematic inconcinnity.

While it may seem like the structure of the book is only loosely related to the overall project of Horace's late work, these two investigations are intimately connected. The fundamental distinctions for other scholars have been in whether they privilege the private voice or the public voice in the poems and whether they treat the encomiastic poems as genuine praise or ironic praise. As I explore below, reading the collection through the lens of desire offers a viable route through these apparent dichotomies.

---

[12] e.g., Dettmer 1983, 506–7.
[13] This also, in a way, realizes Horace's threat of death for Torquatus in 4.7, where Torquatus' individual contributions and accomplishments mean nothing in the face of the eternal abyss.

The originality of *Odes* 4.10

Odes 4.10 appears to suggest its own insignificance through its brevity and erotic theme.[14] Most commentators have thus looked for meaning not within the poem itself, but in how the poem references other poems, other poets, and other genres: anything, it seems, to deflect us from the threatening *puer* with whom the poem puts us face-to-face. The poem's length and content have particularly prompted scholars to view the poem through the interpretive lens of Hellenistic epigram.[15] While several Greek epigrams share features with *Odes* 4.10, I will focus here on two: Asclepiades 46 (=*Anth. Pal.* 12.36) and Diocles 4 (=*Anth. Pal.* 12.35). Both of these poems are part of a run of homoerotic epigrams in the anthology that deal with the motif of the passing of time and its consequences. What we will get from exploring these two poems is a better sense of how *Odes* 4.10 participates in this tradition and what it might do that is different.

First, Asclepiades 46:

νῦν αἰτεῖς, ὅτε λεπτὸς ὑπὸ κροτάφοισιν ἴουλος
  ἕρπει καὶ μηροῖς ὀξὺς ἔπεστι χνόος·
εἶτα λέγεις 'ἥδιον ἐμοὶ τόδε.' Καὶ τίς ἂν εἴποι
  κρείσσονας αὐχμηρὰς ἀσταχύων καλάμας;

Now you ask for it, when the fine fluff spreads under your temples and there is a prickly down on your thighs. And then you say, 'I prefer this.' But who would say that the dry stubble is better than the full-eared corn?

(Transl. Paton, adapted)

This poem not only shares with *Odes* 4.10 the metaphor of facial hair as feathery down, it also shares the layered references to time – νῦν, ὅτε, etc. – and even has the boy assuming a similar speaking role within the poem. Like the cyclicality of *Odes* 4.10 – the end-rhyme of its lines 2, 3, and 4 that then recurs in line 8, for example – Asclepiades 46 'is very symmetrically built,' with the echo of νῦν αἰτεῖς in εἶτα λέγεις and ἂν εἴποι later; similarly, the parallel positions of λεπτὸς... ἴουλος and then ὀξὺς... χνόος.[16]

---

14 For Putnam 1986, 177, the speaker of the poem 'is simply a new Sappho'. Johnson 2004, 138 calls the poem 'thin, but with depth', and quickly goes to work on connecting the poem with Vergil.
15 e.g., Thomas 2011, who sees the poem as a take on Hellenistic epigram, referring to Alcaeus 8 GP, Phanias 1 GP, Mel, 90 GP, Mel. 94 GP, *Anth. Pal.* 12.39, *Anth. Pal.* 12.36, Asclep. 46 GP, among others. See also Pasquali 1920, 461; Syndikus 1973 ii, 368–9.
16 Tarán 1985, 90.

There is an interesting difference between this poem and *Odes* 4.10, one which holds true of most epigrams that we could compare with Horace's poem, and that is the focus on hair coming upon the *legs* (μηροῖς). As Sens has it, hair upon the face is not 'unattractive in itself,' but is instead indicative of an 'end to the boy's sexual desirability in other respects, as evidenced by the thigh-hair referred to in the next line.'[17] Horace may bowdlerize this motif in *Odes* 4.10 because the epigrammatic implication is too crass for lyric.[18] The difference, though, is also one of meaning and motivation. Horace's omission of the expected detail of thigh hair allows the poem to stay focused on the visual details of Ligurinus' self-reflection rather than just his desirability. *Odes* 4.10's vocabulary of mind (*mens*, 7 and *animis*, 8) allows the poem to end on a note of psychological complexity and philosophical reflection from Ligurinus' own viewpoint.

A comparison of *Odes* 4.10 to Diocles 4 also highlights this difference. Diocles 4 is unique among Greek epigrams of this type since, like *Odes* 4.10, it projects a hypothetical future scenario.

> χαῖρέ ποτ' οὐκ εἰπόντα προσεῖπέ τις· ἀλλ' ὁ περισσὸς
>   κάλλεϊ νῦν Δάμων οὐδὲ τὸ χαῖρε λέγει.
> ἥξει τις τούτου χρόνος ἔκδικος· εἶτα δασυνθεὶς
>   ἄρξῃ χαῖρε λέγειν οὐκ ἀποκρινομένοις.

> But a bystander once addressed a boy who did not greet him: 'And so Damon, who excels in beauty, does not even say good-day now! A time will come that will take vengeance for this. Then, grown all rough and hairy, you will be the first to greet those who do not reply to you.'

> (Transl. Paton, adapted)

This poem points to a larger trend in Greek epigram by focusing on the loss that Damon will feel when he has become hairy (δασυνθείς, 3): others will no longer 'greet' him. While epigrams like this one may imagine the transition from *eromenos* to *erastes*, we do not see the reorientation from desired object to desiring subject. In general, these epigrams imagine the future youth growing up and regretting no longer being the object of desire. *Odes* 4.10 is more empathetic in that it imagines in the maturation of Ligurinus the idea that Ligurinus himself will be the one who desires, and it is only in retrospect of this that he regrets not fulfilling the desires of others (e.g., Horace) when he was younger. Ligurinus will not

---

17 Sens 2011, 321.
18 Thomas 2011, 212: 'Horace could not write *ueniet pluma clunibus / cruribus* in the *Odes* (as opposed to the *Epodes*), but that is what is behind the vague *ueniet pluma superbiae*, which conflates two separate themes of models which Horace could write.'

simply mourn the loss of his own desirability; rather, he will recognize a more complex dissonance between what it means to be a lover and what it means to be a beloved. In this way, *Odes* 4.10 presents us with a discourse of desire that is complex in ways that exemplary Greek epigrams are not.

Reading *Odes* 4.10

Now that we have considered the structure of the collection and some of *Odes* 4.10's thematic predecessors, we can consider the poem more closely for what it accomplishes on its own and within its collection. In the reading below, I focus on the relationships that this poem has with other poems in *Odes* 4 as well as the resonances that it has within itself.

> O crudelis adhuc et Veneris muneribus potens,
> insperata tuae cum ueniet pluma[19] superbiae
> et, quae nunc umeris inuolitant, deciderint comae,
> nunc et qui color est puniceae flore prior rosae
> mutatus Ligurinum in faciem uerterit hispidam,   5
> dices, heu, quotiens te speculo uideris alterum:
> 'Quae mens est hodie, cur eadem non puero fuit,
> uel cur his animis incolumes non redeunt genae?'
>
> (Hor. *Carm.* 4.10)

2 *pluma* Ω: *bruma* Bentley *plaga* Lowinski *multa* Housman *palma* Slater, Kershaw
5 *Ligurinum* Ω: *Ligurine* (many)

> O one still cruel and powerful in the gifts of Venus,
> when down comes unexpected upon your pride
> and the hair which now flits about your shoulders falls,
> and the color which surpasses the bloom of the purple rose
> has changed and turned Ligurinus into a shaggy figure,
> 'Alas!' you will say, as often as you see the other you in the mirror:

---

19 Asztalos 2008, 290–3 offers a good summary of the history of the reading of *pluma* and the suggestions. Some critics have had much to say about the allusive dimensions of *pluma*; see, e.g., Asztalos 2008, 297–8 for the *pluma* of 4.10 as a layered allusion through *Aeneid* 10.189–93, which itself alludes to *Odes* 2.20. Other conjectures are also caught up with the meaning of the poem, since there seems to be no critical agreement about whether Ligurinus is becoming an *adulescens*, a *uir*, or a *senex*. These emendations for interpretive sense run the risk of eliding the difficulties of the poem's language.

'What my mind is today, why was it not the same when I was a boy,
or why, with my thoughts as they are, do my cheeks not return unharmed?'

The first line's 'gifts' (*muneribus*) of Venus continue the idea of the 'gifts of the gods' from the previous poem (*deorum muneribus*, *Carm.* 4.9.47–8). They also work as a foil to the gifts of Apollo that Horace possesses at 4.6.29–30: *spiritum Phoebus mihi, Phoebus artem / carminis nomenque dedit poetae* ('Apollo gave me my spirit, Apollo gave me the skill of song and the name of poet'). The power of the gods and their direct impact upon Roman society (in love as in 4.10, in war as in 4.9, and in poetry as in 4.6) play an important role in this central pentad. At a more explicit verbal level, we see 9.5's *prior* ('before') repeat in 10.4 and 9.10's *adhuc* ('still') repeat in 10.1, both occurring only these two times in *Odes* 4.[20] These structural and verbal continuities across disparate themes make the appearance of *potens* ('powerful') all the more interesting, as it transitions us from the military power of 4.9 to the erotic power of 4.10. In doing so, Horace also positions his lasting poetic power against Lollius' precarious military might.

In the second line, the syllable <u>uen</u>- of *cum <u>ueniet</u>* echoes the first line's *et <u>Veneris</u>* in the same metrical *sedes*. The phonetic echo here undercuts the surface reading of the poem: the poem says that desire departs with the onset of *pluma* ('down'), but it lingers in sound through the recurrence of the beginning of Venus' name. This phonetic pattern in 4.10 anticipates a similar phenomenon at the respective conclusions of the final two poems in the collection, where 4.14.52 *compositis <u>uenerantur</u> armis* ('they pray with their weapons set aside') is echoed by 4.15.32's *progeniem <u>Veneris</u> canemus* ('we will sing of the offspring of Venus'). Like the first two lines of 4.10, this feature of the collection quite literally underscores the flexibility of desire (Venus) and its pathways. The opening lines of 4.10 signpost the polyvalence of desire as explored in an erotic poem: desire ('Venus') in the collection is wide-ranging and nimble, with fragments of syllables like *uen* and *uener* appearing here and there to organize Horace's labyrinth of desire.

The opening word of line 2, *insperata*, 'unexpected', is itself unexpected, as it confirms a metrical pattern that Horace has not employed since his first book of odes.[21] It also complements a network of hope (a loose synonym for desire) that runs through the poems.[22] We first saw this in 4.1.30 (*spes animi credula mutui*,

---

20 Thomas 2011, 209, Putnam 1986, 178 n. 1.
21 Horace uses the Greater Asclepiad only in *Odes* 1.11, 1.18, and 4.10.
22 Admittedly, *insperata* usually carries a valence more similar to 'unexpected' than 'unhoped for'—the point is therefore not that Ligurinus does not want his *pluma*, but rather that when it does appear, it will catch him off his guard. Nonetheless, the stem of *spes / sperare* means that the word here participates in a phonetic network with other poems: see earlier 4.7.7 (*immortalia*

'the credulous hope of a common feeling'), where Horace unsuccessfully tries to abandon his erotic desires. It recurs near the end of the first pentad, where Hannibal laments the death of Hasdrubal and, consequently, the end of Carthage (*Carm.* 4.4.70–2, *occidit occidit / spes omnis et fortuna nostri / nominis Hasdrubale interempto*, 'it has died—all hope has died, along with the fortune of our name, now that Hasdrubal is dead'). Horace's logic of desire glides effortlessly from poem to poem, as Hannibal's nightmare at the end of 4.4 is realized in the future portrayed in 4.5. Following the death of Hasdrubal in 4.4 is the rise of Rome in 4.5, but with Augustus rather than with the Nerones.

The balance of 'power' and 'pride' (*potens* and *superbiae*), echoes *Carmen Saeculare* 53 *potentis* and 55 *superbi*, both at line end as here. 'Pride' in *Odes* 4 is otherwise not only political, it is the realm of Roman enemies, such as Hannibal's would-be messengers to Carthage (4.4.69–70 *non ego nuntios / mittam superbos*, 'I will not now send proud messengers') and the Parthians' door-posts that used to hold the stolen Roman standards (*Carm.* 4.15.7–8 *Parthorum superbis / postibus*, 'on the proud doorposts of the Parthians'). This is most explicit at *Carm. Saec.* 55–6, *superbi / nuper et Indi*, 'the Indi, recently proud', where Rome's defeat of the *Indi* results in the loss of their pride through the force of *nuper*: they were recently proud, and now no longer are. By reading *Odes* 4.10's claims about pride and power in love alongside these contemporary references in Horace's poetry, Horace's erotic interests play the role of those Rome has conquered.[23]

Line 3's *inuolitant*, in addition to its ornithological associations,[24] conjures up images that are familiar from elsewhere in the book down to the level of the phoneme. Ligurinus' hair floats over his shoulders like ships on a calm sea (4.5.19, *pacatum uolitant per mare nauitae*) or like Cupid, an instantiation of desire, flies past Lyce (4.13.9–10, *importunus ... transu̱olat*), or even like Ligurinus himself in the first poem, where he is 'swift' (*u̱olucrem*, 4.1.38) and the waves which he speeds over are 'rolling' (*u̱olubilis*, 4.1.40).

The verbal juxtaposition *inuolitant, deciderint*, like the language of the passing of seasons in 4.7.9–12, enacts the passage of time in the line. Ligurinus' hair 'flits (and) falls' as one clause ends with *inuolitant* and another begins with *deciderint*. These two choriambs have an echoing ring, *inuolita̱nt, deciderint*, as the poem builds up a concentration of *in-* compounds (*i̱nsperata, i̱nuolitant, i̱ncolumes*) that eventually culminate in the stuttering elision of *Ligurin-in*. This pattern of *in* works

---

ne speres); and then immediately following the present instance in 4.11.25–30, where *spes* (26) is picked up again by *sperare* (30); then in 4.12.19 *spes donare nouas*.
23 cf. Nisbet and Rudd on 3.10.9 with Lyce's *ingratam superbiam*, 'unpleasant pride'.
24 Putnam 1986, 181 and Thomas 2011 *ad* 1.37–40.

alongside the recurrent end-rhymes in *ae*, which build early in the poem (*superbiae, comae, rosae*), go underground, and then emerge again at its end in *genae*. Odes 4.10 is a poem about loss that ends with a return in rhythm and rhyme: the poem's formal elements seem to compete with its discursive point.

The opening of line 4, *nunc et qui*, rearranges the opening of line 3, *et quae nunc*. The variation here must be intentional: nothing prevents line 4 from repeating like *et qui nunc*. Given the number of other echoes and similarities throughout the structure of the poem, it is difficult to account for this one divergence as a matter of avoiding such a repetition as a general rule of poetic practice. Like the functions of the end rhymes, metrical patterns, and closing questions in the poem, this subtle shift in word order anticipates the 'change' that occurs in the following line. The formal elements here complement the narrative of the poem. Line 4 opening with *nunc* makes us focus on Ligurinus looking into the mirror: the hair which was just now floating on Ligurinus' shoulders now floats away. Line 4's *nunc* concentrates on the poem's complex temporal movement, taking us from youthful hair to the shock of self-recognition that we are about to witness.

There are two words for change in line 5 (*mutatus* and *uerterit*); whether we choose *Ligurin(e)* or *Ligurin(um)*, either elides into the stumbling *Ligurin-in*, a replication that suggests stuttering over the name in a way that erases part of 'Ligurinus'.[25] The choice of the vocative or accusative is driven by a confusion over the precision of the details of the line: the general resistance in accepting the accusative seems to be the metonymical use of *facies* for Ligurinus. But the accusative works here precisely for this very reason for which others would prefer to emend it.[26] The stumbling logic of reducing Ligurinus into nothing but a 'shaggy appearance' (*in faciem ... hispidam*) complements the stuttering effect of *–in in–*, as the reader's comprehension of the image is twisted by the equally twisted logic of the passage.

Facies, too, is a loaded word choice in this collection, as it is what grabs Horace's attention and focalizes his desire at 4.13.22. So, too, the change in Ligurinus' *facies* mirrors aged Lyce's appearance as a *fax* (*Carm.* 4.13.28). Both transformations are entangled in the loss of desire, but it is not the loss of their own desire so much as it is the loss of their status as an object of desire for others. The only

---

25 *contra* Johnson 2004, 142, for whom Horace in this poem 'reels off an invective ... without a stammer.'
26 This confusing logic is in part probably why the debate over *Ligurine* vs. *Ligurinum* exists: the grammar here is purposefully strained. Thus, the fact there may be a textual discrepancy here is more important for my argument than how we resolve it.

other appearance of *facies* in the collection is in 4.5, in a simile where Rome seeking Augustus is like a mother whose face (*faciem*, *Carm.* 4.5.14) is locked on the shore, awaiting her son's return. As Ligurinus looks longingly into the mirror at his *facies*, we can look longingly with our own *facies* out at the sea in a simile, waiting for Augustus to return. The 'look' is simultaneously political and erotic.

This reverses a frequent truism about the erotic poems of *Odes* 4 that they are about Horace's lament for his old age and consequent loss of desire. This is only true of the first poem, and there he does not even make it until the end of the poem before falling under the spell of Ligurinus. So, too, the rest of the collection shows Horace continuing to desire: the complication is that desire keeps manifesting itself in different ways and in different spheres. Through a network of echoes in something as simple as *facies*, we see a desire for Augustus to return conflated with Ligurinus' desire for youth (also implicating Horace's desire for Ligurinus) and his former desire for Lyce. Horace's desire is caught up in the desire of others.

The nuance of *quotiens te speculo uideris alterum* ('as often as you see the other you in the mirror') is critically important, since it points to the contingency of subjectivity that the collection deals with elsewhere.[27] The contingency of the subject is the central issue at stake in this labyrinth of desire. This is, again, most prominent in the opening of *Odes* 4, where Horace states that he is not what he used to be (*non sum qualis eram*, 4.1.3): this forces the reader to ask questions like 'what was he?' and 'what is he?'. The basic question of the hysteric in psychoanalysis is 'who am I?', and these questions thus catch up the reader in a pseudo-analytical experience of transference and countertransference with the poet as he tries to figure them out.[28]

First, let us consider the word order of the line. Like *hispidam* ('shaggy') in line 5, *alterum* ('another') is marked by position as a predicative adjective. In other words, it should read in English something like: 'as often as you see yourself as someone else' rather than 'see the other you'.[29] This is complemented by how the poem perceives the passage of time in its adverbs: *adhuc* ('still', 1), *nunc ... nunc* ('now ... now', 3–4), *hodie* ('today', 9). The *adhuc* spoken by Horace in the present is analogous to the *hodie* spoken by Ligurinus in the future, occupying the same space that Horace does now. In between is Ligurinus' 'change',

---

[27] Compare Ovid's lament for Narcissus at *Fasti* 5.226: *infelix, quod non alter et alter eras!* 'unfortunate, because you were both not someone else and someone else!'
[28] For the hysteric's discourse, see Fink 1997, 129–31.
[29] For Johnson 2004, 143, a grammatical issue is less at stake than one of poetic effect: 'the chiastic separation of *te* from *alterum* saves the surprise for the end of the verse.'

mutatus and *uerterit*, and a dissociation of his former self with what he becomes (*alterum*, 'another').

This change is not only a physical change but also one of mind (*mens, animis*). Thus Ligurinus' change reenacts the change that Horace presents in 4.1.3 with *non sum qualis eram*, 'I am not what I used to be'. As we will see in the next section, this statement implicates contemporary political developments as the Republic transitions into the Empire. *Odes* 4.10, as a poem about desire, is not just an erotic poem, it is also about a changing subject in a changing ideological landscape.

As Ligurinus asks himself questions that continue Horace's statements from earlier in the poem, the final two lines seem to pitch Ligurinus in the role of the aged Horace.[30] This is apparent from a question like *quae mens est*, 'what mind is ...', for example, which picks up on the formulation from line 4 *qui color est*, 'what color is ...'. Furthermore, the questions Ligurinus asks himself (*cur ... cur ... genae*, 'why ... why ... cheeks') echo the questions that Horace asked Ligurinus at 4.1.33–5 (*cur ... genas ... cur*, 'why ... cheeks ... why').[31] Finally, as Fraenkel notes, 4.10.7's *quae mens est hodie, cur eadem non puero fuit?* recalls *Epistles* 1.1.4's *non eadem est aetas, non mens* ('age is not the same, mind is not the same'): in terms of language, Horace has already gone through the experience that Ligurinus can anticipate.[32] But the situation is more complex when we consider it through the lens of desire. Horace in *Odes* 4.1 tries and fails to escape the bond of desire; Ligurinus, in his old age, will desire either his own youth or the same mental change that Horace longs for (and fails to achieve) in *Odes* 4.1. Desire persists despite the rhetoric.

At the end of 4.10, Horace imagines Ligurinus longing for his cheeks to be *incolumes* ('unharmed'). *Incolumis* only appears once elsewhere in the collection, where Romans need not fear foreign enemies so long as Caesar is safe (*incolumi Caesare*, 4.5.27). This furthers the relationship between 4.5 and 4.10 that we saw

---

[30] Some read the poem as Horace addressing his younger self in the guise of Ligurinus. So Fraenkel 1957, 414, where his main interest in 4.10 is not its relationship to the tradition of Hellenistic epigram, but rather its focus on 'regret for the bygone days of youth.' Azstalos 2008 is a more thorough reading in this vein.

[31] So, too, the slightly displaced *heu* and, possibly, the vocative *Ligurine*. As Johnson 2004, 143 puts it 'Horace has retained the structure and vocabulary of his lament for Ligurinus so that literally his words become Ligurinus's.'

[32] Fraenkel 1957, 415. This only partly works: Horace does not erotically appear in the role of the young Ligurinus, i.e., as the object of someone else's desire. He tries to do so politically in his relationship with Augustus and Rome, but he is not here proud or cruel (*superbus, crudelis*) and is powerful (*potens*) in the gifts of Apollo rather than those of Venus.

already above with *facies*. This dialogue between 4.5 and 4.10 creates the outline for the pentadic structure that is fully realized by 4.14 and 4.15. It also points up the contingency of desire for return and stability in the collection. Horace longs for Augustus in the same language as Ligurinus longs for youth, retrospectively incorporating the world of personal change and loss into the political world of 4.5.

What I hope to have illuminated here is that 4.10 both has a close relationship with the rest of the collection it is part of and, just as importantly, has significant resonances within itself that have been underappreciated. These relationships tap into the network of desire that manifests itself in the sounds and patterns of the collection. Word choice and placement are the most crucial aspects of how this works in the poem. This network of desire that emerges from patterns and repetitions pushes *Odes* 4.10 well beyond being a variation on Greek epigrammatic motifs. A fuller interpretation of these features would need to consider the metrical features of the poem more specifically, but my aim from this point is ultimately more conceptual.

Some Lacanian concepts

In what follows, I rely on a few core concepts from Jacques Lacan. Like other scholars of Latin poetry,[33] I have found a psychoanalytic approach particularly valuable for uncovering the layers of desire that are a constituent element of late Republican and early Imperial poetry books. I limit myself to two Lacanian concepts here: *objet petit a* (*a*) and *grand Autre* (*A*).[34] I recognize that readers familiar with Lacan may be frustrated with these boundaries, especially my omission of any discussion of Lacan's Four Discourses and mirror stage, considering that my target poem includes layered voices and a mirror.[35] I have focused on *a* and *A* because these concepts offer an innovative way to think through the interconnectedness of desire in the personal and political realms.

---

33 See note 1 above.
34 The best general introduction to Lacan remains Fink 1997, though the book is targeted at practicing psychoanalysts rather than literary critics. Homer 2005 is good on the reception of Lacan's ideas in various fields, including literature; Bowie 1991 remains valuable. For psychoanalytic literary criticism more particularly, see Wright 1998, Wright 1999, Chaitin 1996, and Felman 1982. More adventurous readers may find value in the interpretive essays collected in Ragland-Sullivan 1991, especially the chapters by Žižek and Soler, and Schneiderman 1980.
35 For the mirror stage, see Lacan 2006, 75–81 [93–100], *LII* 10.58, and Bowie 1991, 21. For the Four Discourses, see Fink 1997, 129f.

Objet petit a is not actually the object of desire *per se*, but is rather the *cause* of desire.[36] The actual object of our desire standing behind *a* is unattainable, as there is in fact nothing there: desire is a representation of lack. It manifests itself as such because this lack or gap would otherwise be impossible to signify, and desire would never enter the Symbolic.[37] Thus, as Lacanian subjects, we misrecognize other things in the Symbolic as if they were actually the objects of desire, though in fact they are false substitutes. We recognize the inability of these objects to satisfy our desire only upon obtaining them. Obtaining them reveals the fiction for us: if we were to get our hands on an object that we have mistaken for *a*, we would find desire manifest itself through some other outlet.

What is perhaps unintuitive about this approach to desire is that desire precedes its targets: we first desire absolutely, and only as a consequence of our environment desire *at* objects.[38] *a* is thus the missing piece of the puzzle that would complete the subject, but which the subject can never obtain. In this sense, it is crucial in *Odes* 4 that objects of desire are always just out of reach: Augustus is always about to return but never arrives, Cinara is only a memory, and Ligurinus is always just out of Horace's reach, even in the dreamwork of the conclusion to 4.1.

Grand Autre (*A*), the big Other, is the system of societal rules in which the subject emerges and which, therefore, circumscribe the subject and his desires.

---

[36] For this refinement, see *LII* 10.68: 'the object, the object *a* … ought to be conceived by us as the *cause* of desire, and… the object is behind desire.' See also Žižek 2012, 664 for the 'paradox' of *a* as both 'an empty, unoccupied place' and 'a rapidly moving, elusive object, an occupant without a place.'

[37] The terms 'Real', 'Symbolic', and 'Imaginary' (often abbreviated 'RSI') are Lacan's way of exploring a complementary tripartite way of understanding the world and our place in it. The three are tied together in a Borromean knot, each informing the other. The Symbolic is the world of symbols: language, in particular, but also the unconscious. Subjects participate in the Symbolic together as a social process. The Imaginary contrasts with the Symbolic by being introverted: here, the Subject repeats and re-enacts, reproducing its own image. The Real remains somewhat mysterious throughout Lacan's thought, but it has a real impact on the Subject. This third part is, in early Lacan, something like the world of primordial trauma, a solid kernel to which everything always returns (Lacan 1998 [1964]). Later, it becomes something more like the realm of what is unable to be expressed. For more on 'RSI', see especially Bowie 1991, 88–121 and the useful *index locorum* in Lacan 2006, 853.

[38] As Fink 1995, 60 describes it, 'object *a*… is an instrument or plaything with which subjects do as they like, manipulating it as it pleases them, orchestrating things in the fantasy scenario in such a way as to derive a maximum of excitement therefrom.' In Horace's formulation, the poet tries to cast out desire completely. This is an impossibility for the subject, and as such Horace's desires continue to occur: as he describes in 4.1, in his dreams, or, as he describes in 4.10, through a mediated surface like the mirror.

A, in other words, is the network of language, culture, family, and politics that pre-exist subjects and in which they participate. Since the Augustan programme was so focused on an individual, the early imperial instantiation of *A* 'should not be reduced to an anonymous symbolic field;' rather, we have one of those 'interesting cases where an individual stands for the big Other [*A*].'[39] Here we can consider Kennedy's formulation of the early principate:[40]

> 'the emergence of the principate might be viewed as the progressive re-organisation of a fragmented discourse, whose previous centre was provided by the institutions of the Republic, around the princeps as the new focus of stable meaning in society. Conventionally we tend to look upon Augustus as a person, but he was more significant as an idea. The power of Augustus was a collective invention, the symbolic embodiment of the conflicting desires, incompatible ambitions and aggressions of the Romans, the instrumental expression of a complex network of dependency, repression, and fear.'

Kennedy, although he is not working from a psychoanalytic angle *per se*, gets at many of the same concerns as we have here. The pivotal movement comes from recognizing that *a* is a fragment or by-product of *A*.[41] At the same time, *a* is also what prevents the subject from being whole. Thus, in a 1966 Venn diagram,[42] Lacan represents *a* as the shared intersection of the subject and *A*. Unpacked, this diagram suggests that the object cause of desire is shared by the subject and the outside world. In consequence a change in *A* will effect a change in *a*, and hence a change in the way that the subject views himself. This brings us back to Horace's statement that he is not what he used to be (*non sum qualis eram, Carm.* 4.1.3), which puts on display the direct impact that seismic shifts in socio-political structures can have on individual desires.

In turn, the relationship between poetry and politics in *Odes* 4 depends less on explicit reactions or articulations of policy than it does on the way that Horace orients his relationships – and not just his political relationships, but his erotic ones as well. This is what allows Horace to flow conceptually from the erotic reign

---

39 Žižek 2012, 92. Žižek qualifies further that for instances like these, 'one should think not primarily of leader-figures who directly embody their communities (king, president, master), but rather of the more mysterious *protectors of appearances* – such as otherwise corrupted parents who desperately try to keep their child ignorant of their depraved lives, or, if it is a leader, then one for whom Potemkin villages are built.' Augustus seems to share in both of these roles. He embodies the community, but only in the sense that he transcends the idea of community by forcing one identity – Roman – upon the world (*Odes* 4.15).
40 Kennedy 1992, 35.
41 *LII* 10.17.
42 *LII* 14.1.

of Cinara (4.1) to Augustus' new world order (4.15).[43] Thus as the patterns in sounds and language participate in a trajectory that reconstructs Venus from the goddess of recursive desire (4.1) to the teleological goddess of the Augustan family (4.15), it is no coincidence that Horace's searching articulation of something like *a* (4.13.18–22) falls right before two of the most overtly panegyrical poems he ever composed. What these poems (4.14, 4.15) celebrate is Augustus as he represents power, order, and stability – that is, as he represents *A*. Yet, through Augustus's absence, he is something of a manifestation of *a* for Horace as well. This is the gap between Augustus as an 'idea' in Kennedy's formulation above and Augustus as an individual.

Erotic and political in *Odes* 4.10

Armed now with a psychoanalytic framework for understanding the connection between the poet, the state, and desire, let us review what links the erotic and the political in *Odes* 4.10. *Odes* 4.10, which focuses on Ligurinus, is the culmination of a pentad, as are 4.5 and 4.15, each of which focuses on Augustus. Ligurinus and Augustus thus occupy analogous places in the structure of the collection. This is reinforced by some verbal parallels between 4.5 and 4.10 that were discussed above. In terms of psychoanalytic theory, we also see an emphasis on absence and return in the erotic space of 4.10 that mirrors the absence and return of Augustus in 4.5 and 4.15. These features are linked by lack and desire, suggesting a conceptual relationship between Augustus and Ligurinus. 4.10, with its layered desire for the recovery of lost time, past decisions, and lost objects of love mirrors the world of desire for Augustus as portrayed in 4.5 and 4.15, where Rome longs for the absent Augustus and the poet longs to be the one who can fulfill Augustus's desires with his poetry.

With Ligurinus swapped in for Augustus as an object of desire, Horace primes us for a subversive political reading. Augustus harbored serious concerns about how the young age at which he came to power affected public perceptions about him. In Cicero's *Philippics* and *Epistulae ad Brutum*, frequent reference is made to Octavian's youth and lack of experience. More telling still is Servius' note on Virgil's *Eclogues* 1.42, where we learn that the young Caesar Augustus had a law

---

[43] Cf. Janan 2012, 379–80 for Woman as a *nom du pere*, associating 'Woman' with the authoritative power of the father; and, consequently, the 'reign' of Cinara with the 'reign' of Augustus. See Miller 2004, 123 for more on the idea of Woman/Father and desire. The idea of Janan 2012, 380 of the 'straight conceptual line from Lesbia to Caesar' in Catullus 11 plays at this same effect.

passed against referring to him as a *puer*.⁴⁴ While *puer* is a common enough word in Horace, it usually refers to anonymous servants or choristers.⁴⁵ In the parallel of how Horace longs for Ligurinus (4.1, 4.10) and how Rome longs for Augustus (4.5, 4.15), Horace runs a subtle risk of placing himself in political danger.

Critics of *Odes* 4 have usually been dismissive of its erotic content. For Putnam the erotic poems highlight, by contrast, 'the more numerous poems on societal, historical time that they introduce.'⁴⁶ Johnson points out the 'obvious dilemma' in the structure of *Odes* 4: it cannot be both very artfully arranged and also include some tangential erotic lyrics without a convincing place in the collection.⁴⁷ For Johnson, the erotic elements of *Odes* 4 become 'part of the poet's public imaging,' and he links them to his rubric of panegyric through lament.

Mitchell is one of the only critics who has seen something political in *Odes* 4.10, though for her the poem is an ethnic allegory. Ligurinus, associated with the Ligurians by long hair and the adjective *puniceae* ('purple' more generally, but also 'Punic' or 'Carthaginian' – the Ligurians had helped Hannibal the battle of Metaurus, the focus of 4.4), shows the promise of the Ligurians 'exchanging their old ethnic identity for a new, Roman one, 'growing up' into a state of Roman civilisation.'⁴⁸ In this way, Mitchell's compelling interpretation helps 4.10 find a place in connection with 4.15, where *Romanitas* takes over the world. It necessarily sets aside, though, the significant erotic component of the Ligurinus narrative as it continues from the dream at the end of 4.1. Political and erotic themes were intertwined in this first poem, which itself undergoes a sort of development from beginning to end. 4.1 opens with Venus (desire) as a system of precepts (*A*, which here Horace tries to reject) and the absent Cinara as its cipher (*a*), and ends in a dream with Rome (manifest in the Campus Martius) as *A* and Ligurinus as *a*. We can here recall Lacan's Venn diagram above: the subject sees both himself and this larger structure as somehow incomplete, and *a* is the missing piece.⁴⁹

---

44 *decreuerat enim senatus, nequis eum puerum diceret, ne maiestas tanti imperii minueretur*, (Servius *ad* Virg. *Ecl.* 1.42 'for the senate had decreed that no one call him a *puer*, in order that the dignity of so great a power not be lessened').
45 For more on the word *puer*, also in the sense of beloved, see Thorsen in the final chapter in this volume.
46 Putnam 1986, 309.
47 Johnson 2004, 134–5.
48 Mitchell 2010, 61–2.
49 A fuller exploration of possible orientations to desire in psychoanalysis (e.g., obsession, hysteria, etc.) would require much more space than I am able to commit here. However, we see Horace himself searching after *a* in poems like 4.1 or 4.11, but figuring himself as Rome's *a* or Augustus' *a* in poems like 4.2 and 4.5. This is what makes 4.15 so significantly different: there no longer

Thus the collection suggests the interrelationship of the erotic and the political through its dynamics of discourse and shifting subject positions.

As a dialogue about power, the political poems come into the light of the erotic poems. Consider Horace's use of *potens* in the collection: Paullus Maximus will laugh at the gifts of his rival as a more powerful contender (*potentior / largi muneribus riserit aemuli*, Carm. 4.1.17–18), while Horace is constrained by the power of desire (4.1.1–4, 4.1.33–40). In 4.8, poets have power (*potentium / uatum*, Carm. 4.8.26–7), but in 4.10 Horace struggles against the might of Ligurinus, who is powerful in the gifts of Venus (*Veneris muneribus potens*, Carm. 4.10.1).[50] Horace's poetic power comes face to face with erotic power in language. And although Ligurinus is *potens* only 'so far' (*adhuc*), the power of Drusus and Tiberius in 4.4 and 4.14 seems effective only when restrained by the nurturing supervision of Augustus.

While modern critical discourse often seeks to distinguish private and public, the Augustan poets were interested in the conceptual overlaps between erotic and political desire.[51] Lowrie made this point more specifically about *Odes* 4.15, where the usual dichotomies in studies of Horatian lyric – 'grand versus light, epic versus lyric, public versus private,' e.g. – fail 'to maintain stability.'[52] In *Odes* 4.15, Horace gives back the remainder of his poetic power, sacrificing it and his identity to the Augustan project. In renouncing his own status as creating subject, he finally achieves the rejection of desire that he sought in *Odes* 4.1. Read through desire, though, these categories were never that stable to begin with. Like the 'idea' of Augustus for Kennedy, the thread of desire in *Odes* 4 that weaves through public and private creates a poetic space where these elements, if they cannot be reconciled, can at least live in a stable tension.

---

seems to be any need for the poet himself, who has his own desire curbed at the beginning of the poem (*uolentem* ... etc.).

50 Cf. the similar collocation of power and gifts at 4.1.17–18 above, as well that in 4.2.19–20 *potiore ... munere*.

51 For more on this feature of elegy, see, e.g., Stahl 1985, who does not rely upon psychoanalysis at all. For the issue in Horace, see Oliensis 1998. Outside of elegy, the entirety of *Aeneid* 4 stages Aeneas' attempt to reconcile erotic and political desire – his desire for Dido, on the one hand, and his divinely order mission of founding a new Troy in Italy, on the other. We see this come together in the language of *Aeneid* 7, where it is Erato who watches over the socio-political action of founding a new city.

52 Lowrie 1997, 347.

Jennifer Ingleheart
Amores Plural: Ovidian Homoerotics in the Elegies

Although the genre is frequently characterized as overwhelmingly interested in heteroerotic love, Latin love elegy is far more homoerotic than most scholars allow. Ovid in particular has been seen as the 'most heterosexual' representative of the genre, and indeed 'the most heterosexual' poet of his age.[1] Ovid has even been characterized as *the* poet of heterosexual love; Tom Habinek went so far as to claim that Ovid 'invents the category of the heterosexual male'.[2] Habinek is far from the only scholar to present us with an Ovid who strikingly departs from the norms of Latin love elegy and, indeed, a much longer Greco-Roman erotic literary tradition of homoerotic poetry, in that his first-person elegies focus almost exclusively on what we would now call heterosexual liaisons. Some readers have claimed that Ovid even displayed hostility towards what we would most conveniently label homosexuality; for example, Peter Green claims that Ovid's 'attitude to adult homosexuality is casual, pragmatic and dismissive' and John Makowski talks of Ovid's 'aversion to pederasty'.[3] Such characterizations of Ovid are highly problematic, for a number of reasons, which will be discussed here. Readers of Ovid who characterize him in this way have ignored the precise terms in which some of his most often quoted elegiac comments on homosexuality are framed, and have consequently failed to explore the rest of his elegies for hints of homoeroticism.

If we look outside Ovid's subjective love elegies, Ovid's other works should emphatically disprove the notion that Ovid was in some way hostile to, or chose mostly to ignore, homosexual love. In the epic *Metamorphoses*, Ovid explores a vast range of human passions, including same-sex desires and liaisons: much of book 10 comprises songs about the loves of gods for beautiful boys, performed by the bard Orpheus, who has himself turned to the exclusive love of boys after the loss of his

---

Earlier versions of this essay were delivered at NTNU and at Durham University; I am grateful to Thea Thorsen for the invitation to think about this theme for my seminar at NTNU, and to all participants there and at Durham whose questions and comments helped to improve this essay, as I am to the editors. Many thanks are also owed to my doctoral student, Joseph Watson, who acted as my research assistant in preparing a final draft of this essay, and provided many useful suggestions and comments.

1 Makowski 1996, 29.
2 Habinek 1997, 31.
3 Green 1982, 355, Makowski 1996, 30. Cf. McKeown 1989, 23 on *Am.* 1.1.19–20.

wife, Eurydice.⁴ Leading in to Ovid's account of the myth of Orpheus is the story at the close of book 9 of Iphis' love for Ianthe. Iphis, born a girl, but raised a boy, falls in love with Ianthe, who loves her back, unaware that Iphis was born female, and Iphis is eventually transformed into a young man so that a marriage between Iphis and Ianthe can be accomplished. Nor are such lengthy episodes the only passages involving homosexuality within the *Metamorphoses*; there are various other references throughout its 15 books to same-sex passions and configurations.⁵ Moreover, if we believe that Ovid wrote *Heroides* 15, the *Epistula Sapphus*,⁶ then he, unlike the majority of writers in antiquity, took an interest in what we would now call lesbian love, as part of his project of exploring the many varieties of human passion; *Her.* 15 is much concerned with how lesbian passion is similar to and different from both heteroerotic love and pederasty, as insightful studies by Judith Hallett and Pamela Gordon have shown.⁷ Even if we do not believe that this poem was actually written by Ovid, it is clear that an imitator took some pains to write it in an Ovidian manner, believing that the treatment of lesbianism was Ovidian, perhaps building on Ovid's brief reference to Sappho's love of girls at *Tristia* 2.365: *Lesbia quid docuit Sappho nisi amare puellas?* 'what did Sappho teach, except how to love girls? / girls how to love'.⁸ Another poem of disputed authorship perhaps suggesting Ovid's interest in homoerotic themes is *Priapeia* 3, attributed to him by Seneca the Elder,⁹ although this attribution has been doubted.¹⁰

---

4 Ovid's depiction of Orpheus as a boy-lover (following a Greek tradition that goes back to at least Phanocles fragment 1), is in marked contrast to Virgil's famous account of Orpheus' loss of Eurydice, in which, as Makowski 1996, 25 observes, Virgil 'does not breathe a word on the subject of homosexuality'. McKeown 1989, 23, in his comments on *Am.* 1.1.19–20 on Ovid's attitude towards homoerotic love, observes: 'Even in the *Metamorphoses*, Ovid makes very sparing use of the rich resources of Greek homosexual mythology, the greatest concentration of such stories being the brief accounts of Cyparissus, Ganymede and Hyacinthus at 10.106–219'.
5 Although McKeown 1989, 23 notes that the longest treatments of homosexual themes in the *Metamorphoses* are cordoned off in Books 9 and 10, briefer, more allusive references appear elsewhere in the text. Most notably, the Callisto episode in Book 2 (404–507), for which see Oliver 2015, and the brief allusion to the homoerotic attachment of Phaëthon and Cycnus at *Met.* 2.367–9.
6 For arguments in favour of authenticity, see Baca 1971, Kirfel 1969, Showerman/Goold 1977, Rosati 1996, Thorsen 2014; 2019c and Elisei, 2019.
7 Gordon 1997, Hallett 2005.
8 See Ingleheart 2010a, 297; either translation contains innuendo about lesbianism, given ancient erotic pedagogy and Sappho's reputation as a teacher.
9 *Controv.* 1.2.22.
10 McKeown 1989, 23 claims that 'Ovid is unlikely to be the author of the homosexual *Priap.* 3', for which also see Buchheit 1962. Whether *Priap.* 3 is Ovidian is immaterial: when Seneca ascribed the poem to him, he clearly did not think the poem's homoerotic themes inappropriate for Ovid; see also Richlin 1992, 141–3.

Even if we leave aside these other works, it would be incredibly anomalous if Ovid departed to such a great extent from the homoerotic tradition of love poetry in his first person subjective elegies, as to either ignore or reject homoeroticism, and this essay argues that he does no such thing. Ovid's *Amores*, the elegies that relate what he presents as his own love affairs, are far from being exclusively heterosexual, and we should take their programmatic titular plurality seriously. These are not poems that are limited to heterosexual passions; they treat many different varieties of love.[11] Extended' scholarly analysis of Ovid's treatment of sexuality has largely focused on studies of the *Metamorphoses*,[12] but there is a great deal to be gained from analysing Ovid's treatment of homoeroticism in his earlier works as well. I argue that Ovid is far more concerned with homoerotic passion, and with homosociality, in the *Amores*, *Ars amatoria*, and *Remedia amoris* than has previously been recognized, and that Ovid's homoeroticism has important consequences for the broader erotics of Ovidian elegy and its place in the wider tradition of love poetry, as well as for the history of sexuality. This essay proposes that homoerotic passion is a programmatic and significant part of Ovidian erotics, demonstrating the breadth of his elegiac world, innovative engagement with the wider tradition of love poetry, and subversion of societal and generic norms.[13]

My starting point, after a brief introductory discussion of the terminology and approach that inform this essay, is the first reference to the possibility of homoerotic passion within Ovid's first person erotic elegies: *Amores* 1.1.19–20. The way in which Ovid programmatically suggests here that a boy may be his beloved, his poetic inspiration, and his theme, has not received sufficient attention. This essay aims to redress this gap in scholarship by exploring in some detail the ways in which *Amores* 1.1 and 1.2 further the hint of homoeroticism in *Amores* 1.1.19–20. I then turn to a poem that is highly loaded in homoerotic terms, Ovid's elegy lamenting the death of his fellow elegiac poet, Tibullus; *Amores* 3.9 has not previously been read in this way,[14] but it is revealing to look for hints of homoeroticism

---

11 Compare the putative use of the title *Amores* for the poems of Cornelius Gallus (Serv. *ad Ecl.* 10.1), who is often portrayed as the poet-lover of Lycoris (e.g. Prop. 2.34.91–2, Ov. *Am.* 1.15.29–30, Verg. *Ecl.* 10); yet Gallus' title suggests other beloveds too, and Virgil seems to suggest that Gallus' affections were not solely heterosexual at *Ecl.* 10.37–43, a claim presumably evidenced by his now lost poetry.
12 E.g. Nagle 1984, Makowski 1996, Hallett 1997, Oliver 2015.
13 My essay is thus parallel to Harrison 2018a's attempt to bring out the (much more obvious) homoerotic elements in Horace's erotic verse.
14 E.g. McKeown 1989, 23, claims *Am.* 3.9 'ignore[s]' the homosexual content of Tibullus' Marathus elegies (1.4, 1.8 and 1.9).

and homosociality in a poem which treats the only Roman love elegist whose surviving poetry presents himself as being in love with a boy. In my final section, I turn to the *Ars amatoria* and its companion piece, the *Remedia amoris*, which have done much to cement the stereotype of an exclusively heterosexual Ovid. The erotodidactic *Ars* purports to teach men how to win over women in its first two books, and instructs women how to pursue men in its third and apparently concluding book. This advice is followed, however, by precepts to both genders on how to get over unhappy love affairs in the *Remedia*, the final instalment of Ovid's didactic elegies. Nevertheless, despite the heavily heterocentric focus of these books, Ovid continues to develop the hints at homoeroticism that are found in his *Amores*, with important consequences for his depiction of love.

At this juncture, I ought to say a few words about the terminology and approach of this essay. Although the term 'homosexual' and its cognates are anachronistic as applied to antiquity, I nevertheless use such terminology as a convenient shorthand when referring to same-sex desire and relations. In order to avoid lengthy and inelegant phrasing, I also refer throughout this essay to ancient poets by their names, both when I make reference to the poet and to the poet-lover who appears as a character in subjective Latin love elegy,[15] but this should not be taken to imply that I subscribe to what I would deem a naive biographical reading of elegy. In fact, biographical interpretations of the elegists' attitudes towards love probably have to bear a large amount of responsibility for readers' failure to explore Ovidian homoeroticism fully. Ovid himself, however, invites us to conflate the poet with the lover *Naso* who appears in his poetry and, ultimately, biographical readings of his poetry must be traced back to Ovid himself.

aut puer aut ... puella

Let us now turn to the start of Ovid's elegiac corpus. As I observed earlier, Ovid dangles out the possibility in *Amores* 1.1 that his first-person erotic elegies will treat homoerotic love: in this programmatic opening poem, Ovid has not yet become a lover but presents himself as already a poet even before the 'narrative' of the elegy begins. Ovid responds to Cupid's theft of a foot of his epic hexameter verse, a theft which forces him to write in the elegiac metre (1.1.1–4), with a lengthy speech complaining about Cupid's interference in the poetic sphere (5–

---

[15] For the *poeta-amator*, see Holzberg 2002, 10–20 = Holzberg 1998.

20). Ovid's protest culminates in the objection that he is not in love, and consequently cannot write love elegy, at lines 19–20:

> nec mihi materia est numeris leuioribus apta,
> aut puer aut longas compta puella comas.
>
> (Ov. Am. 1.1.19–20)

> I do not have material that is suited to lighter metres,
> Either a boy or a girl with beautifully arranged long locks.[16]

The generic necessity for an elegiac love poet to be in love is immediately resolved by Cupid shooting Ovid and forcing him both to fall in love and to accept his new task as a *poeta-amator* (21–30). But this resolution is notably partial: even as Ovid accepts his identity as a love elegist, he teasingly keeps the reader in the dark as to the identity and the gender of the beloved about whom he will write poetry.[17] His focus in the closing lines of this programmatic elegy is upon his own transformation into a poet of love, and we receive no information about the beloved with whom he has fallen in love; by the poem's end, we do not know even whether it is a boy or a girl.

The gender of Ovid's beloved is revealed only at the start of the next but one elegy, when Ovid declares that he has fallen in love with a woman:

> Iusta precor: quae me nuper praedata puella est,
> aut amet aut faciat, cur ego semper amem.
>
> (Ov. Am. 1.3.1–2)

> I pray a just prayer: may the girl who has recently taken me as her prey
> either love me or give me a reason why I should always be in love.

Indeed, when we go on to read the rest of the erotic elegies, the priority, in terms of word order, that was given to the *puer* as love object in *Amores* 1.1.19 seems to be revealed as a generic tease, a playful hint at a possible direction in which Ovid might take his love elegy, that looks to the presence of boy-love in his elegiac predecessors Tibullus, Propertius, and Gallus, and in earlier erotic poetry such as

---

16 Unless otherwise stated, the translations are mine.
17 Ovid may teasingly draw attention to the fact that this is love elegy as yet without a beloved, when he notes that 'Cupid reigns in my empty heart' (*in uacuo pectore regnat Amor*, 1.1.26). McKeown 1989, 27 *ad loc.* argues well for *uacuo* = '(still) fancy-free', suggesting the 'witty paradox that Ovid should be consumed with love even though he does not yet have a beloved'; he notes also the interpretation that *uacuo* may mean 'fancy-free (until Cupid took possession)'.

that of Catullus, the Hellenistic epigrammatists, and the archaic Greek lyricists.¹⁸ Despite what Jim McKeown refers to as Ovid's 'casual attitude to the sex of his beloved' in 1.1.19–20,¹⁹ reflecting an ancient understanding that adult males desired both boys and women, Ovid's erotic elegies go on to be overwhelmingly concerned with the love of *puellae*,²⁰ as many readers have noted. For most readers, then, Ovidian elegiac homoeroticism starts – and ends – with the opening elegy of the *Amores*.

Yet while the *puer* as elegiac beloved/theme may seem to drop out of sight between the first and third elegies, a closer reading of the opening sequence of the *Amores* can help to complicate the characterisation of Ovid's elegiac corpus as focused on heterosexual love. On the way in which *Amores* 1.3.1–2 resolves the tease about the gender of the beloved that is found in *Amores* 1.1.19–20, Katharina Volk has recently noted with reference to *Amores* 1.3 that: 'Once the object of Ovid's desire has been revealed to be a woman, same-sex love is excluded from the *Amores*'.²¹ This is, as we shall see, a partial reading of the erotics of the *Amores*, but it provides us with a useful route into exploring Ovidian homoerotics: that is, I argue that a homoerotic dimension can be detected in *Amores* 1.1 and 1.2, which can be seen as the gap between the lines in which Ovid raises the possibility of same-sex love and *Amores* 1.3, where he appears to shut down that possibility. Crucially for our purposes, *Amores* 1.1 and 1.2 occur at a point in the work at which Ovid has not yet revealed to the first-time reader of the *Amores* that he has a female and not a male beloved;²² a close reading of these poems can illuminate the presence of homoeroticism within the *Amores* and enable us to recognise its programmatic importance for the erotic elegies.

---

18 E.g. Tib. 1.4, 1.8, 1.9, 2.3, Prop. 2.12, Catull. 15, 21, 23, 24, 48, 81, 99, Anac. frs. 1, 14, 62, Thgn. 1259–1380, (Callim.) *Anth. Pal.* 12.43, 12.73, Theoc. 12. Gallus' boy-love does not survive in any of the fragments (for which, see Anderson et al. 1979), but there is allusion to it in Prop. 1.20 and Verg. *Ecl.* 10.37–41. See e.g. Cantarella 2002, Dover 1989, Patzer 1982.

19 McKeown 1989, 23; he provides parallels from elegy and elsewhere in which the beloved is male (Verg. *Ecl.* 10.37–8; Hor. *Epod.* 11.3–4, 27–8, *Carm.* 4.1.29–8, (Mel.) *Anth. Pal.* 12.86. However, McKeown implies that Ovid is antipathetic towards homosexuality, despite quoting a passage (*Ars am.* 2.683–4, see below) in which Ovid insinuates that he feels some level of homosexual sentiment.

20 Volk 2010, 89.

21 Volk 2010, 89.

22 *Contra* Turpin 2014, who argues that the Muse with whom *Am.* 1.1 closes should be understood as Corinna, Ovid's Muse in the sense that she inspires his work; Turpin does not cite perhaps the best evidence I am aware of for the Romans having a concept of a 'Muse' as erotic/poetic inspiration: Catull. 35.16–17 *sapphica puella / musa doctior* ('girl more learned than the Sapphic muse').

I detect complex play with eroticism and, in particular, homoeroticism in *Amores* 1.1.19–20 and in the first elegy of the *Amores* more broadly. While Ovid's poetic *materia* will eventually turn out to be a *puella* rather than a *puer*, Ovid's description of the *longas compta puella comas* recalls homoerotic depictions in both Greek and Latin verse of beautiful boy love-objects as having long hair, which is often in attractive disarray.[23] As scholars have noted, Ovid here recalls Horace, *Epod.* 11.27–8:

> ... alius ardor aut puellae candidae
> aut teretis pueri longam renodantis[24] comam.
>
> (Hor. *Epod.* 11.27-8)

> ... another flame, either for a fair girl
> or a slender boy, knotting up again/unknotting his long locks.

Here, the poet contemplates a future beloved who might set him free from his current passion for the boy Lyciscus. Ovid's readers are encouraged to spot the allusion by the close verbal echo of Horace's *longam ... comam* in the Ovidian *longas ... comas*, as well as the contextual similarity of a poet looking forward to having either a female or a male beloved.[25] Jim McKeown attributes Ovid's change of emphasis in his Horatian allusion to a personal erotic preference: the desirable boy has long hair in Horace, but this attribute is given to the girl of Ovid's poem, showing the real direction of Ovid's desires on McKeown's interpretation, while

---

[23] Mankin 1995, 205, commenting on Hor. *Epod.* 11.27–8 (see below) notes (e.g.) Hor. *Carm.* 1.29.8, 2.5.23, 3.20.14, 4.10.3, Chaerem. fr. 1.5, Theoc. 5.91, Philostr. *Imag.* 1.23.5, Archil. fr. 31; see Nisbet/Rudd 2004, 244. Such hair is often associated with the homoerotic and 'somewhat androgynously handsome' figures of Apollo and Bacchus (McKeown 1989, 376): e.g. at Tib. 2.5.8, Ov. *Am.* 1.1.11, 1.14.31–2, *Ars am.* 3.141–2. For hair and gender, see Pandey 2018. Apollo is regularly found in the homoerotic sphere: e.g. Tib. 2.3.11–14; Ov. *Met.* 10.162–219. However, the eroticism of unkempt hair is not uniquely male: e.g. Daphne (Ov. *Met.* 1.497–8), Naiads (*Fast.* 1.405), and Propertius' Cynthia (4.8.51–2). Ovid himself connects unkempt female hair with eroticism at *Ars am.* 3.153–60; for more on messy hair in Ovid, see Sande 2017, Olson 2017, 139, Pandey 2018, especially 458–9. For the eroticism of messy hair in elegy more broadly, see Burkowski 2012, 184–92.

[24] See Mankin 1995, 205 for the ambiguous meaning of the prefix *re-* of this verb, found here for the first time; Watson 2003, 381 argues convincingly for the sense of 'unbinding'.

[25] Anticipating Ovid's order in which a boy appears before a girl, Horace describes himself as subject to *Amore, qui me praeter omnis expetit / mollibus in pueris aut in puellis urere* ('love/Love [the relative clause suggests the latter is more likely], who seeks me out, more than anyone else, to set me on fire for soft boys or for girls' (*Epod.* 11.3–4).

Ovid's boy receives no distinguishing features whatsoever, in marked contrast to the *puella*, and to Horace's more balanced description.²⁶

McKeown sees the boy as a mere cipher, a nod to the importance of boy-love in earlier erotic verse. While the change of emphasis does matter, it seems highly reductive to approach Ovid's Horatian intertextuality in such biographical terms. Rather, Ovid's play with Horace is significant insofar as it blurs the boundaries between the two genders as love objects, endowing the *puella* with an attractive feature commonly associated with the *puer* as object of homoerotic desire.²⁷ That the *puella* is described with reference to an aesthetically pleasing attribute frequent in poetic descriptions of beautiful boys suggests, then, both that desire will be no simple matter in the *Amores*, and that homoerotic aesthetics will inform the poet's experience of heterosexual desire. This slippage between male and female objects of desire is more than just a matter of Ovidian 'casualness' with respect to the gender of the beloved: it features throughout Ovid's corpus and acts as an important way of keeping homoerotic desire in focus, and, crucially, it has an elegiac precedent.

That precedent is the programmatic opening lines of Propertius' own first elegy, in which Propertius famously rewrites an epigram by Meleager, *Anth. Pal.* 12.101 (= 103 GP):

> Cynthia prima suis miserum me cepit ocellis,
>   contactum nullis ante cupidinibus.
> tum mihi constantis deiecit lumina fastus
>   et caput impositis pressit Amor pedibus,
> donec me docuit castas odisse puellas   5
>   improbus, et nullo uiuere consilio.
>
> (Prop. 1.1.1–6)

---

26 McKeown 1989, 23.
27 Ovid plays with Horace's description of the boy as *renodantis* when he describes the *puella* as *compta*, with well dressed locks; as noted above, *pueri delicati* are often described as having hair that is sexily free. Ovid's reference to the girl as *compta* as to her locks therefore either presents her as different from a boy who is letting his hair down in Horace, or as parallel with the boy who is knotting his hair up in Horace - for the ambiguity of *re-nodantis*, see above. The word *comptas* may also hint at a more metapoetical thrust, in which the literary artefact of the beloved is itself 'composed' by the poet; see Burkowski 2012, especially 3, 21, 36–7, 61. For the connected motif of weaving as metapoetic synecdoche for poetic composition (sometimes tied up with hairstyling), see Nethercut 1975, Papaïoannou 2006, 56–8, Snyder 1981, Zetzel 1996, 77–9. In Ovidian elegy the hair of the beloved woman is a part of her charms that is frequently foregrounded (e.g. *Am.* 1.1.20, 1.5.10, 1.14 *passim*, *Ars am.* 3.141); indeed, some scholars have even gone so far as to call this a 'fetish' (e.g. Kennedy 1993, 73, Frazel 2003, 74). This may in itself respond to references to the hair of the *eromenos* in pederastic verse; see Dover 1989, 78–9, Lear/Cantarella 2008, 28, Harrison 1988.

Cynthia was the first; she captured poor me with her eyes,
   when I had been touched before by no desires.
Then Amor lowered my looks of fixed arrogance
   and pressed on my head with feet imposed
until he taught me to hate chaste girls,   5
   naughty boy, and to live like an elegist.

Τόν με Πόθοις ἄτρωτον ὑπὸ στέρνοισι Μυΐσκος
   ὄμμασι τοξεύσας τοῦτ' ἐβόησεν ἔπος·
'Τὸν θρασὺν εἷλον ἐγώ· τὸ δ' ἐπ' ὀφρύσι κεῖνο φρύαγμα
   σκηπτροφόρου σοφίας ἠνίδε ποσσὶ πατῶ.'
τῷ δ', ὅσον ἀμπνεύσας, τόδ' ἔφην· 'Φίλε κοῦρε, τί θαμβεῖς;   5
   καὐτὸν ἀπ' Οὐλύμπου Ζῆνα καθεῖλεν Ἔρως.'

((Meleager) *Anth. Pal.* 12.101)

Myiscus, shooting me, unwounded by the Loves, in the breast
   with his eyes, shouted out this:
'I have captured the bold one. See, I trample underfoot that insolence on his brow
   that projects sceptred wisdom.'
Just gathering my breath, I said this to him, 'dear boy, why are you amazed?   5
   Love brought down Zeus himself from Olympus.'

In these lines, Propertius could be seen to heterosexualize for Latin love elegy the homoerotic scenario of the Hellenistic epigrammatist, by bringing his female beloved, Cynthia, centre stage, and making her, rather than the boy-beloved Myiscus, responsible for his erotic capture, effected through the eyes. Propertius' readers, versed in Greek epigram, would have been highly alert to Propertius' manipulation of his Hellenistic predecessor and to his switch in the beloved's gender, which nevertheless does not fully erase the homoerotic element of his Greek model. As various scholars have noted,[28] traces of Meleager's homoerotic scenario are not confined to Propertius' inversion of the gender of the beloved, but can also be detected in Propertius' treatment of the role of boy-god of love, who takes on the role of conqueror that Myiscus himself had played in Meleager's epigram. Meleager's depiction of Myiscus had nevertheless aligned the beloved boy strongly with the boy-god of love, an identification that is frequently made in both pederastic Greek epigram and earlier homoerotic Greek lyric.[29] In our epigram in particular, the metaphor of Myiscus shooting (*toxeusas*, 2) at Meleager

---

28 Propertius' play with Meleager, and particularly the implications of the gender switch, are well discussed by Miller 2004, 85–8, Höschele 2011, 20–6, Heslin 2018, 68, see also Ingleheart 2015.
29 E.g. Anac. fr. 396, 413, Ibyc. fr. 287, (Mel.) *Anth. Pal.* 12.127.

recalls the bow and arrows, the usual weapons and attributes, of the love god, even as Meleager's language is revealed as metaphorical by the unexpected combination of this verb with *ommasi* (2). Meleager's opening and closing references to *Pothois* and *Eros* also serve to strengthen the link between Myiscus and Eros, and hint that Myiscus' erotic power and victory have been gained through the workings of the personified god of love. While Meleager's boy-beloved is replaced by Propertius' Cynthia, then, the reader is reminded that the poet is defeated by a boy-beloved in Propertius' model by the boy-god of love performing the same role as the boy himself had done in Meleager. The homoerotic has a significant presence in Propertius 1.1.

This matters, since Propertius' opening poem constitutes an important precedent for *Amores* 1.1, not only as an elegiac opening, but also because Propertius has influenced the specific scenario of Ovid's poem, in which the god of love imposes desire upon a man who has not experienced it previously.[30] Furthermore, traces of Meleager, via Propertius, can be read in Ovid's first poem. Propertius' opening lines offer us a scenario in which the poet-lover simply accepts his ill-treatment and subjugation by forces divine and human, and becomes a passive victim of love, but Ovid's spirited reply to the Cupid who dares to steal a foot of his putative epic work, and who will soon enough shoot him with a love-inspiring arrow, just as Myiscus shoots Meleager, recalls the (much shorter) response of the epigram's Meleager to Myiscus' apparent victory, *Anth. Pal.* 12.101.5–6. Ovid's response to Cupid is quite different from Propertius' passivity and lack of quoted speech, and clearly looks to Meleager's epigram. Jim McKeown's (in many ways excellent) commentary does not note the window-reference to Meleager via Propertius 1.1 in *Amores* 1.1;[31] indeed, he even claims that there are 'no certain conceptual or verbal links' between Propertius' first elegy and *Amores* 1.1.[32] The homoerotic scenario of Meleager's epigram, via Propertius 1.1, nevertheless colours our reading of Ovid; while Propertius had inverted, if never wholly removed from

---

30 In Fowler 2002a's model, poetic 'inspiration is an invasive process, like being the "passive" and "penetrated" partner in intercourse' (150). Fowler does not, however, discuss our passage (Ov. *Am.* 1.1) in his analysis of poetic inspiration scenes.

31 For the 'window reference', see Thomas 1986, especially 188–9. This specific link has not been noted, while some scholars have posited Ovidian play with Propertius/Meleager: for example, Höschele 2011, 21 suggests Amor's theft of one foot in the fourth line of Ovid's *Amores* is 'a witty reversal and metrical elaboration' of Propertius' double allusion to Myiscus *possi pato* with *pressit pedibus* and the verbal echo of *possi* in *impositis*, the participle that qualifies *pedibus*.

32 McKeown 1989, 27 does note that *me miserum* (*Am.* 1.1.25) may allude to Prop. 1.1.1's *miserum me* (see also Hinds 1998, 29–34), and contrasts 'Ovid's light-hearted detachment' with 'the urgency and emotional intensity of Propertius' first elegy' (McKeown 1989, 11).

view, the homoerotic elements of his Hellenistic model, the first-time reader of *Amores* 1.1 cannot be sure that Ovid will follow the same erotic path,[33] of devotion to a one and only female beloved, as his Roman predecessor had done with his Cynthia.

Although I can detect no specific verbal reminiscences of either Propertius 1.1 or Meleager *Anth. Pal.* 12.101 in *Amores* 1.2, the poem as a whole expands upon their scenario of the erotic conquest of the poet-lover. The second poem of the *Amores* creates an entire elegy on the theme of the triumph of Cupid over his victim, drawing on the vocabulary of capture (*eilon*, *Anth. Pal.* 12.101.3; *cepit*, Prop. 1.1.1) and the image of trampling underfoot, the action of the military conqueror, in Propertius and Meleager (*Anth. Pal.* 12.101.4; Prop. 1.1.4). *Amores* 1.2, then, constitutes an important continuation of the homoerotics of Ovidian elegy, not least in its presentation of Cupid as the conqueror of Ovid.

As we have already noted (see note 31), slippage between the beloved boy and Eros, the boy-god of love, was frequent in Greek erotic verse. Such slippage can also be detected in *Amores* 1.2, to homoerotic effect, and it is set up by *Amores* 1.1, a poem in which various erotic slippages and homoerotic hints are found. Some, although not all of these, have been detected in scholarship: the potential homoeroticism in 1.2 of Ovid's presentation of Cupid as his conqueror, effected via his reading of Meleager through Propertius, as discussed above, has not been considered previously. However, Duncan Kennedy has astutely noted homoerotic overtones in the interaction between Cupid and Ovid in 1.1, arguing that, in Cupid's command to Ovid to *accipe ... opus*, 'he ensures that the poet is receptive, thus graphically figuring the passive role which is incorporated in elegy's own representation of itself as *mollis*'.[34] The presentation of Ovid, at the very outset of his corpus, being penetrated by the boy-god Cupid, and therefore being less than manly in Roman terms, matters for our understanding of Ovid's self-presentation in the *Amores*. Ovid in this poem is far from the heterosexually fixated, swaggering lover who boasts about his many female conquests in later poems; indeed, his humiliation in this poem may perhaps account for his later boasting, as a form of overcompensation.

The idea that Cupid and Ovid have an erotic relationship is further hinted at by *Amores* 1.1.26 *uror, et in uacuo pectore regnat Amor* ('I am burned, and Cupid rules in my empty heart'). Traditionally, this description of the dominion of Amor

---

[33] Martelli 2013, 35–8 discusses Ovid's presentation of the *Amores* as a second edition, adapted from a longer, five book original (see *Am.* 1 epigr.); this makes the experience of a 'first-time' reader impossible to reconstruct from the extant text.
[34] Kennedy 1993, 62.

over Ovid has been interpreted as a metaphor for Ovid having fallen in love, although the description of Ovid's heart as 'empty' and the fact that no object for Ovid's love is revealed here has caused readers some disquiet.³⁵ However, perhaps we may recognise that there is no lack of a love relationship in Ovid's life if we are alert to the erotic overtones of this phrasing, for the idea that an individual rules erotically over their lover is a commonplace.³⁶ While we also find Eros/Cupid ruling over others in the sense that he makes them be in love,³⁷ the homoerotic play that we have already detected in *Am.* 1.1 suggests that we should be alert to the former meaning here. Love's dominion over Ovid might precisely be that of a *lover*.

The homoeroticism of Cupid's power over Ovid, and Ovid's erotic submission to Cupid, continues in the portrait of Cupid's triumph in *Amores* 1.2. Before we go on to consider Cupid's triumph, it is worth noting that the initial set up of *Amores* 1.2, before the triumph scene, is homoerotically tinged. For the first four lines, in which Ovid cannot sleep, and wonders why, recall the homoerotically tinged Catullus 50, where Catullus is well aware that his sleeplessness is caused by his (homoerotic) desire to be with his friend and fellow poet Calvus,³⁸ in contrast to the amusingly clueless Ovid. Indeed, Ovid's apparent ignorance about the erotic nature of his insomnia,³⁹ is made even funnier by his apparent lack of awareness of this literary precedent, despite his grandiose claims to literary mastery in *Amores* 1.1. Despite the lack of verbal parallels between the poems, Catullus' homoerotic

---

35 McKeown 1989, 27–8; for a summary of different interpretations of *Am.* 1.1.26, see Turpin 2014.
36 E.g., as noted at Murgatroyd 1980, 276–7, Hor. *Carm.* 3.9.9 (*me nunc Thressa Chloe regit*, 'now Thracian Chloe rules over me'); Prop. 2.16.30 (*subito felix nunc mea regna tenet*, 'now some other man gets lucky all of a sudden and holds my kingdom'); [Tib.] 4.5.3–4 ([Tib] 3.11.3–4) (*Parcae ... seruitium et dederunt regna superba tibi*, 'the Parcae gave slavery and proud sovereignty to you'); Ov. *Am.* 2.17.11 (*non, tibi si facies animum dat et omina regni*, 'not even if your appearance gives you haughtiness and intimations of ruling'). Cf. Prop. 4.7.50 and 3.10.18 (*inque meum semper stent tua regna caput*, 'and may your sovereignty always stand over my head').
37 E.g. Ov. *Met.* 5.369–72: *tu superos ipsumque Iouem, tu numina ponti / uicta domas ipsumque, regit qui numina ponti: / Tartara quid cessant? cur non matrisque tuumque / imperium profers?* ('you rule over the gods and Jupiter himself, you rule over the conquered powers of the sea and he who reigns over the sea; why should Tartarus hold back? Why do you not extend your mother's empire – and your own?'). Cf. Ovid's comments that *regendus Amor [est]* (*Ars am.* 1.4; 'Eros must be ruled') and that his *aetas* is *apta regi* (ibid. 1.10; 'age is appropriate to be ruled over').
38 Catull. 50.11–13: *sed toto indomitus furore lecto / uersare, cupiens uidere lucem, / ut tecum loquerer simulque ut essem* ('but wild I am tossed about in madness over the whole bed, wishing to see the dawn that I might talk with you and be with you').
39 On erotic sleeplessness, see Thomas 1979, 203–5, Miller 2004, 79, Pasco-Pranger 2009.

scenario is very much a precedent for this scene of Ovidian sleeplessness, and ought to be read against it.

The opening lines of *Amores* 1.2 also look back to the sexualized suggestiveness of *Amores* 1.1: the hardness of the covers, described as *dura* in line 1, recalls that the poet has, in the opening poem, been the opposite of *durus*, in terms of Roman ideas about masculine behaviour, as he is emasculated through his penetration by Cupid. Further, the description *lassaque uersati corporis ossa dolent* ('the shagged out bones of my tossed about body ache', 4) begins with two sexually loaded terms: *lassus*, as opposed to its synonym *fessus*, is often found in contexts of *sexual* weariness;[40] indeed, Ovid will use it of the postcoital exhaustion he and Corinna experience at 1.5.25. The fact that this adjective is applied to Ovid's bones may also recall frequent descriptions of Cupid's arrow piercing the bones of those he forces to fall in love, given the previous poem's play on Ovid's sexual penetration by Cupid.[41] The passive participle *uersati* hardly looks innocent in this context, either; for despite the absence of *uerso* from Adams' study of the Latin sexual vocabulary,[42] the vocabulary of turning *is* found with play on its sense of 'turning about in coitus' in Greek texts.[43] Ovid may hint, then, that his body is sexually worn out from its encounter with Cupid in the previous poem. There may well be further innuendo in the next line, as Ovid states *nam, puto, sentirem, siquo temptarer amore* ('For I think I'd know it if / I were being teased by Love', 1.2.5);[44] appreciation of the innuendo has not been helped here for modern readers by the way in which editors are forced to print the 'a' of *amore* either

---

40 E.g. Plaut. *Asin.* 873, Ov. *Am.* 1.5.25; 3.7.80; 3.11.13, Apul. *Met.* 2.17. Cf. the use of the verb *lasso* at Tib. 1.9.55, Juv. 6.130, SHA *Max.* 4.7. See also the noun *lassitudo* at Apul. *Met.* 2.17; Adams 1990, 196.
41 E.g. Ov. *Am.* 2.9a.13–14, *Her.* 16.277–8, *Met.* 1.472–3, cf. the similar, though not osseous, sentiment at Prop. 2.12.17.
42 McKeown 1998, 36 cites for *uersati* Catull. 50.11–12, Prop 1.14.21; 2.22b.47-8, Sen. *Tranq.* 9.2.6 (*quibus difficilis somnus est uersant se*; 'people do toss themselves, as it were to help sleep'), Juv. 13.218. *Verso* does not seem to connote a specific sexual practice, but the contexts in which it is found are ones of heightened sexually frustrated sleeplessness; it seems a metaphor ripe for sexual exploitation and innuendo. Kennedy 2012, 201 suggests some protracted connection between the verb *uerso* and matters sexual, but he does not fully commit to it.
43 See Henderson 1975, 176 for examples, to which should be added Zeus' dirty-minded interpretation of Ganymede's innocent words about tossing on his bed in Lucian, *Dial. D.* 10; a scenario highly relevant to the discussion above. For the motif of 'turning words' relating, eventually, via Greek *tropos*, to words associated with sexuality, see Kennedy 2012, 201 and Gibson 2003, 391.
44 Commenting on *si quo temptarer amore*, McKeown 1998, 36 notes 'I can cite no exact parallel for this phrase', but the sole Ovidian parallel he cites, *Ars am.* 1.365 (*tum quoque temptanda est,*

capitalized or lowercase. If we print *Amore* with a capital A, Ovidian homoeroticism comes into clearer focus,⁴⁵ for *tempto* had been used to refer to feeling up, or 'attempting' in a clearly sexualized sense, at Propertius 1.3.15,⁴⁶ and the line thus seems to look back to Cupid's erotic assault on Ovid in *Amores* 1.1. The sexualized possibilities of *temptarer* in our passage are reinforced by the recall, through the use of the passive voice, of Ovid's sexual position *vis à vis* Cupid in 1.1, and also by the verb *sentirem*, which can be understood have a knowingly *sensual* dimension here,⁴⁷ and so continue the vocabulary of touch and feeling at which *temptarer* hints.

Thus, the erotics of Ovid's submission to Cupid are already established. In the lines that follow, we read of Ovid's acceptance in 9–10 of the need to yield to Amor, and then a description of Cupid's triumph over the poet-lover. We may detect a further erotic charge to Ovid's declaration that *tua sum noua praeda, Cupido* ('I am your new prey, Cupid', 19), not least because Ovid will go on to use the vocabulary of erotic predation of his having fallen in love with the *puella* of 1.3.1: *quae me nuper praedata puella est* ('the girl who has recently taken me as her prey'). Once more, then, we have Ovidian slippage between eroticized males and females, as he refuses to distinguish between the genders, his relations with them, and the terms in which those relations are portrayed. Ovid's description of the beauty of Cupid as he rides in triumph and parades Ovid with his other captives at lines 23–48 is also strongly homoerotic, although it has not previously been read as such. In an article on *Amores* 1.2, Lucia Athanassaki rightly observes that when this description focuses on Cupid's appearance at 1.2.39–46, 'the emphasis is ... on the charioteer's alluring figure and irresistible appeal',⁴⁸ but she

---

cum paelice laesa dolebit; 'then she too must be teased, when she grieves, hurt by a rival'), may include the same sexual innuendo as in Prop. 1.3.13–15 (*iuberent ... / subiecto leuiter positam temptare lacerto*, 'they commanded me to tease the girl with my arm gently beneath her'), not least given that the situations are nearly parallel, as Cynthia in 1.3 suspects that Propertius' absence from her bed earlier in the evening is due to his pursuit of other erotic interests.

45 McKeown 1998, 37 on 5–6 notes that *callidus* in line 6 strongly suggests that '*Amor* is to be extracted from *amore* (5) as the subject of *subit* and *nocet*', reinforcing my reading of *Amore* already at 5.

46 See Preston 1916, 28 and *OLD* 1915 s.v. 'tempto' 9b. See also the presentation of Pygmalion's treatment of his ivory statue at Ov. *Met*. 10.254: *saepe manus operi temptantes admouet* ('often he moved his teasing [I am tempted to translate 'randy'] hands to his work').

47 *Sentio* may suggest sexual submissiveness, as in the innuendo of Cic. *Phil*. 13.24: '*puerum*' *appellat quem non modo uirum sed etiam fortissimum uirum sensit et sentiet* ('he calls him "boy", but he has "experienced" him (and will "experience" him) not only as a man, but as a very masculine man').

48 Athanassaki 1992, 131.

does not consider the specifically homoerotic dimension of Cupid's depiction as supremely attractive, a literal golden boy in these lines.[49] Homoeroticism may further be detected in the early instruction to Cupid, *necte comam myrto* (23) ('bind your locks with myrtle'), given homoerotic descriptions of beautiful boys with their hair unbound in other poems;[50] this is an image that will more readily have occurred to readers thanks to Ovid's allusion in *Amores* 1.1 to the boy of Horace's *Epodes* 11 knotting or unknotting his hair. Ovid's erotic submission to Cupid remains a subtext to the first two books of the *Amores*, and in the programmatic 2.1, he is still Ovid's erotic *dominus*; Ovid clarifies his subservience in the assertion *hoc quoque iussit Amor* (3, 'Cupid also commands this'). Cupid also appears in prominent position, yet again described in wording that implies his erotic dominance over Ovid, at the start of the third book of the *Amores*. The description of Ovid at 3.1.20 as *hic, hic est, quem ferus urit Amor* ('he, he is the one whom savage Love burns') recalls 1.1 and in particular 1.1.26's *uror* (discussed earlier in this essay).

Tibullus and Tibullan homoerotics in *Amores* 3.9

From Ovid's teasing hints that he is himself involved in a homoerotic relationship with the *puer* Cupid in the opening sequence of the *Amores*, I now turn to an elegy in the third book of the collection where scholars have previously seen only the absence of homoeroticism. *Amores* 3.9, Ovid's lament over the death of his fellow elegist Tibullus, has been read as confirming the heterosexual bias that readers have detected in Ovidian elegy: Ovid presents Tibullus as the poet of the two female beloveds who appear in the first and second books of his poetry respectively, Delia and Nemesis, whereas the boy Marathus, Tibullus' other named beloved, is not named in the poem. Yet the absence of Marathus' name in Ovid's poem should not be taken to indicate a lack of homoeroticism in Ovid's portrait

---

49 Ov. *Am.* 1.2.42.
50 There may be homoerotic overtones in the selection of the god Dionysus as a simile for Cupid's appearance as conqueror at lines 47–8; although Amorini were often portrayed in Hellenistic and Roman art with Dionysiac attributes (McKeown 1989, 32, Stuveras 1969, 13, 13–23 and Huwé 2017, 23), Dionysus is portrayed as raping Adonis in the Hellenistic poet Phanocles' elegiac catalogue of the gods' loves for beautiful boys (Phanocles fr. 3: 'and how mountain-haunting Dionysus seized the godlike Adonis, as he visited holy Cyprus'). Ovid's *talis* may be equivalent to Phanocles' ὡς, and the situation of Ovid's poem – a male god makes a same-sex conquest – recalls Phanocles' myth; *domita* (*Am.* 1.2.47), although applied to the land of India, keeps the notion of *erotic* conquest clearly in focus.

of Tibullus; indeed, it would be surprising if this poem did lack homoeroticism. For Ovid is a very attentive and close reader of Tibullus' verse, as this poem shows,[51] and it is highly unlikely that he would ignore completely the homoeroticism that is found in Tibullus' poems: particularly in 1.4, 1.8, and 1.9, but also in 2.3, which treats Apollo's suffering in erotic subjection to Admetus, and so carries on homoeroticism as a theme into Tibullus' second book (although this poem is much less frequently cited in discussions of Tibullan homoeroticism).[52]

Marathus may not be named in *Amores* 3.9 whereas Delia and Nemesis are both named and presented in a manner which draws heavily on their portrayal in Tibullus' poetry,[53] but a teasing hint at Marathus' presence may be found in line 7 of the poem, before either of Tibullus' mistresses have been mentioned: *ecce, puer Veneris fert euersamque pharetram* ('look, the boy of Venus carries a reversed quiver'). While the *puer* of this line is revealed to be Cupid by the word that follows immediately on from it, the reader may initially assume that the *puer* who is mentioned in connection with Tibullus is none other than his beloved Marathus, explicitly characterized as a *puer* in Tibullus' first address to him at 1.4.83: *parce, puer, quaeso* ('spare me, boy, I pray'). Once again, Ovid plays on the interchangeability of boys and the boy-god of love, Cupid. It is surely no accident that Ovid's teasing hint that this poem will treat Tibullus' pederastic relationship recalls the way in which the first elegy of the *Amores* presents us with a *puer* before a *puella* as a possible love object; yet, ultimately, Ovid is only teasing, since here too Marathus fades from view as Ovid concentrates on Delia and Nemesis as Tibullus' beloveds.

Nor is this the only homoeroticism lurking in Ovid's lamentation for Tibullus' death; indeed, Ovid reminds the reader of Tibullus' homoerotic poetry by linking him to other poets whose verses had a homoerotic dimension. For, just as Tibullus had pictured himself in a lover's Elysium in his own poetry (albeit without

---

[51] Cf. Ov. *Tr.* 2.447–64 on Tibullus. In the *Tristia*, Ovid presents Tibullus' erotodidaxis as heterosexually inclined, but the context demands that Tibullus' poetry is presented as a parallel for the offence of Ovid's *Ars*, as I observe at Ingleheart 2010a, 350.

[52] For instance, James 2003, 9–12 omits reference to Tib. 2.3 in her discussion of homoerotic love both in Tibullus and in elegy more broadly.

[53] E.g. Ovid's Nemesis repurposes Tibullus' hyperbolic declaration of love for Delia as a eulogy: *me tenuit moriens deficiente manu* ('as he died, he held me in his ailing hand', Ov. *Am*, 3.9.58) and *et teneam moriens deficient manu* ('may I hold you in my ailing hand as I die', Tib. 1.1.60). For the Tibullan resonances of *Amores* 3.9 more generally, see Taylor 1970, Perkins 1993 and Huskey 2005.

poet-companions),⁵⁴ Ovid depicts Tibullus in the Elysian vale in lines 59–66 and he is accompanied there by a highly suggestive set of companions: Catullus together with his own Gaius Licinius Calvus, and Cornelius Gallus.⁵⁵ There has been scholarly discussion of why Ovid selects these particular poetic companions for the dead Tibullus,⁵⁶ but readers seem to have missed the homoerotic dimension. In a suggestive reference to the heavily eroticized link between Catullus and Calvus in Catullus 50, these two republican love poets are depicted as very close: not just by the fact that they are with each other, but also by the description of Calvus as *tuo*, 'your Calvus', in the address to Catullus, which draws on Catullus' description of Calvus as *meus … Caluos* at 53.3 and self-description in an address to Calvus as *tuum Catullum* (14.13). While this pair of friends whose friendship has highly homoerotic colouring in Catullus' poetry are routinely linked in Latin poetry,⁵⁷ the homoerotic dimension to their portrayal should not be overlooked in this context.

The reader should also recall that Gallus' poetry had a highly homoerotic flavour, at least on the evidence of Propertius 1.20, which alludes to a Gallus' poetry on a male beloved,⁵⁸ and Virgil, *Eclogues* 10.37–8. With this in mind, then, the reader may further find suggestive the fact that the first of the poets with whom Tibullus is aligned in the poem is the mythical bard Orpheus, at 21–2 (*quid pater Ismario, quid mater profuit Orpheo? / carmine quid uictas obstipuisse feras?*, 'what good to Thracian Orpheus was his father, what good was his mother? / What good was the fact that the conquered beasts were stunned by his song?'). While there is no hint at Orpheus' sexuality in this poem, the reader would have recalled Orpheus' prominent placement as a representative of homoerotic love in Phanocles' *Erotes* or *Kaloi* (fr. 1 Powell); the former title translates, of course, into the Latin *Amores*, and it is possible that both Gallus' and Ovid's use of this title for their

---

54 Tib. 1.3.57-8: *sed me, quod facilis tenero sum semper Amori, / ipsa Venus campos ducet in Elysios* ('but, because I am always yielding to gentle Cupid, Venus herself will lead me into the Elysian fields').
55 Compare the first line of Domitius Marsus' epitaph for Tibullus (fr. 7 Courtney), which has Tibullus as *comes* to Virgil (who is much linked with homoerotic love in the biographical tradition, e.g. Donat. *Vit. Verg.* 9 and Apul. *Apol.* 10) in the Underworld; no beloveds are mentioned here at all, with homosociality a strong presence.
56 These discussions tend to revolve around Ovid's inscription into the poetic mode of Latin love poetry (not simply elegy): see e.g. Putnam 2005, 130, O'Rourke 2012, 402 and Ingleheart 2010b, especially 171–2.
57 See Hollis 2007, 58–9.
58 I believe that this Gallus is Cornelius Gallus (on this issue, see e.g. Cairns 2012, 65–6), but this is not a view that is universally held.

collection of love poems has some of this flavour (perhaps also accounting for Gallus' presence in *Amores* 3.9 and his presentation in other poets as homoerotic).[59] Ovid's later reception of Phanocles, in his *Metamorphoses* 10, has been largely responsible for Orpheus' reputation for exclusive pederasty; after the death of Eurydice, the Orpheus of the *Metamorphoses* wanders Thrace and initiates the practice of pederasty there (10.79–85). Ovid, then, may present us, by analogy, with a Tibullus who is separated by death from his mistresses, yet also in death reunited with the company that he may have been happiest in all along: that of his fellow, homoerotically inclined male poets. It is they, not Delia and Nemesis, who provide the conclusion to Ovid's portrait of Tibullus.

si quis ...: homoeroticism in the *Ars amatoria*

Ovidian homoeroticism, then, extends beyond the 'personal' treatment of the theme to teasing allusions to the homoerotic themes and attachments of his poetic predecessors. The *Amores*' mixture of the 'personal' and the more distanced treatment of homoeroticism can also be observed in the didactic *Ars amatoria* and *Remedia amoris*, although only the former has received much attention to date, and this section of my essay aims to redress a gap in scholarly studies as it considers both.

While the *Ars* has been read as almost overwhelmingly heterocentric in terms of its love advice, this is only a partial interpretation. Indeed, the *Ars* begins with the appearance of being a genuinely comprehensive guide to love, as its first couplet tells us:

> Siquis in hoc artem populo non nouit amandi
> hoc legat et lecto carmine doctus amet.
>
> (Ov. Ars am. 1.1–2)

> If anyone among this populace does not know the art of loving, let him read this poem and love, an expert.

Si quis highlights the potential for anyone in Rome, of any gender or erotic persuasion, to become a reader of the *Ars*. Those who pursue homoerotic passions, who, as we shall see, are acknowledged on a few occasions within the text of the poem, would seem to be included in the audience. The suggestion that homoerotic

---

59 I am grateful to the editors for this suggestion.

love is encompassed may also be reinforced by Ovid's frequent references to boys and submission in the prologue: lines 7–10 refer to Ovid's mastery over Cupid:

> me Venus artificem tenero praefecit Amori;
>   Tiphys et Automedon dicar Amoris ego.
> ille quidem ferus est et qui mihi saepe repugnet;
>   sed puer est, aetas mollis et apta regi.
>
> (Ov. *Ars am.* 1.7–10)
>
> Venus has appointed me as the artist of tender Love;
>   I shall be called the Tiphys and Automedon of Love.
> He is certainly savage and prone to fight against me often;
>   but he is a boy, of an age that is soft and can be ruled.

Although the primary sense of *mollis* at line 10 is to the malleability of boys, and hence the ability of Ovid as *praeceptor Amoris* to gain Cupid's submission, the word *mollis* has a very strong sexual charge, suggesting the desirable softness and effeminacy of the boy-god. The sexual sense of *mollis* is increased by the wider context of Ovid's relationship with Cupid, given the opening of the *Amores*. Ovid's claim in the prologue of the *Ars* at 21–2 that he will gain mastery over Cupid suggests perhaps that their erotic situation might have changed after the *Amores*, although there are still strong hints that they have a heavily eroticised dynamic of domination and submission.

Furthermore, the passage contains suggestive hints at erotic pedagogy in Ovid's claims that he is Cupid's teacher, with *me Venus artificem tenero praefecit Amori* ('Venus has appointed me the teacher of tender Love' 7), and line 17's *ego sum praeceptor Amoris*, which has the sense 'I am the tutor to Love', with a capital L, referring to the relationship between Ovid and Amor, as well as the broader sense 'I am the teacher of love', lower case l; that is, 'I am the teacher of the art of love'. Given that erotic pedagogy was indelibly connected with pederastic relationships in antiquity,[60] the homoerotics of Ovid's relationship with Cupid remain to the fore. Alison Sharrock's 1994 *Seduction and Repetition in Ovid's* Ars amatoria argued that homoerotic pedagogy and aesthetics alike are very much a feature of the relationship of Ovid as *praeceptor amoris* with his inexperienced, young male addressees in the *Ars*, and that he seduces them into becoming more appealing to an older lover – that is, himself. Her argument is based for the most part on a passage in *Ars* 2 on how young men can make themselves attractive (2.99–122); the passage includes suggestive references to Ovid's male readers, cast in the

---

60 See Percy 1996, and Provencal 2013.

roles of attractive boys of myth, such as Nireus as loved by Homer, and Hylas as stolen by the nymphs (that is, from his lover, Heracles: *Ars am.* 2.109–10), as well as many allusions to the aesthetics and themes of pederastic poetry. Nevertheless, her argument also applies more widely to the entirety of the first two books of the *Ars*, and the fact that the work as a whole opens with a pedagogic relationship that brings pederasty to the fore very much strengthens her thesis.[61]

The impression that the *Ars* offers love advice for all, and is not heterocentric, is then further suggested within the prologue by Ovid's use of a neuter pronoun when he refers to the object of love at line 35: *principio, quod amare uelis, reperire labora* (Ov. *Ars am.* 1.35, 'in the beginning, work at finding what you might want to love'). Ovid will often go on to denote the beloved with the neuter pronoun in the *Ars*, an idiom that is not found in Propertius and Tibullus, although it is anticipated in the *Amores*.[62] The use of the neuter in the *Ars* has been read as depersonalizing the hunt for an erotic target, and as part of what Hollis referred to as 'the dry and unemotional tone of a technical treatise'.[63] However, the fact that he uses the neuter at this juncture does not just establish Ovid's credentials as the author of a practical didactic manual, nor simply look to the detachment that comes from the fact that the would-be lover of the poem has not yet met the woman he will pursue. *Quod* also serves to hint that the beloved could be of either gender, and is thus equivalent here to *Amores* 1.1.20. However, at line 37, a *puella* is mentioned for the first time as the love object of the male reader and from this point on, the poem *is* focused largely, though not exclusively, on the pursuit of love objects of the opposite sex.

The *Ars amatoria*, then, follows exactly the same pattern as is laid out in the opening poems of the *Amores*: it starts with the possibility of love affairs both homosexual and heterosexual, features the boy-god Cupid and the erotics of submission and domination in prominent positions, and then almost exclusively narrows down to heterosexual possibilities. Yet the *Ars*, as befits the apparently all-embracing nature of its opening announcement of the erotic instruction that it will provide, does also include homosexual configurations, and these are more various than have previously been recognised. The most famous statement of

---

[61] Sharrock 1994, 26–50.
[62] E.g. 1.91–2, 263. For the neuter *quod* of the love object in comedy (and Lucretius 4.1061, *nam si abest quod ames*, 'if your love-object is absent', with obvious didactic crossover with the *Ars*), see Pinotti 1988, 81, commenting on the same usage at Ov. *Rem. Am.* 13.
[63] Hollis 1977, 39 *ad Ars am.* 1.35. James 2016 reads the use of the neuter gender in both Plautus and the *Ars* as a way for male authors to depersonalise the *meretrix*, or sex worker, class.

what has been read as Ovid's attitude towards homosexuality is found at *Ars am.* 2.683–4:

> odi concubitus, qui non utrumque resoluunt;
>   hoc est, cur pueri tangar amore minus.
>
> (Ov. *Ars am.* 2.683–4)
>
> I hate embraces which do not give satisfaction to both partners;
>   that's the reason why I am touched by boy-love – less.

The bathetic and suggestive force of the concluding and comparative *minus* has been overlooked by some readers, who have taken this couplet straightforwardly as expressing Ovid's preference for heterosexual sex, and distaste for sex with boys.[64] Yet Ovid does not here disclaim desire for boys, nor suggest that he does not have sex with boys, but that he is less inclined to pederastic sex because he enjoys it *less* than heterosexual couplings.[65]

Ovid's apparently 'personal' statements of his erotic experience and tastes in the *Ars* and *Remedia* often direct the reader back to his depiction of his erotic adventures in the *Amores*.[66] Yet readers have not been inclined to look to the *Amores* for 'evidence' of Ovid's homoerotic liaisons to support this particular claim. What happens if we do this in this particular case? We may then read Ovid as here encouraging his readers to spot the hints of his erotically unequal relationship with Cupid in the opening sequence of the *Amores*, in which Ovid plays the sexual role usually taken by a penetrated boy. The precise form of Ovid's wording here makes these hints more concrete:[67] the reference to being touched by boy-love (*tangar*) contains a punning allusion to the way in which one particular *puer* had touched Ovid in *Amores* 1.1, that is, to the eroticized touching of the poet by the boy-god, Amor, with a capital A.[68]

---

64 E.g. Habinek 1997, 31, Makowski 1996, 30. Cf. however, e.g., the very clear discussion of the possibility that *minus* here (as elsewhere) has not a comparative but a simple negative force at Sharrock 1994, 27. For the presentation of pederasty as a sexual mode which only pleasures one partner, see (Mel.) *Anth. Pal.* 5.208 = GP 9, Lucian *Am.* 27.
65 Lilja 1983, 79.
66 See Gibson 2003, 195 on how, in the *Ars*, Ovid often refers to his own 'biography' of personal experiences, to be found in the *Amores*.
67 Ovid uses the genitive singular, *pueri*, not the plural, *puerorum*, probably for metrical reasons, but thereby also recalls the singular *puer* of both Cupid and the unspecified boy at *Am.* 1.1.20.
68 We might be tempted to speculate that Ovid may refer not only to the 3-book second edition of the *Amores* which is extant, but to the earlier 5-book edition, which may have contained a

Ovid's few comments within these mostly heteroerotically directed poems concerning males who desire other males have sometimes been read in a very simplistic biographical way, as evidence of his alleged hostility to those who experience such desire. In fact, they are far more interesting than this. At *Ars am.* 1.523–4, Ovid concludes a longer section on male grooming with a comment on taking this to excess, the first explicit reference in the work to males who desire other males:[69]

> cetera lasciuae faciant, concede, puellae,
>   et si quis male uir quaerit habere uirum.
>
> (Ov. *Ars am.* 1.523–4)

> Let wanton girls do anything further than this,
>   and if there is any man, hardly a man, who wants to have a man.

This couplet is fascinating, for even more reasons than those which have usually attracted attention. Adrian Hollis in his commentary takes *male uir* together,[70] translating as 'of doubtful masculinity', and understanding Ovid to subscribe here to typical Roman views of the unmanliness of overgroomed men. Hollis does not note Ovid's allusion to Catullus,[71] who in poem 16 attacks those of his readers who have thought him *male ... marem* ('badly male', 16.13) because of his kiss-

---

greater number of elegies with even more homoerotic flavour. For the 5-book first edition, see Martelli 2013.

69 Similar phrasing, implying effeminate, overgroomed men, is found in what McKeown 1989, 23 labels 'the censorious tone' of *Ars am.* 3.437–8: *femina quid faciat, cum sit uir leuior ipsa / forsitan et plures possit habere uiros?* ('what can a woman do, when her lover is smoother than she herself is, and perhaps has more men than she does?'). I see here, rather than disapproval of effeminate men (who seem to captivate many female beloveds through their appearance at 3.433–6, in line with Roman ideas about the *cinaedus*: see Williams 2010, 227–30), Ovid's acknowledgement of a range of erotic possibilities in Rome. At Rome, male grooming was not forbidden to all men, but was only impermissible to *uiri*, a subset of men who embodied the socio-sexual impenetrability of Roman masculinity (Ov. *Ars am.* 1.505–12; see Tohm 2011, 57–65). For Roman masculine impenetrability, see Walters 1993, 1997.

70 Hollis 1977, 121 *ad loc*. Boswell (1980, 83 n. 106), rather unexpectedly, took *male* with *quaerit* as suggesting a man who wants to have a man by deceit – this seems to stretch the Latin, and the allusion to Catullus' *male marem* (see above) tends not to support this interpretation. However, some support for Boswell's interpretation *is* found in *Ars* 3's advice to women, where a couplet about the overly groomed effeminate man whose desires are homosexual (3.437–8; discussed above) is followed by a longer warning (443–6) to women to be on their guard against deceptive effeminate men – who, it turns out, want to steal female clothes from the women they consort with.

71 Unlike Murgatroyd 1982, 117 *ad loc*.

poems; that is, he is feminised because he has not carried out the proper, penetrative role of a man. Too few readers have noted the significance of the change from Catullus' wording; Ovid refers not, as Catullus had done, to being badly *mas* but to a *uir* who is not properly masculine, and who desires another man, *uirum*. Craig Williams in his ground-breaking *Roman Homosexuality* provides an exception: he notes specifically that Ovid is, unexpectedly, referring here to an adult male's desire to be penetrated by another adult male, an act rendering the penetrated partner effeminate in Roman eyes.[72] It is unexpected to encounter a reference to this particular variety of homosexual desire in Latin love elegy, a genre that otherwise treats pederastic desire,[73] which is far more socially acceptable. The adult male who performs the more usual role of the boy-beloved is a despised and abject figure who normally appears in genres such as Atellan farce, satire, imperial biography, and invective;[74] Ovid's inclusion of such figures in his elegiac world reflects the fact that his brand of elegy is far less romantic, and far more interested in the realities of contemporary Roman life and contemporary Roman love lives, than the poems of Propertius or Tibullus.

Ovid's advice here to the male lover who is assumed to wish to conduct affairs with women further acts as a subtle form of advice to any of his male readers who are in fact erotically interested in other men; that is, the *Ars* genuinely offers advice on how to appeal to your object of desire for anyone, *si quis*, who wants to experience love. Ovid's recall here, via *si quis*, of the opening words of the *Ars amatoria*, seems pointed. Is this echo an acknowledgement that the apparent

---

[72] The precise force of Ovid's phrasing, however, which seems to have been ignored by all readers, may be revealing: Williams 2010, 144 evidently understands *habere* in the sense *haberi* here, in order to see the desiring subject of line 524 as penetrated. This would make sense of the juxtaposition of the two *uiri*: one (the latter) is a true *uir*, acting as the penetrative partner, whereas the other (the earlier *male uir*), is not really a *uir* at all, as he desires to be penetrated.

[73] Ovid may also treat adult males who desire other adult males at *Am.* 1.8.67–8, with Dipsas' scornful portrait of a lover of women who is himself *pulcher* and who has a lover of his own, although there is some ambiguity about the situation. The characterisation of the lover as *pulcher* might suggest that he is a beautiful boy, as may the detail that he has an *amator* who should give him gifts – the gift-giving homosexual *amator* is common (e.g. Tib. 1.4.58, 1.8.29–30, 1.9.11, Juv. 6.35–7; see Koch-Harnack 1983, 191–2 and Krenkel 1979, 181, 183) – but the scenario seems to envisage an adult male who is erotically involved with both a male and female simultaneously. Serv. *ad Aen* 3.119 claims that *exoleti*, adult male homosexuals, were in earlier times referred to as *pulchri*, reinforcing the case that we are, in *Ars am.* 1.523–4, dealing with two adults; for the *exoletus* as an adult male homosexual, not, as it is often taken 'male prostitute', see Butrica 2013, 225–30.

[74] E.g. Juv. 2, Cic. *Phil.* 2.44, Mart. 1.24; 12.42, Suet. *Ner.* 28–9, Tac. *Ann.* 15.37, Dio 62.28, 63.13, 63.22, 79.5, Aur. Vict. *Caes.* 5.5, SHA *Heliogab.* 10.5, 11.5.

catholicity of the opening is in fact just a tease? Or may Ovid hint that erotic advice for such men *is* to be found in the *Ars*? Indeed, the passage on male grooming in *Ars* 1 which contains this reference to effeminate men-who-desire-men could constitute such advice: men are told that, if they achieve anything more than the simple, rugged masculine looks that Ovid advises, they will succeed in attracting homoerotic attention. It is instructive to compare Ovid's advice here with Tibullus 1.8.9–15, addressed to a *puer delicatus*, informing him that over-grooming does not lead to erotic success; Ovid here stealthily rewrites Tibullus' homoerotic didactic. In so doing, he implicitly reverses its thrust: in pointed contrast to Tibullus' focus on male beautification being *frustra*, 'in vain' (Tib. 1.8.13), Ovid suggests that elaborate male self-care in fact leads to *homo*erotic success.

I suggested earlier in this essay that the homoerotic dimension to Ovid's elegies is an important and programmatic feature of these works, demonstrating the great variety of desire that can be found in Roman elegy. I want to suggest that one of the possibilities that Ovid dangles out for the future direction of his love elegies in his supposed 'farewell' to the genre, the *Remedia amoris*, is that his elegiac lovers, unhappily engaged in love affairs with women after successfully following Ovid's advice on how to conduct affairs with them, can turn to homosexual passion. This may be hinted at by the focus on undesirable female bodies that is found in Ovid's address to women almost at the end of book 3 of the *Ars am.*: *nec lucem in thalamos totis admitte fenestris; / aptius in uestro corpore multa latent;* (Ov. *Ars am.* 3.807–8, 'Do not let light into the bedchamber through all the windows; / it is better that many aspects of your body should be hidden'). This advice to women about what to do when they come to bed with their man constitutes the very last bit of erotodidactic instruction of the *Ars*, as the final two couplets of the third book focus on Ovid's didactic achievements, and it is suggestive for the new direction of his *Remedia amoris*. When the male readers at whom this misogynistic comment is clearly actually aimed turn from the love advice of the *Ars* to the *Remedia*, a book that purports to tell them how to get over love, they might reasonably expect that one way to get over the love of women, whose bodies are painted as inadequate by Ovid, would be to turn to sex with boys instead. After all, Ovid insists in the *Remedia* that the cure for love is … another love affair;[75] so, for the man who is thoroughly sick of women, boy-love is an obvious

---

[75] *Rem. am.* 441–88 deals with the theme of using a new love to cure the old one: see especially the advice at 452 that a new love should be found, and the examples of mythical figures getting over love affairs by pursuing love with others at 453–60, 462, and 484.

alternative.⁷⁶ Indeed, Propertius 2.4.17–22 seems to hint at precisely such a scenario when he suggests that boy-love is easier than difficult relations with girls,⁷⁷ although Propertius does not personally follow up on this hint and pursue boys as an antidote to his troubles with Cynthia.

It is no surprise, then, that the prologue to the *Remedia*, significantly, recalls and even intensifies the homoerotic hints of Ovid's relations with Cupid at the start of both the *Amores* and *Ars amatoria*. In the opening 40 lines of this poem, Ovid and Cupid have their longest and most homoerotically charged interaction, as Cupid confronts the poet about the title of a work that seems to declare warfare on Cupid as the god of love. The *Remedia* prologue looks very like a meeting between two lovers. Ovid refers to himself as *tuum uatem* (Ov. *Rem. am.* 3), a possessive which may indicate his erotic possession by and submission to Cupid in *Amores* 1.1 and 1.2. Ovid also looks like a lover in his various professions of loyalty and devotion to Cupid, including his claim at 11 that he has never betrayed Cupid. There may be a homoerotic charge to Ovid's address to Cupid as *blande puer* (11), 'winsome/charming boy', and this is reinforced by the focus on the beauty of the god in the closing lines of this proem, where he appears as golden and bejewelled. While golden hair is a conventional feature of the gods, the reader may recall both Ovidian play on the hair of the beloved in *Amores* 1.1.19–20, and the frequent presentation of desirable boys in pederastic poetry as having precisely this attribute.⁷⁸ There are also further reminiscences of pederastic verse in this encounter: Ovid's insistence on Cupid's boyish and playful nature at lines 23–4 evokes the frequent and homoerotically loaded presentation of the play of Eros and the beautiful boys who are aligned with him in erotic verse, from archaic Greek lyric onwards.⁷⁹

We may also see a hint that it is precisely *heterosexual* love that is rejected in lines 15-16, which focus on the unhappy love of men for women; here, the neuter *quod* (Ov. *Rem. am.* 13) may insist upon homoerotic possibilities in a way that is more charged than ever, given the context of the rejection of heterosexual love. Even the words of Cupid's initial complaint have a homoerotic intertext that has gone unnoticed, but appears highly suggestive in this particular context. Cupid's

---

76 The editors nicely point out that the idea that boy-love follows on from unsatisfactory girl-love finds a notable parallel in *Met.* 10.79–85, where Orpheus (disastrously) moves from loving Eurydice to exclusive boy-love.
77 Cf. the comical claim at Juv. 6.28–38 that marriage with a woman is a fate worse than death, whereas a sexual relationship with a *pusio* would be far easier.
78 E.g. Theoc. 13.36. The line also possibly recalls Anac. fr. 358's χρυσοκόμης Ἔρως ('golden-haired Eros').
79 E.g. Anac. 357, 358.

bella, mihi, uideo, bella parantur 'wars, I see, wars are set in motion against me,' (Ov. *Rem. am.* 2) parallels the opening of another poem, Horace, *Carm.* 4.1.1–2, where the ageing poet asks: *Intermissa, Venus, diu / rursus bella moues? parce, precor, precor,* 'Venus, do you again start a war after a long time? Spare me, I pray, I pray'. Horace's scenario, in which a love poet is clearly unhappy that Venus is waging war against him by making him fall in love, is wittily reversed in Ovid by the complaint of Venus' son, Cupid, that a mortal poet is waging war against him by rejecting love.[80] Ovid further alludes to Horace's poem in line 15 when he talks about the lover who *male fert indignae regna puellae* (Ov. *Rem. am.* 15, 'badly bears the reign of an unworthy girl'), recalling Horace's early reference in *Odes* 4.1 to his previous erotic experience *bonae / sub regno Cinarae* ('under the reign of good Cinara', 3–4). Although Horace's poem refers in lines 29–40 to the possibility of love with either a male or a female partner, in typical Horatian fashion, it suggests precisely that the poet has moved on from his affair with Cinara only to fall in love with a boy, Ligurinus, and, more broadly, that the lover may believe themselves to be over love, but that love comes to them nevertheless. Ovid's poem on the rejection of love, then, recalls a poem in which love returns to Horace, despite his rejection of it, in the form of a boy. These allusions to Horace may hint at homoerotic love as an alternative for the lover of the *Remedia* who wishes to escape from unhappy love with a woman. Yet ultimately the teasing of the *Amores* and the *Ars* continues here too, as the focus of the rest of the *Remedia* remains heteroerotic.

Conclusion

Having examined a number of allusions to homosexual love in Ovidian elegies that have been overlooked, I wish in conclusion to briefly outline some broader consequences of Ovidian homoeroticism.

One wider issue that these homoerotic interpretations of Ovid can illuminate is the erotics of submission. While there have been many studies of the theme of *seruitium amoris* and the elegists' erotic submission to their mistresses, the homoerotic possibilities have escaped scholarly attention. Indeed, Sharon James

---

[80] The likelihood of Ovid's reference to Horace is somewhat heightened by the fact that Venus is explicitly identified as the *mater saeua Cupidinum* ('savage mother of Cupids') at Hor. *Carm.* 4.1.5. Harrison 2018b argues that Ovid is the influence on Horace here rather than vice versa; an ingenious possibility, but one which I do not myself accept.

has argued that the Roman elegists were more interested in heteroerotic than homoerotic love precisely because the latter did not give them the same opportunity for the exploration of the paradoxes of gender inversion and powerplay within a situation where the poets, elite adult Roman males, presented themselves as being under the erotic power of those who occupied a less powerful position in society than themselves. Ovid's presentation of himself as erotically dominated by Cupid, a mere boy, shows that James' interpretation is partial, and indeed should encourage readers of elegy to revisit in particular poems such as Tibullus 1.4 and 2.3 to analyse exactly how the poets present themselves and other men as emasculated through their *homoerotic* subjection.

This study, particularly in its reading of *Amores* 1.2, has also demonstrated that Ovidian elegy contains more sexual innuendo than readers have usually found there, given beliefs about generic decency of elegy. My interpretation enables us to supplement Adams' *The Latin Sexual Vocabulary* with further examples of sexualized vocabulary and imagery in Ovid, and should encourage us to look for parallel instances in the works of the other elegists.

Finally, this study should have helped to demonstrate the inadequacy of conventional readings of Latin love elegy as overwhelmingly concerned with the love of the poet for his *puella*. The *amores* of the Roman elegists, as I hope to have shown, were never so simple and so limited. They were instead genuinely plural.

Thea S. Thorsen
The Beloved: Figures and Words

This chapter explores specific figures and words associated with the role of the beloved in ancient literature. One of the most prominent of these roles is that of Latin love poetry's *puella* (Lat. 'girl'); it therefore offers a natural point of departure for this chapter's investigation. The *puella* resembles and is indeed in current scholarship commonly compared to the figure of the *meretrix* (Lat. 'prostitute') of Attic New/Roman comedy, who may also be an object of love. However, the conspicuous contrast between the frequent occurrence of the word *meretrix* in comedy and the virtual absence of this word from Latin love poetry suggests that the *puella* may also be fruitfully compared to other figures of the beloved. In this regard, the etymologically linked word *puer* (Lat. 'boy'), which appears in that same poetry also in reference to beloved persons, emerges as particularly relevant, especially as both Latin terms may correspond to the Greek gender-inclusive word παῖς ('child'), which can also denote the beloved in Greek poetry. As will be argued, a pursuit of the etymologically linked designations of both male and female objects of love – in both Greek and Latin – offers a fresh perspective on the striking figure of the *puella* in Latin love literature, which arguably helps us to interpret her as an embodiment of a particularly significant moment in the history of literature in the West.

Introduction

Love literature depends on the figure of the beloved, who is readily addressed as a poem's 'you', and also occurs in third-person narratives and descriptions as the 'other'.[1] The beloved thus represents both 'you' and the 'other' in relation to the lover, and their existence may be perceived as strongly as that of the lover's 'I'. This is certainly true of the beloved in poetry at Rome, where the figure acquires a particular complexity. From an overall perspective, this complexity apparently favours and promotes the beloved presented as a female figure. This may seem all as it should be from the perspective of our day and age, which is situated at

---

[1] Cf. Barthes' definition of his *Fragments d'un discours amoureux*: 'C'est un portrait, si l'on veut, qui est proposé, mais ce portrait n'est pas psychologique; il est structural: il donne à lire une place de parole: la place de quelqu'un qui parle en lui-même, amoureusement, face à l'autre (l'objet aimé), qui ne parle pas', 1977, 7.

the end point of a long tradition in the West of male lovers of women beloveds in heterosexual relationships. The allegedly ennobling dynamics of such devotion to the beloved is celebrated in the construct of 'courtly love'[2] and interpreted as a religion of the 'woman',[3] in which – in the words of Johann Wolfgang von Goethe – the allegedly 'eternal feminine draws us on upwards'.[4]

However, this hetero-male-centred perspective, disclosed by the 'us' which is easily understood to mean 'us men' in the Faustian punchline of Goethe, occludes the fact that there are also male beloveds, of both male and female lovers.[5] For in ancient literature there are likewise female figures who may be loving subjects, and from whose perspective the beloved is often male. In fact, in much of ancient literature the beloved seems just as readily to be of the same sex as the lover or of the opposite sex, irrespectively of whether the lover is male or female.[6] Thus, from the perspective of ancient literature, it is rather the dominance of the female figure as beloved in Roman love poetry that requires explanation: why is it that when we arrive at Rome in the Augustan age it is the female beloved who steals the show? Does something happen at this time, in the decades before Christ, and in this place, Rome, which is related to the empowering of feminine qualities and values? Or, perhaps, is what happens here related to a male chauvinist need to possess and exploit female figures in order to celebrate control and power?

Many prominent scholars have approached these questions and given different and important answers.[7] What I hope to add in the following is a fresh approach to some of the underlying dynamics of this process that ended in the predominance of the female beloved. I will do so by looking more closely not only at the figure of the beloved, but also at the vocabulary employed to describe that figure. In the latter regard I am inspired by Antony Corbeill's study, *Sexing the*

---

2 See my first chapter, n. 11.
3 See my first chapter, n. 12.
4 Goethe, *Faust*, Part II, Chorus Mysticus, last two lines: 'das Ewig-Weibliche zieht uns hinan'.
5 And not only in ancient literature, of course; this reminder is perhaps most urgently felt in scholarship on mediaeval love literature, given claims such as 'la femme devint religion' – see my first chapter, n. 12 – despite the fact all the while there were also women singer-songwriters, trobairitz, whose beloveds were male.
6 There are male lovers of male beloveds, female lovers of female beloveds, male lovers of female beloveds and female lovers of male beloveds; see esp. Williams 1990; 2010 2nd ed., Boehringer 2007 and Hubbard 2014.
7 Especially important attempts to explain the historical momentum of this poetry are Lyne 1980, James 2003 and Miller 2004; see also Watson 1983; 1992, Wyke 1987; 1989 = 2002, Sharrock 1991, Keith 1994, Greene 1995, Hardie 2003, Perkins 2011; 2014, Miller 2013, with further references and Hallett 2013, picking up, among other references, Thorsen 2012b.

World: Grammatical Gender and Biological Sex in Ancient Rome (2015), which argues that the categories of grammatical gender in Latin developed out of a transition from one state of the (mostly republican) language in which words occurring in the grammatically feminine gender might *also* occur in the masculine, to a state of the (mostly imperial) language in which words occurring in the grammatically feminine gender could *not* occur in the grammatically masculine gender, and vice versa. Notably, in Corbeill's research material these states represent trends that to a certain extent appear simultaneously, and sometimes even overlap, so that the development in question is not to be imagined as one clear-cut and linear chronological process. I will in the following argue that the beloved in Latin literature undergoes a similar development.

Figures

Curiously, while the prominence in Roman literature of the beloved as female is widely recognized, she famously keeps defying unequivocal definitions.[8] Metapoetically, she represents the poet's work of art,[9] yet as a fictional character, she appears to be more than a projection of the poet-lover's wishes and fantasies;[10] this figure often appears learned, *docta*, sometimes as learned as the poet, and in glimpses almost as a colleague of his in the trade of literature (Prop. 2.3.19–22);[11] moreover, she is not necessarily always attractive and seductive, but can also appear more or less repugnant to the lover (e.g. Catull. 8, 11, 58, 72, 76); the female beloved may readily have forceful aspects (cf. e.g. Prop. 4.7) and repeatedly appears to have a mind and a will of her own (e.g. Prop. 4.8).

She is powerful from the lover's point of view, not just because the poet loves and desires her and she can reject him, but also because she is part of a network of other lovers, rich admirers or even a husband, as is the case in the following poem, where Ovid's poet-lover accepts that his 'beloved girl' (*Am.* 1.4.3, *dilectam ... puellam*) and 'lady' (*mea domina*, see passage quoted below) will have to return home not with him, but with her *uir* ('husband') when the dinner they have all three attended is over:

---

8 Cf. Miller 2013.
9 As stressed by Wyke 2002.
10 This is arguably so even when taking into account the argument of James 2003 that a man who is trying to get sex for free by means of poetry (= the elegiac lover) needs to posit a beloved (= elegiac *puella*) who may – at least potentially – be interested in poetry and hence *docta*.
11 See Keith in this volume.

> me miserum! monui, paucas quod prosit in horas;
>   separor a domina nocte iubente mea.
> nocte uir includet, lacrimis ego maestus obortis,
>   qua licet, ad saeuas prosequar usque fores.
> oscula iam sumet, iam non tantum oscula sumet:
>   quod mihi das furtim, iure coacta dabis.
>
> (Ov. Am. 1.4.59–64)[12]

Miserable as I am, I have urged you to what will help for only a few scant hours; I must be separated from my lady – night will command it. At night your husband will shut you in, and I, all gloomy and pouring forth my tears, shall follow you – as far as I may – up to the cruel doors. Then he will take kisses from you, yes, then he will take not only kisses; what you give me in secret, you will give him as a right, because you must.

(Transl. Showerman and Goold, adapted)

The word *iure* (*Am.* 1.4.64, 'by law') strongly suggests that the status of the relationship between the beloved and the *uir* is that of wedlock.[13]

Even so, Latin love poetry abounds with allegations of greed and readiness to offer sex in return for gifts and money addressed to the beloved, who is accordingly also easily associated with prostitution. In scholarship, the beloved in Latin love poetry is regularly understood in reference to the *meretrix*, mostly in terms of her alleged material greed. The *meretrix* is commonly envisaged as a professional sex worker, who may be a manumitted ex-slave and self-employed businesswoman,[14] but may alternatively be owned by a pimp, as in the following Ovidian passage,[15] where the figure of the *meretrix* is sharply distinguished from that of the beloved:[16]

---

[12] See also e.g. Ov. *Am.* 2.19 and 3.4 and Davis 1999 for the political implications of this configuration, especially as concerns the charge of *lenocinium* (see Treggiari 1991, 288), which made it a punishable crime not to report one's wife if she was having an affair; cf. my first chapter n. 67.
[13] Davis 1993, 67 claims to see 'intentional ambiguities' behind both *uir* (*passim*) and *iure* in *Am.* 1.4.64, with reference to McKeown 1989 *ad loc.*, who only refers to his introduction in McKeown 1987, where information about this ambiguity remains hard to find. Moreover, both McKeown and Davis refer such ambiguites to Ford 1966, who, however, does not discuss the significance of *iure*, but instead consistently translated *uir* as 'husband'. Thus, scholarship has in fact yet to produce arguments on which the interpretation of the relationship between the *puella* and the *uir* in *Am.* 1.4 as non-marital can be based. See also Davis 1999.
[14] Lyne 1980, 8–17, and James 2003, 37.
[15] See Sharrock and Brecke in this volume.
[16] James 2003, 94–6 reads *Am.* 2.10 rhetorically, as an attempt to make the *puella* 'prostitute' herself to the poet-lover without demanding payment of any sort. However, the description of

> stat meretrix certo cuiuis mercabilis aere,
>   et miseras iusso corpore quaerit opes;
> deuouet imperium tamen haec lenonis auari,
>   et quod uos facitis sponte, coacta facit.
>
> (Ov. *Am.* 1.10.21–4)

> The prostitute stands for sale at the fixed price to anyone at all and wins her wretched gains with body on call; yet even she calls down curses on the power of the greedy pimp and does under compulsion what you [non-prostitutes] perform of your own will.
>
> (Transl. Showerman and Goold, adapted)

In these two passages from the *Amores* there is one word that especially stands out: *coacta* (*Am.* 1.4.64; 1.10.24 'forced'). The unique reoccurrence of this word only here in all of the three books of the *Amores* suggests that it is important. And indeed, when it is used in reference to a husband and a pimp respectively, this verbal echo underscores that both a wife and a prostitute share the same fate, inasmuch as one is forced (*coacta*) to have sex with a husband because he has power over her by law (*iure*), while the other is forced (*coacta*) to have sex with the random paying customer because she is under an owner's command (*imperium*). The important contrast between the unwilling, institutionalized sex that a wife/prostitute must have with her husband/customer and the willing lovemaking of a beloved with her lover (cf. e.g. Prop. 2.15 and Ov. *Am.* 1.5) is also underscored by the fact that she can actually reject this lover, which she also does from time to time (cf. e.g. Ov. *Am.* 1.12).

Furthermore, the figure of the female beloved in Latin literature is also associated with Roman citizen status. Catullus' own poems underpin the associations between Catullus' Lesbia and the noble citizen woman Clodia Metelli,[17] however fictitious these associations may be (Catull. 79.1–2; cf. Apul. *Apol.* 10).[18] Sulpicia, who is not only a beloved (cf. [Tib.] 3.8–12), but also a lover ([Tib.] 3.13-18), and indeed one who calls herself a *puella* as such ([Tib.] 3.14.3; 15.1; 17.1),[19] is readily overloaded with costly clothes and adornments of the kind that are easily associated with *meretrices* (cf. [Tib] 3.8),[20] and yet identifies herself as 'the daughter of

---

the line of work of the *meretrix* is arguably compassionate, evoking through the phrasing of *miseras opes* the usual self-complaint of the poet-lover, *me miserum* (see e.g. Ov. *Am.* 1.4.59 above). See also Sharrock, who discusses this poem in this volume.

17 Skinner 2011.
18 See n. 45.
19 Fulkerson 2017, 221–94, makes numerous acute observations on the complexity of the *puella* Sulpicia.
20 '... the visual nature of the description almost forces the readers to look at her', Fulkerson 2017, 222.

Servius', who is most likely Servius Sulpicius Rufus,[21] making Sulpicia niece to Messalla Corvinus, known to be one of the key figures of Augustan literary culture, alongside Maecenas.[22] The lavishly adorned citizen *puella* Sulpicia (also as beloved, cf. [Tib.] 3.8.15; 24, 10.1; 11; 16, 12.2, *docta puella*; 9) is no whore. In fact, that is an allegation she reserves for her rival, whom she calls a *scortum* in the very same line in which her own aristocratic identity is underscored ([Tib.] 3.16.3–4):

> sit tibi cura togae potior pressumque quasillo
> scortum quam Serui filia Sulpicia.
>
> ([Tib.] 3.16.3–4)

> For you, a toga and a whore loaded down with a wool-basket may be worthier of your preference than Sulpicia, Servius' daughter.
>
> (Transl. Postgate and Goold)

As in the case of Sulpicia, Lesbia too, inasmuch as she evokes Sappho, also quite fittingly violates the dichotomy between lover and beloved. For the same dynamic in the case of Sappho herself can moreover be seen in Horace, where Sappho, as lover, both complains about her beloved *puellis* (*Carm.* 2.13.25, 'girls') and is herself referred to as the *Aeolia puella* (*Carm.* 4.9.12, 'the Aeolian girl'). Also, in Ovid's *Heroides* 15.100 Sappho calls herself *puella*, underscoring this word's capacity to accommodate a loving subject.[23] At this juncture we have entered into the realm of a different kind of metapoetics than the one mentioned above. And this kind of metapoetics is arguably not reductive, as the understanding of the *puella* as a product of 'womanufacturing' can be,[24] but enriching, drawing on references to other poetry, including that of women authors, such as Sappho and Corinna.[25]

To sum up, the female beloved in Latin literature is a *locus* of conflicting evocations: on a metapoetic level she is the poet-lover's creation and object, but also his (or her)[26] tribute to preceding poets, including female ones. Moreover, she is attractive, but also intimidating, powerful, but also 'forced', she can be someone else's wife and be compared with a prostitute, and yet brings with her associations with Roman citizenship. The figure of the *meretrix*, who most prominently features in the genre of Roman comedy before that of Latin love poetry, is

---

21 This may also have been her grandfather; see n. below.
22 *OCD* s.v. 'Sulpicia'.
23 For the vexed question of the authenticity of this poem, see Thorsen 2014, 96–122.
24 Sharrock 1991.
25 Thorsen 2019b.
26 If we take Sulpicia into account.

certainly important for understanding the figure of the female beloved in poetry too, as has perhaps been most persuasively argued by Sharon James in her highly influential *Learned Girls and Male Persuasion: Gender and Reading in Roman Love Elegy* (2003). Nevertheless, there is no easy way of referring all these discordant associations to this figure alone, which arguably calls for an additional model of explanation.

Words

Three Latin terms have been used above in relation to the beloved as a female figure: *meretrix*, *puella* and *domina* (cf. above *Am.* 1.4.60), and two bodies of Latin literature have been identified as particularly rich in occurrences of this figure: Roman comedy and Latin love poetry. The main authors of these genres are Plautus, Terence (= comic playwrights), Catullus, Propertius, Tibullus, including Lygdamus and Sulpicia from the *Appendix Tibulliana*, and Ovid in his love elegies (= love poetry).[27] The distribution of the three Latin terms for the female beloved across these authors (whose output varies greatly in size) is as follows:[28]

Tab. 1: Distribution of words.

Author	meretrix	Puella	Domina
Plautus	72	28	ca. 2
Terence	26	6	3
Catullus	1	46	10
Propertius	1	123	32
Ovid	4	221	98

As may be seen from this survey, the application of the word *meretrix* is highly common in comedy, but occurs conspicuously seldom in love poetry, and never unequivocally in reference to the beloved. Catullus uses the word only once (Catull. 110.7), of a certain Aufilena, Tibullus and the *Appendix Tibulliana* never,

---

[27] I include *Heroides* 1–21, *Amores* 1–3, *Ars amatoria* 1–3 and *Remedia amoris* among his love elegies; see Thorsen 2013c.
[28] Generated using the concordance tool of the PHI (https://latin.packhum.org).

Propertius once, of Cleopatra (Prop. 3.11.39), and Ovid five times in his love elegies,[29] of which only one instance includes a certain comparison between the figure of the *puella* and that of the *meretrix* (*Am.* 3.14.9), while another refers to the stock character in Menander's Attic New Comedy plays (*Am.* 1.15.18), one to the beloved of Sappho's brother (*Her.* 15.63), one to the kind of woman who is the direct opposite of the ideal *puella* (*Am.* 1.10.21); and finally, the word is used in reference to the dangers of materially greedy girlfriends in the *Ars amatoria* (*Ars am.* 1.435).[30]

At the same time, the survey above confirms that the genre which arguably displays the most complex figure of the beloved, namely Latin love poetry, most commonly employs the terms *puella* and *domina* for this figure. The latter term occurs less frequently, but is interchangeable with *puella*, as seen e.g. in *Am.* 2.4.3 (*dilectam puellam*) and 60 (*mea domina*). It may therefore be worth scrutinizing the word *puella* first and then that of the *domina* more closely, in order to get a better grasp on the figure she represents.

The word *puella* is a noun in the feminine gender and diminutive form. It is, as such, bound to a male counterpart, and often represented as derived from it, as seen e.g. from the *Thesaurus Lingae Latinae*, which notes 'v.[ide] puellus' ('see "*puellus*"') under the entry '*puella*',[31] even though there are more than 1,300 occurrences of the word in the grammatically feminine gender, against fewer than 20 in the grammatically masculine form in classical Latin.[32] Be that as it may, both forms are etymologically linked to the non-diminutive form of the noun, *puer*. Notably, Varro claims that this word once used to be grammatically gender-inclusive in Latin: *Puer et in feminino sexu antiqui dicebant* (Varro, *Ling.* Fr. 37; Charisius, *Gramm.* I 84.5–11 Keil, '*puer* [child] the ancients used to say also as a feminine'). Varro backs up his claim by quoting e.g. Livius Andronicus, who in his *Odyssey* wrote *mea puer quid uerbi ex tuo ore supra fugit* (Fr. 3, 'my female child, what kind of word flies from your mouth?').[33] Moreover, Varro compares this gender-inclusive usage of the Latin noun with a parallel phenomenon in Greek: *ut Graeci ὁ παῖς καὶ ἡ παῖς ...* (Varro, *Ling.* Fr. 37; Charisius, *Gramm.* I 84.5–11 Keil,

---

29 See n. 27 above.
30 Cf. *procul a scripta solis meretricibus arte* (*Tr.* 2.303 'far from the *Ars amatoria* written only for prostitutes'), which is not as straightforward as it may seem; see e.g. Ingleheart 2010a, 261. See also Sharrock and Brecke in this volume.
31 *TLL* s.v. 'puella'.
32 Figures from PHI (https://latin.packhum.org).
33 There are different versions of this verse in different lines of transmission, which also includes the form *mea puera*; see Kent 1938, 626–9 and *TLL* 2517, 3.

'as the Greeks [use the] masculine article in Greek for παῖς meaning "boy" and feminine article in Greek for παῖς meaning "girl" ...'). The Greek παῖς is thus understood as having been the equivalent of the Latin *puer*,³⁴ in terms of being grammatically gender-inclusive, at least at some point in the history of the Latin language. By comparing the Greek gender-inclusive παῖς (where the grammatical gender distinction is made conspicuous by the preceding articles ὁ and ἡ) to the Latin gender-inclusive usage of the term *puer* at the time of Livius Andronicus, Varro sets up a linguistic trajectory at the other end of which we find the term *puella*. This linguistic trajectory therefore appears suggestively relevant to our understanding of the figure of the beloved *puella* in Latin literature.

In the literary examples Varro uses to back up his claim,³⁵ the significance of the female *puer* seems primarily to be 'daughter'. Similarly, in the *Oxford Latin Dictionary*, which sums up the meanings of the word *puella*, the first of the four main categories is the same: 1) a female child, girl, daughter; 2) a young woman, girl; 3) an object of sexual interest/one's sweetheart and 4) a slave girl.³⁶ Notably, all of these definitions contribute to an image of the *puella* as someone inferior in status and also an object of potential affection, whether non-erotic, as that of a father towards his daughter, or erotic, as that of a lover towards his sweetheart or the customer of a slave-prostitute, whether she is a freedwoman or subject to the ownership of a pimp.

However, as we have seen, the figure of the beloved, who most often goes under the designation *puella*, is complex. Thus, although a relatively young age is the conspicuous common denominator of all the four main categories identified in *OLD*, the *puella* is not always young. Thanks to the association between Clodia and Catullus' Lesbia, one of the most prominent *puellae* appears to be older than the poet who loves her. In the usual chronology, Clodia is thought to have been born in 95/94 BCE and Catullus c. 85 BCE, so that she is in her thirties when addressed by the poet. Thus, the beloved *puella* may violate the convention that the beloved must be young, as well as the word's central connotation of a younger, tender age.³⁷

---

34 And an etymological connection, however insecure, cannot be ruled out: 'The appurtenance of Lat. *puer* < *ph₂u-ero- 'smaller' is not certain', Beekes 2010, 1143. I am grateful to Eystein Dahl for pointing this out to me.
35 Kent 1938, 626–9.
36 *OLD* s.v. 'puella'.
37 So also Phaedra, calling herself *puella* at Ov. *Her.* 4.2, and Sappho at Ov. *Her.* 15.100; both are older than their beloveds. Moreover, Ovid's *praeceptor amoris* recommends senior lovers to both men (*Ars am.* 2.663–702) and women (*Ars am.* 3.555–76); it thus seems that Ovid modifies the presumed fixation on youth in the beloved in antiquity, cf. e.g. Konstan 2000 and 2002.

More importantly, the word's associations with slavery are highly complicated, partly due to the fact that the word *puella* is so closely linked to the term *domina*[38] (i.e. 'mistress of a slave') as another designation of the beloved in Latin love poetry, especially elegy. No doubt, of the two words, *puella* is much more prominent than *domina* in the corpus of Latin love poetry, as seen in the survey above. Yet, even if the word *domina* is less frequently used for the beloved than *puella*, the two terms are, as already pointed out, used interchangeably. According to the *Oxford Latin Dictionary*, the word *domina* denotes power, authority and ownership, as in a 'female head of a household' and 'a female ruler or leader', and expresses 'respect or affection.'[39] Thus, the paradoxical figure of the *puella-domina* might be said to function as a contradictory hendiadys, which may be explained according to the following logic: the lover wants to possess his beloved as one would possess a pet slave, a *puella*, but finds himself enslaved by the beloved as by a *domina*. From this situation arises the topos of *seruitium amoris*, 'slavery of love', which is one of the defining features of Latin love elegy.[40] The *puella-domina* figure thus appears to be a profoundly Roman oxymoron.

However, the double dynamic of an enslaving slave might also be seen as embedded in a poem attributed to the Greek lyric poet Anacreon:

ὦ παῖ παρθένιον βλέπων
δίζημαί σε, σὺ δ' οὐ κοεῖς,
οὐκ εἰδὼς ὅτι ταῆς ἐμῆς
ψυχῆς ἡνιοχεύεις.

(Anac. Fr. 360 PMGF)

O boy with the glance of a virgin, I seek you, but you do not notice, not knowing that you hold the reins of my soul.

(Transl. Campbell, adapted)

The combination of the word 'boy', which carries the connotation of 'slave', and clearly also designates a beloved, with the image of this beloved as a rider or charioteer controlling the soul of the lover seems to capture some of the same dynamic as the oxymoron of the *puella-domina*. The designation of a beloved as παῖς, as seen in Anacreon's poem, also increases the relevance of Varro's observation for our understanding of the figure of the *puella*.

---

38 See e.g. Keith 2012.
39 *OLD* s.v. 'domina'; cf. also de la Bédoyère 2018. For post-Augustan, imperial applications of concepts such as πότνια ('mistress', 'queen', also of a goddess) and δέσποινα ('mistress', 'lady of the house', 'mistress of slaves') in Greek poetry, see Magnelli, 2016.
40 See Fulkerson 2013 and the first chapter in this volume.

Notably, the Liddell-Scott-Jones *Greek-English Lexicon* (*LSJ*) lists only the following three main significances of παῖς, as defined 1) in relation to descent, as a son or daughter; 2) in relation to age, as a male or female child younger than the speaker and 3) in relation to condition, as a male or female slave.[41] Yet the grammatically feminine ἡ παῖς is in fact also a term for the beloved in Greek literature, from Sappho[42] to Philodemus.[43] And, as is also seen in the poem by Anacreon, παῖς is employed more commonly still in the case of beloved boys, from at least as far back as Theognis, to Theocritus and beyond. Seeing a connection between the Greek παῖς and the Latin *puella* should also remind us of how strongly the *puella* is connected to the *puer* as beloved, which also occurs a few times in the diminutive form *puellus*.[44] Grammatically, the word *puella* is thus an example of a word in the feminine gender bound to a grammatically male counterpart, which, as demonstrated by Corbeill, was once a pervasive phenomenon in earlier Latin, though it later became evanescent.

The beloved: from both through two to the one and only

Against the background of these observations, an alternative to the *meretrix* figure as a point of comparison for the *puella* is offered by the etymologically connected term *puer*, which may also represent the beloved in Latin literature. As Corbeill points out, men and women, or girls and boys, have more in common than not. And this is arguably the case for the *puella* and the *puer* in the role of the beloved, too.[45] Both carry connotations of the erotic pet slave, such as Alexis

---

41 *LSJ* s.v. 'παῖς'.
42 E.g. Sappho, Fr. 49 Voigt, which includes both love and distaste for the παῖς Atthis in a way that is reminiscent of the figure of the *puella* as outlined above.
43 For Philodemus, see Keith in this volume.
44 *OLD* s.v. 'puellus'; Stephen Harrison kindly suggests that the occurrences of this word are either 'in archaic or archaising texts ... suggesting that this like feminine *puer* is an early usage', as in Apuleius; see my first chapter in this volume.
45 Cf. Apuleius *Apol.* 10, which is usually quoted as a source of information on the alleged historical identities behind the pseudonyms of elegiac *puellae* only, but in addition to informing us that Catullus' Lesbia was Clodia, Ticidas' Perilla was Metella, Propertius' Cynthia was Hostia and Tibullus' Delia was Plania, Apuleius reveals in this passage the identity of Vergil behind the name Corydon and of his beloved (whose real name we are not told) behind that of Alexis. When we add the real names of the boy loves of Lucilius, also mentioned in this passage, we get a fairly even distribution of same- and other-sex beloveds in Latin erotic poetry.

in Virgil's second *Eclogue*, who is *delicias domini* ('darling of his lord') and therefore inaccessible to others (Verg. *Ecl.* 2.2). Thus, the unnamed *puer* of Catullus' homoerotic verse in poems 15.5 (*puerum*) and 21.11 (*puer*), often assumed to be the beloved boy Juventius, but otherwise designated only as *meos amores* (15.1; 21.4), seems also to be such a pet slave and object of love, just like the *tenerae puerorum turbae* ('the tender throng of boys') at Tibullus' elegy 1.4.9.

That same elegy, which professes the poet's love for the boy Marathus, includes a lengthy passage on the perishable beauty that will fade with time, a concern shared with the poetic 'I' of Horace *Odes* 4.10 in regard to his beloved boy Ligurinus.[46] The concern for the preservation of beauty, particularly in the face of age, not only functions as a reminder of the present attractiveness of the beloved, but also creates a bridge between such accounts of the beloved as a *puer* with those of *puellae* and their looks, particularly in the works of Ovid.[47]

Furthermore, just like the *puella* figure, the beloved boy, too, may not reciprocate the lover's advances. Thus, Catullus is vehemently rejected by Juventius, who is mentioned explicitly as the male object of love in Catull. 24, 48, 81 and 99, and whom the poet wants to give as many as 'three hundred thousand kisses' (Catull. 48.3, *usque ad milia basiem trecenta*), but from whom he eventually steals but one:

> surripui tibi dum ludis, mellite Iuuenti,
>   sauiolum dulci dulcius ambrosia.
> uerum id non impune tuli: namque amplius horam
>   suffixum in summa me memini esse cruce,
> dum tibi me purgo nec possum fletibus ullis   5
>   tantillum uestrae demere saeuitiae.
> nam simul id factumst, multis diluta labella
>   guttis abstersti mollibus articulis,
> ne quicquam nostro contractum ex ore maneret,
>   tamquam commictae spurca saliua lupae.   10
> praeterea infesto miserum me tradere amori
>   non cessasti omnique excruciare modo,
> ut mi ex ambrosia mutatum iam foret illud
>   sauiolum tristi tristius helleboro.
> quam quoniam poenam misero proponis amori   15
>   numquam iam posthac basia surripiam.

(Catull. 99)

---

[46] Cf. also Hor. *Carm.* 4.1 and Palmore in this volume.
[47] Cf. e.g. *Am.* 1.14, *Ars am.* 3.124–320 and, of course, the fragmentary *Medicamina faciei feminarum*, 'Cosmetics for female beauty.'

> I stole a kiss from you, honey-sweet Juventius, while you were playing, a kiss sweeter than sweet ambrosia. But not unpunished; for I remember how for more than an hour I hung impaled at the top of the gallows tree, as I excused myself to you, yet could not with all my tears take away ever so little from your anger; for no sooner was it done, than you washed your lips clean with plenty of water, and wiped them with your dainty fingers, that no contagion from my mouth might remain, as though it were the foul spit of some filthy whore. Besides that, you made haste to deliver my unhappy self to angry love, and to torture him in every manner, so that that kiss, changed from ambrosia, was now more bitter than bitter hellebore. Since then you impose this penalty on my unlucky love, henceforth I will never steal any kisses.
>
> (Transl. Cornish)

However, such bitter experiences as those of Catullus in this poem are not the only lessons to be learned by a lover in Latin poetry. This is demonstrated by the homoerotic teachings of Priapus in Tibullus 1.4:

> tunc tibi mitis erit, rapias tum cara licebit
>   ascula : pugnabit, sed tibi rapta dabit.
> rapta dabit primo, post adferet ipse roganti,   55
>   post etiam collo se inplicuisse uelit.
> heu male nunc artes miseras haec saecula tractant:
>   iam tener adsueuit munera uelle puer.
> at tu, qui uenerem docuisti uendere primus,
>   quisquis es, infelix urgeat ossa lapis.   60
> Pieridas, pueri, doctos et amate poetas,
>   aurea nec superent munera Pieridas.
>
> (Tib. 1.4.53–62)

> Then will he be gentle with you; then you may snatch the precious kiss: he will struggle, but let you snatch it. He will let you snatch it first; but later will he bring it for the asking, and presently even he will be fain to hang upon your neck. But now, alas! Our perverse age plies wretched art. Now gentle boys have learned to look for gifts. Whoever you are who first taught the sale of love, may an unhallowed stone weigh heavy on your bones. Love the Pierians, boys, and learned poets, do not let the Pierians succumb to golden gifts.
>
> (Transl. Cornish)

The element of force and Priapus' advice to interpret the beloved's 'no' as really a 'yes' might also compare with Ovid's advice in his *Ars amatoria* to use a bit of force in the case of *puellae*: *Vim licet appelles: grata est uis ista puellis: / Quod iuuat, inuitae saepe dedisse uolunt* (Ov. Ars am. 1.673–4, 'You may call it violence; that kind of violence is welcome to girls; that which is pleasing they often wish to have given unwillingly').⁴⁸ Thus, Ovid's seemingly male-chauvinist piece of advice to take 'no' as a 'yes' may in fact be mirroring Tibullan *erotodidaxis* regarding beloved boys.⁴⁹

In addition to being hard (if not impossible) to get, the beloved *puer* may be unfaithful, susceptible to the wealth of rich suitors, who get sex in return for gifts and money, much to the lament of the poet-lover, who wants the *puer* to accept the gift of poetry instead (cf. Tib. 1.4.61–2), which exactly resembles the case of *puellae* (cf. e.g. Ov. *Am*. 1.10 and 3.8, the latter adding a political aspect to the riches with which one may achieve sex by linking these to Augustan military victories).

Finally, the beloved *puer* may also be associated with Roman citizenship, as seen from Catullus' designation of Juventius as *flosculus Iuuentiorum* (Catull. 24.1, 'the flower of the Juventii'), a phrase which seems to suggest the noble Roman family of that name.⁵⁰

The status of the beloved *puer* is thus highly composite, and encompasses beauty and attraction, freedom to reject a lover, connotations of prostitution, as well as associations with the aristocracy, just like the figure of the beloved *puella*. Considering the similarities between the *puer* and the *puella* as figures of the beloved as well as their semantic connection, it is attractive to see the development outlined by Corbeill, from gender fluidity to more fixed and heterosexualized representations of grammatically male and female words in the history of the Latin language, as parallel to a development in Latin literature, in which Catullus' Juventius, the male beloveds of Virgil's *Eclogues*, Tibullus' Marathus, Horace's Ligurinus and even Ovid's plural *amores*⁵¹ are a part of a vital yet vanishing feature, which is eventually eclipsed by the figure of the *puella*. For while one might have expected, due to these similarities between male and female beloveds,

---

48 See Zuckerberg on the issue, 2018, 105–22.
49 Ovid's piece of advice is further complicated by the fact that it alludes to the female figure Oenone's accusation of Helen as constantly saying 'no' but meaning 'yes' – see Brecke in this volume; however, there is also the narrative of Achilles and Deidamia to back up the theory, at *Ars am*. 1.681–704.
50 The Juventii were a Roman noble family from Tusculum; cf. Cicero, *Tu es e municipio antiquissimo Tusculano, ex quo sunt plurimae familiae consulares, in quibus est etiam Iuuentia* (*Planc*. 19, 'you are from the ancient Tuscan municipality, from which come several consular families, among them even the Juventii').
51 See Ingleheart in this volume, who explores the homoerotic aspects of Ovid's *Amores*. There are others too, such as the poet Valgius' Mystes, and, as Maltby points out in his commentary on Tibullus, 'The theme occurs …, on the evidence of Verg. *Ecl*. 10.37–41, probably also in Gallus', Maltby 2002, 215.

mostly from the point of view of a male lover, that there would be male dominance on both the subjective and the objective side of love in Latin poetry, this is not the case. The conundrum of the prominence of the *puella* remains, in the sense that her presence, most concretely represented by the large number of verses dedicated to this figure, is not overshadowed by that of the *puer*, but quite the opposite.

I will close this chapter with an example that may be interpreted as a dramatization of this trajectory from the Greek gender-inclusive term παῖς to a *puella* who, not only as an object, but also as a subject in an erotic setting, acquires a presence so profound as 'you' and as the 'other' that she threatens to break loose from the role of beloved altogether. The example I have in mind is the reworking of Callimachus' story of Acontius and Cydippe (*Aet.* Frr. 67–75 Harder) in Ovid's *Heroides* 20–1, where the hero and heroine each pen their own letter.[52]

In the extant fragments of his *Aetia*,[53] Callimachus unfolds the tale of how the boy Acontius managed to trick Cydippe into unwittingly swearing to marry him in the temple of Artemis, and how the goddess struck Cydippe with illness every time she tried to marry the fiancé she was already engaged to, how her father eventually asked the oracle of Apollo what was the matter, and how his oracular response was that she had to marry Acontius, which she did, and was cured. The poet then closes his tale by divulging that he found the legend in the chronicles of Xenomedes, 'from which the child's story moved swiftly to our Calliope' (Fr. 75.76–7 Harder, ἔνθεν ὁ παιδὸς / μῦθος ἐς ἡμετέρην ἔδραμε Καλλιόπην).

I will make but one brief point, which is that the phrase ὁ παιδὸς μῦθος, 'the child's story', has been interpreted strikingly differently in scholarship; Constantine Trypanis translates it as 'the maiden's story', as does Giulio Massimilla, yet Anette Harder reads this as 'the boy's story' and Susan Stephens as the 'story of a boy'. In fact, as I have pointed out elsewhere,[54] there are three instances of the word παῖς in the extant fragments of the story in Callimachus; the first refers to Acontius (Fr. 67.2 Harder), the second to Cydippe (Fr. 75.16 Harder) and the third may, as the diverging translations suggest, refer to either (Fr. 75.76–7 Harder).

The potential gender-inclusiveness of the final παῖς in the extant Callimachean fragments is arguably exploited in Ovid's *Heroides* 20–1. In scholarship, Acontius has been regarded as the more prominent of two, not least as an

---

[52] The following observations necessarily overlap with Thorsen 2019a, which nevertheless differs in terms of the arguments offered.
[53] See Thorsen 2019a, n. 1 for a brief overview on the scholarship on the state of the *Aetia*.
[54] See n. above.

embodiment of the poet,⁵⁵ especially as (author-like) he carves 'Cydippe is beautiful' into the bark of trees as he walks about in the woods and longs for her (Fr. 73 Harder). Yet Cydippe must at least be literate to have read the oath Acontius inscribed on the apple he threw at the feet of her nurse, who picked it up and, herself illiterate, asked Cydippe to read it aloud in the temple of Artemis (cf. Fr. 75.39 Harder).⁵⁶ And so, in Ovid's *Heroides* the two παῖδες who both know their way around words emerge as fully fledged writers of their own letters.

In these letters both Acontius and Cydippe identify Cydippe as a *puella* (*Her.* 20.26; 37; 66 and 21.59; 122; 159), thus signalling that her role is that of the beloved. But the love story, which seems unproblematic as such in Callimachus, is rather disturbing in Ovid's presentation. A considerable body of scholarship has detected disquieting features in Acontius' interest in Cydippe, such as his violent threats, stalking and jealousy,⁵⁷ not to mention the suffering on the part of Cydippe, who is literally on the verge of death because of Acontius' so-called 'love', which he himself calls 'madness' (*Her.* 20.207, *furoris*).⁵⁸ Such features are confusing when they occur in what is supposed to be one of the founding myths of love literature, and to have a happy ending. At the same time, precisely against the background of this confusion, Cydippe, the 'you' and 'other' to Acontius, emerges not only as a writing subject, but also as one of the more remarkable personalities in ancient literature.

I will in the following illustrate this point with the help of two examples, one of Cydippe's learnedness and one of her sarcasm. At the beginning of her letter, Cydippe compares herself to Hippolytus and implies that she – because she too is a virgin⁵⁹ – ought to be protected by the goddess Artemis/Diana, who now punishes her for breaking her oath (*Her.* 21.7–12). What is more, she also elegantly

---

55 Acosta-Hughes 2009.
56 See also Thorsen 2019a, 136.
57 Unlike Callimachus' Acontius, Ovid's has come from his own Island of Ceos to that of Cydippe, and claims that he lurks outside her door as she reads her letter, *Her.* 20.130; his letter abounds with violent images, such as the following threats: *si noceo quod amo, fateor, sine fine nocebo / teque ... Her.* 20.35–6, 'if I hurt what I love, I confess, I will hurt you without end ...' and *si non proficient artes, ueniemus ad arma, Her.* 20.47, 'if art/tricks will not work, I will resort to arms'; finally, in *Her.* 20.135–70 Acontius rants against his rival, claiming his right over Cydippe's body, which he compares to material property such as crops, fenced land and chattel.
58 For such interpretations, see Rosenmeyer 1996, Kuhlmann 2005, Rynearson 2009, Alekou 2011, Alekou (forthcoming) and Thorsen 2019a and Thorsen (forthcoming b).
59 By referring to herself by the elegiac designation *puella* and the non-elegiac term *uirgo*, Cydippe further contributes to the above-mentioned confusion, see also Brecke in this volume.

alludes to Euripides' *Hippolytus*[60] when she magisterially lectures Acontius on the juridical difference between the letter and the spirit of the law, thus:

> quae iurat, mens est ; sed nil iurauimus illa ;   135
>   illa fidem dictis addere sola potest.
> consilium prudensque animi sententia iurat,
>   et nisi iudicii uincula nulla ualent.
> si tibi coniugium uolui promittere nostrum,
>   exige polliciti debita iura tori;   140
> sed si nil dedimus praeter sine pectore uocem,
>   uerba suis frustra uiribus orba tenes.
> non ego iuraui – legi iurantia uerba;
>   uir mihi non isto more legendus eras.
> decipe sic alias – succedat epistula pomo: 145
>   si ualet hoc, magnas ditibus aufer opes.
> fac iurent reges sua se tibi regna daturos,
>   sitque tuum toto quidquid in orbe placet.
>
> (Ov. *Her.* 21.135–48 Kenney)

It is the mind that swears, and I have taken no oath with that; it alone can lend good faith to words. It is counsel and the prudent reasoning of the soul that swear, and, except the bonds of the judgment, none avail. If I have willed to pledge my hand to you, exact the due rights of the promised marriage-bed; but if I have given you naught but my voice, without my heart, you possess in vain but words without a force of their own. I took no oath – I read words that formed an oath; that was no way for you to be chosen as husband by me. Deceive thus other maids – let a letter follow an apple! If this plan holds, win away their great wealth from the rich; make kings take oath to give their thrones to you, and let whatsoever pleases you in all the world be yours.

(Transl. Showerman, rev. by Goold)

The punchline about all the things Acontius might achieve through his non-juridical (i.e. criminal) methods is easily read as irony. And an ironic attitude arguably permeates Cydippe's whole letter, as seen e.g. when she calls Acontius *magne poeta* (*Her.* 21.110, 'great poet') in the same line in which she identifies his inscribed words on the apple as *insidias tuas* ('your ambush'), and when she characterizes her own body, the health of which is ruined due to her repeated illnesses, as *ingenii ... magna tropaea tui* (*Her.* 21.114, 'your artistic talent's great trophy'). These are only a few of many examples of the Cydippe's strong personality as expressed through Ovid's poem.

---

[60] ἡ γλῶσσ' ὀμώμοχ', ἡ δὲ φρὴν ἀνώμοτος, Eur. *Hipp.* 612, 'My tongue swore, but my mind is not under oath.'

It thus seems – along the lines that have so far been investigated in this chapter – that Ovid, in the case of Acontius and Cydippe, has taken the ambiguous, grammatically gender-inclusive ὁ παιδὸς μῦθος of Callimachus and turned it into the story not only of Acontius, but also of the *puella* Cydippe. Moreover, the larger-than-life character of Cydippe as *puella* appears to break loose from the constraints of the role of beloved – also in the sense of a product of 'womanufacturing' – while simultaneously assuming the literary realness of a person in her own right.

Conclusion

As has been maintained throughout this chapter, the words παῖς, *puer* and *puella* all appear connected, yet evoke at the same time seemingly irreconcilable associations, which arguably refer not so much to historical facts about real working girls (*meretrices*) as to an imposing literary presence of increasing complexity. This complexity arguably culminates in the figure of the *puella*. The beloved, especially in the guise of this figure, becomes far more than a pretty face, and impossible to ignore, even as this figure evokes categories of socially inferior status such as that of a slave or a girl. The ultimate argument of this chapter is, therefore, that Roman love poetry, precisely because of its sustained focus on the beloved, and especially in the figure of the *puella*, might be regarded as a decisive moment in the emergence of the reality of 'you' and the 'other' in the history of literature in the West.

List of Contributors

Benjamin Acosta-Hughes is Professor of Greek and Latin at the Ohio State University. He has published extensively on Hellenistic poetry, and is the author of *Polyeideia – The Iambi of Callimachus and the Archaic Iambic Tradition* (2002) and *Arion's Lyre. Archaic Lyric into Hellenistic Poetry* (2010), and co-author of *Callimachus in Context. From Plato to the Augustan Poets* together with Susan Stephens (2012). He is co-editor of several volumes, including *Brill's Companion to Callimachus* (2011) with Luigi Lehnus and Susan Stephens, *Euphorion. Oeuvre poétique et autres fragments* (2012) with Christophe Cusset and *The Door Ajar: False Closure in Greek and Roman Literature and Art* (2013) with Farouk Grewing and Alexander Kirichenko.

Iris Brecke is affiliated with the research group The Classical Ages at the Norwegian University of Science and Technology. She is the author of *Ovid's Terence: Tradition and Allusion in the Love Elegies and Beyond* (doctoral thesis, 2020), and has published Norwegian verse translations of Terence's *Eunuchus* (2017) and *Hecyra* (2018).

Paola D'Andrea is affiliated with the research group The Classical Ages at the Norwegian University of Science and Technology. She is the author of *Classical Reception in Sir Walter Scott's Scottish Novels. The Role of Greece and Rome in The Making of Historico-National Fiction* (doctoral thesis, 2016) and *Il latino allo specchio. Riflessi dell'antico nel romanzo di Stendhal* (2021).

Stephen Harrison is Professor of Latin Literature at the University of Oxford and a Senior Research Fellow in Classics at Corpus Christi College. He has published extensively on Augustan Poetry, the Roman novel, and the reception of Latin literature. He is the author of several books, including *Generic Enrichment in Vergil and Horace* (2007), *Framing the Ass: Literary Form in Apuleius' Metamorphoses* (2013), *Horace: Odes II* (2017), *Victorian Horace: Classics and Class* (2017), and *How to Be Content: An Ancient Poet's Guide for an Age of Excess* (2020). He is the editor and co-editor of numerous volumes, including *Intratextuality and Latin Literature* (2018) with Theodoros Papanghelis and Stavros Frangoulidis, *Roman Receptions of Sappho* (2019) with Thea S. Thorsen, and *Cupid and Psyche: The Reception of Apuleius' Love Story since 1600* (2020) with Regine May.

Jennifer Ingleheart is Professor of Latin at Durham University. She has published widely on topics such as Roman homosexuality and its reception, Latin poetry and its reception, and is the author of *A Commentary on Ovid, Tristia, Book 2* (2010) and *Masculine Plural: Queer Classics, Sex, and Education* (2018), and the co-author of *Ovid, Amores 3: A Selection: 2, 4, 5, 14* (2011) together with Katharine Radice. She is the editor of *Two Thousand Years of Solitude: Exile After Ovid* (2011) and *Ancient Rome and the Construction of Modern Homosexual Identities* (2015).

Boris Kayachev is a Marie Curie Research Fellow at the Faculty of Classics, University of Oxford and a Non-Stipendiary Research Fellow at Wolfson College, Oxford. He specialises in the literary and textual criticism of Roman and Hellenistic poetry; besides numerous articles, he is the author of *Allusion and Allegory: Studies in the Ciris* (2016) and *Ciris: A Poem from the Appendix*

Vergiliana (2020), and the editor of *Poems Without Poets: Approaches to Anonymous Ancient Poetry* (2021).

Alison Keith is Professor of Classics and Director of the Jackman Humanities Institute at the University of Toronto. Her research addresses the intersection of gender and genre in Latin literature and Roman society. She has written books on Ovid, Propertius, and Vergil, and edited or co-edited volumes on Latin epigram and elegy, women in classical literature and ancient society, and the reception of philosophy in Latin epic.

Aaron Palmore teaches Classics at Loyola University Maryland. He is currently producing an edition of Christian Wedsted's transatlantic Latin poetry for the Bloomsbury Neo-Latin Series. He is also the author of *Desire Interrupted: Erotics, Politics, and Poetics in Horace, Odes 4* (doctoral thesis, 2016) and an article on Callimachus' *Victoria Berenices*.

Alison Sharrock is Hulme Professor of Latin at the University of Manchester. She has published extensively on Latin poetry, and is author of *Seduction and Repetition in Ovid's Ars Amatoria 2* and *Reading Roman Comedy: Poetics and Playfulness in Plautus and Terence* (2009), and co-author with Rhiannon Ash of *Fifty Key Classical Authors* (2002). She is the co-editor of numerous books, including *The Art of Love: bimillennial essays on Ovid's Ars Amatoria and Remedia Amoris* (2006) with Roy Gibson and Steven Green, *Metamorphic Readings: Transformation, Language, and Gender in the Interpretation of Ovid's* Metamorphoses (2020) with Mats Malm and Daniel Moller, and *Maternal Conceptions in Classical Literature and Philosophy* (2020) with Alison Keith.

Peter Astrup Sundt is Teacher of Latin and Modern Foreign Languages at Sutton High School GDST. He is the author of *Looking backwards and forwards – Orpheus in love and metapoetical complexities* (doctoral thesis, 2021), an article on classical reception in Tolkien and a Norwegian verse translation of Horace's *Ars Poetica*.

Thea S. Thorsen is Professor of Classical Studies at the Norwegian University of Science and Technology. She is the author of numerous publications on Greek and Roman literature and their receptions, including the monograph *Ovid's Early Poetry* (2014). She is the editor of *Greek and Roman Games in the Computer Age* (2012) and the *Cambridge Companion to Latin Love elegy* (2013), and co-editor of *Dynamics of Ancient Prose* (2018) and *Roman Receptions of Sappho* (2019), both with Stephen Harrison. She has published Norwegian metrical translations of all of Ovid's eroto-elegiac works (2001-2009).

Bibliography

Acosta-Hughes, B. (2008), 'Unwilling farewell and complex allusion (Sappho, Callimachus, and *Aeneid* 6.458)', *PLLS* 13, 1–12.
Acosta-Hughes, B. (2009), 'Ovid and Callimachus: rewriting the master', in: Knox, P.E. (ed.), *A Companion to Ovid*, Chichester, 236–51.
Acosta-Hughes, B. (2010), *Arion's Lyre: Archaic Lyric into Hellenistic Poetry*, Princeton.
Acosta-Hughes, B./Stephens, S.A. (2002), 'Rereading Callimachus' *Aetia*, fr. 1', *CPh* 97, 238–55.
Acosta-Hughes, B./Stephens, S.A. (2012), *Callimachus in Context: From Plato to the Augustan Poets*, Cambridge.
Adams, J.N. (1990²), *The Latin Sexual Vocabulary*, Baltimore, MD.
Alekou, S. (2011), *La représentation de la femme dans les* Héroïdes *d'Ovide: Parole et mémoire dans les Lettres XII, XX et XXI*, doctoral diss. Paris-IV Sorbonne.
Alekou, S. (forthcoming), 'The art of death in Ovid's *Heroides*', *ICS*.
Aloni, A. (1998), *Cantare glorie di eroi. Comunicazione e performance poetica nella Grecia arcaica*, Torino.
Alvares, J. (2012), 'Considering desire in the Greek romances employing Lacanian theory: some explorations', in: Futre Pinheiro, M./Skinner, M./Zeitlin, F. (eds.), *Narrating Desire: Eros, Sex, and Gender in the Ancient Novel*, Boston, 11–28.
Álvarez Hernández, A.R. (2014), '*Deductum carmen – deducere ornos*: acerca del programa bucólico virgiliano en la *Égloga 6*', *REC* 41, 13–35.
Anderson, R.D./Parsons, P.J./Nisbet, R.G.M. (1979), 'Elegiacs by Gallus from Qaṣr Ibrîm', *JRS* 69(1), 125–55.
André, J.-M. (1967), *Mécène*, Paris.
Andrisano, A.M. (2007), *Biblioteche del mondo antico. Dalla tradizione orale alla cultura dell'Impero*, Roma.
Armstrong, D. (1993), 'The addressees of the *Ars poetica*: Herculaneum, the Pisones and Epicurean protreptic', *MD* 31, 185–230.
Armstrong, D. (2004), 'Horace's *Epistles* 1 and Philodemus', in: Armstrong, D./Fish J./Johnston, P.A./Skinner, M.B. (eds.), *Vergil, Philodemus and the Augustans*, Austin, TX, 267–98.
Armstrong, D. (2014), 'Horace's Epicurean voice in the *Satires*', in: Garani, M./Konstan, D. (eds.), *The Philosophizing Muse: The Influence of Greek Philosphy on Roman Poetry*, Newcastle upon Tyne, 91–127.
Armstrong, J.M. (1998), 'Aristotle on the philosophical nature of poetry', *CQ* 48, 447–55.
Armstrong, R. (2006), *Cretan Women: Pasiphae, Ariadne, and Phaedra in Latin Poetry*, Oxford.
Asztalos, M. (2008), 'The poet's mirror: Horace *Carmen* 4.10', *HSPh* 104, 289–302.
Athanassaki, L. (1992), 'The triumph of love and elegy in Ovid's *Amores* 1, 2', *MD* 28, 125–41.
Austin, J.L. (1975²), *How to Do Things with Words*, Oxford.
Baca, A.R. (1971), 'Ovid's epistle from Sappho to Phaon (*Heroides* 15)', *TAPhA* 102, 29–38.
Baker, R.J. (ed.) (2000), *Propertius I. With an Introduction, Translation and Commentary*, Warminster.
Baldwin, B. (1970), 'Horace on sex', *AJPh* 91, 460–5.
Barbantani, S. (2009), 'Lyric in the Hellenistic period and beyond', in: Budelmann, F. (ed.), *The Cambridge Companion to Greek Lyric*, Cambridge, 297–318.
Barchiesi, A. (1984), *La traccia del modello: effetti omerici nella narrazione virgiliana*, Pisa.

Barchiesi, A. (1986), 'Problemi d'interpretazione in Ovidio: continuità delle storie, continuazione dei testi', *MD* 16, 77–107.
Barchiesi, A. (1987), 'Narratività e convenzione nelle *Heroides*', *MD* 19, 63–90.
Barchiesi, A. (2009), 'Lyric in Rome', in: F. Budelmann (ed.), *The Cambridge Companion to Greek Lyric*, Cambridge, 319–35.
Barsby, J.A. (1996), 'Ovid's *Amores* and Roman comedy', *PLLS* 9, 135–57.
Barsby, J.A. (1999a), 'Love in Terence', in: Braund, S.M./Mayer, R.G. (eds.), *Amor, Roma: Love and Latin Literature: Eleven Essays (and One Poem) by Former Research Students Presented to E. J. Kenney on his Seventy-Fifth Birthday*, Cambridge, 5–29.
Barsby, J.A. (ed.) (1999b), *Terence. Eunuchus*, Cambridge.
Barsby, J.A. (ed. and transl.) (2001), *Terence. The Woman of Andros, The Self-Tormentor, The Eunuch*, Cambridge, MA.
Barthes, R. (1977), *Fragments d'un discours amoureux*, Paris.
Becker, C. (1963), *Das Spätwerk des Horaz*, Göttingen.
Beekes, R. (ed.) (2010), *Etymological Dictionary of Greek*, Leiden.
Benner, A.R./Fobes, F.H. (eds.) (1949), *The Letters of Alciphron, Aelian and Philostratus*, Cambridge, MA.
Bessone, F. (2013), 'Latin Precursors' in: Thorsen, T.S. (ed.), *The Cambridge Companion to Latin Love Elegy*, Cambridge, 39–56.
Bierl, A./Lardinois, A. (eds.) (2016), *The Newest Sappho. P. Sapph. Obbink and P. GC inv. 105, Frs. 1–4. Studies in Archaic and Classical Greek Song, vol. 2. Mnemosyne* Suppl. 392, Leiden.
Binder, G. (2000), *Dido und Aeneas: Vergils Dido und Aspekte seiner Rezeption*, Trier.
Bing, P./Höchele, R. (eds.) (2014), *Aristaenetus. Erotic Letters*, Atlanta, GA.
Blank, D. (2019), 'Philodemus', E.N. Zalta (ed.), *Stanford Encyclopedia of Philosophy*. <https://plato.stanford.edu/archives/spr2019/entries/philodemus/>.
Boehringer, S. (2007), *L'homosexualité féminine dans l'antiquité grecque et romaine*, Paris.
Booth, J. (ed. and transl.) (1991), *Ovid, Amores II. With Commentary*, Warminster.
Booth, J. (2001a), 'Problems and programmatics in Propertius 1.1', *Hermes* 129, 63–74.
Booth, J. (2001b), 'Moonshine: intertextual illumination in Propertius 1.3.31–3 and Philodemus, *Anth. Pal.* 5.123', *CQ* 51(2), 537–44.
Booth, J. (2011), 'Negotiating with the epigram in Latin love elegy,' in: Keith, A. (ed.), *Latin Elegy and Hellenistic Epigram. A Tale of Two Genres at Rome*, Newcastle upon Tyne, 51–66.
Boswell, J. (1980), *Christianity, Social Tolerance, and Homosexuality: Gay People in Western Europe from the Beginning of the Christian Era to the Fourteenth Century*, Chicago.
Bowditch, P.L. (2012), 'Roman love elegy and the eros of empire' in: Gold, B.K. (ed.), *A Companion to Roman Love Elegy*, Chichester, 119–33.
Bowie, E. (1986), 'Early Greek elegy, symposium and public festival', *JHS* 106, 13–35.
Bowie, E. (2016), 'How did Sappho's songs get into the male sympotic repertoire?', in: Bierl, A./Lardinois, A. (eds.), *The Newest Sappho. P. Sapph. Obbink and P. GC inv. 105, Frs. 1–4. Studies in Archaic and Classical Greek Song*, vol. 2. *Mnemosyne* Suppl. 392, Leiden, 148–64.
Bowie, M. (1991), *Lacan*, Cambridge.
Brecke, I. (2020), *Ovid's Terence. Tradition and Allusion in the Love Elegies and Beyond*, doctoral diss., The Norwegian University of Science and Technology.
Breed, B.W. (2000), 'Imitations of originality: Theocritus and Lucretius at the start of the *Eclogues*', *Vergilius* 46, 3–20.
Briffault, R. (1945), *Les troubadours et le sentiment romanesque*, Paris.
Brink, C.O. (1971), *Horace on Poetry*, vol. 2: *The 'Ars Poetica'*, Cambridge.

Brink, C.O. (1982), *Horace on Poetry*, vol. 3: Epistles *Book II*, Cambridge.
Brown, P.M. (ed. and trans.) (1993), *Horace, Satires I*, Warminster.
Brown, R.D. (ed. and trans.) (1987), *Lucretius on Love and Sex: A Commentary on* De Rerum Natura *IV, 1030–1287*, Leiden.
Buchheit, V. (1962), *Studien zum Corpus Priapeorum*, Munich.
Budelmann, F./Philips, T. (eds.) (2018), *Textual Events: Performance and the Lyrics in Early Greece*, Oxford.
Burkowski, J.M.C. (2012), *The Symbolism and Rhetoric of Hair in Latin Elegy*, doctoral diss., Oxford University.
Butrica, J.L. (2013²), 'Some myths and anomalies in the study of Roman sexuality', in: Verstraete, B.C./Provencal, V. (eds.), *Same-Sex Desire and Love in Greco-Roman Antiquity and in the Classical Tradition of the West*, New York, 209–70.
Cahoon, L. (1987), 'The anxieties of influence: Ovid's reception by the early troubadours', *Mediaevalia* 13, 119–55.
Cairns, F. (1975), *Further Adventures of a Locked-out Lover: Propertius 2.17*, Liverpool.
Cairns, F. (1977), 'Horace on other people's love affairs (*Odes* I 27; II 4; I 8; III 12)', *QUCC* 24, 121–47, Repr. Cairns 2012, 262–83.
Cairns, F. (1979), *Tibullus: A Hellenistic Poet at Rome*, Cambridge.
Cairns, F. (1989), *Virgil's Augustan Epic*, Cambridge.
Cairns, F. (2006), *Sextus Propertius, the Augustan Elegist*, Cambridge.
Cairns, F. (2011), 'Philodemus *AP* 5.123, the epigrammatic tradition, and Propertius 1.3', in: Keith, A.M. (ed.), *Latin Elegy and Hellenistic Epigram. A Tale of Two Genres at Rome*, Newcastle upon Tyne, 33–50.
Cairns, F. (2012), *Collected Papers on Catullus and Horace*, Berlin.
Calame, C. (1999), *The Poetics of Eros in Ancient Greece* (trans. Lloyd, J.), Princeton.
Campbell, D.A. (ed. and transl.) (1988), *Greek Lyric, Anacreon, Anacreontea, Choral Lyric from Olympus to Alcman*, vol. II, Cambridge, MA.
Cantarella, E. (1992), *Bisexuality in the Ancient World* (trans. Ó Cuilleanáin, C.), New Haven, CT.
Cantarella, E. (2002²), *Bisexuality in the Ancient World* (trans. Ó Cuilleanáin, C.), New Haven, CT.
Cantarella, E./Lear, A. (eds.) (2008), *Images of Ancient Greek Pederasty: Boys Were Their Gods*, London.
Carey, C. (2013), 'Pimps in court', in: Harris, E.M./Leão, D.F./Rhodes, P.J. (eds.), *Law and Drama in Ancient Greece*, London, 169–84 (first published by Bristol Classical Press, 2010).
Carson, A. (1986), *Eros the Bittersweet*, Princeton.
Casali, S. (1992), 'Enone, Apollo pastore e l'amore immedicabile: giochi ovidiani su di un topos elegiac', *MD* 28, 85–100.
Casali, S. (1997), 'Review: The Cambridge *Heroides*', *CJ* 92, 305–14.
Cautadella, Q. (1950), 'Filodemo nella satira 1.2 di Orazio', *PP* 5, 18–31.
Cazzato, V./Obbink, D./Prodi, E.E. (eds.) (2016), *The Cup of Songs. Studies on Poetry and the Symposion*, Oxford.
Chaitin, G. (1996), *Rhetoric and Culture in Lacan*, Cambridge.
Christenson, D.M. (2013), 'Eunuchus', in: Augoustakis, A./Traill, A. (eds.), *A Companion to Terence*, Oxford, 262–80.
Clark, J.G./Coulson, F.T./McKinley, K.L. (eds.) (2011), *Ovid in the Middle Ages*, Cambridge.
Clausen, W. (1994), *A Commentary on Virgil*, Eclogues, Oxford.
Cohen, D. (1991), 'The Augustan law on adultery: The social and cultural context', in: Kertzer, D.I./Saller, R.P. (eds.), *The Family in Italy from Antiquity to the Present*, New Haven, 109–26.

Coleman, R. (1977), *Vergil: Eclogues*, Cambridge.
Conte, G.B. (1986), *The Rhetoric of Imitation, Genre and Poetic Memory in Virgil and other Latin Poets* (trans. Segal, C.S.), Ithaca.
Conte, G.B. (1989), 'Love without elegy: The *Remedia amoris* and the logic of a genre', *Poetics Today* 10, 441–69.
Conte, G B. (1994a), *Genres and Readers: Lucretius, Love Elegy, Pliny's* Encyclopedia (trans. Most, G.W.), Baltimore/London.
Conte, G.B. (1994b), *Latin Literature: A History* (trans. Solodow, J.), Baltimore.
Conte, G.B. (2007), *The Poetry of Pathos* (ed. Harrison, S.J.), Oxford.
Conte, G.B/Most, G.W. (1996), 'Genre', in: Hornblower/S. Spawforth, A. (eds.), *The Oxford Classical Dictionary*, 3rd edition, 630–1.
Cooley, M.G.L. (ed.) (2013), *The Age of Augustus*, London.
Copley, F.O. (1956), Exclusus Amator: *A Study in Latin Love Poetry*, Madison, WI.
Corbeill, A. (2015), *Sexing the World: Grammatical Gender and Biological Sex in Ancient Rome*, Princeton, NJ.
Cornish, F.W./Postgate, J.P./Mackail, J.W. (eds. and trans.) (1913), *Catullus. Tibullus. Pervigilium Veneris*, rev. by Goold, G.P, Cambridge, MA.
Courtney, E. (1990), 'Ovid and an epigram of Philodemus', *LCM* 15(8), 117–18.
Courtney, E. (1993), *The Fragmentary Latin Poets*, Oxford.
Cox, F. (2011), *Sibylline Sisters: Virgil's Presence in Contemporary Women's Writing*, Oxford.
Cribiore, R. (2001), *Gymnastics of the Mind: Greek Education in Hellenistic and Roman Egypt*, Princeton, NJ.
Crosland, J. (1947), 'Ovid's contribution to the conception of love known as "l'amour courtois"', *The Modern Language Review* 42, 199–206.
Csillag, P. (1976), *The Augustan Laws on Family Relations*, Budapest.
Cucchiarelli, A. (2012), *Publio Virgilio Marone:* Le Bucoliche, Rome.
Currie, B./Rutherford, I. (eds.) (2020), *The Reception of Greek Lyric Poetry in the Ancient World: Transmission, Canonisation and Paratext*, Leiden.
Czapla, B. (2006), 'Der Kuß des geflügelten Eros: Figurationen des Liebesgottes in Moschos 1 und Bion Aposp. 13 Gow als hellenistische Kontrafakturen des γλυκύπικρον ἀμάχανον ὄρπετον', in: Harder, M.A./Regtuit, R.F./Wakker, G.C. (eds.), *Beyond the Canon*, Leuven, 61–82.
Dahlmann, H. (1958), 'Die letzte Ode des Horaz (carmen IV 15)', *Gymnasium* 65, 340–55.
Dahlmann, H. (1979), 'Ein Gedicht des Apuleius? (Gellius 19, 11)', *Akademie der Wissenschaften und der Literatur, Abhandlungen der Geistes-und Sozialwissenschaftlichen* Klasse 8, Wiesbaden, 3–18.
Davidson, J.N. (2001), 'Dover, Foucault and Greek homosexuality: penetration and the truth of Sex', *P&P* 170, 3–51.
Davidson, J.N. (2007), *The Greeks and Greek Love: A Radical Reappraisal of Homosexuality in Ancient Greece*, London.
Davidson, J.N. (2008), *The Greeks and Greek Love: A Bold Exploration of the Ancient World*, New York, NY.
Davies, M. (1988), 'Monody, choral lyric and the tyranny of the handbook', *CQ* 38, 52–64.
Davis, G. (2011), '"A, uirgo infelix, quae te dementia cepit?": the Epicurean critique of *amor insanus* in Vergil's sixth eclogue', *Vergilius* 57, 35–54.
Davis, P.J. (1993), 'Thou shalt not cuddle: *Amores* 1.4 and the law', *Syllecta Classica* 4, 65–9.
Davis, P.J. (1999), 'Ovid's *Amores*: a political reading', *CPh* 94(4), 431–49.
Day, A.A. (1938), *The Origins of Latin Love Elegy*, Oxford.

de la Bédoyère, G. (2018), Domina: *The Women Who Made Imperial Rome*, New Haven, CT.
De Lacy, P.H. (1983) 'Lucretius and Plato', in: *Συζήτησις: Studi sull'epicureismo greco e romano offerti a Marcello Gigante*, Naples, 291–307.
de Rougemont, D. (1939), *L'amour et l'Occident*, Paris.
de Rougemont, D. (1962), *Passion and Society* (trans. Belgion, M.), 3rd revised edition, London.
de Rougemont, D. (1983), *Love in the Western World* (trans. Belgion, M.), Princeton, NJ (based on the 1940 and 1956 editions, New York).
Deacy, S./Pierce, K. (eds.) (1997), *Rape in Antiquity*, London.
DeBrohun, J.B. (2003), *Roman Propertius and the Reinvention of Elegy*, Ann Arbor, CT.
Delvigo, M.L. (1995), [review] Lyne, R.O.A.M (1989), *Words and the Poet: Characteristic Techniques of Style in Vergil's* Aeneid, *Gnomon* 67, 211–17.
Detel, W. (2005), *Foucault and Classical Antiquity: Power, Ethics and Knowledge* (trans. Wigg-Wolf, D.), Cambridge.
Dettmer, H. (1983), *Horace: A Study in Structure*, New York, NY.
Doblhofer, E. (1966), *Die Augustuspanegyrik des Horaz in formalhistorischer Sicht*, Heidelberg.
Dover, K.J. (1973), 'Classical Greek attitudes to sexual behavior', *Arethusa* 6, 59–73.
Dover, K.J. (1978), *Greek Homosexuality*, Cambridge, MA.
Dover, K.J. (1989²), *Greek Homosexuality*, Cambridge, MA.
Drago, A.T. (ed. and trans.) (2007), *Aristeneto: Lettere d'amore. Introduzione, testo, traduzione e commento*, Lecce.
Drinkwater, M.O. (2015), 'Irreconcilable differences: pastoral, elegy, and epic in Ovid's *Heroides* 5', *CW* 108(3), 385–402.
Dronke, P. (1965–1966), *Medieval Latin and the Rise of European Love-Lyric*, (2 vols.), Oxford.
Eder, W. (2005), 'Augustus and the power of tradition', in: Galinsky, K. (ed.), *The Cambridge Companion to the Age of Augustus*, Cambridge, 13–32.
Edwards, C. (1993), *The Politics of Immorality in Ancient Rome*, Cambridge.
Elder, J.P. (1961), '*Non iniussa cano*: Virgil's sixth eclogue', *HSCPh* 65, 190–225.
Elisei, C. (2019), 'Sappho as a Pupil of the *praeceptor amoris* and Sappho as *magistra amoris*. Some lessons of the *Ars amatoria* anticipated in *Heroides* 15', in: Harrison, S.J./Thorsen, T.S. (eds.), *Roman Receptions of Sappho*, Oxford, 227–47.
Fantuzzi, M. (2012), *Achilles in Love. Intertextual Studies*, Oxford.
Farrell, J. (1991), *Vergil's* Georgics *and the Tradition of Ancient Epic: The Art of Allusion in Literary History*, New York, NY.
Fedeli, P. (ed.) (1980a), *Sesto Properzio. Il primo libro delle elegie*, Florence.
Fedeli, P. (1980b), 'Properce et la tradition hellénistique', in: Thill, A. (ed.), *L'Élegie romaine; enracinement, thèmes, diffusion. Actes du colloque international organisé par la faculté des lettres et sciences humaines de Mulhouse en mars 1979*, Bulletin de la faculté des lettres de Mulhouse X, Mulhouse.
Fedeli, P. (ed.) (1984), *Propertius*, Stuttgart.
Fedeli, P. (ed.) (1985), *Properzio. Il libro terzo delle elegie*, Bari.
Fedeli, P. (ed.) (2005), *Properzio. Il libro secondo*, ARCA 45, Cambridge.
Fedeli, P./Ceccarelli, I. (2008), *Q. Horati Flacci, Carmina, Liber IV. Testi con commento filologico*, Firenze.
Fedeli, P./Dimundo, R./Ceccarelli, I. (eds.) (2015), *Properzio, Elegie Libro IV*, Nordhausen.
Feeney, D.C. (1983), The taciturnity of Aeneas, *CQ* 33, 204–19.
Feeney, D.C. (1993), 'Horace and the Greek Lyric Poets', in: Rudd, N. (ed.), *Horace 2000: A Celebration, Essays for the Bimillennium*, London, 41–63.

Felman, S. (1982), *Literature and Psychoanalysis: The Question of Reading, Otherwise*, Baltimore, MD.
Ferrari, F. (2010), *Sappho's Gift. The Poet and Her Community*, Ann Arbor, MI.
Figueira, T.J./Nagy, G. (eds.) (1985), *Theognis of Megara: Poetry and the Polis*, Baltimore, MD.
Fink, B. (1995), *The Lacanian Subject: Between Language and Jouissance*, Princeton, NJ.
Fink, B. (1997), *A Clinical Introduction to Lacanian Psychoanalysis: Theory and Technique*, Cambridge.
Fiorentini, L. (2007), 'Lirici greci nella biblioteca di Virgilio: qualche appunto sulla presenza di Saffo, Alceo e Stesicoro nell'*Eneide*', in: Andrisano, A.M. (ed.), *Biblioteche del mondo antico. Dalla tradizione orale alla cultura dell'Impero*, Roma, 127–45.
Fitzgerald, W. (1992), 'Catullus and the reader: the erotics of poetry,' *Arethusa* 25, 419–43
Fitzgerald, W. (1995), *Catullan Provocations. Lyric Poetry and the Drama of Position*, Berkeley, CA.
Ford, G.B. (1966), 'An Analysis of *Amores* 1.4', *Helikon* 6, 645–52.
Foucault, M. (1984a), *Histoire de la sexualité: L'usage des plaisirs* (Vol 2), Paris.
Foucault, M. (1984b), *Histoire de la sexualité: Le souci de soi* (Vol. 3), Paris.
Foucault, M. (1985a), *The History of Sexuality: The Uses of Pleasure* (Vol. 2) (trans. Hurley, R.), London.
Foucault, M. (1985b), *The History of Sexuality: The Care of the Self* (Vol. 3) (trans. Hurley, R.), New York.
Foucault, M. (2018), *Histoire de la sexualité: Les aveux de la chair* (Vol. 4), Paris.
Fowler, D. (2002a), 'Masculinity under threat? The poetics and politics of inspiration in Latin poetry', in: Spentzou, E./Fowler, D. (eds.), *Cultivating the Muse: Struggles for Power and Inspiration in Classical Literature*, Oxford, 141–60.
Fowler, D. (2002b), *Lucretius on Atomic Motion: A Commentary on* De Rerum Natura, *Book Two, Lines 1–332*, Oxford.
Foxhall, L. (1998), 'Pandora unbound: a feminist critique of Foucault's *History of Sexuality*', in: Larmour, D.H.J./Miller, P.A./Platter, C. (eds.), *Rethinking Sexuality: Foucault and Classical Antiquity*, Princeton, 122–37.
Fraenkel, E. (1957), *Horace*, Oxford.
Fraser, P.M. (1972), *Ptolemaic Alexandria*, I–II, Oxford.
Fratantuono, L. (2007), *Madness Unchained. A Reading of Virgil's* Aeneid, Lanham, MD.
Fratantuono, L. (2017), 'Ovid's *Metamorphoses*', *Oxford Bibliographies Online*, DOI: 10.1093/OBO/9780195389661–0251, Oxford.
Frazel, T.D. (2003), 'Priapus's two rapes in Ovid's *Fasti*', *Arethusa* 36 (1), 61–97.
Fredrick, D. (1997), 'Reading broken skin: violence in Roman elegy', in: Hallett, J.P./Skinner, M. (eds.), *Roman Sexualities*, Princeton, NJ, 172–93.
Fredrick, D. (2012), 'The gaze and the elegiac imaginary' in: Gold, B.K. (ed.), *A Companion to Roman Love Elegy*, Chichester, 426–39.
Freudenburg, K. (1993), *The Walking Muse. Horace on the Theory of Satire*, Princeton, NJ.
Fulkerson, L. (2004), '*Omnia vincit amor*: why the *Remedia* fail', *CQ* 54, 211–23.
Fulkerson, L. (2005), *The Ovidian Heroine as Author. Reading, Writing, and Community in the* Heroides, Cambridge.
Fulkerson, L. (2013), '*Seruitium amoris*: The Interplay of Dominance, Gender and Poetry', in: Thorsen, T.S. (ed.), *The Cambridge Companion to Latin Love Elegy*, Cambridge, 180–93.
Fulkerson, L. (2017), *A Literary Commentary on the Elegies of the Appendix Tibulliana*, Oxford.

Fumo, J.C. (2017), 'Ovid in the Middle Ages', *Oxford Bibliographies Online*, DOI: 10.1093/OBO/9780195396584–0224, Oxford.

Gagliardi, D. (1995), '*Horatius ludibundus* (Per l'interpretazione di *Carm.* II 4)', in: Gigante, M./Cerasuolo, S. (eds.), *Letture orazione*, Naples, 137–46.

Gale, M.R. (1991), 'Man and beast in Lucretius and the *Georgics*', *CQ* 41, 414–26.

Gale, M.R. (1994), *Myth and Poetry in Lucretius*, Cambridge.

Gale, M.R. (2000), *Virgil on the Nature of Things: The* Georgics*, Lucretius and the Didactic Tradition*, Cambridge.

Gardner, J. (1993), *Being a Roman Citizen*, London.

Gasti, H. (2010), 'Narrative self-consciousness in Virgil's *Aeneid* 3' *Dictynna* 7, [https://journals.openedition.org/dictynna/348].

Gentili, B. (1984), *Poesia e pubblico nella Grecia antica*, Rome.

Gentili, B. (1990), 'Die pragmatischen Aspekte der archaischen griechischen Dichtung', *A&A* 36, 1–17.

Germany, R. (2016), *Mimetic Contagion: Art and Artifice in Terence's* Eunuch, Oxford.

Ghiselli, G. (2004), *Enea e Didone e altre coppie di amanti tragici: l'amore come guerra, ferita, follia e morte*, Catania.

Giangrande, G. (1973), 'An epigram of Philodemus', *Maia* 25, 65–6.

Gibson, R.K. (1998), '*Meretrix* or *matrona*? Stereotypes in Ovid Ars Amatoria 3', *PLLS* 10, 295–312.

Gibson, R.K. (2003), *Ovid:* Ars Amatoria*, Book 3*, Cambridge.

Gibson, R.K. (2007), *Excess and Restraint: Propertius, Horace and Ovid's* Ars Amatoria I, London.

Gibson, R.K. (2009^2) [2003], *Ovid:* Ars Amatoria*, Book 3*, Cambridge.

Giesecke, A.L. (2000), *Atoms, Ataraxy, and Allusion: Cross-Generic Imitation of the* De Rerum Natura *in Early Augustan Poetry*, Zurich.

Gigante, M. (1983), *Ricerche filodemee*, Naples.

Gigante, M. (1993), *Orazio: una misura per l'amore: lettura della satira seconda del primo libro*, Venosa.

Gigante, M. (2004), 'Vergil in the shadow of Vesuvius', in: Armstrong, D./Fish, J./Johnston, P.A./Skinner, M.B. (eds.), *Vergil, Philodemus and the Augustans*, Austin, TX, 85–99.

Gigante, M./Capasso, M. (1989), 'Il ritorno di Virgilio a Ercolano', *SIFC* 7, 3–6.

Gillet, L. (1941), *Dante*, Paris.

Glazebrook, A. (2015), 'Sexuality' in: *Oxford Bibliographies Online*, DOI: 10.1093/OBO/9780195389661–0220, Oxford.

Gold, B.K. (ed.) (2012), *A Companion to Roman Love Elegy*, Chichester.

Golden, M./Toohey, P. (eds.) (2011), *A Cultural History of Sexuality in the Classical World*, London.

Goldhill, S. (1995), *Foucault's Virginity: Ancient Erotic Fiction and and the History of Sexuality*, Cambridge.

Gordon, P. (1997), 'The lover's voice in *Heroides* 15: or, why is Sappho a man?', in: Hallett, J.P./Skinner, M.B. (eds.), *Roman Sexualities*, Princeton, NJ, 274–91.

Gow, A.S.F./Page, D.L. (eds.) (1965), *The Greek Anthology: Hellenistic Epigrams*, 2 vols., Cambridge.

Gowers, E. (ed.) (2012), *Horace,* Satires *Book I*, Cambridge.

Gram, L.M. (2019), '*Odi et amo*: On Lesbia's name in Catullus', in: Thorsen, T.S./Harrison, S., *Roman Receptions of Sappho*, 95–117, Oxford.

Grandsen, K.W. (1996), *Virgil in English*, London.
Green, P. (1982), *Ovid: The Erotic Poems*, London.
Greene, E. (1995), 'Elegiac woman: fantasy, *materia* and male desire in Propertius 1.3 and 1.11', *AJPh* 116(2), 303–18.
Greene, E. (1998), *The Erotics of Domination: Male Desire and the Mistress in Latin Love Poetry*, Baltimore.
Greene, E. (1999), 'Re-figuring the feminine voice: Catullus translating Sappho', *Arethusa* 32(1), 1–18.
Griffin, J. (1985), *Latin Poets and Roman Life*, London.
Griffin, J. (2006), 'Herodotus and tragedy', in: Dewald, C./Marincola, J. (eds.), *The Cambridge Companion to Herodotus*, Cambridge, 46–59.
Griffith, R.D. (1995), 'Catullus' *Coma Berenices* and Aeneas' farewell to Dido', *TAPhA* 125, 47–59.
Griffiths, A.H. (1970), 'Six passages in Callimachus and the anthology', *BICS* 17, 32–43.
Gunderson, E. (2015), *Laughing Awry*, Oxford.
Gutzwiller, K. (1998), *Poetic Garlands: Hellenistic Epigrams in Context*, Berkeley, CA.
Habinek, T. (1997), 'The invention of sexuality in the world-city of Rome', in: Habinek, T./Schiesaro, A. (eds.), *The Roman Cultural Revolution*, Cambridge, 23–43.
Hall, E.W. (2011), '"And Cytherea smiled": Sappho, Hellenistic poetry, and Virgil's allusive mechanics', *AJPh* 132(4), 615–31.
Hallett, J.P. (1997), 'Female homoeroticism and the denial of Roman reality in Latin literature', in: Hallett, J.P./Skinner, M.B. (eds.), *Roman Sexualities*, Princeton, NJ.
Hallett, J.P. (2005), 'Catullan voices in *Heroides* 15: How Sappho became a man', *Dictynna* 2(1), https://journals.openedition.org/dictynna/129.
Hallett, J.P. (2013), 'Intersections of gender and genre: sexualizing the *puella* in Roman comedy, lyric and elegy', *EuGeStA* 3, 195–208.
Halliwell, S. (1986), *Aristotle's Poetics*, London.
Halperin, D.M. (1990), *One Hundred Years of Homosexuality and Other Essays on Greek Love*, New York, NY.
Halperin, D.M. (2002), *How to Do the History of Homosexuality*, Chicago, IL.
Hardie, P. (2003), *Ovid's Poetics of Illusion*, Cambridge.
Hardie, P. (2006), 'Cultural and historical narratives in Virgil's *Eclogues* and Lucretius', in: Fantuzzi, M./Papanghelis, T. (eds.), *Brill's Companion to Greek and Latin Pastoral*, Leiden, 275–300.
Harrison, E. (1988), 'Greek sculptured coiffures and ritual haircuts', in: Hägg, R./Marinatos, N./Nordquist, G. (eds.), *Early Greek Cult Practice: Proceedings of the fifth International Symposium at the Swedish Institute at Athens*, Athens, 247–54.
Harrison, S. (ed.) (1991), *Vergil* Aeneid *10*, Oxford.
Harrison, S. (1992), '*Apuleius eroticus*: Anth. Lat. 712 Riese', *Hermes* 120, 83–9.
Harrison, S. (2007), *Generic Enrichment in Virgil and Horace*, Oxford.
Harrison, S. (ed.) (2017), *Horace, Odes Book II*, Cambridge.
Harrison, S. (2018a), 'Hidden voices: homoerotic colour in Horace's *Odes*', in: Matzner, S./Harrison, S. (eds.), *Complex Inferiorities: The Poetics of the Weaker Voice in Latin Literature*, Oxford, 169–84.
Harrison, S. (2018b), 'Ovid's literary entrance: Propertian and Horatian traces', in. Harrison, S./Frangoulidis, S. (eds.), *Life, Love and Death in Latin Poetry: Studies in Honor of Theodore D. Papanghelis. Trends in classics. Supplementary volumes* 61, Berlin, 111–24.

Harrison, S. (2019), 'Shades of Sappho in Vergil', in: Harrison, S./Thorsen, T.S. (eds.), *Roman Receptions of Sappho*, Oxford, 137–50.
Harrison, S./Frangoulidis, S./Papanghelis, T. (eds.) (2018), *Intratextuality and Latin Literature*, Berlin.
Heath, J. (1994), 'The failure of Orpheus', *TAPhA* 124, 163–96.
Heath, M. (1991), 'The universality of poetry in Aristotle's *Poetics*', *CQ* 41, 389–402.
Heinze, R. (1915), *Virgils epische Technik*, Leipzig.
Hemker, J. (1985), 'Rape and the founding of Rome', *Helios* 12, 41–7.
Henderson, J. (1975), *The Maculate Muse: Obscene Language in Attic Comedy*, New Haven, CT.
Henderson, W.J. (2000), 'Aspects of the Ancient Greek *Symposion*', *Akroterion* 45, 6–26.
Henkel, J.H. (2009), *Writing Poems on Trees. Genre and Metapoetics in Vergil's* Eclogues *and* Georgics, doctoral diss., University of North Carolina.
Heslin, P.J. (2018), *Propertius, Greek Myth, and Virgil. Rivalry, Allegory, and Polemic*, Oxford.
Hexter, R. (2010), 'On first looking into Vergil's Homer', in: Farrell, J./Putnam, M.C.J. (eds.), *A Companion to Vergil's* Aeneid *and its Tradition*, London, 26–36.
Heyworth, S.J. (2007), *Cynthia. A Companion to the Text of Propertius*, Oxford.
Heyworth, S.J./Morwood, J.H.W. (2010), *A Commentary on Propertius, Book 3*, Oxford.
Hinds, S. (1987a), *The Metamorphosis of Persephone. Ovid and the Self-Conscious Muse*, Cambridge.
Hinds, S. (1987b), 'Generalising about Ovid', *Ramus* 16, 4–31.
Hinds, S. (1998), *Allusion and Intertext. Dynamics of Appropriation in Roman Poetry*, Cambridge.
Hines, C. (2014), 'Rufinus and Ovid', M.A. Thesis, University of Toronto.
Hobden, F. (2013), *The* Symposion *in Ancient Greek Society and Thought*, Cambridge.
Hollis, A.S. (1977), *Ovid: Ars Amatoria: Book I*, Oxford.
Hollis, A.S. (2007), *Fragments of Roman Poetry c. 60 BC–AD 20*, Oxford.
Hollis, A.S. (2009[2]) [1977], *Ovid: Ars Amatoria: Book 1*, Oxford.
Holzberg, N. (1998[2]), *Ovid. Dichter und Werk*, Munich.
Holzberg, N. (2001), 'Lesbia, the poet, and the two faces of Sappho: "womanufacture" in Catullus', *PCPS* 46, 28–44.
Holzberg, N. (2002), *Ovid: The Poet and his Work*, Ithaca, NY.
Homer, S. (2005), *Jacques Lacan*, New York, NY.
Hopkinson, N. (1988), *A Hellenistic Anthology*, Cambridge.
Höschele, R. (2006), *Verrückt nach Frauen: der Epigrammatiker Rufin*, Tübingen.
Höschele, R. (2010), *Die blütenlesende Muse: Poetik und Textdualität antiker Epigrammsammlungen*, Tübingen.
Höschele, R. (2011), 'Inscribing epigrammatists' names: Meleager in Propertius and Philodemus in Horace', in: Keith, A.M. (ed.), *Latin Elegy and Hellenistic Epigram. A Tale of Two Genres at Rome*, Newcastle upon Tyne, 19–32.
Housman, A.E. (1972) [1890], 'Horatiana', in: Diggle, J./Goodyear, F. (eds.), *The Classical Papers of A.E. Housman*, Cambridge, 136–61.
Howatson, M.C. (trans.) (2008), 'The Symposium ('The drinking party')', in: Howatson, M.C./Sheffield, F.C.C. (eds.), *Plato: The Symposium*, Cambridge, 1–63.
Hubbard, M. (2001), *Propertius*, London.
Hubbard, T.K. (1998), *The Pipes of Pan: Intertextuality and Literary Filiation in the Pastoral Tradition from Theocritus to Milton*, Ann Arbor, MI.
Hubbard, T.K. (ed.) (2014), *A Companion to Greek and Roman Sexualities*, Chichester.

Hullinger, D. (2016), 'Chasing a dark horse. Pursuit and identity in Anacreon's 'Thracian filly' Fragment 417 *PMG*', *Mnemosyne* 69, 5, 729–41.
Hult, D.F. (1996), 'Gaston Paris and the Invention of Courtly Love', in: Block, R.H/Nichols, S.G. (eds.), *Medievalism and the Modernist Temper*, Baltimore, MD, 192–224.
Hunter, R. (1992) 'Callimachus and Heraclitus', *MD* 28, 113–23.
Hunter, R. (2006), *The Shadow of Callimachus. Studies in the Reception of Hellenistic Poetry at Rome*, Cambridge.
Hunter, R. (2018), *The Measure of Homer. The Ancient Reception of the* Iliad *and the* Odyssey, Cambridge.
Huskey, S.J. (2005), 'In memory of Tibullus: Ovid's remembrance of Tibullus 1.3 in *Amores* 3.9 and *Tristia* 3.3', *Arethusa* 38(1), 367–86.
Huwé, C. (2017), *Cupidon dans l'art romain*, Paris.
Ingleheart, J. (ed.) (2010a), *A Commentary on Ovid*, Tristia, *Book 2*, Oxford
Ingleheart, J. (2010b), 'The literary "successor": Ovidian metapoetry and metaphor', *CQ* 60(1), 167–72.
Ingleheart, J. (ed.) (2011), *Two Thousand Years of Solitude: Exile after Ovid*, Oxford.
Ingleheart, J. (2015), '"Greek" love at Rome: Propertius 1.20 and the reception of Hellenistic verse', *EuGeStA* 5(1), 124–53.
Irigoin, J. (2003), *La tradition des textes grecs. Pour une critique historique*, Paris.
Jacobson, H. (1974), *Ovid's* Heroides, Princeton, NY.
Jacoby, F. (1905), 'Zur Entstehung der römischen Elegie', *RhM* 60, 38–105.
Jakobson, R. (1987), 'Linguistics and poetics', in: Pomorska, K./Rudy, S. (eds.), *Language in Literature*, Cambridge, MA, 66–71.
James, S.L. (1998), 'From boys to men: rape and developing masculinity in Terence's *Hecyra* and *Eunuchus*', *Helios* 25(1), 31–48.
James, S.L. (2003), *Learned Girls and Male Persuasion: Gender and Reading in Roman Love Elegy*, Berkeley, CA.
James, S.L. (2006), 'A courtesan's choreography: female liberty and male anxiety at the Roman dinner party', in: Faraone, C.A./McClure, L. (eds.), *Prostitutes and Courtesans in the Ancient World*, Madison, WI, 224–62.
James, S.L. (2012a), 'Elegy and New Comedy', in: Gold, B.K. (ed.), *A Companion to Roman Love Elegy*, Chichester, 253–68.
James, S.L. (2012b), 'Teaching rape in Roman love elegy, part II', in: Gold, B.K. (ed.), *A Companion to Roman Love Elegy*, Chichester, 549–57.
James, S.L. (2012c), 'Case study V: Vergil's Dido' in: James, S.L./Dillon, S. (eds.), *A Companion to Women in the Ancient World*, Chichester, 369–71.
James, S.L. (2016), '*Fallite fallentes*: rape and intertextuality in Terence's *Eunuchus* and Ovid's *Ars amatoria*', *EuGeStA* 6, 86–111.
Janan, M. (1994), *When the Lamp is Shattered: Desire and Narrative in Catullus*, Carbondale, IL.
Janan, M. (2001), *The Politics of Desire: Propertius IV*, Berkeley, CA.
Janan, M. (2012), 'Lacanian psychoanalytic theory and Roman love elegy', in: Gold, B.K. (ed.), *A Companion to Roman Love Poetry*, Chichester, 375–89.
Johnson, T. (2004), *Symposion of Praise: Horace Returns to Lyric in* Odes *IV*, Madison, WI.
Kallendorf, C. (2015), *The Protean Virgil: Material Form and the Reception of the Classics*, Oxford.
Kania, R. (2012), 'Orpheus and the reinvention of Bucolic poetry', *AJPh* 133, no. 4, 657–85.
Kaster, R. (ed.) (2011), *Macrobius'* Saturnalia, Cambridge, MA.

Kayachev, B. (2012), 'The so-called Orphic gold tablets in ancient poetry and poetics', *ZPE* 180, 17–37.
Kayachev, B. (2013), 'The ideal biography of a Roman poet: from *lusus poetici* to *studia philosophica*', *Latomus* 72, 412–25.
Kayachev, B. (2015), 'Walking barefoot on hoarfrost (Virgil, *Eclogues* 10.49 and Propertius 1.8.7)', *Indo-European Linguistics and Classical Philology* 19, 358–62 [in Russian, abstract in English].
Kazazis, J.N/Rengakos, A. (eds.) (1999), *Euphrosyne. Studies in Ancient Epic and its Legacy in Honour of Dimitris N. Maronitis*, Stuttgart.
Keith, A.M. (1994), '*Corpus eroticum*: elegiac poetics and elegiac *puellae* in Ovid's *Amores*', *CW* 88(1), 27–40.
Keith, A.M. (1999), 'Slender verse: Roman elegy and ancient rhetorical theory', *Mnemosyne* 52(1), 41–62.
Keith, A.M. (2008), *Propertius, Poet of Love and Leisure*, London.
Keith, A.M. (ed.) (2011a), *Latin Elegy and Hellenistic Epigram. A Tale of Two Genres at Rome*, Newcastle upon Tyne.
Keith, A.M. (2011b), 'Latin elegiac collections and Hellenistic epigram books', in: Keith, A.M. (ed.) *Latin Elegy and Hellenistic Epigram. A Tale of Two Genres at Rome*, Newcastle upon Tyne, 99–115.
Keith, A.M. (2012), 'The *domina* in Roman elegy', in: Gold, B.K. (ed.) *A Companion to Roman Love Elegy*, Chichester, 285–302.
Keith, A.M. (2013), 'Propertius', in: Thorsen, T.S. (ed.), *The Cambridge Companion to Latin Love Elegy*, Cambridge, 97–113.
Kennedy, D.F. (1992), '"Augustan" and "anti-Augustan": reflections on terms of reference', in: Powell, A (ed.), *Roman Poetry and Propaganda in the Age of Augustus*, Bristol, 26–58.
Kennedy, D.F. (1993), *The Arts of Love: Five Studies in the Discourse of Roman Love Elegy*, Cambridge.
Kennedy, D.F. (2012), 'Love's tropes and figures', in: Gold, B.K. (ed.), *A Companion to Roman Love Elegy*, Chichester, 189–203.
Kenney, E.J. (ed.) (1996), *Ovid: Heroides XVI–XXI*, Cambridge.
Kent, R.G. (ed.) (1938), *Varro on the Latin Language*, Cambridge, MA.
Kershaw, A. (1994), 'Horace, *Odes* 4.10.2: the sweet bird of youth', *CQ* 44, 544–5.
Khan, H.A. (1999), 'Horace's *Ode* to Virgil on the death of Quintilius: 1.24', in: Anderson, W.S. (ed.), *Why Horace? A Collection of Interpretations*, 73–84, Wauconda, IL.
Kilpatrick, R. (1990), *The Poetry of Criticism: Horace,* Epistles *II and* Ars Poetica, Edmonton.
Kim, J-h.P. (2010), '"L'amour courtois" de Gaston Paris: une lecture décadente du "Chevalier de la Charrette"?', *The French Review*, 589–606.
Kim, J-h.P. (2012), *Pour une littérature médiévale moderne: Gaston Paris, l'amour courtois et les enjeux de la modernité*, Paris.
Kirfel, E.A. (1969), *Untersuchungen zur Briefform der Heroides Ovids*, Bern.
Kivilo, M. (2010), *Early Greek Poets' Lives: The Shaping of the Tradition, Mnemosyne* 322, Leiden.
Klingner, F. (1982), *Q. Horatius Flaccus, Opera*, Leipzig.
Knox, P.E. (1990), 'In pursuit of Daphne', *TAPhA* 120, 183–202.
Knox, P.E. (2007), 'Catullus and Callimachus', in: Skinner, M.B. (ed.), *A Companion to Catullus*, Malden, MA, 151–71.
Knox, P.E. (ed.) (1995), *Ovid,* Heroides: *Select Epistles*, Cambridge.

Koch-Harnack, G. (1983), *Knabenliebe und Tiergeschenke: ihre Bedeutung im päderastischen Erziehungsystem Athens*, Berlin.

Konstan, D. (1986), 'Love in Terence's *Eunuch*: The origins of erotic subjectivity', *AJPh* 107, 369–93.

Konstan, D. (1994), *Sexual Symmetry: Love in the Ancient Novel and Related Genres*, Princeton, NJ.

Konstan, D. (1995), *Greek Comedy and Ideology*, Oxford.

Konstan, D. (2000), 'The Pre-Pubescent Lover in Greek Literature', in: https://diotima-doctafemina.org/essays/the-pre-pubescent-lover-in-greek-literature/

Konstan, D. (2002), 'Women, boys and the paradigm of Athenian pederasty', *Difference: A Journal of Feminist Cultural Studies* 13, 35–56.

Konstan, D. (2018), *In the Orbit of Love: Affection in Ancient Greece and Rome*, Oxford.

Konstan, D./Raval, S. (2018), 'Comic violence and the citizen body', in: Gale, M.R./Scourfield, J.H.D (eds.), *Texts and Violence in the Roman World*, Cambridge, 44–62.

Kovacs, D. (2015), 'Phyllis's high-born parents: Horace, *Odes* 2.4.13–20', *Mnemosyne* 68, 866–71.

Krenkel, W. (1979), 'Pueri meritori', *WZRostock* 28(1), 49–56.

Kretschmer, M.T. (2013), 'The love elegy in medieval Latin literature (pseudo-Ovidiana and ovidian imitations),' in: Thorsen, T.S (ed.), *The Cambridge Companion to Latin Love Elegy*, Cambridge, 271–89.

Krostenko, B.A. (2001), *Cicero, Catullus and the Language of Social Performance*, Chicago, IL.

Kuhlmann, P. (2005), 'Akontios und Kydippe bei Kallimachos (67–75 Pf.2) und Ovid (*Epist.* 20–21): eine romantische Liebesgeschichte?', *Gymnasium* 112(1), 19–44.

La Penna, A. (1963), *Orazio e l'ideologia del principato*, Turin.

Labate, M. (2006), 'Erotic aetiology: Romulus, Augustus, and the rape of the Sabine women', in: Gibson, R./Green, S./Sharrock, A. (eds.), *The Art of Love. Bimillennial Essays on Ovid's Ars Amatoria and Remedia Amoris*, Oxford, 193–215.

Lacan, J. (1998^2) [1964], *The Seminar of Jacques Lacan: The Four Fundamental Concepts of Psychoanalysis* (Seminar XI) (ed. Miller, J.-A. /trans. Sheridan, A.), New York, NY.

Lacan, J. (2006) [1966], *Écrits* (trans. Fink, B.), New York, NY.

Larmour, D.H.J./Miller, P.A./Platter, C. (eds.) (1998), *Rethinking Sexuality: Foucault and Classical Antiquity*, Princeton, NJ.

Lear, A./Cantarella, E. (2008), *Images of Greek Pederasty: Boys Were Their Gods*, London.

Lee, E.M. (2016), *Laetus Amor: Love and Memory in Latin Elegy*, doctoral diss., University of Michigan.

Lefèvre, E. (1975), 'Nil medium est. Die früheste Satire des Horaz 1.2', in: Lefèvre, E. (ed.), *Monumentum Chiloniense. Studien zur augusteischen Zeit: Kieler Festschrift für Erich Burck zum 70. Geburtstag*, 311–46, Amsterdam.

Lefkowitz, M.R. (2012, 1981), *The Lives of the Greek Poets*, Baltimore, MD.

Leisner-Jensen, M. (2002), '*Vis comica*: consummated rape in Greek and Roman New Comedy', *C&M* 53, 173–96.

Leo, F. (1895), *Plautinische Forschungen Zur Kritik Und Geschichte Der Komödie*, Berlin.

Lewis, C.S. (1936), *The Allegory of Love: A Study in Medieval Tradition*, Oxford.

Lewis, J.M. (1985), '*Eros* and the *polis* in Theognis' Book II', in: Figueira, T.J./Nagy, G. (eds.), *Theognis of Megara: Poetry and the Polis*, Baltimore, MD, 197–222.

Licht, H. (1994), *Sexual life in Ancient Greece* (trans. Freese, J.H.), London.

Lieberg, G. (1962), *Puella Divina*, Amsterdam.

Lieberg, G. (1987), 'Les Muses dans le papyrus attribué à Gallus', *Latomus* 46, 527–44.
LII 10 = Lacan, J. (1961–2), *Anxiety*, trans. Gallagher, C., Ongoing online translation project, http://www.lacaninireland.com/web/published-works/seminars/
LII 14 = Lacan, J. (1966–7). *The Logic of Phantasy*, trans. Gallagher, C., Ongoing online translation project, http://www.lacaninireland.com/web/published-works/seminars/
Lilja, S. (1983), *Homosexuality in Republican and Augustan Rome*, Helsinki.
Lindberg, C. (2008), *Love: A Brief History through Western Christianity*, Oxford.
Lindheim, S.H. (2000), '*Omnia vincit amor*: or, why Oenone should have known it would never work out (*Eclogue* 10 and *Heroides* 5)', *MD* 44, 83–101.
Lindheim, S.H. (2003), *Mail and Female: Epistolary Narrative and Desire in Ovid's* Heroides, Madison, WI.
Lindsay, W.M. (ed.) (1903), *T. Macci Plauti Comoediae I*, Oxford.
Lipka, M. (2001), *Language in Vergil's* Eclogues, Berlin.
Lissarague, F. (1990), *The Aesthetic of the Greek Banquet: Images of Wine and Ritual*, Princeton, NJ.
Liveley, G. (2012), 'Teaching rape in Roman elegy, part I', in: Gold, B.K. (ed.), *A Companion to Roman Love Elegy*, Chichester, 541–8.
Liveley, G./Salzman-Mitchell, P. (eds.) (2008), *Latin Elegy and Narratology: Fragments of Story*, Columbus, OH.
Lowinski, A. (1873), 'Scheda Horatiana', *Jahrbücher für classische Philologie* 107, 255–66.
Lowrie, M. (1997), *Horace's Narrative Odes*, Oxford.
Luck, G. (1969^2), *The Latin Love Elegy*, London.
Ludwig, W. (1961), 'Die Anordnung des vierten Horazischen Odenbuches', *MH* 18, 1–10.
Ludwig, W. (1963), 'Plato's love epigrams', *GRBS* 4, 59–82.
Lyne, R.O.A.M. (1980), *The Latin Love Poets: From Catullus to Horace*, Oxford.
Lyne, R.O.A.M. (1989), *Words and the Poet: Characteristic Techniques of Style in Vergil's* Aeneid, Oxford.
Lyne, R.O.A.M. (1995), *Horace: Behind the Public Poetry*, New Haven, CT.
MacLeod, C.W. (1982), *Iliad Book XXIV*, Cambridge.
MacLeod, C.W. (1983), 'Horatian *imitatio* and *Odes* 2.5', in: MacLeod, C.W. (ed.), *Collected Essays*, Oxford, 245–61.
MacQueen, J.G. (1982), 'Death and immortality: a study of the Heraclitus epigram of Callimachus', *Ramus* 11, 48–56.
Magnelli, E. (2016), '*Potnia* and the like: the vocabulary of domination in Greek love epigram of the imperial period', in: Santin, E./Foschia, L. (eds.) *L'Épigramme dans tous ses états: épigraphiques, littéraires, historiques*, Lyon, 40–59.
Makowsky, J.F. (1989), 'Nisus and Euryalus: a Platonic relationship', *CJ* 85, 1–15.
Makowski, J.F. (1996), 'Bisexual Orpheus: pederasty and parody in Ovid', *CJ* 92(1), 25–38.
Maltby, R. (2002), *Tibullus: Elegies*, Cambridge.
Maltby, R. (2011), 'The influence of Hellenistic epigram on Tibullus', in: Keith, A.M. (ed.), *Latin Elegy and Hellenistic Epigram. A Tale of Two Genres at Rome*, Newcastle upon Tyne, 87–97.
Mankin, D. (ed.) (1995), *Horace: Epodes*, Cambridge.
Marshall, L.A. (2015), 'Tracking down love: A new interpretation of κεχρημένος in Callimachus 31.3', *SIFC* 2, 227–31.
Martelli, F.K.A. (2013), *Ovid's Revisions: The Editor as Author*, Cambridge.
Mayer, R. (ed.) (2012) [1994], *Horace*, Odes Book I, Cambridge.

McCarthy, K. (1998), '*Servitium Amoris: Amor Servitii*', in: Joshel, S.R./Murnaghan, S. (eds.), *Women and Slaves in Greco-Roman Culture: Differential Equations*, London, 174–92.
McCoskey, D.E./Torlone, Z.M. (2014), *Latin Love Poetry*, London.
McGinn, T.A.J. (1998), *Prostitution, Sexuality, and the Law in Ancient Rome*, New York, NY.
McKeown, J.C. (ed.) (1987), *Ovid's* Amores. *Vol. I: Text and Prolegomena*, Liverpool.
McKeown, J.C. (ed.) (1989), *Ovid: Amores. Vol. II: A Commentary on Book One*, Liverpool.
McKeown, J.C. (ed.) (1998), *Ovid: Amores. Vol. III: A Commentary on Book Two*, Liverpool.
Meyer, D. (2005), *Inszeniertes Lesevergnügen. Das inschriftliche Epigramm und seine Rezeption bei Kallimachos*, Stuttgart.
Miller, P.A. (1993), 'Sappho 31 and Catullus 51: the dialogism of lyric', *Arethusa* 26(2), 183–99.
Miller, P.A. (2004), *Subjecting Verses: Latin Love Elegy and the Emergence of the Real*, Princeton, NJ.
Miller, P.A. (2013), 'The *puella*', in: Thorsen, T.S. (ed.), *The Cambridge Companion to Latin Love Elegy*, Cambridge, 166–79.
Minnis, A.J. (2001), *Magister Amoris: The Roman de la Rose and Vernacular Hermeneutics*, Oxford.
Mitchell, E. (2010), 'Time for an emperor: old age and the future of the empire in Horace *Odes* 4', *MD* 64.1, 43–76.
Monti, R.C. (1981), *The Dido episode in the* Aeneid: *Roman social and political values in the Epic*, Leiden.
Montiglio, S. (2017), *The Myth of Hero and Leander: The History and Reception of an Enduring Greek Legend*, London.
Morgan, L. (1995), 'Underhand tactics: Milanion, Acontius and Gallus P. Qaṣr Ibrîm', *Latomus* 54, 79–85.
Morton Braund, S. (1998), 'Speech, silence and personality: the case of Aeneas and Dido', *PVS* 23, 129–47.
Mozley, J.H. (trans.) (1979), *Ovid. The Art of Love and Other Poems*. rev. by Goold, G.P., Cambridge, MA.
Murgatroyd, P. (1980), *Tibullus I: A Commentary on the First Book of the Elegies of Albius Tibullus*, Pietermaritzburg.
Murgatroyd, P. (1981), '*Seruitium amoris* and the Roman elegists', *Latomus* 40, 589–606.
Murgatroyd, P. (1982), *Ovid with Love: Selections from* Ars Amatoria *I and II*, Wauconda, IL.
Murray, O. (1990), Sympotica: *A Symposium on the* Symposion, Oxford.
Myers, K.S. (1996), 'The poet and the procuress: The *lena* in Latin love elegy', *JRS* 86, 1–21.
Myers, K.S. (2009) 'Ovid', *Oxford Bibliographies Online*, DOI: 10.1093/OBO/9780195389661-0039, Oxford.
Mynors, R.A.B. (ed.) (1958), *C. Valerii Catulli Carmina*, Oxford.
Nagle, B.R. (1984), '*Amor, ira*, and sexual identity in Ovid's *Metamorphoses*', *ClAnt* 3(2), 236–55.
Nagy, G. (1996), *Poetry as Performance*, Cambridge.
Nagy, G. (2004). 'Transmission of archaic Greek sympotic songs: from Lesbos to Alexandria', *Critical Inquiry* 31, 26–48.
Nethercut, W.R. (1970), 'The ironic priest. Propertius' "Roman Elegies" III, 1–5: imitations of Horace and Vergil', *AJPh* 91, 385–407.
Nethercut, W.R. (1975), 'Weaving. A point of art in the *Ciris*', *CB* 61(1), 62.
Newlands, C. (2016), 'Trilingual love on the bay of Naples: Philodemus *AP* 5.132 and Ovidian elegy', *EuGeStA* 6, 112–28.

Nilsson, I. (ed.) (2009), *Plotting with Eros: Essays on the Poetics of Love and the Erotics of Reading*, Copenhagen.
Nisbet, G. (2013), *Greek Epigram in Reception. J. A. Symonds, Oscar Wilde, and the Invention of Desire, 1805–1929*, Oxford.
Nisbet, R.G.M. (ed.) (1961), *Cicero in* L. Calpurnium Pisonem Oratio, Oxford.
Nisbet, R.G.M./Hubbard, M. (eds.) (1970), *A Commentary on Horace* Odes, *Book I*, Oxford.
Nisbet, R.G.M./Hubbard, M. (eds.) (1978), *A Commentary on Horace* Odes, *Book II*, Oxford.
Nisbet, R.G.M./Rudd, N. (2004), *A Commentary on Horace:* Odes *Book III*, Oxford.
Norberg, D. (1952), 'Le quatrième livre des *Odes* d'Horace', *Emerita* 20, 95–107.
Nuttal, A.D. (1998), 'Inconstant Dido', in: Burden, M. (ed.), *A Woman Scorn'd: responses to the Dido myth*, London, 89–104.
O'Hara, J.J. (1996), *True Names: Vergil and the Alexandrian Tradition of Etymological Wordplay*, Ann Arbor, MI.
O'Rourke, D. (2012), 'Intertextuality in Roman elegy', in: Gold, B.K. (ed.), *A Companion to Roman Love Elegy*, Chichester, 390–409.
Ogilvie, R.M. (1965), *A Commentary on Livy: Books 1–5*, Oxford.
Oliensis, E. (1998), *Horace and the Rhetoric of Authority*, Cambridge.
Oliensis, E. (2009), *Freud's Rome: Psychoanalysis and Latin Poetry*, Cambridge.
Oliensis, E. (2019), *Loving Writing/Ovid's* Amores, Cambridge.
Oliver, J.H. (2015), '*Oscula iungit nec moderata satis nec sic a virgine danda*: Ovid's Callisto episode, female homoeroticism, and the study of ancient sexuality', *AJPh* 136(2), 281–312.
Olson, K. (2017), *Masculinity and Dress in Roman Antiquity*, Abingdon.
Omitowoju, R. (2002), *Rape and the Politics of Consent in Classical Athens*, Cambridge.
Ormand, K. (2008), *Controlling Desires: Sexuality in Ancient Greece and Rome*, Westport, CT.
Otis, B. (1976), 'Virgilian narrative in the light of its precursors and successors', *Studies in Philology* 53, 1–28.
Pandey, N.B. (2018), '*Caput mundi*: female hair as symbolic vehicle of domination in Ovidian love elegy', *CJ* 113(4), 454–88.
Papaïoannou, S. (2006), 'The poetology of hairstyling and the excitement of hair loss in Ovid, *Amores* 1, 14', *QUCC* 83(1), 45–69.
Papanghelis, T.D. (1999), '*Relegens errata litora*: Virgil's reflexive *Odyssey*', in: Kazazis, J.N./Rengakos, A. (eds.), *Euphrosyne. Studies in Ancient Epic and its Legacy in Honour of Dimitris N. Maronitis*, Stuttgart, 275–90.
Paraskeviotis, G.C. (2014), 'Verg. *Ecl.* 6,13–30: mimic humour in Silenus' scene', *Arctos* 48, 279–93.
Paris, G. (1883), 'Études sur les romans de la table ronde. Lancelot du lac: II Le "Conte de la charrette"', *Romania* 12, 459–534.
Paschalis, M./Putnam, M.C.J. (eds.) (2002), *Horace and Greek Lyric*, Rethymnon.
Pasco-Pranger, M. (2009), 'Sustaining Desire: Catullus 50, Gallus and Propertius 1.10', *CQ* 59(1), 142–6.
Pasquali, G. (1920), *Orazio lirico*, Florence.
Paton, W. (ed. and trans.) (1918), *The Greek Anthology, Volume IV*, Cambridge, MA.
Patzer, H. (1982), *Die griechische Knabenliebe*, Wiesbaden.
Pecere, O. (1972), 'Selene e Endimione (*Anth. Lat.* 33 R.)', *Maia* 24, 304–16.
Peraki-Kyriakidou, H. (2003), 'The bull and the bees', *LEC* 71, 151–74.
Percy, W.A. (1996), *Pederasty and Pedagogy in Archaic Greece*, Chicago, IL.
Perkins, C.A. (1993), 'Love's arrows lost': Tibullan parody in 'Amores 3.9"', *CW* 86(6), 459–66.

Perkins, C.A. (2011), 'The figure of elegy in *Amores* 3.1: elegy as *puella*, elegy as *poeta*, *puella* as *poeta*', *CW* 104, 313–31.
Perkins, C.A. (2014), '*Corinna dubitans*: rhetorics of seduction and failure in Ovid, *Amores* 1.11', *CW* 107, 347–65.
Pfeiffer, R. (1968), *History of Classical Scholarship: From the Beginnings to the Hellenistic age*, Oxford.
Piazzi, L. (2013), 'Latin love elegy and other genres', in: Thorsen, T.S. (ed.), *The Cambridge Companion to Latin Love Elegy*, Cambridge, 224–38.
Pierce, K.F. (1997), 'The portrayal of rape in New Comedy', in: Deacy, S./Pierce, K. (eds.), *Rape in Antiquity*, London, 163–84.
Pilipović, J. (2013), '*Ad sidera*: tree-space symbolism in Plato's *Phaedrus* and Vergil's *Eclogues*', *AAntHung* 53, 221–44.
Porter, D. (1975), 'The recurrent motifs of Horace, *Carmina* IV', *HSCPh* 79, 189–228.
Porter, D. (1987), 'From separation to song: Horace, *Carmina* IV', *ICS* 12(1), 97–119.
Porter, J./Buchan, M. (2004), 'Introduction', *Helios* 31, 1–20.
Preston, K. (1916), *Studies in the Diction of the Sermo Amatorius in Roman Comedy*, doctoral diss., University of Chicago.
Privitera, T. (1996), *Didone mascherata: per il codice genetico di Emma Bovary*, Pisa.
Provencal, V. (2013), '*Glukus himeros*: pederastic influence on the myth of Ganymede', in: Verstraete, B.C./Provencal, V. (eds.), *Same-Sex Desire and Love in Greco-Roman Antiquity and in the Classical Tradition of the West*, New York, NY, 87–136.
Pucci, P. (1978), 'Lingering on the threshold', *Glyph* 3, 52–73.
Putnam, M.C.J. (1985, repr. 1995²), *Virgil's Aeneid: Interpretations and Influence*, Chapel Hill, NC.
Putnam, M.C.J. (1986), *Artifices of Eternity: Horace's Fourth Book of Odes*, Ithaca, NY.
Putnam, M.C.J. (1992), 'The languages of Horace "*Odes*" 1.24', *CJ* 88(2), 123–35.
Putnam, M.C.J. (2005), 'Virgil and Tibullus 1.1', *CPh* (2), 123–41.
Putnam, M.C.J. (2007), 'Horace *Carm*. 4.7 and the epic tradition', *CW* 100(4), 355–62.
Ragland-Sullivan, E./Bracher, M. (eds.) (1991), *Lacan and the Subject of Language*, New York, NY.
Ramsby, T.R. (2007), *Textual Permanence. Roman Elegists and the Epigraphic Tradition*, London.
Rand, E.K. (1925), *Ovid and his Influence*, Atlanta, GA.
Reddy, W.M. (2012), *The Making of Romantic Love: Longing and Sexuality in Europe, South Asia, and Japan, 900–1200 CE*, Chicago, IL.
Reed, Joseph D. (ed.) (1997), *Bion of Smyrna: The Fragments and the Adonis*, New York, NY.
Richlin, A. (1992²), *The Garden of Priapus: Sexuality and Aggression in Roman Humor*, Oxford.
Richlin, A. (1993), 'Not before homosexuality: the materiality of the *cinaedus* and the Roman law against love between men', *JHSex* 3, 523–73.
Richlin, A. (1998), 'Foucault's *History of Sexuality*: a useful theory for women?', in: Larmour, D.H.J./Miller, P.A./Platter, C. (eds.), *Rethinking Sexuality: Foucault and Classical Antiquity*, Princeton, NJ, 138–70.
Rimell, V. (1999), 'Epistolary fictions: authorial identity in "*Heroides*" 15', *PCPS* 45(1), 109–35.
Rolfe, J.C. (ed. and trans.) (1927–8), *The Attic Nights of Aulus Gellius*, Cambridge, MA.
Rosati, G. (1996), 'Sabinus, the *Heroides* and the Poet-Nightingale. Some observations on the authenticity of the *Epistula Sapphus*', *CQ* 46, 207–16.

Rosen, R.M./Farrell, J. (1986), 'Acontius, Milanion, and Gallus: Vergil, *Ecl*. 10.52–61', *TAPhA* 116, 241–54.
Rosenmeyer, P.A. (1996), 'Love letters in Callimachus, Ovid and Aristaenetus or the sad fate of a mailorder bride', *MD* 36, 9–31.
Rosenmeyer, P.A. (1992), *The Poetics of Imitation: Anacreon and the Anacreontic Tradition*, Cambridge.
Rosivach, V.J. (1998), *When a Young Man Falls in Love: The Sexual Exploitation of Women in New Comedy*, London.
Ross, D.O. (1975), *Backgrounds to Augustan Poetry: Gallus, Elegy and Rome*, Cambridge.
Rossi, L.E. (1971), 'I generi letterari e le loro leggi scritte e non scritte nelle letterature classiche', *BICS* 18, 69–94.
Rossi, L.E. (1983), *Il Simposio greco arcaico e classico come spettacolo a se stesso*, in: *Spettacoli conviviali dall'antichità classica alle corti italiane del '400. Atti del VII convegno di studio. Viterbo, 27–30 maggio 1982*, Viterbo, 41–50.
Rudd, N. (1966), *The Satires of Horace*, Cambridge.
Rudd, N. (1981), 'Romantic love in classical times?', *Ramus* 10, 140–58.
Rudd, N. (1989), *Horace: Epistles, Book II and* Ars Poetica, Cambridge.
Rudd, N. (ed.) (1993), *Horace 2000: A Celebration, Essays for the Bimillennium*, London
Rudd, N. (ed. and trans.) (2004), *Horace, Odes and Epodes*, Cambridge, MA.
Rumpf, L. (1996), Extremus labor: *Vergils 10. Ekloge und die Poetik der* Bucolica, Göttingen.
Rutherford, I. (2010), 'Greek poetry, elegiac and lyric', in: *Oxford Bibliographies Online*, DOI: 10.1093/OBO/9780195389661–0048, Oxford.
Rynearson, N. (2009), 'A Callimachean case of lovesickness: magic, disease, and desire in *Aetia* Frr. 67–75 Pf', *AJPh* 130, 341–65.
Sage, P. (1994), 'Vatic admonition in Horace *Odes* 4.9', *AJPh* 115(4), 565–86.
Said, S. (2002), "Herodotus and Tragedy", in: Bakker, E.J./de Jong, I.J.F./van Wees, H. (eds.), *Brill's Companion to Herodotus*, Leiden, 117–47.
Sande, S. (2017), 'The female hunter and other examples of change of sex and gender on Roman sarcophaugs reliefs', *AAAH* 22(1), 55–86.
Sankovitch, T. (1999), 'The trobairitz', in: Gaunt, S./Kay, S. (eds.), *The Troubadours: An Introduction*, Cambridge, 113–26.
Schneiderman, S. (1980), 'Lacan et la littérature', *Tel Quel* 84, 39–47.
Schrötter, W. (1908), *Ovid und die Troubadours*, Halle.
Segal, E. (1987²), *Roman Laughter: The Comedy of Plautus*, Oxford.
Sens, A. (2011), *Asclepiades of Samos: Epigrams and Fragments*, Oxford.
Shackleton Bailey, D.R. (ed. and transl.) (2015), *Statius Silvae*, rev. by Parrott, C.A., Cambridge, MA.
Sharrock, A.R. (1991), 'Womanufacture', *JRS* 81, 36–49.
Sharrock, A.R. (1994), *Seduction and Repetition in Ovid's* Ars Amatoria *II*, Oxford.
Sharrock, A.R. (1995), 'The drooping rose: elegiac failure in *Amores* 3.7', *Ramus* 24, 152–80.
Sharrock, A.R. (2000), 'Constructing characters in Propertius', *Arethusa* 33, 263–84.
Sharrock, A.R. (2008), 'The theatrical life of things: Plautus and the physical', *Dictynna* 5, https://journals.openedition.org/dictynna/419.
Sharrock, A.R. (2009), *Reading Roman Comedy: Poetics and Playfulness in Plautus and Terentius*, Cambridge.
Sharrock, A.R. (2013a), 'The *poeta-amator*, nequitia and recusatio', in: Thorsen, T.S. (ed.), *The Cambridge Companion to Latin Love Elegy*, Cambridge, 151–65.

Sharrock, A.R. (2013b), 'Terence and non-comic intertexts', in: Augoustakis, A./Traill, A. (eds.), *A Companion to Terence*, 52–68.
Sharrock, A.R. (2016), 'Genre and social class, or Comedy and the rhetoric of self-aggrandisement and self-deprecation', in: Frangoulidis, S./Harrison, S./Manuwald, G. (eds.), *Roman Drama and Its Contexts*, Berlin, 97–126.
Sheffield, F.C.C. (2006), *Plato's* Symposium*: The Ethics of Desire*, Oxford.
Showerman, G. (ed. and trans.) (1977²), *Ovid,* Heroides *and* Amores, rev. by Goold, G.P., Cambridge, MA.
Sider, D. (ed. and transl.) (1997), *The Epigrams of Philodemos: Introduction, Text, and Commentary*, New York, NY.
Skinner, M.B. (1997), '*Ego mulier*: the construction of male sexuality in Catullus', in: Hallett, J.P./Skinner, M.B. (eds.), *Roman Sexualities*, Princeton, NJ, 129–50.
Skinner, M.B. (2005), *Sexuality in Greek and Roman Culture*, Malden, MA.
Skinner, M.B. (2007), *A Companion to Catullus*, Malden, MA.
Skinner, M.B. (2011), *Clodia Metelli: The Tribune's Sister*, Oxford.
Slater, D.A. (1913), 'Horace, *Carmina* 4.10.2', *CR* 27, 194–5.
Snyder, J.M. (1981), 'The web of song: weaving imagery in Homer and the lyric poets', *CJ* 76(1), 193–6.
Soler, C. (1991), 'Literature as symptom', in: Ragland-Sullivan, E./Bracher, M. (eds.), *Lacan and the Subject of Language*, New York, NY, 213–19.
Spentzou, E. (2013), *The Roman Poetry of Love: Elegy and Politics in a Time of Revolution*, London.
Stahl, H.-P. (1985), *"Love" and "War": Individual and the State Under Augustus*, Berkeley, CA.
Stendhal [= Marie-Henri Beyle] (2014 [= 1822]), *De l'amour*, Paris.
Strong, A.K. (2016), *Prostitutes and Matrons in the Roman World*, New York, NY.
Stuveras, R. (1969), *Le putto dans l'art romain*, Brussels.
Sullivan, J.P. (1961), 'Two problems in Roman love elegy', *TAPhA* 92, 522–36.
Sutherland, E.H. (1997), 'Vision and desire in Horace's *Carm.* 2.5', *Helios* 24, 23–43.
Svenbro, J. (1993), *Phrasikleia: An Anthropology of Reading in Ancient Greece*, New York, NY.
Syme, R. (1939), *The Roman Revolution*, Oxford.
Syndikus, H.P. (1972/3), *Die Lyrik des Horaz. Eine Interpretation der* Oden, 2 vols., Darmstadt.
Tait, J.I.M. (1941), *Philodemus' Influence on the Latin Poets*, doctoral diss., Bryn Mawr University.
Tarán, S. (1985), '*EISI TRIXES*: an erotic motif in the Greek anthology', *JHS* 105, 90–107.
Taylor, J.H. (1970), '*Amores* 3.9: a farewell to elegy', *Latomus* 29(2), 474–7.
Thom, S. (1996), '"That no man lives forever": Horace on the death of Quintilius (1.24)', *Akroterion* 41(3–4), 114–23.
Thomas, R.F. (1979), 'New Comedy, Callimachus, and Roman poetry', *HSCPh* 83(1), 179–206.
Thomas, R.F. (1986), 'Virgil's *Georgics* and the art of reference', *HSCPh* 90(1), 171–98.
Thomas, R.F. (1988), *Virgil,* Georgics, vol. 2, Cambridge.
Thomas, R.F. (1999), *Reading Virgil and His Texts: Studies in Intertextuality*, Ann Arbor, MI.
Thomas, R.F. (2001), *Virgil and the Augustan Reception*, Cambridge.
Thomas, R.F. (ed.) (2011), *Horace* Odes *IV and* Carmen Saeculare, Cambridge.
Thomson, D.F.S. (ed.) (1997), *Catullus*, with a commentary, Toronto.
Thorsen, T.S. (2012a), 'Sappho, Corinna and colleagues in ancient Rome: Tatian's catalogue of statues (*Oratio ad Graecos* 33–34) reconsidered', *Mnemosyne* 65, 695–715.

Thorsen, T.S. (2012b), *'Puella* poetry – a useful term in the history of Latin literature?' Paper at the American Philological Association meeting 2012.

Thorsen, T.S. (ed.) (2013a), *The Cambridge Companion to Latin Love Elegy*, Cambridge.

Thorsen, T.S. (2013b), 'Introduction: Latin love elegy', in: Thorsen, T.S. (ed.), *The Cambridge Companion to Latin Love Elegy*, Cambridge, 1–22.

Thorsen, T.S. (2013c), 'Ovid the love elegist', in: Thorsen, T.S. (ed.), *The Cambridge Companion to Latin Love Elegy*, Cambridge, 114–29.

Thorsen, T.S. (2014), *Ovid's Early Poetry: From his Single* Heroides *to his* Remedia Amoris, Cambridge.

Thorsen, T.S. (2017), 'Ovid's Love Poetry', *Oxford Bibliographies Online*, DOI: 10.1093/OBO/9780195389661–0279, Oxford.

Thorsen, T.S. (2018), 'Intrepid intratextuality: the epistolary pair of Leander and Hero (*Heroides* 18–19) and the end of Ovid's poetic career', in: Harrison, S./Frangoulidis, S./Papanghelis, T.D. (eds.), *Intratextuality and Latin Literature*, Berlin, 257–71.

Thorsen, T.S. (2019a), 'Cydippe the Poet', *CJ* 115(2), 129–45.

Thorsen, T.S. (2019b), 'Sappho: transparency and obstruction', in: Thorsen, T.S./Harrison, S. (eds.), *Roman Receptions of Sappho*, Oxford, 27–44.

Thorsen, T.S. (2019c), 'The newest Sappho (2016) and Ovid's *Heroides* 15', in: Thorsen, T.S./Harrison, S. (eds.), *Roman Receptions of Sappho*, Oxford, 249–63.

Thorsen, T.S. (forthcoming a), 'Oenone (*Her.* 5), Acontius (*Her.* 20), and the Ovidian *seruitium amoris*', *ICS*.

Thorsen, T.S. (forthcoming b), 'In sickness or in health? Love, pathology and marriage in the letters of Acontius and Cydippe, Ovid's *Heroides* 20–21', in: Kanellakis, D. (ed.), *Pathologies of Love*, Berlin.

Thorsen, T.S./Harrison, S. (eds.) (2019), *Roman Receptions of Sappho*, Oxford.

Thorsen, T.S./Berge, R.E. (2019), 'Receiving receptions received: a new collection of *testimonia sapphica* c. 600 BCE–CE 1000', in: Thorsen, T.S./Harrison, S. (eds.), *Roman Receptions of Sappho*, Oxford, 289–402.

Tissol, G. (2017), 'Ovid's exile poetry', *Oxford Bibliographies Online*, DOI: 10.1093/OBO/9780195389661–0280, Oxford.

Tohm, S.K. (2011), *Contesting Masculinity: Locating the Male Body in Roman Elegy*, doctoral diss., University of Michigan.

Totola, G. (2012), 'Donne e follia nell'*Eneide* di Virgilio: tre invasamenti per l'azione epica', *MedSec* NS 24(3), 689–704.

Treggiari, S. (1991), *Roman Marriage:* Iusti Coniuges *from the Time of Cicero to the Time of Ulpian*, Oxford.

Treggiari, S. (1996[2]), 'Social status and social legislation', in: Bowman, A.K./Champlin, E./Lintott, A. (eds.), *The Cambridge Ancient History, Vol. X: The Augustan Empire, 43 B.C.–A.D. 69*, Cambridge, 873–904.

Troia, A.M.d.l.F. (2016), *The Epitaph for Bion: Agonism and Fictional Biography as Literary Criticism in Late Bucolic*, doctoral diss., Brown University.

Turpin, W. (2014), 'Ovid's new Muse: *Amores* 1.1', *CQ* 64(1), 419–21.

Van Sickle, J.B. (2000), 'Virgil *vs.* Cicero, Lucretius, Theocritus, Plato, and Homer: two programmatic plots in the first bucolic', *Vergilius* 46, 21–58.

Verstraete, B.C./Provencal, V. (eds.) (2013), *Same-Sex Desire and Love in Greco-Roman Antiquity and in the Classical Tradition of the West*, New York, NY.

Vetta, M. (ed.) (1983), *Poesia e simposio nella Grecia antica*, Rome.

Veyne, P. (1983), *L'élégie érotique romaine: L'amour, la poésie et l'occident*, Paris.
Veyne, P. (1988), *Roman Erotic Elegy: Love, Poetry, and the West*, Chicago, IL.
Veyne, P. (2005), *Sexe et pouvoir à Rome*, Paris.
Veyne, P. (2008), *Foucault: Sa pensée, sa personne*, Paris.
Veyne, P. (2013), *Foucault: His Thought, his Character*, Cambridge.
Volk, K. (2010), *Ovid*, Chichester.
von Albrecht, M. (transl.) (2001), *P. Vergilius Maro:* Bucolica – *Hirtengedichte*, Stuttgart.
Walsh, G. (1990), 'Surprised by self: audible thought in Hellenistic poetry', *CP* 85, 1–21.
Walters, J. (1993), '"No more than a boy": the shifting construction of masculinity from ancient Greece to the middle ages', *Gender & History* 5(1), 20–33.
Walters, J. (1997), 'Invading the Roman body: manliness and inpenetrability in Roman thought', in: Hallett, J.P./Skinner, M.B. (eds.), *Roman Sexualities*, Princeton, NJ, 29–47.
Wardy, R. (2007), 'Virgil's sacred duo: Phaedrus' *Symposium* speech and *Aeneid* IX', in: Scott, D. (ed.), *Maieusis: Essays on Ancient Philosophy in Honour of Myles Burnyeat*, Oxford, 154–75.
Watson, L.C. (2003), *A Commentary on Horace's* Epodes, Oxford.
Watson, P. (1983), '*Puella* and *virgo*', *Glotta* 61 (1/2 H), 119–43.
Watson, P. (1992), '*Erotion: puella delicata?*', *CQ* 42(1), 253–68.
White, P. (1993), *Promised Verse: Poets in the Society of Augustan Rome*, Cambridge.
Whitmarsh, T. (2018), *Dirty Love: The Genealogy of the Ancient Greek Novel*, Oxford.
Wili, W. (1948), *Horaz und die augusteische Kultur*, Basel.
Williams, C.A. (1999), *Roman Homosexuality: Ideologies of Masculinity in Classical Antiquity*, Oxford.
Williams, C.A. (2010^2), *Roman Homosexuality: Ideologies of Masculinity in Classical Antiquity*, Oxford.
Williams, G. (1968), *Tradition and Originality in Roman Poetry*, Oxford.
Williams, G. (1972), *Horace*, Oxford.
Williams, G. (1998^2), *Tradition and Originality in Roman Poetry*, Oxford.
Williams, R.D. (1963), 'Virgil and the *Odyssey*', *Phoenix* 17, 4, 266–74.
Wills, J. (1998), 'Divided allusion: Virgil and the *Coma Bernices*', *HSCPh* 98, 277–305.
Wirshbo, E. (1980), '"Lesbia": A Mock Hypocorism?', *CPh* 75 (1), 70.
Wright, E. (1998^2), *Psychoanalytic Criticism: A Reappraisal*, Cambridge.
Wright, E. (1999), *Speaking Desires Can Be Dangerous: The Poetics of the Unconscious*, Cambridge.
Wright, F.A. (1921), 'Horace and Philodemus', *AJPh* 42, 168–9.
Wyke, M. (1989), 'Reading female flesh: *Amores* 3.1', in: Cameron, A. (ed.), *History as Text*, 111–43, London.
Wyke, M. (2002), *The Roman Mistress: Ancient and Modern Representations*, Oxford.
Yardley, J.C. (1972), 'Comic influences in Propertius', *Phoenix* 26(2), 134–9.
Yardley, J.C. (1987a), 'Propertius 4.5, Ovid *Amores* 1.6 and Roman Comedy', *PCPS* 33, 179–89.
Yardley, J.C. (1987b), 'The elegiac paraclausithyron', *Eranos: Acta Philologica Suecana* 76, 19–34.
Yatromanolakis, D. (2007), *Sappho in the Making: The Early Reception*, Washington, DC.
Yona, S. (2018), *Epicurean Ethics in Horace. The Psychology of Satire*, Oxford.
Younger, J.G. (2005), *Sex in the Ancient World from A to Z*, New York, NY.
Zetzel, J.E.G. (1996), 'Poetic baldness and its cure', *MD* 36(1), 73–100.
Zink, M. (1987), 'Chrétien et ses contemporains', in: Norris, J./Douglas, K./Busby, K. (eds.), *The Legacy of Chrétien de Troyes*, Amsterdam, 5–32.

Žižek, S. (1991). 'The truth arises from misrecognition', in: Ragland-Sullivan, E./Bracher, M. (eds.), *Lacan and the Subject of Language*, New York, NY, 188–212.
Žižek, S. (2012), *Less Than Nothing: Hegel and the Shadow of Dialectical Materialism*, New York, NY.
Zuckerberg, D. (2018), *Not All Dead White Men: Classics and Misogyny in the Digital Age*, Cambridge, MA.

Index Locorum

Alciphron
Letters of Fishermen
11   9

Anacreon
fr. 358 PMGF   209
fr. 360 PMGF   222
fr. 376 PMGF   137
fr. 402c PMGF   22, 137
fr. 407 PMGF   137
fr. 450 PMGF   137

Apollonius
Argon.
3.96   116

Apuleius
fr. 6 Courtney   10

Aristaenetus
1.14.1–5   21
1.15.33   8
1.15.41–2   8

Aristotle
Poet.
1451b   120

Asclepiades
46   171

Bion
fr. 6, 1–2   44

Callimachus
Aet.
fr. 1.2 Pf./Harder   121
fr. 1.21–2 Pf./Harder   35
fr. 1.25–6 Pf./Harder   121
fr. 67.1 Pf./Harder   116
fr. 67.3 Pf./Harder   117
fr. 75.76–7 Pf./Harder   227, 230
Epigr.
2 Pf. (34 GP)   31
31 Pf. (1 GP)   37
56 GP (27 Pf.) 3–4   35

Catullus
3.13–14   32, 34
14.13   201
15.1   224
15.5   224
21.4   224
21.11   224
24.1   226
32.8   163
35.16–17   190
48.3   224
50   33–4
50.11–13   196
51   49–50
53.3   201
66.39   129
85   159
99   224

Charisius
Gramm.
i 84.5–11 Keil   220

Cicero
Phil.
13.24   198
Pis.
70   146
Planc.
19   226

Diocles
4   172

Euripides
fr. 663 (in *TGF* Nauck)   117
Hipp.
612   229

Gallus
fr. 2.6 Courtney   122

Homer
Il.
1.5	23
6.496	30
19.324–5	30
24.1–18	29–30
24.9	32

Od.
18.327–30	32

Horace
Ars P.
438–9	54
442	54
445–6	54
449	54

Carm.
1.24	53
1.24.17	55
1.33	150
2.4	151–2
2.4.21	153
2.4.23	153
2.5.2	154
2.8.13–16	154
2.13.25	218
3.9.9	196
4.1.1–2	210
4.1.3	36, 177, 178, 181
4.1.3–4	210
4.1.5	210
4.1.17–18	184
4.1.29	38
4.1.29–32	36
4.1.30	174
4.1.33–5	178
4.1.33–40	36
4.1.38	175
4.1.40	175
4.2.19–20	184
4.4.69–70	175
4.4.70–2	175
4.5.1–2	169
4.5.9–16	170
4.5.14	177
4.5.19	175
4.5.27	167, 178
4.6.29–30	174
4.7.7	174–5
4.8.26–7	184
4.9.12	218
4.9.47–8	174
4.10	173
4.10.1	184
4.10.7	172, 178
4.10.8	167, 172
4.12.19	175
4.13.9–10	175
4.13.28	176
4.14.52	174
4.15.7–8	175
4.15.17	170
4.15.32	174

Carm. saec.
53	175
55	175
55–6	175

Epist.
1.1.4	178

Epod.
11.3–4	191
11.27–8	191

Sat.
1.2.30	149
1.2.90–4	147
1.2.116–24	146
1.2.125–7	149

Lucretius
1.1	108
1.15–6	109
1.16	109
1.19	108
1.924–5	108
2.172	108
2.258	107, 108
2.261	107
3.3	109
3.3–6	109
4.1061	204
4.1160	153
4.1177–9	64
6.94	108

Meleager
Anth. Pal. 12.101   193
Anth. Pal. 12.101.3   195

Moschus
Runaway Eros
21   115
28   115

[Moschus]
Ep. Bion.
14–19   42
83–4   46
93–7   41
114–26   43

Ovid
Am.
1.1.19–20   189
1.1.25   194
1.1.26   189, 195
1.2.4   197
1.2.5   197
1.2.19   198
1.2.23   199
1.2.47   199
1.3.1   198
1.3.1–2   189
1.4.3   215
1.4.59–64   216
1.4.64   216, 217
1.5.10   162
1.5.12   150
1.5.17–24   161
1.5.25   164
1.6.49–52   66
1.7.17–18   100
1.7.19–23   100
1.7.29–30   102
1.7.45–50   100
1.7.63–5   101
1.8.2–4   164
1.10.21–4   217
1.10.33–6   74
1.10.63–4   75
2.1.3   199
2.4.3   220
2.4.60   220
2.4.45   164
2.9.9–10   37
2.17.11   196
3.1.20   199
3.6.45–58   93
3.6.73–4   94
3.6.79–82   94
3.7.15–16   163
3.7.17–18   163
3.7.23–6   163
3.7.41–2   163
3.7.65–6   163
3.9.7   200
3.9.21–22   201
3.9.58   200
Ars am.
1.1–2   202
1.4   196
1.7   203
1.7–10   203
1.17   203
1.31–4   95
1.35   204
1.37   92
1.89–92   89
1.101–2   89
1.109–10   91
1.117–29   90
1.129   94
1.131   97
1.131–32   90
1.365   197–8
1.523–4   206
1.673–4   225
2.157   80
2.198   81
2.643–4   162
2.683–4   205
3.436   106
3.437–8   206
3.807–8   208
Fast.
5.226   177
Her.
5.133   97
5.140–6   96

5.155	97	22.4 Sider	149
18.101–18	11–12	On Vices	
19.59–70	12	P.Herc. Paris 2	145
20.35–6	228		
20.47	228	**Plato**	
20.207	228	Anth. Pal. 5.78	9
21.110	229	Symp.	
21.114	229	176a	111
21.135–48	229	176b	111
Met.		177d	116
5.369–72	196	196e	117
10.254	198	197a–b	118
Rem. am.		201d	110
2	210	205d	112
3	209	209b	114
11	209	209b–c	119
13	209	210a	114
15	210	210c	119
Tr.		211b	114
2.7–8	85	211c	114
2.207	85	213b	111
2.212	85	213e	111
2.303	220	214c	111
2.365	186	215c	111
		215d	112
Parmenides		220a	111
fr. 1.27	121	220b	112
fr. 6.4	121	222b	112
		223c	111
Phanocles			
fr. 1.9–10	48	**Plautus**	
		Bacch.	
Philodemus		50–6	73
Epigr.		Curc.	
1.3–4 Sider	159	147–54	70
4 Sider	154	172	67
5 Sider	153	173–4	67
7.6 Sider	164	175–7	67
10 Sider	149	178–80	67
12 Sider	147	Mil.	
14 Sider	156	110	78
16.1 Sider	154	Mostell.	
17 Sider	152	213	77
19 Sider	162	270	77
19.4 Sider	163	286	98
22 Sider	148	Pers.	
22.2 Sider	149	1–6	63

Index Locorum

Pseud.
273 — 62

Plutarch
De mul. vir.
16 — 8

Propertius
1.1.1 — 194
1.1.1–6 — 192
1.3.13–15 — 198
1.3.27–33 — 156
1.6.36 — 72
1.8.39–40 — 75
1.8b.27–32 — 75
1.9.17–18 — 159
2.3.19–22 — 159
2.3.21 — 25
2.4.9–10 — 159
2.8.11–12 — 74
2.10.8 — 25
2.15.1–4 — 158
2.15.9–10 — 158
2.15.15–16 — 157
2.16.30 — 196
3.3.49 — 66
3.5.19–20 — 160
3.5.23–5 — 160
3.5.45–6 — 160
3.8.1 — 69
3.10.18 — 196
3.25.10 — 70

Quintilian
Inst.
12.1.1 — 54

Sappho
fr. 1.27–8 Voigt — 24
fr. 16.2–3 Voigt — 23
fr. 31 Voigt — 32, 67
fr. 94.5 Voigt — 129
fr. 130 Voigt — 24
fr. 188 Voigt — 24

Seneca (the Younger)
Tranq.
9.2.6 — 197

Solon
fr. 23 West — 139

Terence
Eun.
293 — 91
307–9 — 86
308–9 — 89
342 — 91
372 — 90
372–3 — 86
373 — 90
601–2 — 91
645–6 — 87
647–8 — 101
657–9 — 87
819–20 — 87
832 — 92
859–60 — 101
861–3 — 102
Hec.
69 — 73
817 — 90

Theocritus
Id.
1.82 — 106
3.42 — 106
5.35–41 — 46
5.134–5 — 47

Theognis
27–8 — 131

Tibullus
1.1.1 — 68
1.1.46 — 68
1.1.55–62 — 71
1.1.60 — 200
1.1.73–8 — 69
1.2.7–10 — 70–1
1.2.33–4 — 164
1.3.57–8 — 201

1.4.9	224	6.17	111
1.4.53–62	225	6.18–19	112
1.4.83	200	6.19	111
1.5.39	164	6.24	111
1.6.85–6	72	6.25	111
1.8.13	208	6.40	106
		6.46	105
[Tibullus]		6.47	106
3.16.3–4	218	6.49–50	107
3.11.3–4	196	6.52	106
		6.55	107
Varro		6.58	106
Ling.		6.59	107
fr. 37	220	6.59–60	108
		6.63–5	107
Virgil		6.64	106, 114
Aen.		6.65	108, 115
1.94–6	138	6.66	115, 117
1.437	138	6.69	115
1.573–4	134	6.70	115
1.749	132, 136	6.71	108, 123
1.688	137	6.73	117
4.14	135	6.74	107
6.460	128	8.41	106
Ecl.		10.2–3	116
2.2	224	10.22	106
2.64	107	10.38–9	153
2.68	106	10.49	112
3.12–13	116	*G.*	
3.13	115	3.11	123
6.3	117	3.285	108
6.5	116	4.469–70	55
6.10	106, 116	4.488	106
6.11	117	4.494–5	55
6.15	111	4.507–9	56

Index Rerum

Achilles 3, 23, 25, 29, 30, 32, 50, 83, 152, 227
Acontius 6, 116, 117, 227, 228, 229, 230
Adams, J.N., *The Latin Sexual Vocabulary* 197, 211
Admetus 200
Aeneas 5, 125, 126, 127, 128, 129, 130, 132, 133, 134, 135, 136, 138, 139, 140, 141, 142, 143, 144, 184
adulescens (of comedy) 3, 21, 61, 73, 76, 78, 79, 85, 89, 103, 173
Agathon 3, 9, 10, 111, 117
Alcaeus 50, 130, 136, 138, 171
Alciphron 3, 8
Alexis 107, 223–4
allusion 29, 32, 44, 45, 46, 47, 52, 71, 81, 90, 91, 107, 110, 112, 115, 116, 121, 122, 128, 132, 141, 147, 156, 157, 158, 160, 173, 186, 190, 191, 194, 199, 205
Amor/*amor*/Cupid 24, 105, 106, 112, 137, 141, 154, 175, 189, 190, 194, 195, 196, 197, 198, 199, 200, 201, 203, 204, 205, 209, 210, 211
Anacreon 22, 50, 130, 136, 137, 222, 223
Anchises 140
Andromache 30
Andromeda 148, 152, 162
Anio 4, 93, 94
Aphrodite/Venus 9, 23, 24, 36, 38, 46, 47, 65, 67, 108, 109, 115, 116, 131, 137, 140, 141, 150, 152, 154, 162, 164, 173, 174, 178, 182, 183, 184, 200, 201, 203, 210
Apollo 4, 83, 96, 97, 105, 110, 117, 118, 121, 122, 158, 174, 178, 191, 200, 227
Apollonius, *Argonautica* 17, 116
Appendix Tibulliana 219
Ares/Mars 23, 83, 93, 95
Aristaenetus 8, 21
Aristotle 113, 120
– *Poetics* 120
Armstrong, D. 155
Artemis 8, 23, 227, 228
Ascanius 137, 141

Asclepiades 5, 171
Atalanta 105
ataraxia 148
Ate 23
attraction 107, 108, 112, 114, 129, 226
Aufilena 219
Augustus 5, 27, 85, 95, 145, 167, 168, 169, 170, 175, 177, 178, 179, 180, 181, 182, 183, 184
Aulus Gellius 9, 10, 11
Bacchylides 136, 138
Barsby, J. 60, 77, 99
Bessone, F. 61,
Bion 39, 40, 41, 42, 43, 44, 45, 46, 47, 48, 49, 57
Booth, J. 61, 155
bucolic/pastoral poetry 40, 41, 42, 44, 46, 47, 48, 80, 99
Cahoon, L. 17
Cairns, F. 127, 128, 155, 164
Calaïs 3, 40, 47, 48
Callimachus 3, 8, 29, 31, 31, 32, 33, 35, 37, 38, 117, 121, 122, 123, 151, 156, 227, 228, 230
– *Aetia* 35, 116, 121, 122, 227
Calliope 66, 108, 227
Calvus 33, 56, 196, 201
Carthage 128, 130, 133, 134, 138, 140, 175
Catullus 3, 6, 17, 18, 25, 33, 34, 35, 37, 39, 49, 50, 51, 52, 57, 65, 128, 129, 136, 141, 159, 163, 182, 190, 196, 201, 206, 207, 217, 219, 221, 223, 224, 225, 226
Cicero 146, 147, 182, 226
Cinara 36, 38, 180, 182, 183, 210
Cleopatra 220
Clodia Metelli 217, 221, 223
Coleman, R. 110, 111, 115
Comatas 46, 47, 49
Corbeill, A. 6, 214, 215, 223, 226
Corinna 24, 25, 158, 163, 218
Cory, W.J. 33, 35
Corydon 107, 223
courtly love 7, 14, 15, 19, 214

https://doi.org/10.1515/9783110633030-016

Cydippe 6, 116, 117, 227, 228, 229, 230
Cynthia 25, 51, 69, 72, 75, 158, 159, 191, 193, 194, 195, 198, 209, 223
Danaë 87
Dante 24, 138
Daphnis 41, 47, 115, 116
death 3, 8, 11, 13, 23, 24, 31, 32, 34, 42, 43, 45, 53, 54, 55, 56, 67, 163, 175, 187, 199, 200, 202, 209, 228
declamation 60, 71
Deidamia 83, 226
Delia 25, 72, 199, 200, 202, 223
de Rougemont 16, 17, 18
Dido 125, 126, 127, 128, 130, 132, 133, 134, 135, 137, 138, 139, 140, 141, 142
Diocles 5, 171, 172
door 64, 65, 66, 67, 68, 69, 70, 71, 77, 175, 216, 228
drama 2, 62, 65, 157
Dronke, P. 17
Drusus 169, 184
durus pater 80
education 59, 130, 131
elegiac couplet 20, 32, 139
epic 32, 98, 126, 127, 128, 134, 136, 139, 142, 143, 144, 159, 184, 187, 194
epicureanism/Epicurean philosophy 5, 109, 113, 114, 145, 146, 148, 149, 150, 151, 155, 156, 160, 161, 164
Epicurean love 105, 112, 148
Epicurus 27, 105, 109, 112, 151, 161
Epistula Sapphus 186
epithalamia 3, 51
erastes/ἐράστης 37, 172
eromenos/ἐρώμενος 127, 130, 133, 172, 192
Eros/eros 24, 110, 113, 115, 116, 117, 118, 121, 122, 131, 136, 194, 195, 196, 209
erotodidactic poetry 60, 65, 66, 80, 91, 188, 200, 208, 226
Euripides 117
– *Hippolytus* 23, 229
– *Iphigenia in Aulis* 66
Eurydice 3, 39, 40, 43, 44, 48, 49, 55, 56, 57, 186, 202, 209
exclusus amator 65, 68, 71
exile 26, 134, 138, 139

Fedeli, P. 155, 157
fellatio 50, 51
Foucault, M. 19
Fraenkel, E. 168, 169, 178
Freudenburg, K. 155
friendship 19, 55, 201
Fulkerson, L. 61
furor 55
Gale, M. 109, 112
Gallus 20, 105, 106, 108, 113, 114, 115, 116, 117, 119, 122, 145, 153, 187, 189, 190, 201, 202, 226
generic enrichment 125
gifts 47, 74, 86, 97, 142, 174, 184, 207, 216, 225, 226
Gigante, M. 155
Glaucippe 3, 8, 9
von Goethe, Johann Wolfgang 214
Gordon, P. 186
Greek lyric poetry 5, 32, 125, 126, 127, 128, 130, 135, 136, 137, 138, 141, 142, 143, 144, 193, 209
Greek novel 3, 19, 22, 25, 26
Green, P. 185
grief 3, 11, 32, 39, 42, 43, 56, 61, 62, 69, 96, 101, 151
Griffin, J. 60, 73
Habinek, T. 185
Hades 31, 32, 34, 43
Hall, A.E.W. 128
Hallett, J.P. 186
Halliwell, S. 120
happiness 1, 112, 113, 114
Harder, A. 227
Harrison, S. 125, 129
Hector 30, 31, 151, 152
Helen 23, 97, 98, 103, 226
Hellenistic epigram 5, 65, 156, 157, 171, 178
Heracles/Hercules 4, 43, 63, 105, 142, 204
Heraclitus 32
Hermesianax, *Leontion* 50
Hero (see Leander and Hero)
Herodotus, *Histories* 139, 140
Hesiod 106, 108, 115, 116, 119
– *Theogony* 115

hetaera 21, 51, 52, 130
heteroerotic love 6, 22, 38, 39, 40, 45, 48, 49, 50, 53, 57, 144, 185, 186, 210, 211
heterosexuality 19
Hippolytus 23, 228
Hippomenes 105
Hollis, A. 204, 206
Holzberg, N. 51, 52
Homer 1, 3, 30, 46, 47, 119, 143, 204,
– *Iliad* 3, 15, 23, 25, 29, 30, 32, 38
– *Odyssey* 3, 32, 132
homoeroticism/homoerotic love 3, 4, 5, 6, 22, 23, 26, 37, 38, 39, 40, 46, 48, 49, 50, 51, 52, 53, 56, 57, 126, 128, 141, 142, 144, 185, 186, 187, 188, 190, 191, 195, 196, 198, 199, 200, 201, 202, 210, 211, 224, 225
homoerotic poetry 3, 5, 33, 39, 144, 167, 171, 185, 186, 187, 188, 191, 193, 194, 195, 196, 200, 201, 202, 208, 224, 225
homosexuality 19, 26, 127, 185, 186, 190, 205, 207
Hopkinson, N. 32
Horace 3, 5, 36, 37, 38, 39, 40, 49, 53, 54, 55, 56, 133, 136, 145, 146, 147, 148, 149, 150, 151, 153, 154, 155, 160, 161, 164, 165, 167, 168, 170, 172, 174, 175, 176, 177, 178, 179, 180, 182, 183, 184, 187, 191, 192, 210, 219, 224, 226
– *Ars Poetica* 54, 155
– *Epistulae* 146, 164
– *Epodes* 172, 191, 199
– *Odes/Carmina* 3, 5, 6, 36, 37, 38, 39, 49, 53, 56, 133, 136, 150, 151, 153, 154, 155, 164, 167, 168, 170, 171, 172, 173, 174, 175, 176, 177, 178, 179, 180, 181, 182, 183, 184, 210, 218, 224
– *Satirae/Sermones* 37, 145, 147, 148, 149, 150, 151, 154
Höschele, R. 154, 155
Hubbard, M. 152, 153, 154
Hubbard, T.K. 41, 47
Hunter, R. 32, 149
Hylas 4, 105, 204
Ianthe 186

Ilia/Rhea Silvia 4, 83, 93, 94, 95, 98, 103, 149
Ilioupersis 134, 140
intertextuality 3, 59, 61, 71, 129, 192
intratextuality 167
Iphis 186
James, S.L. 21, 22, 25, 61, 72, 79, 81, 84, 89, 90, 204, 210, 211, 215, 216, 219
Johnson, T. 169, 176, 177, 178, 183
Jupiter (see Zeus)
Juventius 224, 225, 226
Kania, R. 42, 48
katabasis 44, 45, 46, 48, 49, 55, 56, 57
Kennedy, D. 181, 184, 195
Khan, H.A. 55
kiss/kissing 9, 10, 12, 46, 47, 64, 137, 148, 158, 206-7, 216, 224, 225
Konstan, D. 19, 22, 26, 76
Lacan, J. 5, 167, 179, 180, 181, 183
Labate, M. 92
Lacon 46, 47, 49
Latin love elegy 3, 5, 6, 14, 20, 21, 22, 51, 59, 60, 61, 83, 85, 127, 185, 188, 193, 207, 211, 222
Lavinia 128, 140, 141
law 4, 80, 98, 182, 216, 217, 229
Leander and Hero 3, 11, 12, 13, 20
lena 76, 77, 78
Lesbia 18, 24, 50, 51, 52, 57, 182, 186, 217, 218, 221, 223
lesbianism 50, 186
lesbian love 57, 186
Lewis, C.S. 16, 17
Lieberg, G. 17
Ligurinus 5, 36, 38, 167, 172, 173, 174, 175, 176, 177, 178, 179, 180, 182, 183, 184, 210, 224, 226
Livius Andronicus 220, 221
Livy 89, 90, 91, 94
Lucilius 223
Lucius Calpurnius Piso Caesoninus 145
Luck, G. 60
Lucretius 4, 64, 65, 67, 89, 105, 108, 109, 112, 113, 151, 160, 204
Lygdamus 219
Lyne, R.O.A.M. 17, 18
madness (love as) 23, 55, 106, 228

Makowski, J. 185
Maecenas 5, 80, 145, 155, 156, 165, 218
Maltby, R. 164
Marathus 187, 199, 200, 224, 226
marriage 4, 9, 25, 63, 67, 68, 70, 71, 72, 73, 75, 76, 79, 80, 83, 84, 85, 88, 90, 92, 93, 94, 95, 97, 99, 102, 103, 128, 130, 140, 186, 209
Mars (see Ares)
Massimilla, G. 227
McKeown, J.C. 61, 80, 99, 190, 191, 192, 194
Meleager 6, 156, 192, 193, 194, 195
memory 3, 30, 32, 33, 34, 38, 46, 180
Menander 4, 60, 68, 77, 84, 99, 220
– *Dyskolos* 4, 68
– *Kolax* 69
– *Misoumenos* 65, 77
– *Perikeiromene* 99
Mercury 53, 54, 55
meretrix (see also prostitute) 6, 21, 25, 61, 86, 90, 97, 98, 148, 204, 213, 216, 217, 218, 219, 220, 223
Messalla 5, 80, 165, 218
Mitchell, E. 183
militia amoris 20, 24
Minos 4, 105
Moschus 115, 116, 151
mourning 30, 31, 32, 42, 46, 54
Muse/Muses 41, 50, 105, 108, 113, 115, 118, 122, 123, 137, 154, 160, 190
mutual love 67
Myers, S.K. 77, 78
Myiscus 193, 194
Nemesis 34, 199, 200, 202
New comedy 59, 60, 61, 72, 83, 84, 99, 157, 220
Nisbet, R.G.M. 152, 153, 154
Odysseus 31, 32, 43, 132
Oenone 4, 83, 96, 97, 98, 101, 103, 226
oratory 60, 77
Orpheus 3, 39, 40, 42, 43, 44, 45, 46, 47, 48, 49, 53, 54, 55, 56, 57, 111, 185, 186, 201, 202, 209
Oscan Flora 148, 158, 159
otium 50

Ovid 1, 2, 4, 5, 6, 11, 16, 17, 25, 37, 60, 64, 65, 66, 74, 79, 80, 81, 83, 84, 85, 88, 90, 91, 92, 94, 95, 97, 98, 99, 100, 102, 103, 138, 145, 147, 161, 162, 163, 164, 165, 185, 186, 187, 188, 189, 190, 191, 192, 194, 195, 196, 197, 198, 199, 200, 201, 202, 204, 205, 206, 207, 208, 209, 210, 211, 219, 220, 224, 226
– abortion poems 25, 26
– *Amores* 4, 5, 6, 17, 37, 61, 64, 65, 66, 67, 71, 74, 75, 76, 77, 83, 84, 93, 94, 95, 97, 98, 99, 100, 101, 102, 150, 158, 161, 162, 163, 164, 186, 187, 188, 189, 190, 191, 192, 194, 195, 196, 197, 198, 199, 200, 205, 207, 215, 216, 217, 219, 220, 224, 226
– *Ars amatoria* 4, 6, 23, 64, 65, 70, 80, 81, 83, 88, 89, 90, 91, 92, 94, 95, 106, 158, 162, 187, 188, 190, 192, 196, 202, 203, 204, 205, 206, 207, 208, 209, 220, 221, 224, 225, 226
– *Heroides* 11, 13, 17, 20, 50, 83, 86, 96, 97, 101, 127, 162, 186, 197, 218, 219, 220, 221, 227, 228, 229
– *Metamorphoses* 11, 185, 186, 187, 191, 196, 197, 198, 202, 209
– *praeceptor amoris* 89, 203, 221
– *Remedia amoris* 6, 64, 65, 187, 188, 204, 208, 209, 210
– *Tristia* 85, 158, 186, 200, 220
paraclausithyron 64, 65, 66, 68, 70
Paris 23, 96, 97, 98
Parmenides 4, 121, 122
Pasiphae 4, 105, 106, 107, 108
passion 6, 16, 17, 34, 105, 106, 107, 109, 127, 130, 132, 138, 139, 149, 151, 186, 187, 191, 208
pastoral poetry (see bucolic poetry)
Patroclus 3, 23, 29, 30, 31, 32
pedagogy 48, 186, 203
pederastic poetry 2, 37, 46, 47, 127, 192, 193, 204, 209
pederasty/pederastic love 37, 40, 46, 47, 48, 127, 130, 185, 186, 200, 202, 203, 204, 205
Peleus 30
Perilla 223

Persephone 43, 44, 45
Phanocles 48, 186, 200, 202
– *Erotes/Loves* or *Kaloi/Beautiful Boys* 40, 47, 48, 200, 201
Phaon 50, 9
Philodemus 5, 109, 113, 145, 146, 147, 148, 149, 150, 151, 152, 153, 154, 155, 156, 157, 158, 159, 160, 161, 162, 163, 164, 223
Philomela 4, 105
Phrygius and Pieria 3, 8
Phyllis 152, 153
Piazzi, L. 61, 65
Pieria (see Phrygius and Pieria)
pimp 66, 68, 216, 217, 221
Plato 3, 4, 9, 10, 27, 105, 110, 112, 113, 114, 118, 119, 120, 121, 122
– *Symposium* 4, 110, 111, 112, 114, 115, 116, 117, 118, 119, 121
Platonic love 10, 105, 112, 115
Platonism/Platonic philosophy 4, 10, 113, 114, 120
Plautus 4, 59, 60, 62, 65, 66, 67, 68, 70, 71, 72, 73, 77, 78, 79, 83, 84, 89, 98, 167, 204, 219
– *Amphitruo* 73, 79
– *Asinaria* 73, 78, 79, 83, 197
– *Aulularia* 73, 79, 84
– *Bacchides* 4, 62, 68, 73, 79
– *Captiui* 73, 79
– *Casina* 73, 79
– *Cistellaria* 78, 79, 84
– *Curculio* 4, 65, 66, 67, 68, 70, 76, 77, 78, 79
– *Epidicus* 62, 79, 84, 89
– *Mercator* 79, 106
– *Miles gloriosus* 73, 78, 79
– *Mostellaria* 62, 76, 77, 78, 79, 98
– *Persa* 4, 62, 63, 76, 79
– *Poenulus* 79
– *Pseudolus* 62, 73, 79
– *Rudens* 79
– *Stichus* 73, 79
– *Trinummus* 79
– *Truculentus* 76, 79, 84
– *Vidularia* 73, 79
Plutarch 8, 15

Pluto 43, 44, 45, 55
poeta-amator 188, 189
Ponticus 159
Porter, D. 169
Priapeia 186
procreation 26, 92
Propertius 2, 4, 6, 20, 25, 51, 60, 61, 64, 66, 67, 69, 70, 71, 72, 74, 75, 76, 77, 80, 83, 127, 145, 147, 150, 155, 156, 157, 158, 159, 160, 161, 162, 164, 165, 187, 189, 190, 191, 192, 193, 194, 195, 196, 197, 198, 201, 204, 207, 209, 215, 217, 219, 220, 223
prostitute/prostitution (see also *meretrix*) 19, 21, 22, 26, 61, 62, 63, 66, 68, 70, 72, 73, 75, 76, 78, 79, 80, 98, 130, 149, 150, 207, 213, 216, 217, 218, 220, 221, 226
'Pseudo-Moschus'/the Epitaphist 40, 42, 43, 44, 45, 46, 47, 48, 49, 56, 57
– *Lament for Bion* 40, 42, 43, 44, 45, 46, 47, 48, 49, 56, 57
psychoanalysis 5, 18, 167, 177, 183, 184
Pudor/*pudor* 54, 55
puella 6, 24, 25, 51, 66, 74, 75, 83, 88, 89, 90, 92, 96, 97, 98, 99, 100, 102, 103, 157, 158, 162, 188, 190, 191, 192, 198, 200, 204, 210, 211, 213, 215, 216, 217, 218, 219, 220, 221, 222, 223, 224, 225, 226, 227, 228, 230
puer 6, 36, 38, 167, 171, 183, 188, 189, 190, 191, 192, 199, 200, 205, 208, 209, 213, 220, 221, 223, 224, 226, 227, 230
Putnam, M. 56, 168, 169, 183
Pyramus and Thisbe 3, 11
Quellenforschung 21, 59
Quintilius Varus 39, 53
Rand, E.K. 16
rape 4, 23, 68, 69, 70, 76, 83, 84, 85, 86, 87, 88, 89, 90, 91, 92, 93, 94, 95, 96, 97, 98, 99, 100, 101, 102, 103, 105
– of the Sabine women 83, 88, 89, 90, 92, 94, 98, 103
Reddy, W. 15
remythologisation 112
Roman Comedy 3, 14, 20, 21, 25, 59, 60, 61, 62, 65, 76, 77, 84, 87, 213, 218, 219

Roman love elegy (see Latin love elegy)
romanticism 59
romantic love 7, 10, 14, 15
Romulus 89, 90, 92, 93, 94, 170
Ross, D.O. 113, 114
Rudd, N. 17
Sage, P. 169
Sapphic stanza 32, 52
Sappho 3, 5, 8, 9, 15, 23, 24, 27, 32, 35, 36, 38, 39, 49, 50, 51, 52, 53, 57, 67, 128, 129, 130, 131, 136, 138, 140, 141, 148, 151, 158, 171, 186, 218, 220, 221, 223
Schrötter, W. 16
Scylla 4, 105, 107
Segal, E. 62
Selene 156, 157, 158
Seneca the Elder 186
senex (of comedy) 61, 73, 79
Septuagint 8
seruitium amoris 20, 61, 64, 103, 196, 210, 222
Servius Sulpicius Rufus 218
sexuality 1, 2, 5, 14, 15, 18, 19, 51, 95, 144, 164, 187, 197, 201
Shakespeare 11
– *A Midsummer Night's Dream* 11
– *Romeo and Juliet* 11
Sharrock, A. 3, 4
Sider, D. 148, 149, 155, 157, 164
slavery 20, 222
sleeplessness 30, 35, 196, 197
Solon 5, 138, 139, 140, 141
Spenser, E. 16
status 26, 52, 63, 71, 79, 80, 84, 87, 89, 92, 95, 98, 101, 102, 103, 120, 130, 138, 140, 151, 162, 176, 217, 221, 226, 230
Stephens, S. 227
stuprum 98, 103
Sullivan, J.P. 17
Sulpicia 21, 217, 218, 219
synkrisis 46
Terence 4, 59, 60, 62, 72, 73, 78, 79, 83, 84, 87, 90, 91, 103, 219
– *Adelphoe* 68, 73, 84, 97
– *Andria* 73, 84

– *Eunuchus* 4, 19, 25, 62, 68, 76, 80, 81, 83, 84, 85, 86, 87, 89, 90, 91, 92, 93, 95, 96, 97, 99, 100, 101, 102, 103
– *H(e)autontimorumenos* 80
– *Hecyra* 73, 78, 84, 90
– *Phormio* 84
Tereus 4, 105
Theocritus 41, 44, 46, 47, 106, 115, 223
– *Idylls* 41, 46, 47, 49, 106
– *Thalysia* 115
Theognis 2, 131, 138, 190, 223
Thersites 31
Thisbe (see Pyramus and Thisbe)
Thorsen, T.S. 52
Tiberius 169, 184
Tibullus 4, 5, 6, 20, 25, 60, 64, 66, 68, 69, 70, 71, 72, 77, 83, 127, 145, 151, 156, 164, 165, 187, 189, 190, 191, 197, 199, 200, 201, 202, 204, 207, 208, 211, 219, 223, 224, 225, 226
triumph 152, 195, 196, 198
Troia, A. 40, 42, 45
troubadours 14, 15, 16
trobairitz 14, 15, 214
Troy 69, 130, 132, 133, 138, 184
'true love' 2, 4, 7, 8, 11, 13, 14, 16, 18, 19, 20, 22, 23
Trypanis, C. 227
uirgo 84, 85, 92, 97, 98, 101, 102, 228
uitta 95
underworld 40, 43, 44, 45, 48, 128, 160, 201
Varius 145, 155, 160
Varro 220, 221
Venus (see Aphrodite)
Veyne, P. 18, 19
violence 4, 7, 21, 26, 68, 69, 70, 83, 84, 85, 87, 88, 92, 94, 97, 98, 99, 100, 103, 225
Virgil 3, 4, 13, 40, 53, 54, 55, 56, 57, 105, 106, 107, 108, 109, 110, 111, 113, 114, 115, 116, 119, 120, 121, 122, 128, 129, 132, 135, 136, 160, 186, 187, 201
– *Aeneid* 5, 15, 110, 125, 126, 127, 128, 129, 130, 132, 133, 134, 135, 136, 137, 138, 139, 141, 142, 143, 144, 145, 155, 173, 184

– *Eclogues* 4, 80, 105, 106, 107, 108, 109, 110, 111, 112, 113, 114, 115, 116, 117, 118, 119, 121, 122, 123, 153, 158, 182, 187, 190, 201, 224, 226
– *Georgica* 13, 55, 56, 106, 108, 110, 112, 123, 160

Volk, K. 190
Wills, J. 34
Yardley, J.C. 60
Yona, S. 155
Zeus/Jupiter 23, 71, 79, 87, 193, 196, 197

www.ingramcontent.com/pod-product-compliance
Lightning Source LLC
Chambersburg PA
CBHW020225170426
43201CB00007B/322